PETER STEWART

# ESSENTIAL RADIOSKILLS

## HOW TO PRESENT AND PRODUCE A RADIO SHOW

 A & C BLACK · LONDON

*For my parents Margaret and John*
for their love and support through school, university and life
*For Bob and Marjorie Alexander*
for his great friendship and support especially as I started my broadcasting career

*For Mike Eaton and Brinley Page*
Communications BA, University of Central England, 1986–9
who both died soon after

First published 2006
A & C Black Publishers Limited
38 Soho Square
London W1D 3HB
www.acblack.com

© Peter Stewart 2006

ISBN-10: 0–7136–7913–1
ISBN-13: 978–0–7136–7913–7

A CIP catalogue record for this book is available from the British Library.

This book is produced using paper that is made from wood grown in managed, sustainable forests. It is natural, renewable and recyclable. The logging and manufacturing processes conform to the environmental regulations of the country of origin.

Typeset by Palimpsest Book Production Ltd, Grangemouth, Stirlingshire

Printed and bound in Great Britain by MPG Books Limited

# Contents

## Part One OFF AIR

**4  OTHER PEOPLE AT THE STATION**

**5  THE RADIO STATION**

**6  THE AUDIENCE**

# Part Two **PRE PRODUCTION**

## 16   AUDIO IMAGING

# Part Four GOING LIVE!

## 17   STAND BY STUDIO

## 18   HOW TO TALK

## 22  PRESENTING MUSIC

## 23  COMPETITIONS

## 27 WHEN IT ALL GOES WRONG

## 28 AT THE END OF THE SHOW

# Part Five GETTING IN

## 29 WHERE TO START

## 30 MORE CAREER ADVICE

# Part Six

**1**  THE BACK ANNO

**2**  APPENDICES

# Foreword

It was dark. That's chiefly what I remember – the darkness, the bumping into furniture, and seeing a figure in the far corner. The man was sitting with his back to me, head bobbing left and right. Above him a single bulb threw light into his wavy hair.

I don't know what I had been expecting, but my first visit to a radio studio was not exactly a walk on the wild side. It was 1977. Aged twelve, I was the young DJ on that week's Kenny Everett show on Capital – 'Don't be nervous! Don't be rocky! You're our teenage disc-jockey!' – but Kenny wasn't there and I was pre-recording with Maggie Norden.

Disgracefully, I chose a James Galway record in the middle of the punk explosion; I blame a sheltered upbringing for that. After we had taped a few halting links in my squeaky voice, Maggie said: 'Hey, I'll show you round.' And so, a floor later, I ended up in the darkness, knocking the '70s sofa and watching Roger Scott in the other corner of the room.

The visual experience only captured about fifteen kilobytes of my memory, so I may never understand why it had such an extraordinary impact on my young life. I got back home and announced I was going to be a DJ. Then I fired off a letter to every single radio station in Britain asking for work (why did none reply?) while my mum and dad kindly encouraged me in the craziness, perhaps sensing that impossible dreams were not always a waste of time.

As time went by they added the sensible rider: 'You'll probably want to do something else when you're older, Jeremy. Playing records for a living is, well . . .' Like I say, good advice.

Life moved on and seemed to prove them right. At school I did hospital radio, but by Durham University I was in the middle of what the army call mission creep. Editing the student newspaper was a different career – journalism. Surrounded by serious people who remain friends twenty years later, I decided my Roger Scott phase must be over. The Coventry Evening Telegraph trained me; moving to the BBC, I reported everywhere from Westminster to Timbuktu. As baffled as anyone by the timing of tides in the corporation, I then found myself dropped into the Newsnight chair by a surfer's wave.

But if life springs surprises, a media career is an endless string of them. Suddenly a lateral thinker at Radio 2 was asking if I would consider taking over Jimmy Young's show when he left. 'You realise,' they said, 'this'll be music too? I mean, you're a serious journalist and all that, are you sure you can be enthusiastic about *records*?'

I won't even try to write down what I said and thought by way of reply. A quarter of a century after walking into that dark room with one of the great music presenters aglow in the other corner, I had finally found my way back to it. The bug that bit that day at Capital had never left the system – when I tease my parents about their 'playing records for a living' stuff, we all end up laughing in astonishment and delight that a job could be such a perfect fit and so much fun.

If you're reading this book it might just be because you feel the same way about radio. Take nothing from television, it has enormous impact – like a wrecker's ball swung into your living room – but radio has intimacy to make up for it. 'I drop a word into the nation's ear,' said the irrepressible Brian Redhead. Maybe; to be allowed to drop even one word into even one ear is enough privilege for anybody.

While reporting for Radio 4's Today programme in the early nineties I would watch Brian with fascination – he always smiled just as they turned on his microphone, and then when he spoke, you heard the smile in his voice. Observing his successor John Humphrys, I saw how he could take forty pages of information and, in a trice, remove the 39 that weren't helping and find the one question that mattered. Steve Wright, now my next-door neighbour on Radio 2, brings enough energy to the microphone to power a small village – I could go on and on about the lessons learnt watching these guys.

If you're reading this book it's because you want to learn too, and it's a great place to start. You'll see what makes radio the uplifting, enthralling, exasperating profession it is. Take Peter Stewart's advice would be my advice; push and push and don't give up, be sure of yourself, and don't be afraid to have quite inappropriate amounts of fun.

Above all, don't be surprised when radio suddenly gives you the best job in the world, because it has quite a lot of them.

*Jeremy Vine*
*Presenter BBC Radio 2*
*Spring 2006*

# Preface

Congratulations! So, you want to get into radio? You've made a great start by buying this book. Over the next few hundred pages I'm going to show you everything you need to know about producing and presenting a radio programme. From behind the scenes to behind the mic, there's more information on the fast-changing world of radio right here than has ever been gathered in one place before.

The basic broadcasting techniques I'm going to share with you will make you fighting fit as radio enters a war zone with new technology. Perhaps the greatest challenge that stations and radio presenters and producers face worldwide is the iPod. Users can listen to their own choice of music; content that's advert-free; available where they want and when they want it. All things that radio can't always provide.

But that challenge is also our greatest opportunity for two reasons. First, the iPod (and the same goes for digital and internet stations) can never be local: most of those technologies work everywhere, but they're not from anywhere specific. Digital services beamed across the country or non-stop tracks on an MP3 player can't give information of value such as local news, weather, traffic and sport. Your MP3 loaded with 20 albums can't surprise you with a new release or give you personalities that make you laugh, think, and send you prizes.

Radio can.

Secondly, iPods give the opportunity for radio stations to produce podcast programmes. Often broadcasters can't include commercially-available music on these, because of royalty payments. That means that the downloadable mini-programmes consist entirely of 'content': personality links, humour, observations and team interaction. All of which I'm going to show you how to produce and present.

This book won't show you how to create hot music mixes in the style of a club DJ, but it will tell you how to blend music with information that is relevant, interesting and compelling for your listener. I'll also show you how to combine those elements with travel, temperature and time checks, ads, events and OBs: the information that's not just 'geographically local' but also local to the listeners' sphere of interest, relevant to how they live their lives.

The more relevant, interesting and compelling you are, the more likely it is that listeners will listen. The more often they will be late for work as they sit in the car waiting for you to finish a link. The more often they will eat a cold meal after standing in the kitchen listening to you. And the longer they listen, the more successful your career and station.

Over the years, as radio journalist, music presenter, head of news, programme manager, TV presenter and now radio trainer for the BBC, I've collated many thoughts and ideas on programming and presentation. Some of them are from what I've been told and some from what I've learnt through my own trial and error. My personal notebook of ideas has now manifested itself into this Handbook. Here are a few quick points that'll help you get the most from the next couple of hundred pages:

- *Essential Radio Skills* is written from a local radio perspective as that's where most presenters and producers start their careers. That makes it ideal for those on RSLs (Restricted Service Licence), community radio and university and hospital radio, too.

- My background is in both BBC and commercial radio and I've covered both areas with examples and quotes. I use BBC and commercial terms and these are explained both in the text and in the Glossary. For clarity, I've tended to use commercial terminology as 'presenter' is more straightforward than 'BJ', 'programme controller' more obvious than 'SBJ programmes' and so on.

- There are dozens of quotes in the book from presenters, station managers, programme controllers, managing directors, chief executives, a vice president and chief engineer, a brand marketing director and a content director, from across the BBC and commercial sectors. Look out for these comments from people who've worked their way up to be industry experts: there's no doubt they know what they're talking about.

- There are more examples in the form of transcripts of 'Actual Audio' of what has been broadcast. A little speaker in the text marks these: ◀. All of these are what actually went out on air, but I haven't named the stations concerned because I want to make points, not make enemies!

- Ways of working are different not only between the BBC and commercial sectors, but also within the BBC and commercial groups, and between stations and between programmes. I outline the general tried-and-tested way of doing certain things, and explain why they're done that way, but do check with your programme controller (or in your station's House Style book) whether they're appropriate for your station.

- Occasionally, I say something like, 'Never do this . . .' or 'You shouldn't do that . . .' and a few days later you'll hear someone successful doing just what I warned against. Yes, there are many people who break the rules, but I think you've got to know what the *accepted* ways of working are, and why they're there, before you can change them for dramatic or creative effect.

- I haven't divided the book too much between the two roles of presenter and producer. That's because at many stations they're one and the same person; because roles are often interchangeable; and because I think it'll be of value for those with either job title to read about what the other has to do. Producing can mean several things: setting up a show, directing it and making the items. I've concentrated in this edition on the first two roles and not gone into other elements such as vox pops, packages, drama and music recording and so on.

- There is a section on basic law, but you're strongly advised to get some formal legal training as well. Although there's no substitute for a classroom setting where you can talk through questions and examples with a trainer, at the very least buy *Essential Law for Journalists* and read it. Note: there have been cases where presenters have been fined thousands of pounds, lost their job, or have been a hair's-breadth away from going to jail because they said things on-air they shouldn't have. It is your employer's responsibility to provide some legal training, but you've also got a responsibility to yourself and your career to ask for it.

- I've used 'he' and 'she' interchangeably, but usually 'they', and I have broken rules of grammar. The Handbook is written as it would be said if I was in the room with you. After all, in radio we write as we speak.

o   Unlike other books, there's no long list of addresses here. These change regularly and such information uses up valuable space when most people have access to the internet for such basic research. There is, however, an appendix with some internet addresses of trade organisations.

o   Although much of what follows comes from my experience in and around radio, some of my suggestions have been adapted from other sources. That's because over the years I've taken notes from different books, style guides, handouts and presentations. Some sources are therefore not credited – I simply have no way of finding out where they started life – it may be, for example, that a handout I've been given by one person, may have been 'borrowed' from another publication. However, if you recognise something here that you originally wrote, I apologise. Please let me know and I'll happily credit you in the future.

If you're starting out in radio I think most of this Handbook will be invaluable. If you've been in the business a few years you'll know some of what's here, but may also be able to take on some ideas and adapt others. But, I'm not saying this is the *only* way. I'm just showing you *one* way.

It'd be great to get your feedback and suggestions for future editions. Perhaps you've got a great tip, or do something differently, or have a great example. E-mail me and I'll try to include as much as I can next time around: EssentialRadioSkills@hotmail.com

Perhaps I'll hear *from* you in an e-mail, and *of* you on-air one day soon!

Thanks for buying this Handbook and best wishes for your future broadcasting career.

*Peter Stewart*
*Spring 2006*

# The author

**Peter Stewart** is an award-winning broadcaster, radio consultant and author with 20 years' experience in speech and music radio, and TV.

He started on hospital radio and RSLs, then student radio before getting his first professional role presenting news and magazine programmes. He has hosted music shows, celebrity interview programmes and chart countdowns, and handled phone-ins, competitions and election coverage.

Peter's been heard on national and local radio, commercial stations, the BBC and BFBS, and in almost every time slot.

In radio management he has been group head of news and head of presentation, and in TV has hosted programmes, written scripts and recorded voice-overs.

He received an award for Best Personality Newsreader at the New York International Radio Awards in 1997, and has been UK Chairman of Judges since 2000. He's also judged awards for the CRCA, Skillset and the Student Radio Association.

As well as training hundreds of presenters, producers and managers for the BBC's national and local radio and television stations, Peter's also coached commercial radio staff in Britain and around the world.

He's written a weekly column in *The Radio Magazine* since 2001 and for RadioJam.co.uk since 2006, and is co-author of *Basic Radio Journalism*.

Away from radio, Peter has a BA in Communications and a Diploma in Marketing and Advertising, and has studied forensics and psychology.

Peter runs his own websites at www.PeteStewart.co.uk and www.FindaLine.co.uk

# Acknowledgements

It's customary for authors to list those who've helped make their book possible. The thanks are particularly deserved in this case because of the short lead-time between the proposal being accepted and the manuscript deadline date.

Thanks to John Ryan, Managing Editor at BBC Radio Manchester who reviewed the final draft version and gave incomparable and invaluable insight and advice. Thanks also to the following who also came up with additional feedback: Ray Clark at BBC Essex; Will Jackson; Danny Pike at Southern FM; Richard Waghorn at the BBC.

Each chapter was reviewed by those working in the appropriate area, and who offered suggestions and corrections: Nick Alliker at BBC Essex; Paul Atkinson at the BBC; Martyn Blunt at Goose Communications; Shelley Bradley at the BBC; Mark Chapman at the BBC; John Cushing at LBC 97.3; Mark Hall at Heart 106.2; Faye Hatcher at BBC Radio Gloucestershire; Claire Jaggard at journojobs.com; Will Kinder at Radio 1; Sarah Knight at BBC South East Today; Neil Pringle at BBC Southern Counties Radio; Bob Symons at the BBC; Kevin Steele at BBC Training; Jo Walker at suzylamplugh.org; Jane Wickens; Jonathan Witchell at BBC Radio Kent.

More information and assistance was provided by Paul Chantler at paulchantler.com; Simon Furber at BBC Radio Devon; Margaret Hyde at BBC Essex; Lucy Mackay at The Radio Academy; Louise Hall at the BBC; Mike Skinner at the Hospital Broadcasters' Association; Kirsten Smith at Broadcast Bionics; the University of Central England, Birmingham.

For the pictures, thanks to Shona Harvey at GCap Media; Brian Cantwell at Radio St Helier, Carshalton; Fiona Clarke and Dawn Baxter at BBC Radio Scotland; Claire Martin at Essex FM; David Robey and Nikki O'Donnell at BBC London 94.9.

Many hours were spent by Ruth Evans typing handwritten notes and by John Stewart copy editing – my thanks to them both.

I am grateful to Jeremy Vine at BBC Radio 2 for his excellent Foreword and to the great and good of British radio who were kind enough to provide some terrific (and humbling) testimonial quotes for the cover. Many of the quotes in the book are courtesy of Paul Boon and my other colleagues at *The Radio Magazine*.

Jenny Ridout, Katie Taylor and Suzi Nicolaou at A&C Black steered me in the right direction from pitch to publication – I hope to work with all again soon.

Finally, to all those who over the last 20 years have given me the knowledge to be able to write this book . . .

Thank you!

A studio at BBC Radio Leeds

# OFF AIR

What's in this part:

o There's a quick overview of the UK radio landscape and the different broadcasting platforms and the stations which don't actually broadcast.

o An outline of the ups and downs, the qualities and qualifications of good presenters and producers, and an explanation of what they do and how much they earn.

o Then I take a look at the station as a whole: the other people you'll be working with, the importance of the station's name and branding, how it makes its money and who we do all this for.

# 1 The structure of UK radio

Radio is everywhere. Despite its premature death knell being sounded with the increased popularity of multi-channel television, CDs and iPods, almost everyone in the UK listens to radio every day. It may be on in the factory, on a personal stereo as you walk to the station, a recorded and downloaded programme that you listen to on an MP3 player as you work out, a digital station playing in your car or even through the TV. It may be a music station playing chart hits, rock, easy listening or gold music. It may be a speech station with a diet of news and sport, book-readings or phone-ins. Or possibly it is a station with a combination of speech and music, perhaps targeted towards a certain age-group, people with a certain income, interest, culture or sexual orientation. Whatever the medium, the message or the music, radio is becoming more popular rather than less, despite the competition.

This is mainly because radio is cheap to provide and consume, the cheapest 'tranny' is just a few pounds, and because there's so much radio to choose from. Even if you don't become a presenter on 'Bedroom FM' and compile, record and upload your own programme on to the internet for others to hear, there are hundreds of other choices available to work for or listen to.

As well as the five national analogue BBC stations (on FM, MW and LW), there are three national commercial stations (INR – Independent National Radio) which can be heard across the UK. Then there are 46 BBC local and regional stations, 282 (at the last count and increasing) local and regional commercial ones (ILR – Independent Local Radio), community stations and short-term RSLs. If you add the UK's national analogue commercial stations, the UK has more national stations than any other country in the world. Add to these the dozens of stations run by volunteers at hospitals and on university campuses and the hundreds more on digital radio and thousands 'broadcasting' on the internet – you can see that the world of radio is growing very quickly.

## The BBC

You'll no doubt be familiar with the BBC national services Radio 1, Radio 2, Radio 3, Radio 4 and Radio Five Live, but there are also local stations and others available on digital services.

Programmes in network radio (the national stations BBC Radio 1, 2, 3, 4, Five Live, 1 Xtra, BBC 6 Music, BBC 7 and the Asian Network) have programme teams to help put the shows together. There may well be a studio manager, producer and other staff to book guests, answer calls or even appear on the show itself as other characters (such as Steve Wright's programme on Radio 2 or with Chris Moyles on Radio 1). Most presenters will still be driving the show themselves, but with more back-up staff to help them both on and off-air.

BBC local stations usually broadcast local output from 5am until 7pm, with 'regionally shared' programmes usually transmitted from 7pm until midnight, with a simulcast of Radio Five Live or the BBC World Service from then until 5am. A 'regional share' is when five or six nearby stations join together and broadcast the same programme. This is particularly cost effective at a time of day when few people are listening.

Elsewhere in the day, BBC local breakfast programmes are speech-only featuring lots of news, interviews and packages (pre-recorded interviews or features). The afternoon drive programme may also be quite speech heavy with other programmes more balanced between music and talk.

A BBC local presenter is likely to have a BA (Broadcast Assistant or producer) to help them put their programme together and to be with them as they broadcast. This may seem staff-heavy when compared to commercial radio, indeed those who move from commercial radio to the BBC see it as a luxury, but the extra pair of hands is often for practical reasons: as BBC local programmes have a higher speech content, the presenter can't be doing an interview and answering calls at the same time.

The BBC is in a bit of a cleft stick. On one hand it has a public service remit to provide programmes to those who would otherwise not be catered for by the commercial sector. In other words, it should be broadcasting programmes for minority audiences – the ones commercial stations don't want to target because smaller audiences may mean less income. On the other hand there's the universal licence fee. This argument says that because everyone in the UK with a television pays a licence fee (some of which goes to BBC radio), the BBC has a duty to broadcast programmes that everyone will want to hear.

You can see how these two factors are largely at odds with each other, and this is why the BBC has to tread a careful line. If the BBC broadcasts programmes that are said (by its commercial competitors) to be too popular then it is accused of abusing its remit and providing programmes that they could make money from. If the BBC programmes are *not* popular the cry goes up that it is poor value for money and why should people pay for a service that they don't use?

# Commercial stations

Started in 1973, there are now at least 282 local and regional commercial stations (and three national ones), which sell airtime to advertisers to generate their income. To put it simply, the more popular a programme or station, the higher the cost of advertising on it and the greater the amount of money made by the station's owners.

But the opposite is also true: a station that loses an audience has to charge less for its airtime (it's offering fewer listeners to its clients), and so has a lower income. That's less money to spend on presenters, so arguably they're not as good. They may attract fewer listeners, which means less money for competitions and prizes, and less money to market the station. It's a difficult spiral to get out of.

Some stations turn over a good profit even with a small audience because they're 'super-local'. The percentage of people listening within the transmission area is high, even though the actual number is low, and that means that advertisers have less 'wastage'. Similarly specialist music stations charge a premium because of the specific kind of person (the demographic) attracted to its output.

Commercial stations are, understandably, always looking for ways to cut costs without cutting corners. That's why some of the most-heard words are 'automation', 'syndication' and 'consolidation'.

'Automation', is where live presenters are replaced by computers playing out pre-recorded programmes; 'syndication' where one show is broadcast on several stations at once; 'consolidation' where individual stations are bought by larger groups to reduce overheads.

'Commercial radio players need to get bigger if they are to compete more effectively with the BBC for listeners.'

Paul Brown, Chief Executive, Commercial Radio Companies Association, *The Radio Magazine*, 18 December 2004

A larger group usually means job losses in areas of the business where consolidation can be effectively achieved, but can also have benefits. There's more expertise available and more opportunity to move from one of its stations to another. Some complain it leads to a more homogenised sound (shared formats and some shared programmes), but audience figures stand up well – larger groups still seem to give audiences what they want to hear.

The station management may decide which group of people in the area is the biggest and has the most spending power as the one they want to attract as listeners, and 'sell' them to the advertisers as the people who'll be able to hear their commercials.

Alternatively, a new station may decide to target a different kind of listener who is currently underserved by existing stations. Instead of going head-to-head with three chart-based stations, a new company may decide to play dance music to siphon off a small group of young people from each station which combined would make a large and well-defined core audience. Another new station may target older people from each existing station. Put simply, commercial stations sell advertisers 'pairs of ears'.

Most commercial stations target a very similar audience: the biggest and richest. That's usually 25–34 year olds, described as 'the age that younger ones want to be and the older ones wish they still were'! News bulletins, travel news, what's ons and even adverts all inform the audience what's happening in the area. Add requests, roadshows and charity appeals and you'll see that commercial stations may not have a strict public service remit, but they still serve the public.

Commercial stations have to put forward a proposal to run a radio station when the regulatory body Ofcom advertises a licence. It considers which of several plans, often put forward by small local groups as well as by large multi-station groups, is likely to be of most benefit to the people of the area, and actually do what it promises.

The winning station provides a one-page Format to Ofcom describing their output (types of music and speech), target audience and how much will be presented locally. Every Format is different as it caters for the needs of the specific audience in each area, and the different conditions each station faces.

The 12-year licence can be sold by the winner (it's immediately worth a potential fortune), but the promised format of the station has to remain. If a station breaks broadcasting regulations Ofcom can impose a fine, shorten the licence period if it's a serious transgression, or take the licence away completely.

Ofcom charges a fee to national, regional and local commercial stations for the right to broadcast. In 2005 this was 0.627% of the qualifying revenue of that station.

Most local radio presenters will do everything in the studio themselves: playing in the songs and the commercials, answering the phone-in line, recording and editing callers, and so on. Off air they'll devise their own links, book guests and research competitions and features. After the shows they'll package and post prizes and possibly also help out in another department for the rest of their shift.

# RSLs

Cheaper equipment and lower operating costs have opened up the airwaves as never before. Small-scale, low-power, short-term stations have operated since the early 1990s. Called RSLs (Restricted Service Licences) they broadcast to a very local area (3km radius in urban areas, 5–7km in rural areas) and are usually staffed by volunteers. The stations are allowed to broadcast for up to 28 days a year and usually cover special events. It may be to give travel and tennis information on Radio Wimbledon, to celebrate a religious festival such as Christmas FM, or as an on-air training event or outreach project (Youth FM). You can see that RSLs are a great place for hands-on experience if you're thinking about making radio your career.

Another common reason for applying for an RSL licence is so a group of broadcasters can gauge demand for a full-scale licence before it is advertised by Ofcom. It can be seen as a trial run, but does not guarantee success.

It costs £200 to apply for an RSL licence, with no guarantee of success. Add to that a daily fee that has to be paid for the duration of the licence (on a sliding scale of whether the station is on AM or FM), music licensing and the hire of equipment, facilities and premises, and it's not necessarily a cheap station to run.

# Community radio

'Expertise, imagination and determination, plus a strong interest in the community radio concept, all exist outside the ranks of the current radio practitioners, so I confidently forecast there'll be no shortage of more than useful volunteers when groups set up . . . Community radio has been a very long time coming in the UK — some of its early protagonists have probably already gone to the great studio in the sky — but at last it's almost with us and it should be fun and worthwhile. It could also be of very considerable help to the commercial stations by providing the flow of applicants with real radio experience (rather than media studies degrees) that the industry has always said it lacked.'

Brian West, former Director and Chief Executive of the Association of Independent Radio Contractors, *The Radio Magazine*, 17 April 2004

The community radio movement started in the early 1980s, pushing for really local stations, locally run and not for private financial gain. In 2005 the communications regulator Ofcom started awarding new community radio licences, the new third tier of commercial radio broadcasting (after national commercial and local/regional commercial stations), and by spring 2006 a total of 93 had been won.

This new sector was set up to complement the mix of services already provided by the BBC and commercial radio. As Ofcom explains: 'The characteristics of community radio are distinct from commercial radio in that the services will cover a small geographical area and be provided on a not-for-profit basis focusing on the delivery of specific social benefits to enrich a particular geographical community or a community of interest.'

Ofcom does not specify where these radio stations should be. Instead, it invites applicants to apply for a five-year licence identifying the community or communities they want to serve, on either the FM or AM waveband. Each licence contains a list of commitments that the licence-holder will work to, providing a yardstick against which to measure the station. One of those commitments is to get the community involved in the broadcasts, and so it's another great training ground for you.

Stations cover their costs through advertising, sponsorship (so long as it is not more than 50% of their annual income, unless there's a big overlap with an existing commercial station in which case they can't take *any* advertising or sponsorship) and local grants. And of course, most of their staff work for free. Any profits from running adverts on the station are ploughed back into the station itself and used to pay annual fees to Ofcom (£600 and 0.627% of its commercial revenue).

## Digital radio

The main advantages of digital radio are that it can be much clearer than the ordinary (analogue) signal; you can tune by searching for the name of the station rather than its frequency; extra information can be sent to the receiver such as the name of the song being played or the station's competition number; and on some digital radio receivers you can pause and rewind output as it's broadcast.

Since 1998 there have been dozens of digital stations available. Although take-up of the receivers was slow, what the industry had been hoping for came in Christmas 2004 when a combination of cheaper prices and an advertising campaign helped boost sales (although the BBC had been broadcasting its five national stations digitally since 1995).

Digital radio is available on several different systems or platforms: through your digital TV via satellite, cable and Freeview; on the internet and terrestrially via a DAB digital radio receiver.

'Next to terrestrial radio, digital TV remains the second most popular platform (for radio listening) with 5.9 million listeners compared with 4.8 million DAB listeners. The internet clocks up 3.6 million listeners.'
*The Radio Magazine*, 23 November 2005

On digital TV, listeners can receive about 80 radio stations on satellite, and about 30 on cable services and Freeview. On the internet, you can access literally thousands of radio stations from right across the world.

Digital radio is also available terrestrially in the UK on DAB digital radio. There are two multiplexes across the UK (one operated by the BBC and one operated by commercial operator Digital One). Each multiplex carries a number of radio services and coverage is about 85% of the UK. Locally, there are 46 multiplexes serving local and regional markets carrying a number of commercial and BBC stations. DAB offers more choice; for example, in Cornwall audiences have a choice of six BBC stations and four commercial on FM/AM. On DAB that choice increases to some 25 national and local stations. By autumn 2005 there were 43 BBC digital stations available in the UK and 172 commercial ones, of which 40 were digital-only.

Digital stations have extended listener choice. There are niche music stations playing rock, easy listening or country music, or targeting demographic groups such as the Asian community, children or business people. Many of the stations can afford to do this because they are automated: presenters record links for a whole programme in a few minutes and then load them into the computer which plays them out at the correct point in the programme. The presenter still appears to be broadcasting live, but without the expense of paying them a full shift.

Some people say DAB quality is worse than FM and that is usually down to the bit-rate (the bandwidth of the signal) which is often squeezed to fit in extra stations or data services.

The Ofcom fees for a local digital multiplex is £500 a year, and for a national multi-plex licence, £10,000.

# Student radio

Volunteers run about 70 such stations, usually to a very high standard, on university and college campuses across the UK. These are often at places that also have broadcasting, communication or media studies courses. If you're considering a career as a presenter and are yet to go on to further education it'll be hard to beat the head-start you'll get by studying where there's a student station.

> 'Student radio stations provide a useful and vibrant autonomous channel for student communication. Gigs, sports events, clubs, essential announcements can all be broadcast to the student body with their own voice. This ... is an invaluable asset to any educational institution.'
> Phill Jupitus, presenter BBC 6Music, *The Radio Magazine*, 1 February 2006

Many broadcasters on these stations go on to present shows on professional stations after, or even while they're students.

# Hospital radio

This is another great training ground for the aspiring broadcaster. To split a hair, often these stations (around 480 of them) aren't actually broadcasting as they send the signal around the wards on cable which is heard on headsets rather than through a domestic radio. Others do, though, broadcast on low power signals within the hospital perimeter via LRSLs (Long-term Restricted Service Licences) for up to five years.

Again, many are very professional and although you may have to serve your indenture by collecting dedications on the wards for months or even years before you get a show of your own, your time may pay off when you broadcast for the first time.

# Internet radio

An increasing number of stations use their websites to simulcast their on-air programmes and reach not only those people who are working at their desks and have access to a computer, but also people abroad. BBC local stations have had success with their commentary of local football matches, which are heard by ex-pats who've moved out of the transmission area to other parts of the UK or to other countries. Some programmes are stored on a website so they can be listened to later, rather than listened to live; see Podcasting below.

Thousands more radio stations are broadcast solely via the internet (if that's not a contradiction in terms, as the stations do not broadcast on the airwaves in the traditional way). This is more accurately called webcasting or streaming, and because licences don't have to be fought for and won, and staff can be kept to a minimum, programmes are very cheap to produce.

This means that there's a huge range of stations to listen to and that the range of quality is just as wide. As there are no licences for internet stations, there's also no regulation which means anyone can webcast anything. That can be good or bad depending on your viewpoint. It means instant access to a potential audience for almost anyone, but it can lead to uninformed, legally dubious or racist material being distributed. All you need is the appropriate computer program, a pile of CDs and a microphone and you can talk to the world, though whether anyone will listen is another matter. Of course, an internet station can be picked up by your wireless broadband home computer, which can then send the signal, wirelessly, to a unit such as a Skygnome (which looks just like a radio) for you to hear anywhere in the house. That means that ironically, at the receiving end of the process the internet station is still technically being broadcast.

Free, wireless audio? There's another name for that: radio!

# Podcasting

'Just three years ago, if you'd asked listeners what an iPod was you wouldn't be sure of an answer. Now everyone has got one . . . or has a cameraphone or broadband. It's a transfer from the idea of the radio market in to a digital media market.'
Andy Parfitt, Controller Radio 1, *Media Guardian*, October 2005

There are three kinds of podcast available:
o Programmes of convenience – a complete programme made available so it can be listened to again, a 'best bits' compilation, or a version of a previously broadcast show put on the internet for convenience.
o Direct audio – these are audio versions of other media, for example, those produced by journalists and columnists from *The Daily Telegraph* and *The Guardian* newspapers.
o Bedroom audio – recordings compiled and presented by amateurs in their own studios or bedrooms. Although the content and quality of these is often poor, that may not concern downloaders who've made a specific decision to listen.

The audio available on internet sites can be downloaded onto an iPod (or similar device) and listened to whenever and wherever is convenient.

Although I used the word 'amateur' (it is thought 95% of the world's downloaders listen to the same 5% core of podcasts), many of these presenters are professional in as much as they attract sponsorship or advertising for their programmes. Some are well-known names, personalities and comedians who want to speak their mind or test new material. (Indeed podcasting could be the place where new presenters may be found in the future, as a radio programmer hears a 'bedroom broadcast' and hires the presenter for a show on-air.)

Amateur podcasters aren't bound by the usual rules and regulations of broadcasting, so they can plug records for money ('payola') or get paid for product placement. Reputable broadcasters, though, often don't include commercially-available music on downloads to avoid paying royalties. It's an emerging technology, but currently the BBC can only make programmes (or clips from them) available for download once they have been broadcast. In other words, they can't make shows specifically for the internet.

Now more programmes (and advertising, which equals revenue) can be produced at very little extra cost, commercial broadcasters are discovering a source of extra revenue by charging for additional, non-broadcast, programmes from their most popular personalities.

As I write, such podcasts are still in their early days, but a few lessons are being learnt in how to produce them:

- You could simply make available the whole programme, in which case edit out the music and time-sensitive information (news, travel, weather, and the time-checks themselves).
- The speech content can be the best bits from a previously broadcast show. Stations re-wire their desk so the feed from the mics is recorded separately, without any music, to allow for easy editing.
- Additional speech audio could be recorded (subject to the conditions of the BBC mentioned above) to make the podcast more personal and so downloaders get 'added value' and feel part of an exclusive club. This could be branded 'Unfit for Broadcast' or 'The Secret Recordings' to engage the audience.
- Comedy is an important battleground in creating original content, so too are really useful items such as film reviews.
- Consider including trails to promote the website and the radio show and station, where listeners' presence can be recorded (by page impressions or Rajar) to help cause a rise in advertising rates.
- Your speech content could be as a single programme or in the style of short individual links. Using the latter technique would mean that on 'shuffle' mode, listeners would hear *your* links and *their* music, in the style of a truly personalised radio station.
- Reconsider the running order of your podcast. It may be tempting to leave an interview with a big-name guest till the end of the show as you might do on radio, to give you plenty of time to promote it. But listeners to a podcast can easily fast forward through the download, so you may want to put that cracking audio first to ensure they hear it.
- Music from unsigned bands can be of interest to downloaders, and there's no problem with paying royalties. But even if royalties weren't an issue, to include scheduled music from your radio show rather defeats the object of a podcast. Listeners are a touch away from hearing their own choice that's already on their device, and won't want to hear tracks chosen for them. Plus, listeners download the podcast of, say, Chris Moyles, because they want to hear Chris Moyles – not for the music.
- In the future producers of podcasts ('pod-ucers'?) may consider making available even more content: scrolling text information; bookmarks so listeners can go straight to a specific part of the programme; and pictures or clips of bands and movies that are being talked about.

Earlier I said that more programmes can be produced at very little extra cost, but that opens up a new problem for stations and their presenters. Downloads and podcasts featuring a station's main presenter may very well raise their profile, but also that of the station. So there's an argument to say that, as their talent is being heard across several media (or plat-forms) those presenters should be paid more. Radio with pictures? That sounds like televi-sion. You can see how different technologies are colliding.

# Pirate radio

The heyday of the pirates were in the '60s when stations such as Radio Caroline and Radio London broadcast from ships in international waters off the coast of Essex. The excitement and need was lost somewhat with the arrival of the BBC's Radio 1 which provided the pop music that the pirates said had being missing from the Corporation's output up till then.

Pirate radio still exists today, more accurately called 'unlicensed radio', and catering to specialist niche listeners. The arguments against pirates are often the same as they've been for years: that they broadcast illegally on frequencies that may interfere with those of the emergency services; that they pay no royalties on the music they play; that because of the proliferation of choices on legal stations there's no need to work for or listen to them.

Although the 1990 Broadcasting Act brought about many more licensed stations, causing some illegal ones such as Kiss FM to apply for and win licences and became legitimate, the operators of pirate stations still claim they're disenfranchised in the way radio is run, and that their views and music are not heard anywhere else.

Operators face heavy fines (£50,000 is not unheard of) and even jail sentences, and the risk that its staff are never employed on official stations in the future. Indeed, licensees sign a declaration that they won't employ anyone convicted within the previous five years of an unlicensed broadcasting offence. Bear this in mind if you're tempted to learn your trade on such an outfit.

# 2 So you want to present?

'There's no identikit for the making of leading local presenters.
They're often as different as the local landscape and as
characterful. But they're invariably well-rounded, well-informed
broadcasters with a commitment to the locality, some verve,
a "good listen", thought provoking, quirky even, but with that
unmistakable knack of being in tune with the lives of listeners
and the temper of the locality. Research shows that listeners
can't abide presenters who are jokey with no wit; glib
with no weight; trivial with no insight; or just plain dull.
They warm to presenters who have intelligence, zest
and who lighten their day.'
Connecting England, BBC, 2001

'The presenter's role:
Defining and delivering our brand personality and values.
Providing the "packaging" — the variety, humour and passion
that listeners crave. Making a connection and building a
relationship with our listeners — presentation plays a vital
role in building listener loyalty.'
GWR Brand Handbook 2000

After reading those two quotes it should be clear how important a presenter is to a station, and also how important it is for you to get it right! Presenters are the public face of the station, with a job to entertain and inform, but crucially to keep people listening for as long as possible through the day and to come back the next. As a presenter you're the glue that holds the other elements together. Your specific job will be different from station-to-station and from show-to-show, depending on the size of station, the style that's needed, the timeslot that you're on and the help that's available.

Before a show you might research topics (perhaps for an interview or for your own short links), write scripts (either for longer features or short anecdotes) and select music (although not necessarily *choose* it, see p. 79).

During a show you'll most likely operate the studio desk, play music and jingles, interview guests, and read or introduce items such as the weather, travel news, what's ons and interact with listeners.

After the show there'll be a meeting to review how it went and to come up with ideas for the next one, and that may be followed by a public appearance.

James Bassam, Su Harrison, Alex Williamson in the Essex FM studios, Chelmsford. Note the number of screens, keyboards and mice! Courtesy of GCap Media.

# What are the plus points?

In short: fun, freebies and fame.

It's not really hard work is it, being on the radio? Not like being a farmer or a fire-fighter? A few hours on air playing some music and being daft, then off to do some lucrative voice-over work before swanning off to a showbiz party to get free drinks and have beautiful people fall at your feet. Instant friends!

And then there's the money! If you're good (or perhaps I should say, if you're popular) the financial rewards can be great.

You may have the whole country as your stage, performing in front of millions, be sent free tickets and CDs, get to meet people you would never have had the chance to meet and go to places you would never have had the chance to go.

# What are the negatives?

Well, actually it *is* hard work. At least it is if you do it properly. You're always trying to come up with things to say in a relevant, interesting and compelling way because you know you're only as good as your last show, and if your audience figures slip you may be out of a job.

Other work? Unlikely. There's usually no time. Stations, BBC as well as commercial, are increasingly run by money-men rather than programme-makers. The commercial stations have to report to their owners or shareholders about how much profit they're making, and the BBC has to report to its shareholders too: the licence-fee payers on whether its services are value for money. That means that a four-hour air-shift is only the start of your work at the radio station. There's pre- and post-production and a programme to do six days a week, as well as voice-tracking a show for another station in the group.

Showbiz parties? Possibly at the big stations, but not for the vast majority of presenters. And those 'friends' probably want to know you for what you do and how much they reckon you earn (vastly inaccurate), rather than because they genuinely like you, or maybe they're after a celebrity notch on their bedpost.

Consider all these other potential drawbacks:

- Unusual, unsocial or unpredictable hours and the knock-on with a disrupted personal life.
- Intense competition to get work and then stay in work.
- A low starting salary until you hit the big time. In commercial radio especially, but not exclusively, there's no job for life. And there's 'multi-skilling', the definition of which seems to be 'more work, no more money'.
- Meeting people who recognise your talents and stab you in the back to get the job that you were after, or being taken advantage of by the boss who knows that you're keen to impress ahead of your big break.
- Facing the same questions again and again:
  'Are you that bloke off the radio? You're rubbish. I never listen . . .'.
- Having to travel to a hotel, hang around, get five minutes in which to ask three censored questions to a rude and arrogant celebrity.
- Few training schemes – isn't that why you've bought this book?!.

And here are some more points to ponder:

Do you like your bed? A breakfast presenter will have to be at work at 5am. That probably means getting up at 4am, which means going to bed at 8pm to get an 8-hour sleep. Think of the logistics for a midnight to 4am shift. What about working on Friday and Saturday nights, or weekends? How will these hours suit your metabolism and family life?

Can you force yourself to be happy? Your role on the radio is usually to be entertaining, but if you've just split up with your partner, the dog's got fleas and your car's been stolen, how will you feel about doing the act then?

Worried about your old age? It's precarious being a presenter. If your act gets stale or listeners aren't listening, you may be shown the studio door. Do you fancy hawking yourself around to find another gig? You may still be at the station if trends change, but not on air. How will you feel about that?

Fancy living as a goldfish? You'll be encouraged to reveal a bit of yourself on air to connect better with your audience. You may have your picture in the local papers, appear on stage at a roadshow and be asked to sign photos of yourself, and be stopped in the supermarket. Some people love all that, but what about being asked for your autograph while you're waiting in the doctor's surgery, or being stopped for a chat while you're in a toilet, or being stared at as you try and discipline your toddler in the high street?

Are you interested in presenting because you've been told you've a good radio voice? What *is* one of those? If it's 'dark and chocolatey' you may be pigeonholed presenting love songs for your whole career. Is that what you want? Good voice or bad, you'll certainly need more qualities to back it up.

If you've considered all of those points and you still think you've got what it takes, are willing to learn more and want to go for it – great!

# Your qualifications

All sorts of people become radio presenters. You may be 'The Idiot' who presents the outside broadcasts and the Saturday phone-in competition show, or 'The Intellectual', perhaps the anchor for the all-speech breakfast programme or who fronts the budget and election programmes. You may be neither of these and have other talents. You may have been to university and completed a postgraduate course in radio journalism, or you may have worked your way from work experience to producer, with your sights set on being a presenter and then programme controller. Skills honed from time in further education can be useful: working to deadlines, having an appreciation of the wider world, knowing how to question and how to cut through complex ideas, having a life and interests outside radio.

A presenter might be a 'celebrity', either because they've been at the station so long, or because they are (or have been) a famous television presenter, or years ago had their own show on Radio 1. You'll be more likely to get through the door of the station if you can show that you have some background in radio. That may be practical experience in RSL, community, hospital, or university radio. Although qualifications may be useful, skills, interest, and passion probably count for more. What's on paper is less important than what's in your heart.

# Your qualities

Whatever makes good radio, no one has been able to pin it down exactly. Listeners don't buy it, and you can't smell or taste it, but you can *feel* it. That is, the station and all its integral parts have an overall attitude, and your attitude is part of it. Here, in alphabetical order, are the top ten qualities it'd be good to have:

## Adaptability

Have this and you're much more likely to get on. Put yourself out, help where it's needed and you may well be rewarded with a show, or another one in a better time slot, with more potential listeners. You also need to be adaptable in case of any change to your programme while you're on air: maybe an emergency news flash which has the potential to throw the rest of the programme running-order out of the window, or something as basic as moving around features to cope with the late arrival of a guest.

## Confidence and friendliness

You'll certainly have to speak in front of an audience of hundreds, or thousands or maybe hundreds of thousands, but they'll most often be unseen. On other occasions you'll have to speak to a group where you can see 'the whites of their eyes' – half a dozen co-workers at an ideas meeting, a few dozen people at a Rotary group, or an auditorium-full when introducing a band on stage, or in the station's Christmas panto! Confidence is also needed to keep calm in a crisis (see p. 327–334, When It All Goes Wrong).

## Courtesy

On air and off air you are representing the radio station as well as yourself. Unless you decide to become a 'shock jock', whose persona is one of being rude and arrogant to callers to gain more listeners (a format that works in the States, but less well in the UK), you'll lose an audience and maybe your job if you're plain rude to the people who pay your salary either directly (the radio station) or indirectly (the listeners).

## Good personality

In your broadcasting role you want to be someone who your audience can trust and warm to. Someone they like and can relate to, and that needs to be reflected in the office as well. It's highly likely that you'll be earning more than those who are working in the background of the radio station (although their jobs are no less important than yours). They'll resent that salary if you're abrupt, unprofessional, late, rude, or even refuse to make the tea. There are plenty of stories in the industry about household names who are one person on air and another off air – don't let your name be added to the list.

## Humour

'There is,' as the saying goes, 'a time and a place for everything.' And that's especially true with humour. Part of being funny is being sensitive to the mood and expectation of the audience, but when you're on the radio the instant feedback that a club comic might get isn't there. This is why it's important to picture a typical listener in your mind as you broadcast. By doing this, and meeting your listeners as often as possible, you'll get an idea of what they like. Even if you're not a presenter who's cracking gags every link (and most aren't) you must still be able to laugh at the idiocies of life, and at yourself, especially if things go wrong.

## Lots of interests

All work and no play . . . as the saying goes. If you spend so much time at the radio station that all you can talk about is the radio station, you are, frankly, going to be a dull broadcaster. You need to have a life away from radio, doing things that your listeners do so you will have something to talk about on your next programme. You'll have read books and newspapers, lived life, have anecdotes to tell and a yardstick by which to measure other experiences.

'The more things you can do outside work; be it seeing family and friends, keeping fit, reading, cooking, going to the cinema or theatre — whatever — the more your life will feed your work, and the more interesting your work will be. If you live, eat and breathe radio then you're probably doing it wrong. All you have to do is love it and work hard at it.'
Francis Currie, Programme Director, Heart 106.2,
*The Radio Magazine*, 3 July 2004

## Sociable

Being a presenter is not the job for a wallflower. You may find yourself eating things on sticks with a glass of warm white wine at a school prize-giving ceremony, or meeting prospective advertising clients of the radio station. Develop techniques on everything from making small talk to making people laugh. You must love meeting and working with people.

## Talkability

You should be able to articulate sometimes complex ideas in an interesting and compelling way, as well as being able to talk to listeners on air or at an OB, to children or grannies, poets, priests and politicians, as well as be able to ad-lib if it all goes wrong!

## Team worker

Work well with the people around you and get to know those at the station in other departments. Your job will be easier if you make friends at an early stage with key staff such as the receptionist and the engineer, but don't forget those in the promotions or sales team, the staff who schedule the ads and so on. Make a point of going in to their office to say hello each week. It can only help everyone — including you. Treat others how you want to be treated. Despite the growing number of stations, UK radio is still a small industry and the chances are you'll keep coming across the same faces. Some of them, like you, will be on the way up and others will be on the way down. Some will make your heart leap when you bump into them again and others will make your heart sink. Some will be able to help you, others to hurt you. If you hurt them before, what do you think they will do the next time they meet you?

## Well-organised

Presenting a three-hour show, six days a week seems straightforward enough, doesn't it? You just wander in with the newspapers and a list of friends to call on the studio phone while the songs are playing. There's more to presenting than that as we'll see, and that's off air as well as on air. You need to prepare your show, research your guests, devise and produce competitions, find the prizes for those competitions and send them off, conduct studio tours and appear at roadshows or outside events.

Each week you'll have to be able to pick up information on dozens of subjects, assimilate it and be able to interview someone about it intelligently on air. You may have to read books if you're interviewing authors and certainly read the newspapers each day to know what's going on in the world. If you're freelance, multiply all that by the number of different jobs you have and then add cold-calling prospective employers and sorting out your tax and national insurance paperwork; you can see that you have to be organised to be able to survive.

The above are all things you should strive to be. But there is one more — OK, that makes eleven.

## Be yourself

Don't copy other presenters, although you may benefit from listening closely to what they do and work out why they're successful. If you put on an act you'll be found out as your real personality comes through and then your programme controller will wonder who they've hired.

> **INFORMATION FOR INSPIRATION:** It's better to be a good version of you than a poor version of someone else.

> 'The listener can tell if you're bullshitting, they can hear it in your voice.'
> Jono Coleman, presenter BBC London 94.9,
> Radio Academy event, November 2005

In these pages you'll learn tips and techniques about what to do, what to say and what to sound like. What I can't do, though, is to teach you an overall style. You'll come to realise that your style has to fit with that of the station. Beyond that, 'style' is an imprecise 'something' that can be elusive to some and natural to others.

If two presenters were given the same programme elements (songs, features, and competition prizes) and a list of bullet points to communicate to the audience, each one would provide a programme that was completely different. Neither would be wrong, or bad, or unprofessional, but one may be better than the other. It may be because of their voice, their style, their personality, their life experience, their vitality, their humour, their empathy or their connection with the audience.

All those qualities add up to some kind of magic, a gift, a spark. Most presenters don't have it. The ones that do are invariably major stars (if they also have the self-belief, get the break, and don't mind moving themselves and their families to another city). You may be able to develop it, but you won't be able to learn it from scratch.

I can show you the mechanics. The magic has to come from inside.

# Your name

Should you change your name to be on the radio? It's one of the big questions that aspiring presenters consider, especially those who set out to hit the big time.

Why would you want to change it and what would you change it to? Some people say that the answer to the former question is because their current name is boring and easily forgettable; others because it's awkward to say. The truth is that for everyone who's changed a 'boring' name to a more 'flamboyant' or 'showbiz' one, there's someone else who's changed theirs in the other direction.

Certainly some names are considered more radio friendly. I was asked very early in my career whether my name was my real one (it is) as it's supposed to be good for radio to have a first name and surname that are interchangeable (Peter Stewart, Stewart Peters). Others may think that a good strong name with hard first letters makes for better announcements on the radio, such as Radio Kent's Dominic King (again, his real name). Perhaps you consider your name is tricky to say, but then Mariella Frostrup hasn't been held back. Maybe you think that what you are called doesn't fit with what you do: perhaps Agatha Clutterbuck presenting the sexy late night love songs show may sound a surprising juxtaposition, but then it would be instantly memorable. Getting people to remember your name is half the battle as you forge ahead with your career.

If other people find your name awkward or even impossible to say then that could be another reason why you may consider changing it (I'm not saying you should, just that it may be easier than having to explain it to every caller to your show, or spell it out every time you give out your e-mail address). You may have a fantastically long Asian or eastern European name, full of heritage but a tongue twister for most English speakers.

You may want to pick a new name so you can be anonymous when you're off the air (see the section on personal safety later, p. 144), to protect you if you present a controversial show or to add mystery. Perhaps you think your name sounds funny and people crack the same joke every time you say it. Then again, maybe you share a name with someone else in the radio business and you don't want to be confused with them or maybe you share a name with someone who's famous. I once worked with a Paul McCartney, not a bad name to have if it's got to be someone else's but imagine if it was Tony Blair or Peter Sutcliffe; someone who was disliked by some or all of your listeners.

A changed name can cause confusion in the office (on salary slips, for example, or if someone calls and asks to speak to someone in the office that no one's ever heard of) and also on air if you say your real name instead of your stage one. If you're worried about this, perhaps you need to change your name by deed poll and only have one.

You can legally call yourself what you want as long as it's not for illegal reasons (like fraud or impersonation) so let your imagination run riot. Simply go to a high street solicitor and sign a sworn declaration in front of them. A few weeks and a few pounds later, you can be whoever you want to be. The choice is yours but remember, once you've changed your name there's little chance of you changing it back without great confusion.

A few final thoughts – some people think that making up another name can sound rather pretentious; what will your parents think? Will they be offended that you've denounced part of your heritage and history? Your name is part of what makes you, you.

Some people call themselves by a nickname: BamBam, The Fridge and so on but this is rare; so is a one-name name. If you're simply known as JoJo you may want to ask whether the image that you have on-air is really the one that you want: a single name (usually given to female presenters) can sound childlike and a touch demeaning.

# Possible earnings

It used to be said that you wouldn't get rich working in radio. Certainly the highest earners in TV get more than most of the highest earners in radio, but arguably the gap has narrowed over recent years. As radio becomes more cut-throat, stations are willing to pay some large sums to attract and then retain the best talent, but a presenter in the middle of the night on a small local station may work for free.

Here's a very rough guide, bearing in mind that most people's salaries are confidential and those reported by the papers are usually either over-inflated, or over several years.

In the BBC, presenters may be BAs (Broadcast Assistants) who will anchor a show as part of their job. Their basic salary may be (according to length of service and experience), around £20,000. They may be a Broadcast Journalist (BJ) whose salary grade can be between £20,000–35,000, but again the higher level will depend on your experience and popularity as a presenter. A Senior Broadcast Journalist will be on anything from £35,000.

A local BBC presenter may be a freelance (with a fee decided between them and the station management for each show they present), who may get less than £100 a programme. There will be a contract between each party over the duration of the show, any preparation they have to do for it (either at the station or at home) and any notice the presenter has to give for holiday. They may, though, get paid much more than this.

I have no way of knowing how true this next figure is, but a correction never appeared:

'Triple Sony winner Jon Gaunt has . . . criticised BBC bosses for sacking him from his job as breakfast presenter of . . . BBC Coventry & Warwickshire (after he started writing a column in The Sun) . . . Gaunt was replaced on his £3,000 a week breakfast show . . .'
*The Radio Magazine*, 26 October 2005

At national level the presenters will be freelancers and will negotiate their salaries on an individual and confidential level. They may be higher than £100,000 a year, but remember they're big audience-builders for the station and as soon as their popularity wanes they may be forced to accept a lower fee or not get their contract renewed. Then they may find themselves slipping back down the ladder and becoming presenters at local level, where, as we've seen, the salaries are substantially lower.

In commercial radio, the salaries tend to start lower, but end higher than the BBC's. Indeed on a community station the presenters won't get paid at all as it's a not-for-profit set up, run by local people for local people. At a small local station a presenter may get as little as £10,000 (or maybe as little as £50 for a four-hour programme) and also be expected to work six days a week and do other jobs at the station as well (such as selling advertising time, writing commercials or inputting data into the music scheduling system). The breakfast presenter, whose show invariably attracts the biggest audience, will get more than the other hosts, but even that may be as little at £15,000. At some stations, presenters aren't paid at all because the managers have so many people wanting to be on air. If you have this opportunity and you can afford the time and travel expenses, don't turn it down. Working at any station, even for a few months, is worth the experience, and you'll have some on-air material that you can use in your next demo for a paid gig (see p. 348 for more on work placements).

At a larger station, perhaps a countywide, city or regional one, the salaries will be based on the audience figures. Pay may start at around £25,000 and rise to two or three times that. At the country's biggest commercial stations, either those in major cities or national ones, the sky is virtually the limit.

Remember: many commercial stations don't have staff presenters. The company's income is so much governed by the numbers of those listening that it's better for them to be able to end a short-term contract with a freelancer and replace them with another potentially more popular presenter, if necessary, without warning.

# Career prospects

Radio can be run on a shoestring budget, especially at local level. It's quite conceivable that when you start you may be the producer, technical operator and performer all at the same time. This kind of experience is why starting off at a low level is so useful. You get the opportunities and get to understand the whole process of radio much more than if you suddenly find yourself involved with a programme at a national level.

If you're good you can make a good living, and with more and more stations on the way, there'll be lots of openings. There's the opportunity to boost your income at the station (depending on what your contract allows) by taking part in roadshows, personal appearances, writing a newspaper column and even pantomime. As you progress you'll be able to use the skills you have learnt in radio in other areas and make more money: maybe TV presenting, continuity, voice-overs, endorsing products and writing. But for all radio presenters, especially freelancers (and there'll be more and more of them over the next few years) job security is certainly precarious.

Competition for jobs in radio can be stiff, but the following pages will not only help you get in to radio, but also get on in radio.

# 3 So you want to produce?

Producer on the Vanessa Feltz Programme, Rory Barnett. He's got line of sight to Vanessa to whom he's sending a message on the visual talk back system. On another screen he has his running order open. Courtesy: BBC London 94.9

'How will you get the best out of one of the industry's most talented presenters?
How will you create compelling radio that really connects with its audience?
How will your previous industry experience elevate a breakfast team that's already flying high, to even greater heights?'
Advert for Breakfast Show Producer, 96.3 Radio Aire, Leeds,
The Radio Magazine, 21 September 2005

The radio producer is the person who helps a presenter put a programme together, and who directs them while they're on-air. The job is different depending on whether the role is at a BBC or commercial local radio station. In fact, the job can vary widely between stations and between programmes partly depending on the role of each individual presenter.

Many large commercial stations will have a producer for each main show, for example, Radio Aire in the job ad above, although at smaller stations, the breakfast show is often the only one with a producer because it is the most important one of the day. In general, other programmes are more music-driven.

The more speech-heavy BBC local stations have a producer for each programme because of sheer practicalities: there are more items and stories to arrange, and because a presenter can't talk on air and take calls or answer the door to a guest at the same time. The producer may be called a Broadcast Assistant or the higher graded Broadcast Journalist. But for the sake of clarity, I'll refer to a producer.

Before the programme you will originate programme ideas that are creative and relevant to the show and station (such as links, competitions, phone-in elements, guests and so on, each of which have their own chapters in this Handbook); do the paperwork – getting money or authorisation for projects, setting up technical facilities, PRS returns, arranging fees; booking guests, facilities and studios and so on.

During the show you will keep the programme and presenter on track and on time, keeping an eye and an ear on the balance of the programme, its direction, technical quality and legality. If it's a news programme, you'll have to respond to breaking stories – what many producers relish as the perk of the job. That means thinking of who to contact for comment and reaction, writing a cue and questions for the presenter, and moving around other features and guests to accommodate the new items.

After the programme you may need to edit the show (if it's recorded), log it and store it. You'll have to arrange payment for contributors (although this is rare in local radio) and correspond with listeners.

Other administrative parts of your possible job spec:

- Making contact with the contributors, booking them and welcoming them when they visit.
- Researching and writing scripts and running orders.
- Attending programme planning meetings and liaising with and briefing presenters.
- Making sure that programmes fit a given brief, are appropriate for the station and its listeners and conform to station style and editorial guidelines.
- Keeping the presenter organised, producing them as they do pre-recorded interviews before the show.
- Maintaining a personal (or contributing to a station's) contacts file of regular contributors and callers.
- Co-ordinating the presenter's appearances with venues and/or the station's promotion/ marketing department.
- Working as a foil for the presenter for links and bits such as skits and sketches.
- Collating and possibly presenting programme elements such as weather or traffic details, requests and so on.
- Getting the show talked about.

Technical parts of your role:

- Editing, timing and checking pre-recorded programmes.
- 'Driving' studio desks to record, mix and play out programmes.
- Answering phones to the show as it is broadcast and deciding which callers go to air and in which order.
- Directing the presenter in matters such as timings and content.
- Editing phone conversations recorded by the presenter while they're on-air, for later broadcast.
- Identifying clips from on air items for programme trails, which you also write.
- Identifying longer items for 'best of' compilation shows.
- Producing drop-ins and beds (see p. 179) for the show.
- Becoming a roving reporter out on the streets in a branded vehicle to do live call-ins, stunts and so on.

As a producer you will have to lose your ego, as listeners will give a lot of the credit for the show to the presenter (the 'name' or the 'voice'). You'll have to cope with the personality of the presenter. Most didn't get to where they are today by being a shrinking violet! Then you have to cope with the programme controller. They're in charge of everything that goes out on the station as their title suggests. *They* want one thing, but the presenter wants to do something else and you're caught in the middle!

Remember, if you're a producer, you're a producer; not the presenter! One thing that rattles some presenters more than anything is producers who want to be on air themselves. So, if that's your aspiration watch and learn, but it may be wise to keep your planned career path to yourself. It's not going to make for a good working relationship if the presenter's always wondering if you really *are* working as hard as possible to make them as sound as good as possible.

# What are the plus points?

The work is fun to do, partly because it is so varied. You may be talking to famous guests, getting comment on a breaking news story or arranging an outside broadcast. There's nothing like the feeling you get just before a live show whose agenda can change while you are on air. Or the feeling when you're involved with making a programme whose content you love. Of coming up with new ideas or developing old ideas so they still sound fresh. It may be a long-form programme, perhaps a documentary, or maybe a consumer affairs phone in, or maybe a show whose music you're passionate about. There is nothing like loving your job, and with so many stations and programmes around there's a show just waiting for you to be its producer, and if there's not, write your programme proposal and get it on air yourself.

As well as those 'buzzes' there's also relief: relief when you get the guest you've been chasing for hours or weeks and when a fraught show is over without any mistakes. There's also a feeling of power! Often producers have more say about the content and direction of a programme than a presenter, both as it's produced and as it goes out.

Finally, for some people the biggest comfort of being a producer is that they're not the person whose name is on the credits. They don't want to be a star but they do want to be in radio and contribute to a successful show without the hassle of being famous.

# What are the negatives?

The hours can be long, unpredictable and unsocial. If a programme needs to be edited and its transmission time (tx) is Saturday morning, you'll have to stay late on Friday to get it done. As presenters rarely want to work on Christmas Day and New Year's Day it is often producers who have to go in to work to play out pre-recs (pre-recorded programmes).

Here's something you'll see a producer do more than almost anyone else: look at their watch. Even though most have an in-built feel of what the time is (developed from years of working with deadlines and backtimes) they still need to check because in radio there's never enough time to get done what you need to get done. Being a producer can be highly pres-sured both before the show goes on air and especially while it's on. When that red light is lit all hell can break lose — equipment failure; a no-show from a guest; a competition that doesn't work; a phone in with no one phoning in; a pre-rec going out with a bad edit included; a presenter with a tantrum. No wonder the second strange trait of a producer is waking up at night in a cold sweat!

# Your qualifications

As with many entry-level jobs in the media, qualifications are not always as important as practical experience. An understanding of radio, perhaps through student, hospital, community or RSL stations, or work placement, will stand you in great stead. Some producers may have completed a post-graduate course in journalism or communications, or a basic media course, for example a BTEC in media. These will help you identify stories, be able to research them and know what to do with them, as well as being able to spot possible legal pitfalls (outlined later). A year-long post grad course will go into these skills, and more, in greater depth to well equip you for your first producer position.

# Your qualities

Here in alphabetical order is a top ten list of qualities that a potential employer would love to see in your application to be a producer. Read them and find something in your character that illustrates as many points as you can. Then when you write your CV make sure that you highlight them to prove to the programme controller that you're the right person for the job.

## Assertiveness

You'll be able to explain clearly what you want and when to colleagues, including your presenter who may be older, more famous and on a larger salary. Often this will have to be said at times of great pressure or when there's little time. Assertiveness may also be needed when you're speaking with a PR person who's changed their mind about giving you access to their star, or to a regular caller who only phones in to whinge. It's not your job to be best friends with the host, it's not your job to make them feel good – it's your job to make them *sound* good. A producer may find themself the mediator between the presenter and the programmer; that means that you may hear things from both sides that they don't want the other to know. You'll need to be diplomatic and respect their confidence. (See also p. 142.)

## Creativity

Come up with outstanding ideas for programmes, contributors and treatments (the ways of doing an item) and you'll make a good radio producer. If you can find new guests, approach problems in a creative and resourceful way, write fresh cues and questions and know how it'll all *sound*, then you could be a *great* one. Remember, from outside broadcasts and roadshows to one-off stunts, part of the job of the producer is to help attract *new* listeners as well as keep the ones you've got.

## Good general knowledge

Stay informed by reading newspapers and magazines, watch TV, go to films. Like presenters, do what your listeners do – and more. You need to know what their interests are, and also what their interests may be. Go to a museum exhibition you may not have been to before, read an unusual book. This will help you connect and be creative.

## Immediacy

A good producer will be able to see the crux of issues very quickly – what the main argument really is, what needs to be done or said to make an item or interview work better.

## Organised

As you may be working on the production of several shows at the same time, being able to manage your time and be systematic with your paperwork is essential. You may also be sorting out a long-term project as well, like an outside broadcast or a Christmas show; and dealing with the presenter's paperwork; and liaising with the programme controller. Did I mention listeners' calls and letters too? Deadlines are appropriately named: if they're not met, the programme is as good as dead and buried.

## Practical and adaptable

Don't just know your job, know other people's jobs too. That means understanding the cabling for rigging an OB, how to use the newsroom computer system and being an ace at fixing a mis-feed on the photocopier, as well as knowing how to make tea and coffee. You're at an outside broadcast and something goes wrong: will you know how to repair the bit of kit, or at least know who to call? Although I can't give you engineering lessons here, it's worth paying attention when you're shown the basic workings of equipment that you use, not so you can whip out a soldering iron, but so you can make an educated guess whether the problem is a dead battery or a faulty lead.

## Research skills

Could you find a clown to lead the station's float in the carnival, and kit out the float like a studio, and a get celebrity on board – and have the day recorded, all within 48 hours? Talents from finding funny stories to phone numbers, biographies and a whole lot more, will be second nature to you. You'll need to use the internet, books and your own contacts to come up with the accurate information the presenter will need. But gathering material is not enough, you also have to be able to sift it and question it: 'Who's telling me this? Do they have a vested interest in this story or angle? Are they accurate? Can they prove it? Why are they telling me, and why now?'

## Resilience

Not everyone works well under pressure, but a good producer thrives on it. More than that, your attitude will have a calming effect on others who'll look to you to respond calmly in times of change or emergency. Resilience is also shown if you can cope with a heavy work-load and aggressive or temperamental colleagues.

## Self-confidence

You'll be able to deal confidently with people at all levels, and give colleagues confidence in your ability. In addition, you'll have a belief in your own capacity and be able to say 'no' or to question managers when necessary. When you build trust with contributors and listeners, you get the best out of them. You do that by putting them at their ease and speaking to them on their own level, by understanding what their needs are. But communication is a two-way process that involves listening, as well as talking, and then perhaps negotiation to reach compromise: you'll be good at this too.

## Writing ability

As well as coming up with ideas are you able to put them down on paper? A more-than-basic grasp of writing, spelling and punctuation will serve you well from writing a letter asking for a work placement, to putting together a CV for a better job in a larger market and when submitting programme proposals for a controller's consideration. Could your writing skills be tailored for a management job for writing reports, presentations and appraisals in a few years' time? You'll also have to be quick and accurate with numbers especially when calculating timings – adding up item durations, and working out backtimes (see p. 272).

# Possible earnings

Typical salaries in local radio range from about £15,000–£25,000 although, as I said earlier, the roles vary between stations, and so too do salaries. A more experienced producer at a city station, on a high-profile breakfast show may get a salary more like £30,000–£40,000.

# Career prospects

You work your way up the radio ladder in a similar way that a presenter does – producing on a variety of programmes which are more demanding (for technical or creative reasons) or more high profile, and in a variety of larger and larger markets (station areas). Jump at any chance to develop your skills: perhaps sit in and watch another producer work on a phone-in or outside broadcast, then stand in for them when they go on holiday.

It's quite common for a producer to stay at a station for two or three years and then move on after building a bridge from local to national radio, or from radio to TV. Some producers work so well with their presenter, that they follow them from job to job. If the hotshot presenter goes to a big station with big bucks and wants you to produce them, you could be in line for big bucks too.

The rule of thumb will come as no surprise: the bigger the show/the bigger the market/the more experience you have, the more money you'll get.

Down the line you could be a presenter yourself. After all, you know what makes a good one. Or you may decide to jump in to the world of marketing or PR. With your experience of dealing with those kinds of people while producing, and after selling the show on and off air to listeners and clients, it'll be a doddle: or a really competent producer could wind up as a programme controller.

# 4 Other people at the station

I thought this would be a good time to give you a quick guided tour of the other departments at the typical station, so you know who else you might come across and what they do.

Some of the titles may be different where you'll be working, and some of the roles might not exist at all, but this is a good overview. Most stations will have no more than about 30 people working for them, and others may have as few as half a dozen, but at those stations numbers will often be boosted by freelance staff.

## Your manager

This is the boss of the station. In BBC local stations it's the managing editor (commonly abbreviated to 'man ed') and in commercial stations it's usually the managing director.

In the BBC they're usually a radio person through and through, they've probably been a presenter at some stage and most likely have a journalistic background. In commercial radio they're less likely to have been a presenter and more likely to be from a money background, perhaps in radio sales, or from accounts. (You can see that in commercial radio, the station is a business for making money.) A BBC local radio station's managing editor will typically earn £40,000–60,000 and it's said that an MD's salary is broadly equivalent to the station's monthly ad revenue!

## Programme controller/ director or SBJ programmes

This person is likely to be someone with previous presenting or production experience. They're in direct control of the programmes on a day-to-day basis (making sure that everything is in format) and also long term (devising strategies to win new or bigger audiences). They're the people who do the hiring and firing, and are the manager with direct responsibility for presenters and producers. A good PC will work closely with members of the on-air team. Together with the man ed (or, less usually, the MD), they'll hold daily meetings with the breakfast team to review that day's show and help plan the next. They'll also hold regular feedback sessions with all presenters to help them develop a style that fits the station's sound.

A programme controller will work with the promotions team to help market the show on air and with the manager to help make sure that the station delivers its promises to the shareholders and/or listeners.

## Journalists

Led by a news editor or head of news, this small team will prepare bulletins, read scripts and conduct interviews with a content that is relevant to the station's target audience. At BBC stations the journos may also present a news programme, or 'dep' (deputise for) a presenter.

In small independent stations, the news team may consist of just two people (one in the morning who also does Saturday, and one in the afternoon who also works Sunday). In a BBC local station there'll be a team of around half a dozen although boundaries are blurred: some journalists may also have a programme, or may also be producers.

Some reporters have a hankering to be a music jock – I was one and got the chance at Essex FM. On weekdays I was head of news and breakfast newsreader, on Sunday nights I had a three-hour music show.

BBC stations present more news than commercial stations, but length isn't important. Content is. Long bulletins, which aren't focussed on the interests of those listening, are pointless to produce and present. As a lot of my background is in commercial radio news, I'm keen to stress that it's not the length – it's what you do with it.

## Other producers or broadcast assistants

While we're with on-air staff let's mention other producers. In 2005, BBC Radio Leeds led the way in a new division of skills between the traditional news and producers roles. Led by Managing Editor John Ryan, the station created a 'lives' desk and a 'futures' desk and all the news staff and production staff worked on each. The 'lives' dealt with what was happening that day, the breaking stories for the bulletins and the speech-led programmes. They were responsible for reporting live from the scene of a fire or crash, for example, and for setting up guests and interviews for that day's shows.

Staff on the 'futures' desk dealt with everything else for the station's output, from the next day onward. So all the planning, setting up guests and features, etc, fell to them. It meant there was a more cohesive and long-term strategy for the station: that programmes weren't 'islands', and that an idea or theme could flow through the day. Staff get to spend time on both desks to extend their skills and keep the station sounding fresh.

A presenter may spend more of their time with their producer than their partner! A four-hour show plus prep time before and after it, maybe e-mails and texts at other times and OBs and roadshows – it all mounts up. So learn to appreciate your producer and get along with them.

Let's also mention here the trails producer. It's their job to write and produce adverts which sell promotions or programmes on the station, as well as making some of the jingles.

## Other presenters

There can be a bit of friendly rivalry between presenters. The breakfast show is seen as the plum job, though it's one that not every presenter is able to do or wants. Yes, you get more listeners and more money, but you also get less sleep. Traditionally, the afternoon presenter has replaced a departing breakfast host, but that's becoming less and less the case: breakfast hosts are a breed apart and can't be made to order!

A problem at many stations is that most of the presenters never actually meet each other:

a breakfast and evening host will pass like ships in the night. The same for an overnight presenter and one on mid-mornings. That's why it's important for station managers to arrange socials so all of their staff can meet, so they know who they're promoting the next time they are on air.

# Promotions team

Let's move on to some of the backroom people who, although not on air, are no less important members of the radio station family.

A promotion is anything that gets your station talked about in the local community, and persuades current listeners to listen longer and new people to sample the station. This team is responsible for setting up the outside broadcasts (usually with a sponsor) and on-air competitions (usually with a company paying for the association of their name with the contest, and/or supplying the prizes). The team may additionally set up everything from the design and printing of the car stickers, to running listener holidays.

Promotions is usually one person with several freelancers who help out (especially at weekends). The young women who hand out stickers on OBs were traditionally called 'goodie girls', although now are often referred to as 'promotions staff'.

# Marketing and brand management team

Not every station will have these roles, and those that do may absorb it into the promotions team; it's all about promoting the radio station, but in a bigger way. These staff are the ones who are behind the nightclub events, the back-of-bus advertising or even the station-branded CDs that you often see for sale.

# The sales team

Still with money, these experts (who obviously don't exist in a BBC station, as their revenue comes from a slice of the TV licence fee) help local businesses promote themselves by selling them airtime so their message reaches the ears of listeners. Selling that airtime brings income to the station, which pays for everything from the staff to the use of the transmitter. You can see why this department has so much influence at a commercial station.

Sales staff are keen (they have to be: often a percentage of their salary is based on their income for the station) and are expert at selling the benefits of the station to potential advertisers and then closing the deal. You won't see a good salesperson very often, as they're out on the road in their patch (or area) visiting, persuading and selling.

They also have to work with other departments such as accounts, traffic and commercial production.

# Commercial production

This is the team which actually writes and records the adverts and is often known as 'com prod'. Few stations apart from the largest have their own department. Instead, they employ independent com prod companies to work with the client and deliver the final ad to the station for broadcast.

## Traffic department

These people have nothing to do with the road and rail news. They're the staff who 'traffic' the adverts and trails on the station: positioning them in the slots that the client's paid for, arranging billing for their airplay, producing documented proof they went out on time and so on. These are the people to tell if there's a product clash or voice clash in an ad-break. The first of these is when two similar companies are in the same break (for example, two car garages). The second is where the same voice-over artist appears in the same break (or worse, on two ads in a row). Both of these situations could reduce effectiveness of the commercial.

## Accounts, finance and admin

These are important people too – they make sure you're paid! These staff may not be radio people through and through, they've often come from other companies, but as I mentioned earlier they often make it to the dizzy heights of managing director.

## Music librarian and scheduler

Often if this person exists at all, they're one and the same person. Years ago you needed someone to catalogue all the songs. Nowadays, a computer does that automatically. Years ago a station would have its own mix of music that would be handpicked by one person. Now many stations (BBC as well as commercial) have a central group playlist, which is also on computer. This is the person to tell if there's a scheduling problem with the music, such as a song clash where two songs featuring the same singer appear close to each other on your playlist (for example, a song by The Spice Girls and then one by Emma Bunton), or to speak to about PRS payments.

## Community affairs producer

If this job exists it may be an additional role for a programme producer, or at a BBC station may be a role that's part-funded by the charity CSV (Community Service Volunteers). This person co-ordinates publicity of charity activities and announcements on what might be called the station's Helpline, or Careline.

## Engineer

The engineer should be your best friend. As well as doing the studio maintenance their role has increased over recent years and may also include fixing the phones, helping with IT, filling the coffee machine, mending the air conditioning or putting up shelves. They may not exist in many smaller stations. Even though there's more technology than ever, most of it is pretty reliable and so radio station groups often organise their engineers on a regional basis with one person looking after several stations. But wherever they're based, you can see why you need to make friends with them.

## Receptionist

Make sure you're friends with the receptionist too; they're the gatekeepers at the station. They answer the phones, greet guests, send the post, meet listeners and so usually are the first to know what's happening at the station. Keep in with them! Gone are the days when listeners would hang around the reception area to spot their favourite presenter, or pop in and buy a T-shirt and that's why many commercial stations now don't have receptionists. The salary is saved and the work divided up: in-coming calls are re-directed by whoever picks up the phone and the post is sorted by someone as part of their regular job.

# 5 The radio station

Radio's a strange thing. You don't buy it in the traditional sense, you can't taste it or even see it, and even though you can hear it and experience it, those are rather subjective qualities: each listener may feel something quite different depending on their assumptions and needs.

'Radio delivers things other than music — it communicates with people through debate and advice and it's tailored to its audience. It gives something to its listeners, so it is definitely not just background noise.'

Bruno Brookes, ex-Radio 1 presenter, *Campaign* magazine, 17 June 2005

The on-air sound is made up of the music, presenters (including voices and accents and sense of humour and style), links (including their duration and content), the jingles, competitions, listener interaction and so on. But it's also what happens off air: things like how the news journalist greets an interviewee and how well a prize is wrapped when it arrives at a winner's house. That's what we'll be looking at in this part of the book. From the station's name to its sound: what makes a radio station a radio station.

## The station's name

It may seem pretty basic, but it's very important. A lot of time and research goes into choosing just the right name for a radio station. Consideration must be given to how it reflects the area it serves, what it says about the overall style of the station, how it sounds when it's said (or sung on the jingles) and even how it'll look on a car sticker.

Existing station names fall into a few distinct categories:

▫ Names with a geographical reference such as Capital Radio, Essex FM, Fox FM — **F**irst **Ox**fordshire radio company — or the BBC local stations.
▫ Those which refer to some historical reference — Mercia, Invicta, The Bear.
▫ Ones which refer to local landmarks — Tower FM, Spire FM.
▫ Names which create a certain image — Kiss, Heart.
▫ Those which are extensions of other brands — Virgin, Saga, Kerrang.
▫ Names which carry other messages — 'This is Real Radio', 'This is Your FM', 'This is Your Choice FM'.
▫ Stations whose names 'do what they say they do' — Virgin Classic Rock, talkSPORT.
▫ Others which give no clue as to their content and are rather generic — The Arrow, The Eagle.
▫ And those that have no meaning at all — BRMB although some claim it stands for BiRminghaM Broadcasting, other say it was chosen just because it sounded good.

'There are two famous towers in the area — Turton Tower near Bolton and Peel Tower in Bury. It was therefore a name that was relevant to both towns, unifying them at the same time as being a powerful and recognisable station signature.'

Danny Holborn, Station Manager Tower FM,
Bolton and Bury, *X-Trax* magazine, June 2005

'Now when we're doing the travel news, we can be talking about somewhere that is a good 10 or 54 miles away from where a listener might be. You still want to relate it to the people who are listening, so it's "your travel", "your sport" and "your news."'

Derek McIntyre, Programme Controller, Your Radio,
Scotland, *X-Trax* magazine, July 2005

'The official story is that the station's founders wanted a name that people said at least once a day. People always talk about the weather and sunshine always puts a smile on people's faces. However, after a bit of digging I discovered the name had really emerged because they needed a jingle package that could be adapted . . . and there happened to be a radio station in Ireland called Sunshine that was coming to an end.'

Ginny Murfin, Managing Director, Sunshine 855, Ludlow,
*X-Trax* magazine, August 2005

Although some stations have the word 'radio' in their name (the BBC locals for example), a lot of commercial names include a frequency and the suffix FM. I suppose the question is whether, in the days of digital broadcasting where people tune by station *name*, those details are needed.

It makes you wonder about 2-Ten FM (in Reading, Berkshire), whose name is purely a frequency and waveband; that frequency isn't even the FM one, but the one on MW when they started life as Radio 210 in 1976!

In January 2006, 95.8 Capital FM changed its name to Capital Radio as part of its re-launch and started a return to the use of 'radio' in stations' names, and in that case a full-circle to what the station was called when it started in 1973.

Whatever the name of the station, one of your jobs is to say it loud and often, with pride and enthusiasm. Doing that will help someone when they come to complete a Rajar (listener survey) diary, or when they want to find you again. It may also mean that they're aware of how their licence fee is being spent.

I can't think of a situation where you could say the name of the station too often. But just because you say it often (and here's a theme we'll come back to later), that doesn't mean that it's not important. You say it so often because it *is* important, so don't throw it away, mumble or stumble through it.

Audience figures are calculated by asking people what they *remember* listening to – not what they actually *did* listen to. So again: say it loud and often, with pride and enthusiasm. You can do this in a number of ways. See on pp. 197–219 the chapter on links.

However often you say the name, there'll always be a core minority of people who'll call the station by another name, or simply don't know what they're listening to. People often ring a station's newsroom to comment on a story that hasn't been run by that station, and take some convincing that they've been listening to someone else!

One day in April 2000, the on-air presenter at Essex FM got a bone fide call from police HQ in Chelmsford saying that they'd received a bomb threat made against the station building. Staff were told to evacuate the studios and offices immediately. Emergency tapes were put on and a full evacuation was carried out. Nothing happened. Not only was there no explosion but also no police ever arrived. Twenty minutes later a call was made to police HQ to ask what was going on. Officers then admitted they'd actually meant to call BBC Essex instead and had got confused.

> **INFORMATION FOR INSPIRATION:** Say your station's name often and with pride. Quantity *and* quality. Repetition arouses recall.

# Station logo

The choice of a station's logo also has to be thought through carefully. Does it reflect the area, is it a graphical representation of the name, will the colours stand out, can the logo be seen from a distance? Even consider whether the combination of colours will be too expensive to print.

Some groups have a common theme running through their station logos, the obvious ones being the BBC local stations with a similar colour and a background of local place names.

Then there are other considerations:

> 'We've tried to have a generic logo that's immediately recognisable as being a Saga radio station brand, so the colours are broadly similar but with different use of colour and, of course, different frequency numbers. The colours are chosen for each area, and very often they're dictated by avoiding the local football team's colours, because if you've chosen Aston Villa's colours in Birmingham, City fans won't want to know you, so we try to be neutral'
>
> Ron Coles, Director Saga Radio, *X-Trax* magazine, July 2005

# Station slogan

From logos to slogans or what are sometimes called 'positioning statements' or 'station straplines'.

This is the phrase heard on jingles and often written under the station logo, that helps establish and maintain the brand. It may show what kind of station it is ('Your better music mix', 'Live news and sport'), remind people why they should listen ('Your kind of music') and/or include a location to reinforce localness ('The sound of south-west London', 'The heart of the south'). However, not every station has a strapline: Radio 1 doesn't.

A positioning statement should be:

- Brief.
- Understandable.
- Memorable.
- Sell the benefits.

That last point is an important one: the slogan is advertising the station in the same way that a commercial is selling the benefits of the product. So even though 'more music variety' is OK-ish as a slogan, the addition of the line '. . . so you can listen longer' is better as it makes it clear to the listener what the advantages mean to them. Another example? 'Travel news at breakfast every 15 minutes . . . so you get to work on time'.

A lot of time and research goes in to devising the best slogan, so don't change around how it's said ('Your better music mix' to 'Your better mix of music', for example), or make up your own. When I was a station manager one new presenter decided to do just that. His reasoning: 'I wanted to hear how it sounded'! This waters-down the station's message.

When commercial radio stations started in the UK in the 1970s they served, in the main, cities or counties. More recently, smaller stations were set up covering more localised communities that sometimes straddled county borders. Therefore it's not always easy to talk about your broadcasting area as 'across Blankshire', so you may need to check whether your reference is something like 'west Kent', 'the Lake District' or something even more intangible such as 'the Radio X area'.

# The station brand

A brand is much more than the music a station plays. A station has to understand its listeners and their lives and build a relationship with them. Hopefully that will be one that lasts for many years. Proving to the listener that the station understands how they live their lives should be illustrated in everything that the station does both on and off air: its name, logo, jingles, the presenters, the speech content, the music that's played, the location and look of the building, the spec of the radio or sales cars, the outside events or roadshows that the station attends, the station merchandise . . . its 'attitude'.

In other words, branding is the association the public makes with the name of the station, and is important because it helps sell the station to advertisers and listeners.

> 'Our brand personality is
> Spontaneous — a switched on character
> who's exciting to be with.
> Infectiously confident — a positive outlook, always
> looks on the bright side of life, but mature enough to
> have seen and done quite a bit
> Likes a laugh — finds the funny side when it's right —
> doesn't laugh at your expense though
> Easy to talk to — natural, honest and unpretentious
> Down to earth — in touch with people's real lives,
> grounded through natural character and a bit of
> "nous" that carries us through.'
> *GWR Brand Handbook 2000*

Let's take a look at a few distinct examples:

*Saga Radio*
Target audience:                50–69 year olds.
Brand values:                   High quality, value for money, customer service.

*Smooth FM*

| | |
|---|---|
| Target audience: | 35–54 year olds, more likely to be female (especially during the day), up market, affluent and fun. |
| Brand values: | Human, personal, welcoming, reliable, surprising. |

*Classic Gold*

| | |
|---|---|
| Target audience: | 25–55 year olds, probably in their 40s and 50s but with a young attitude. |
| Brand values: | Warm, friendly, fun, approachable, playing your kind of music. |

Source: *X-Trax*, July, August, September 2005

'We're about attitude, having fun, energy, laughing at the world and ourselves and communicating with our listeners in the way in which they communicate with one another. We don't want to preach from the rooftops; we'd rather be sitting in a pub with our listeners having a beer and a chat about what's on telly or what they did last night . . .'

Andrew Jeffries, Programme Controller Kerrang 105.2,
*X-Trax* magazine, June 2005

'(Great stations have) . . . a defining sound — where the whole is more than the sum of its parts.'

Jeremy Vine, presenter, BBC Radio 2,
*The Radio Magazine*, 6 April 2005

As each station is slightly different in its sound, most usually issue a House Style Guide that advises on things such as the music that's played, the duration and content of links, how often news, travel and sport bulletins are broadcast and how they're introduced (see p. 176). A station without some sort of Guide is opening the airwaves up to free interpretation of style from the various presenters, who may each go their way and ultimately dilute the identity of the station.

'Our tone of voice (on BBC local radio) is cheerful, friendly, down to earth and welcoming. We're very good company. But although good company is a valuable part of our mix, it's not enough by itself. We need to make sure that we're informative too.'

BBC 'Project Bullseye' document

'With so many different radio stations on the dial, it's crucial that Five Live stands out from the rest. We need to make sure we're distinctive in what is now a highly competitive world — a world in which style is as important as substance.
When listeners tune in, they should know within minutes that they're listening to Five Live, simply by the tone of our programmes.

That doesn't mean that everything should sound the same —
just that there should be a recognisable "core style"
running through all that we do.'
BBC Radio Five Live Style Guide

Own everything you do on the station, and brand it with your name – the weather is always with 'Blank FM's Pete Wrong', the travel with 'Blank FM's Emma Leven' and the sport with 'Blank FM's Barney Sausage'.

## Advertising the station

These are all the off-air events that help publicise the station: the marketing and promotions. Most radio stations need this to happen continuously so they stay top of people's minds. Marketing includes the use of paid-for media. Ads in cinemas, on bus-backs, on taxis and in the local paper are all called mass marketing (as they reach the masses). Direct marketing is cheaper and arguably more effective as it involves contacting specific people through the likes of mail shots and e-mails. If you target people specifically, rather than with a mass campaign, there's less waste. Or to put it anther way, you're more likely to be talking to the people who're already interested in hearing your message. Termite marketing is less obvious and is the drip-drip effect of lots of small references to the station, such as on car stickers, T-shirts and car parking tickets.

If you're stuck in a jam and see this advert in front of you, you'd be very tempted to tune in! Courtesy: GCap Media

Promotions are the other activities where the station usually works by itself, such as giving out car stickers or having an outside broadcast.

Advertising the station in these ways may add to the reach of the station (the number of people who listen), by:

- Creating an awareness of the radio station among potential new listeners, so more people sample the station.
- Reminding lapsed listeners of the station's existence so they're tempted to listen again.
- Building awareness of the station and its name to current listeners so they give credit to the right station if they are sampled by Rajar.

Promotions may also persuade people to listen for longer, by:

- Promoting the 'positioning' of the radio station (its style, what it does, what makes it different from the others).
- Building a loyalty with the current listeners.

**INFORMATION FOR INSPIRATION:** The overall reason for marketing and promotion is to steal from other stations. There are only 100 points in a percentage scale, so if you're marketing and they're not, and your figures go up, theirs will go down automatically.

'External advertising (through car stickers to cinema advertising) represents a marvellous means of strengthening the extent and nature of the relationship we have with our listeners. It's a complex and potentially very expensive area, though, that requires careful handling.'

*GWR Brand Handbook, 2000*

It is important to advertise in the right place. The choice of location can do damage to the station's brand (you wouldn't advertise on cards in phone boxes, for example, or perhaps before an adult film in a cinema).

'One of the first moves our MD Paul Cooney made when he took on the role was to increase the outdoor marketing presence of Clyde 1 and Clyde 2. Our logos are visible now in all the major shopping centres in the TSA, at Celtic Park and Ibrox and at ice rinks and concert venues. We've got a number of permanent branded sites in and around Glasgow and we even sponsor a River Clyde waterbus! Tickets for shows at the SECC carry our logos on the back and we've staged some amazing live events where artists like the Stereophonics, Dido, Keane and Westlife have performed to Clyde 1 winners only.'

Gavin Pearson, Presenter Clyde 1, *The Radio Magazine*, 29 January 2005

Make sure that the product (your output) is right, before you start promoting it. I can think of several stations that spent a lot of money on publicity ahead of a launch only for the first weeks of output to be fairly poor. Those who'd been tempted to listen returned to their previous station and it became much harder and more expensive to get them to sample the new station again.

Let's take a look at some of the basic promotions run by stations.

## Appeals

One way a station can interact and connect with its audience is by promoting a charity. The most effective tie-ins (for both parties) are ones where the fundraising is for a group which is appropriate to the target audience and which links with the style of the station. If you choose a charity that your community cares about, it helps the charity and helps the station get closer to its listeners. That shows that you have a heart and are not just a moneymaking machine, although if you can do good while also reaping the benefits of additional publicity, so much the better.

Other points to consider:

- Make sure the charity is either based locally or has a strong local relevance.
- Get everyone at the station involved in the one or two large pushes for the cause that you'll have each year.
- You may want to have different causes or stick to the same one – the local children's hospital will always be an emotional one with which to be associated.
- Consider sticking to the same mechanic for each charity you support so you don't confuse the listener, and to make things easier for you. For example, an annual walkathon in aid of a different charity each year will stick in the listeners' mind more than a walkathon one year, a baked-bean-sitting contest the next and a jeans-to-work-day the one after.
- As well as these scheduled supports of charity, always keep an eye out for sudden opportunities. Responding to a plea by a nursery that's gutted by fire and needs to restock its toy store, gains extra points with listeners.

Some BBC local stations have their own annual fundraising events for local groups, as well as linking with the main BBC charity Children In Need, and sometimes Comic Relief as well. Commercial stations also raise money for local good causes. A huge success was UK Radio Aid, when stations as diverse as Classic FM and Capital FM came together with hundreds of other commercial stations to raise money for the victims of the 2004 Asian Tsunami.

## Social action campaigns

The profile of your station is heightened if it covers campaigns that are of interest to its core audience.

'Social action broadcasting (is an area) of importance, helping us to bond with different sections of the community . . . Campaigns of relevance to local communities make for good programming, powerful public relations and add another tier of public value to our public purpose. They combine useful information with material that conveys the grain and texture of the community.'

Connecting England, BBC, 2001

For example, Radio 1 runs features on drug abuse and sex, BBC local radio campaigns have covered topics such as caring for elderly relatives.

What to consider:

- Make the topic relevant.
- Make the content interesting and compelling. If it's too preachy or do-goody, the campaign may, as far as audience figures go, do more harm than good. Consider the language, voice over, music and so on.
- Reach out to potential listeners and engage with the ones already listening.
- Carefully schedule the features so they don't swamp the everyday content.
- Provide help and advice perhaps in the form of a fact pack or a phone-in to an expert.

As a presenter your role is to get behind these campaigns (both the charity events and social action features), to promote the benefits of listening and getting involved. An unnamed and unknown voice-over on one of these features will have less impact than a personal recommendation from you, a presenter the audience knows. A presenter telling how Parkinson's affected his mother and how the family coped with caring for her, or giving blood at the local town hall (perhaps as an outside broadcast, together with newspaper photographer) will encourage many more people to connect with and support the campaign.

## Concerts

Every opportunity to meet your audience or potential audience has to be taken. It is another opportunity for you to get your logo across, to tempt people with the sound of your station, to lure people into trying the station for the first time or to get them back if they've migrated elsewhere.

One of the biggest possible showcases for this is an outside event  not just a roadshow or outside broadcast (which are discussed later on pp. 123–133), but a full-scale concert.

'We will broadcast from around 25 major live events and festivals in the UK and abroad.'
BBC Radio 1 Programme Policy, 2005/6

'We're consistent and distinctive in our offering. In the past few years we've worked hard to take the brand to new and exciting places. We've always done the V Festival but now also cover the Isle of Wight Festival note for note and really bring them alive for our listeners. This year has seen us do two of the largest outside broadcasts ever; for four weeks live from Lisbon for Euro 2004, and a week live from Vegas. We're working more on charity events such as Roger Daltrey's Teenage Cancer Trust concerts at the Royal Albert Hall from which we broadcast live. We have a better understanding of what our listeners want and in turn are better able to reflect that in our strategy for Virgin Radio'
Paul Jackson, PD Virgin Radio, *The Radio Magazine*, 4 December 2004

'Promotion of concerts is a revenue stream for the commercial radio sector. Typically concert promoters will pay a radio station to promote a concert on air; arrange radio station branding at the event, and provide a number of free tickets and merchandise as competition prizes for listeners. Occasionally, when the artist is particularly big, instead of paying for promotion, a contra deal will be negotiated, with the value of the broadcast rights and on-site branding off-set against the airtime promotional value.'
GCap Media's response to the Green Paper on BBC Charter Renewal, 2005

Not many stations have the budget, the expertise or the potential audience to be able to run such an event, but those who do, understandably, reap the benefits. Radio 3 runs The Proms and for several years Capital held their annual Party in the Park (in Hyde Park) in aid of the Prince's Trust. Music pluggers know that without the stations playing their artists' songs they wouldn't be hits, so arranging a personal appearance on stage for half an hour is a back-scratching exercise.

Most stations promote concerts in association with an artist or venue. They talk about the event on-air, interview the stars, and give away free tickets to competition winners. In return, the station gets its name and logo on the tickets and on stage, and a presenter (maybe you) introduces the band on stage.

The artist the station promotes must fit with the station's core values. BBC local stations successfully promoted Elton John in the late '90s, in his tour playing in the grounds of stately homes across the UK. Gold format commercial stations may link with a '70s reunion concert, while their FM Top 40 counterparts may promote a concert with Robbie Williams.

Concerts, then, are good for the station (links with successful and popular singers and the opportunity to get the station name in front of listeners and potential listeners), listeners (goodwill shown to the station for helping bring the singer to town) and the sales team, because such an event gives them an opportunity to get free tickets in a VIP area for representatives from local businesses who buy adverts on the station (as a thank you) or those who don't (as an inducement).

## Street patrols

Many commercial stations have a team of staff who tour their area in branded vehicles, wearing branded clothes, to raise awareness. They go to major events and smaller community events and may be seen at shopping centres handing out stickers, reporting from fairs and fêtes, delivering sandwiches to an office of listeners, and might even perform publicity stunts live on-air – all to promote the station.

**INFORMATION FOR INSPIRATION**: If you hand out free stickers, badges or balloons, people will wear them and become walking billboards for your station.

The trouble is, you then have no control over how the logo is used. What's the image if your free stickers are plastered all over an official sign, your leaflets litter a car park, or your stylish new logo is stuck in the back window of a 20 year old rust bucket?

Such teams (GWR called their vehicles the Black Thunders, Heart 106.2 has the Ground Patrol) have a vital part to play in brand building in a local area. In their highly visible 4x4s they add spontaneity and celebrity to events and provide face-to-face contact with the local community outside the confines of the studio, which helps strengthen the station's local credentials.

They're best used at places where:

◻ Their presence is creative and fun – just handing out stickers is not as interesting or fun as taking part in the town's pancake race.

◻ They complement other promotions – say, delivering morning doughnuts to an office ten minutes after they were won on-air.

◻ They provide obvious benefit to the public – not only give-aways, but also on-location involvement perhaps in a competition or on-air request and all this is done in public to build awareness and maybe generate free publicity in the local press.

◻ Their presence is spontaneous – reacting to opportunities as they arise, for example, delivering pizza to road workers on the by-pass so they can get the resurfacing finished sooner and your listeners aren't stuck in the delays.

## Local logos

It's important to stay uppermost in people's minds, so the more places you can get your logo the better. The station may have a deal with the local taxi firm to put stickers in their cabs, or in the shop window of every one of its advertisers, maybe a programme leaflet with every Saturday night take-away (promoting your party music programme that's on at that time).

Some stations sponsor the local football team, with logos on players' shirts and hoardings at the ground. Match commentaries and interview access to players and the manager are included in the deal.

Radio Jackie has taken over its TSA of southwest London. 'Banner hangers' have put up two-metre-long signs of their logo and frequency on central reservations, pub railings and the outside of multi-storey car parks across the area. It also runs a sticker spotter campaign. Listeners put a car sticker in their vehicle and if their registration number is read on air, they will win a prize. Such endorsement (even without inducement) may be worth more than an anonymous billboard.

## Out and about

You don't have to go to the time, trouble and expense of mounting a full OB. Many school and church fairs and fêtes would be glad to have a local celebrity cutting the ribbon to open the event and spend a few minutes talking to visitors. It helps them and the station.

Radio Pembrokeshire was at 315 local events in the summer of 2003. Some of those visits were only flying but at almost every one a presenter did a quick phone interview into the on-air programme and recorded a few clips (vox pops) with visitors that were played out in their own show a few days later. Think of the publicity and goodwill generated. (See Chapter 12 on outside broadcasts).

## Press publicity

It is important to build good relations with the local press. However, I appreciate that's easier said than done. Commercial stations often have a tricky time as local papers consider they steal their advertising revenue. BBC stations often come in for stick from the paper because, as the licence fee pays for them, they're an easy target.

Perhaps get one of the paper's reporters involved in helping out at the station, suggest a series of interviews with the presenters or backroom staff. Maybe the paper's news editor can come in and review the national papers once a week, or say what's in their own edition. These kinds of activities should all help foster good relations.

But you also have to give them what they want. It would take a particularly sour news editor to turn down a good story and picture from their local radio station. Send them press releases and pictures about your charity event, new presenter line-up, or competition winner. Let them know about the bad news too: the reporter who filled the car with petrol instead of diesel, the vandals who tore down the transmitter, and the leaking roof that flooded the basement. Then there are the fun stories such as the ghost that haunts studio 1, the lost cat that's made the newsroom her new home or how a programme helped reunite two pals from the Second World War. Push for publicity.

## Publicity stunts

These can also be very effective ways of getting into the paper, getting talked about by your listeners or passers-by.

A good stunt may have some or all of the **Six As of Attention**.

◻ Activity – drama and movement is inevitably more interesting than something that's static.
◻ Anticipation – that something will happen: someone may be covered in gunge, win a huge prize or lose everything.
◻ Audience involvement – for those involved, those watching and those listening at home.
◻ Audacity – a stunt that's outrageous, unconventional or extravagant will simply make better radio.
◻ Availability – there has to be a low entry level for people who want to take part.
◻ Actuality – it all has to sound good on the radio.

You may have a presenter living in the shop window of the local department store for a week, a competition to win a car where the winner is the contestant who stays touching it the longest, or simply stand in the street and hand out fivers! It could be to take a young listener to school in a limo or have a male presenter live like a woman for a week. Almost anything where there's a memorable and effective way to get your message across.

> **INFORMATION FOR INSPIRATION:** The amount spent on putting on a good stunt is often less than what would have been spent on paying for the advertising that the stunt generates.

A few points to consider though:

◻ The health and safety of you and others. There's not enough room to go into the H&S rules here, but suffice to say that you should think through the whole stunt for possible problems and then think it through again. One radio station got a lot of media attention for a competition to see who could sit longest on a block of ice, but they used dry ice instead of wet ice, and the contestant ended up with nasty burns.
◻ How the audience will perceive the station. Is the stunt fun or stupid? Is it wild or reckless? Is it creative or embarrassing? Does it do the station harm or good?
◻ Some of those problems are diminished if you get on board with another group. For example, if you do a publicity stunt for charity you'll not only get away with much more silliness, but you've also got the expertise of the charity fundraisers to help you organise

the event. For example, one station collected hundreds of old bras to stretch the length of a bridge in their area, to raise awareness of breast cancer.

Often the most effective way to get publicity is to arrange a world record attempt. Flick through the pages of the *Guinness World Records* and see what you can do individually (longest non-stop broadcast), as a station (the biggest collection of something) or with your listeners. As I write this, one station is planning an attempt at the world snow angel record, which only stands at a thousand or so. Surely you could get your listeners together and borrow a local football pitch or school field for the attempt? Make sure though, before you go careering off to set a record, that you do it officially and through the Guinness World Record people. You don't want all that trouble wasted.

## Guerrilla promotions

This is cost-effective and surreptitious marketing of the station, with a drip-drip effect:

- Sales staff sign for a client lunch with a station-logoed pen and leave it on the table.
- When you go for after-works drinks, leave station-branded coasters on the pub tables.
- Get the work-experience people to walk into electronics stores and retune the radios to your station.

## Industry competitions

There are three main competitions for radio presentation each year in the UK. Winning one of them, or even being nominated, not only heightens the profile of the station and gets lots of publicity both in the industry and on-air, but also helps your own career. Perhaps you'll get a bonus or a longer contract, or be made an offer you can't refuse by another station.

The Sony Radio Academy Awards are open to BBC and commercial presenters and producers. The Gillard Awards (named after the founder of BBC local radio Frank Gillard) are for those in BBC local stations, and the awards for commercial radio stations' staff are run by the trade association for independent radio, The RadioCentre.

The New York Radio Awards are open to presenters and producers at stations around the world. Even though the three UK-based gongs are highly prized, I know personally that there's something extra special about being judged on a worldwide platform.

## Advertising on the station

Many people see radio commercials as a necessary evil. The presenters don't like playing them as they interrupt the programme. Many people don't like listening to them for the same reason. And the advertisers would rather not have to pay for them! But without them there would be no independent radio. Although ads may be called local input (and they certainly do advise listeners of sales and so on which are happening locally, and help boost the local economy), no one actively tunes to a radio station for its commercials.

**INFORMATION FOR INSPIRATION:** An ad-break is the most likely time for a listener to leave the station.

There's one important thing to be aware of: in commercial radio, your customer is not first and foremost your listener.

> 'The way we make money in commercial radio is not by selling advertising, it's by renting our audience to advertisers. And it's on this basis that we succeed or fail. Good programming and presenters will deliver the audience; good listener figures will bring in the advertisers; the advertisers bring in the revenue and that will flow to the bottom line and deliver profit.'
> Norman Quirk, MD Saga 105.2, *The Radio Magazine*, 11 September 2004,

As Norman says, commercial stations exist to make money for their owners and share-holders. They get the money by selling airtime to businesses. The companies that buy their series of 30-second spots have been promised that in return, a certain number of pairs of ears will hear their message, and those ears will belong to a particular kind of person who'll be interested in their message. The longer those ears listen in any week, the more chance there is that they'll hear (and potentially act on) the sales pitch from the business.

So, your customer is not your listener. After all, they don't pay you: the advertiser does. The advertiser is really the reason the station is there in the first place, not because of some desire to entertain and inform the local public for free.

**INFORMATION FOR INSPIRATION:** If your station plays nine minutes of ads an hour, that's 15% of your total output.

## What's in the adverts

There are regulations regarding what products can and can't be advertised on the radio, and regarding the wording of scripts for others. Your sales team and commercial production department will have the up-to-date information from the regulators. This will include, for example, how the word 'free' can be used in an ad; in what way one product can be compared with another; the control of commercials for medicines, tobacco and alcohol; and even the use of sound effects.

Just as a scheduling system works out the music playlist, another creates the running order for a station's commercials. Criteria are similar: the mood, content, rotation (how often it has to be broadcast according to the contract with the client) and even who's on the voice-over. The adverts will be loaded automatically into a presenter's on-screen running order in the studio.

## Four listener turn-offs

### 1. Too many ads

The more ads a station plays, the greater its income but the more likely the audience is to reach for the off button. Where that tipping point is, is difficult to gauge. A station can set its own limit on the amount of ad 'minuteage' it will run in each hour. That's usually up to about nine minutes although some stations in the US may have as much as 20. A really low minuteage may increase the number of listeners (tempted back by the increase in music), but unless the cost of that remaining airtime is raised at the same time, the station could lose a lot of money.

This is the route that Capital Radio took in December 2005 in an effort to get more listeners. It cut its ad-minutes from nine minutes an hour to six at peak times (and from ten to five off peak), also pledging that there would be no more than two adverts in a break and that no break would be longer than one minute. It also kept the amount it charged advertisers for those slots, the same, even though the ads would stand out more (being in a less cluttered environment). The thinking was that Capital would charge more for the ad-space when audience figures rose. With analysts calculating that the changes would need to attract 30% more people tuning in to offset the cut in ad-minutes, it was a risky game (turning away money or turning off listeners) and one that's still being played as I write.

What Capital's move immediately did though, was to create a point of difference between it and other stations in the market (that there were never more than two ads in a row, therefore 'we play more music'). The amount of music is where another balancing act occurs in commercial radio.

## 2. Long ad breaks

Ad breaks are traditionally scheduled evenly through an hour, say at :15, :30, :45 and just before the news at :58, often called the '58 break'. That gives four roughly 15-minute slots in which to play music, do links, run competitions and so on. There's rarely an ad break coming out of the top-of-the-hour news, so the station can get back to the music faster. The exception is the Newslink advert on those commercial stations that take news from IRN. Stations get the news service for free in return for giving IRN prime next-to-the-news airtime, which it then sells to an advertiser.

Balanced breaks through the hour are fine, but it is a bit formulaic and can disrupt the flow of the music which will inevitably appear as two or three-in-a-row: that doesn't attract or keep listeners. By moving the breaks closer together, or by making the breaks longer and having fewer of them, a programmer can create a longer time without adverts elsewhere in the hour, and still keep the same income.

As I say, that's another balancing act. You could have half an hour of music from the news until 30 minutes past, followed by three longer ad breaks (say at 30, 45 and 57) in the second half of the hour. The interruption to the music lasts longer, but happens less often. The argument is that many people may tune away from the station between :30 and :00, but at least they were listening for the full half-hour between :00 and :30. The big question is: do listeners stay listening longer if there are fewer breaks which are longer or if there are shorter breaks but more of them?

**INFORMATION FOR INSPIRATION:** One long break is a benefit to the programmer but a drawback to the salesperson. Several shorter breaks are a drawback to the programmer, but a benefit to the salesperson.

## 3. Poor ads

What turns people off adverts? Is it their content, their style or irrelevance? Their intrusiveness or repetition? Adverts have less of a tune-out factor if they are relatable, interesting and compelling. And those three points add up to one thing: the benefit of buying the product should be made clear.

A good ad isn't one that's startlingly creative or terribly funny. It's one that *works*, by persuading someone that the product or service will help make their life easier, more enjoyable or whatever.

A commercial for a garage that says, 'We have a dozen mechanics, hi-tech engine tuning, four service bays and free courtesy cars' is all about the garage, not about the customer. It's rich in boasts, but poor on benefits. It needs the addition of a line such as '. . . so we can service your car faster' or '. . . so we cut the hassle of getting your car serviced'.

> **INFORMATION FOR INSPIRATION:** Ads should be like every other element on a station — relevant, interesting and compelling.

Adverts are not inherently bad: millions of people buy local newspapers every week just for the property, motoring and classified pages. So, potentially, the adverts on the radio are as important to the listener as every other programme element. Perhaps we don't need fewer adverts after all — just better ones.

### 4. The same ad, too often

Over-exposure to the same message over and over may actually 'inoculate' the listener from the message. If they don't turn off physically they may do mentally. Alternatively, the commercial may become so annoying that it triggers negative emotions that become associated with the brand or product being advertised.

## Playing the adverts

'Commercials pay your wages, so play them or you don't get paid. Simple'
*Neptune Radio Style Guide, 1997*

You have a duty to make sure that the commercials are played and played on time. The advertisers have paid money to have their 30-second slot go out at a certain time of day (an ad in the breakfast show is more expensive than one at night, because of the number of listeners), so you're breaking a contract by moving them or not playing them at all. Additionally, some advertisers pay more to have their commercial by itself in a break (solus), or in a certain position (usually either first or last) because adverts in these positions are more noticeable.

Playing the break shouldn't be difficult. The complete sequence will be loaded onto the playout system automatically. All you have to do is press 'go' and watch it count down so you're ready to fire a jingle and the next song. Then sign and time the ad log that helps prove that the break was played when it should have been.

You may additionally have to listen to different transmitters during the break on split-headphones — a different output in each ear — to ensure that all the ads have fired. If they don't (perhaps a commercial hasn't been loaded onto the system, is out of date, or has been mistimed so that one break ends up longer on one transmitter than another), make sure that the commercial scheduling department knows about it as soon as possible.

In January 2005 a presenter on a radio station in the east of England was dismissed for not playing 33 scheduled commercials during his shift on the previous Christmas Day. Station managers decided, 'dismissal was the only way as he had breached our trust and confidence in him'. Quoted in *The Radio Magazine*, the MD said, 'It's a standing order that DJs play the adverts as scheduled'. A subsequent tribunal pronounced, 'we are satisfied that the respondents dismissed the claimant for a potentially fair reason, namely that he had failed to carry out his duties deliberately on 25 December and compounded that decision by failing to make any efforts to rectify the situation, either by informing station management or by rescheduling the relevant advertisements himself. The decision to dismiss for that misconduct was within the range of reasonable responses.' You have been warned!

Never go from music *into* an ad-break – always 'throw ahead' first and talk about what's the other side of the commercials (see p. 230 for ideas). Many stations also say that you should never talk *out of* a break: simply play a jingle and get back to the music as soon as possible.

Never refer to the break on air. Don't call it a 'break' as that sub-consciously gives the listener an opportunity to turn off. Don't call them adverts or commercials – don't refer to them at all. That is, unless the break is really short, as listeners are conditioned to believe that a break will last for three minutes, you can highlight the fact that it's only one minute as a way to stop them tuning to another station.

> **INFORMATION FOR INSPIRATION:** Just say what you're going to do the other side of them, play them and then do what you said you would.

## How presenters can help the sales team
You'll understand the whole sales process much better if you go out with one of the sales executives to a client meeting. Your appearance may also help them secure the advertising campaign – you never know, if that client is say, a car dealership, then they may offer to give you a logoed car or sponsor your show.

## Sponsorship
A sponsor's credit or 'tag' (note. not an advert) is played solus (by itself) and associated with a station feature. You've probably heard them, usually in the weather jingle: 'The weather is brought to you in association with Cozy Boilers, keeping you warm whatever the weather . . .'. They may also be linked with a feature: a DVD chart may be run as a sponsor feature with a DVD rental shop, or tour dates may have to be mentioned to promote the station's ticket line. In these situations it's up to the presenter to make the feature sound as relevant, interesting and compelling as possible, even though the sponsorship may be the only reason the feature is on!

Clients can sponsor almost anything on the station – the time-checks, the travel bulletins, groups of songs, competitions, even the show itself – but they can't sponsor the news. That's to keep the bulletins impartial. What if a petrol company sponsored the news and your station then had to report on one of its tankers causing a crash on the motorway? You could be tempted not to run the story. Ofcom guidelines say, 'A sponsor must not influence the content and/or scheduling of a programme in such a way as to impair the . . . editorial independence of the broadcaster'.

Some of the sponsor credits are pre-recorded, the presenter says others live. If you have to read one of these make sure that you say it word for word, as it has been given to you. The sponsor has paid a lot of money and invested a lot of time in deciding just the right line and won't want it altered. However, that doesn't mean that you should throw the line away without thinking; sound enthusiastic and interested in the line. Sell it as you say it.

The point of sponsored features is that the advertiser pays for credits that are shorter than an advert, so are cheaper, but have a long-term place next to a feature that's fun or informative. Because the sponsorship helps the listener get the programme or feature free of advertising, a closer link is created between them and the brand.

In some cases a sponsor won't give money to the station itself, for example, a bank sponsoring the Premiership, or a margarine company lending its name to the London Marathon. If that's the case consider whether they need to be credited at all, especially when the event is well known in its own right. If you do have to mention the company, limit the number.

## Ads, sponsorship and the BBC

Ads and sponsorship have nothing to do with the BBC — or do they?

'Although the BBC does not compete with independent radio for advertising revenue, it does compete for audiences. And as audience size is the currency upon which advertising is bought, any increase in BBC audience will have an adverse effect on commercial radio's revenue . . . As a result direct competition by BBC radio for commercial radio's audiences and revenue sources has real, depressive consequences.'
GCap Media's response to the Green Paper on BBC Charter Renewal, 2005

## Advertising the station, on the station

I've mentioned advertising the station via other media, and other brands advertising on our media — now here's the third spoke in the wheel.

**INFORMATION FOR INSPIRATION:** Nothing sells your radio station better than your radio station.

The adverts that mention other programmes or features on the station are called trails, and of course they appear on independent *and* BBC stations.

There are three main types of trails:

- Pre-recorded and mixed trails, which are scheduled (like adverts) to be played at certain times.
- Pre-scripted trails which the presenter will be asked to read at a certain time.
- (Usually) ad-libbed teasers (also called teases). I've devoted a whole section to these later in the Handbook on p. 220.

Playing a trail won't attract more people to the station (they simply won't hear it). They're used to tempt current listeners to listen again on another occasion. That'll increase the station's 'hours' (or TSL: 'time spent listening') and increase the station's market share. I'll explain why these are important later, but for the moment let's just say that the longer someone listens to the station, the more chance there is of them hearing the advert paid for by a company, and therefore the more the station can charge for that airtime.

Additionally, but no less importantly, trails also reinforce the name of the station and its strapline and prompt people to realise what they're listening to in the first place!

Trails are placed carefully to lure listeners into listening again. For example, one for the

Saturday sports show is best scheduled next to the weekday mornings' sports reports, so you're talking to those who're most likely to be interested.

On a commercial station a trail will go within or next to an ad-break, rather than being played solus, so there aren't as many stops. Some stations say the first ad in a break is the one people pay most attention to, so that's where the trail should go. Others say that the last spot (position in a break) is the one that should be claimed by the station. And yes, you've guessed it, other stations say that a trail should go mid-break!

If the trail is last in a break, it may very well end with a station jingle, or similar announcement: '. . . that's right here, on Tuesday at 9, on 99FM Radio Black . . .'. Be aware of how it ends; it sounds awful for a line like that to be followed by the presenter playing in a jingle that sings '99FM Radio Black . . .'.

Make sure you know what the trail is for. First, this will avoid nasty clashes (such as playing Elton John's *Candle in the Wind* followed by a trail for the station's travel bulletins) and secondly it'll make you better prepared to improve the trail's impact (for example, if you followed an interview with the organiser of the county show, with a trail mentioning your station's OB from it). Picking up on that last point, the effect of a trail is heightened considerably if you, the presenter, react personally and positively to it. It's like your own endorsement. Listeners like you, and will like what you like.

As I mentioned at the start of the Handbook, there are stations whose house style is different from these suggestions: that you *should* go from a trail to a jingle, or that you *shouldn't* talk off the back of a trail. Check what yours says, and follow it.

**INFORMATION FOR INSPIRATION:** Everything you say about the station *off air* should encourage sampling. Everything you say about it *on air* should communicate a benefit and extend TSL and recall.

## Cross-platform promotions

This is when a station uses several media to get the message across, while a 'cross-promotion' is where a radio station teams up with say, a newspaper or other company to share an event, to increase the reach of the message. Both these have to be carefully planned, not only so all media is saying the same thing, but also so they all say it at the right time.

A good example is what staff did at BBC Radio Devon in 2004. A Christmas Murder Mystery was conceived to help raise money for charity, publicise the station to potential new listeners and to maintain reach and share through Christmas.

Billed as the UK's first ever interactive radio drama where listeners would solve the crime, the Mystery was a 3-hour on-air programme (☑ Interactivity, ☑ On-air programme).

Big names (Noel Edmonds, Greg Dyke) with local connections took part (☑ local and national media exposure, ☑ local links). The show was promoted on ☑ radio, ☑ BBC regional television, ☑ online, ☑ in local and national newspapers, ☑ billboard posters and ☑ word of mouth from other fundraising events. ☑ 2000+ letters were sent to those on the listener database and ☑ free adverts appeared in Devon's community magazines.

☑ Leaflets were distributed at large-scale events (Navy Days in Plymouth, the Exeter Festival) and at community locations (pubs, health clubs, football grounds). ☑ Partnerships were established with local companies to gain extra promotion through their newsletters, websites and notice boards. ☑ Presenters endorsed the Mystery on air and ☑ different trails targeted different ages and sexes with individual angles (executions).

Inside each Detection Pack sold to listeners was ☑ a Christmas schedule for BBC Radio Devon along with other promotional literature or packs could be ☑ downloaded from the station website.

The campaign was ☑ tested before launch, ☑ planned (the team produced a campaign timetable) and ☑ consistent (with the music, voice-over artist and single core strapline throughout, across all media).

In the Mystery itself, specially produced trailers promoted BBC Radio Devon's Christmas schedule, inviting new listeners to ☑ sample other programmes and services, and included ☑ an incentive for new listeners to keep listening to win a luxury weekend break.

The Murder Mystery campaign raised more than £30,000 for the appeal and the subsequent Rajar figures confirmed that BBC Radio Devon extended its reach, listening hours and share of audience. It went on to win a Gold Gillard Award for Simon Furber and his promotions team after the judges said the '*extremely well-planned, highly original and creative campaign, (with) excellent production values both on and off-air . . . simply ticked all the boxes.*'

# 6 The audience

A radio station is nothing without its listeners.

There are so many newer technologies available for people to listen to their favourite music, why do people still use one of the oldest? With record players, cassettes, CD players, MP3 devices and the internet, people can choose exactly what they want to listen to and when – but perhaps that gives us a clue to radio's biggest selling points.

Radio is easy to use: you just turn it on and there's a service. OK, it may need retuning occasionally (and that's even easier on a digital radio with the names of stations, rather than their frequency). It doesn't need to power up or download. There are no moving parts to go wrong or licences or subscriptions to buy. It runs on mains power, batteries or in the case of wind-up radios, elbow grease. It's portable, personal (speaking on a one-to-one basis) and, with headphones, non-intrusive.

Radio is interactive. You can call a phone-in and tell thousands of others your opinion, take part in a competition and, bizarrely, phone a radio presenter and ask them to play a song on the radio that would be just as easy for you to select on your MP3 player.

'On one occasion a listener lost her purse while out shopping and rang us for help. Within twenty minutes of broadcasting this message the owner of a local restaurant called us to say that the purse had been found. No other station in the area would have broadcast such a request, but Lakeland Radio exists to provide news and information just for local people.'

Peter Fletcher, Station Director, Lakeland Radio,
*The Radio Magazine*, 22 January 2005

**INFORMATION FOR INSPIRATION:** The number of people listening to a radio station can affect both its output and the careers of those employed. If listening figures are down, stations will make on-air changes to boost the station's popularity. Commercial stations do this so they can charge more money for delivering a larger audience to the advertisers, and BBC stations so they can justify the licence fee.

## The target audience

Commercial radio stations want the biggest and most easily identifiable audience that they can deliver to potential advertisers. That usually means that most of them target the 'masses', the 18–34 year olds, with a mix of current chart hits and favourite older songs.

Another consideration may be to target a section of the potential audience that's not already catered for. That may be people in a geographical area (like the community stations), or those interested in a specific kind of music or information (Classic FM, the talk station Oneword or the Christian station Premier Radio), or it might be a certain demographic (the breakdown of a group of people by their age and income), such as Saga Radio or Capital Disney. However, in general, a niche output may have to broadcast to a large area to get a large enough audience to be viable.

'The Saga company provides services for people aged 50 and over, but that's quite a broad spectrum, so for radio we needed to narrow it down a bit. Our core target audience is 50—69 and commercially people in that age group have the most disposable income so from a business viability point of view it's a very important age demographic.'
Ron Coles, Director Saga Radio, *X-Trax* Magazine, July 2005

Once a station has chosen its demographic, it may further sub-divide that group into the different kinds of people according to their interests, which helps the station programmers ensure that everyone's being catered for.

'Their personality — unpretentious, young-at-heart, fun, gregarious and impetuous.
Their demographic profile — they are best thought of as: 25—34 year old, more likely to be female than male.
This definition is important for two reasons:
• Commercially, it's vital that our profile is strong across a much broader target of adults 15—44. By targeting 25—34s we stand the strongest chance of appealing to this broad profile.
• A female skew again is used as a means of attracting the largest possible brand franchise. Whilst men will willingly listen to a station directed towards women, the converse is definitely not the case. We are not, though, a female brand. It's crucial to understand that men remain a vital half of our audience whose perceptions of our station are just as important as those of females.
Nothing we do should alienate them.'
*GWR Brand Handbook* 2000

The BBC targets an audience in a similar way.

'The Sparkler research found there are three groups of listeners among the 15—24 year old audience. The majority according to Parfitt (Andy Parfitt, Controller Radio 1), are the "contended grouping" who might go to a Robbie Williams show but don't buy music magazines. The second group, "Radio 1 heartland" are active gig goers and downloaders, and then there are the "scenesters" who are making music themselves or are DJs.'
*The Independent,* 16 May 2005

BBC local radio has similarly identified three distinct groups of people who it wants to target. There's the over 55s, the 'heartland' audience which is currently its biggest and most loyal listeners. (This demographic has been 'personalised' by the BBC as two typical listeners, Dave and Sue. Station staff are given facts and lifelines about these 'composite listeners', to help them focus on the heartland's needs and wants.) The next group is the 45–54 year old age group, the 'replenishers' who gradually come into the above age range and start tuning to BBC local stations more as they become older. Then the under 45s, the 'cherry pickers', who come to the stations occasionally for specific information or programmes such as news, sport, travel and weather.

Student radio is funded by the college or student union, so it stands to reason that their music and speech content should reflect their target audience. That is, young men and women between 18 and 23.

# Non-target listeners

As a programmer you aren't going to actively discourage people from listening if they don't fit into your model of an audience member. After all, those people are just as likely to get a Rajar survey diary as anyone, but you mustn't be diverted into thinking that you should pander to their desires – if a 50 year old woman writes in to your Top 40 station and says she listens all the time but wants more '60s music played, you shouldn't do as she asks. That would water down the programming for those who you are actively targeting.

People tend to listen to stations that are not actively targeted at them for one of two reasons. They might wish they were in that targeted audience, or they can't get what they want from a single station and prefer to dip in and out of several (a chart hits fan who additionally tunes to Radio 4 for the comedy and Radio Five Live for the news, for example).

# Rajar and ratings

The majority of listeners will never want to tell you who they are. Certainly some will want to write and ring, but most will be quite happy to just listen. So how do you find out how many of them you've got?

This used to be done by the BBC counting listeners to its stations and the commercial radio industry doing the same for its stations. But using two different survey methods led, unsurprisingly, to figures that quite literally didn't add up. Put together, the stats would show that there'd be more people listening to the radio, than there were people!

In 1992, BBC and commercial stations joined forces to contract Rajar (Radio Joint Audience Research) to work out for them how many people listen; when they listen; and for how long. Thirty-thousand people are surveyed across the UK on an ongoing basis (a survey 'sweep') and reports are published every three months. Each of these is known as a 'Quarter': Quarter 1 is the survey for January, February and March, Quarter 2 is for April, May and June and so on. Some stations ask for reports every *six* months (over two Quarters) because it effectively doubles the sample and so increases the accuracy

Because stations have to pay Rajar (on a sliding scale according to their size) to survey their TSA (Total Survey Area), many small stations decide not to be included, but this does mean that they don't have 'industry standard' audience figures to show prospective advertisers.

The audience is counted by choosing a typical cross-section of people in a certain area. Those people are initially asked in a face-to-face, individual briefing what stations they're likely to listen to, and stickers of those stations (mentioning the name, logo, strapline and description of the station) are put on to each page of a special diary. The person is then asked to note what station they remember listening to in each 15-minute segment of each day in the seven-day survey period. Later, the diaries are collected and the numbers are crunched. The resulting figures show whether the audience for each station is increasing or decreasing.

Rajar provides Quantitative Research as it quotes actual figures (or quantities). Qualitative Research is the type of information that comes from focus groups and deals with thoughts and feelings about the station ('I like the choice of music', 'It's best for travel news', and so on).

## Reading the stats

This will be the job of the managers of the station, so you won't have to know that much about it at this stage. Having said that, it's good if you understand the basics and the terminology so you know what they're talking about.

Weekly Reach is the number of people over 15 who listen to the station for at least 15 minutes over the course of the average week and is shown either in thousands of listeners, or as a percentage of the total population. (The three-month total is averaged out to give a weekly figure.) Note that in any area this will add up to more than 100% as people listen to more than one station.

Total Weekly Hours is a simple addition of the total number of people and how long they listen for. Divide this by the reach and you get the Average Hours: how long a typical listener listens. This is often called Time Spent Listening, or TSL. (Earlier I mentioned trailing other features on the station, so existing listeners would tune in again on another occasion. Doing that should increase your TSL.)

Market Share is the percentage of radio-listening your station has compared to others in the area (so it measures your relative success). This always adds up to 100% as it's a division of all radio listening between all the stations in the area.

The Total Survey Area is the area that is surveyed for the listening figures. This can be reduced by the station to capitalise on the likelihood of having more listeners in the core area rather than on the fringes. This has the effect of boosting the percentage reach of the station, although not the actual number of listeners.

A station might have quite a small *share*, but a large *reach*, and that's what's usually most important in terms of radio listening: get lots of listeners first, then tempt them to listen longer. As people can only listen to one station at a time, the more your figures go up, the more your rivals' go down.

Headline figures come under these headings published by Rajar for everyone to see. Fuller figures, available only to individual stations, show the demographic breakdown of every half-hour segment through the day at that station.

Rajar statistics have a caveat attached to them: their accuracy (like most polls) are accurate only to +/- three percentage points. That means that if your station is shown to have a reach of 26%, it may in fact be 23% or 29%. So small rises or falls in quarterly figures should be treated with caution.

## Interpreting the stats

You can compare the Rajars from one three-month sweep to the next (quarter on quarter), but this may not be very accurate because of the small number of people with diaries. Although it may show if you've done spectacularly well or badly, unless you can pinpoint a specific reason for that (for example, your coverage of severe storms, or a huge cash-give-away caused more people to tune in), these stats must be treated as more of a guide than as the 'holy grail'. Also bear in mind that people's listening habits change during a calendar year: with more people on holiday in the summer, there are fewer people available to listen. It is probably better to compare the figures with what you had this time last year (year on year). Then you get a much clearer picture, although it also means there's a long time before any change that is made to the sound of the station (a new feature or presenter) is reflected in the figures.

**INFORMATION FOR INSPIRATION:** It's thought that it takes at least 18 months for a show to 'bed' in and become truly accepted by an audience, and any trend on Rajar will only really be evident after a similar length of time. So, only after that should the data be used as an accurate indication of the station's, or a programme's, popularity.

## Alternatives to the diary system

Critics to the diary system have several gripes. They say:

- It's old-fashioned to ask people to tick boxes on pieces of paper.
- The shortest time between results is three months, which makes the results of changes difficult to measure.
- People simply forget, or never know or realise, what stations they listen to (with digital stations and analogue ones, there are hundreds of stations that someone could be exposed to during a day).
- 'Heritage stations' (those which have been around for a long time) often do better than newer ones simply because people remember their name more readily.
- People's measurement of the length of time they listened for is not always reliable.
- The 'sample size' is too small to be accurate. (30,000 people are sampled each quarter with a new sample each week, providing a sample of 130,000 across the year. That's out of an adult population of 48.8 million, a survey sample of 0.25%.)
- The stats produced are only quantative and not qualitative. In other words, they give the number of people who heard the broadcast not whether they enjoyed it or not – or even whether they were the person who chose that station (what if it was on in a shop, cab or friend's home?).
- Why should those asked to fill in a diary be bothered? They don't pay to hear the radio, so it doesn't matter to them what they tick, if anything.

**INFORMATION FOR INSPIRATION:** It's often said that if your station does well in Rajar; the system is accurate. But if it does poorly, the stats are wrong!

As I write, there are moves to change the paper diary system into one relying more on technology. This may be an automatic device that hears either inaudible tones or snippets of sound broadcast by stations, but that still won't show if someone was actually *listening* to the programme, or just *hearing* it. It still won't differentiate between stations actively chosen by the survey sample or those heard by accident.

## Rajar analysis

It's often worth getting more detailed analysis of the Rajar results than purely the headline figures. By digging deeper you can work out listening patterns: for example, what kind of person turns off which programmes on your station, and what do they listen to instead? This 'switching analysis' may show that people are turning on specifically for a mid-morning presenter, and a controller may consider that if that person is such a draw maybe they should be on at, say, drivetime instead.

## Tracking

Specialist companies can provide stations with additional weekly information over several months. It's collected in a different way to Rajar figures, by phone or online, so it's not directly comparable, but it can give a useful trend of the audience's perception of the station. Answers to questions such as 'Which station's got the best music?' or 'Which station runs the best competitions?' are tracked over a set period and compared with the programme controller's strategy for the station. The stats are then used as an on-going reality check on how the station's performing, and perhaps provide evidence for the need for change.

## Focus groups

These groups are used to find out qualitative information (not *what* station people listen to but *why* they listen to it). A small group of people (usually six to ten) are asked their opinions about a certain topic to do with the station. An expert who remains objective throughout moderates over the course of a couple of hours and then produces a report on the key themes and trends that came to light.

## LACs

Another quite different way of monitoring the audience's reaction to programming has been the BBC local stations' Local Advisory Councils. These were made up of a carefully-selected cross section of the community from the station's area which may have represented interested groups (perhaps a councillor, a church leader, a headmaster) or were members of the public.

The panels would meet a few times a year to give their feelings about the programmes and presenters, but sometimes the panel felt so close to the station that they wanted to please. On other occasions individuals had delusions of grandeur and demanded presenters be dropped or programme elements changed to fit with their personal listening habits. I once attended a listener panel meeting and was told that one member of the panel lived outside the station transmission area and rarely heard the programmes!

Notice that those paragraphs are in the past tense. That's because as I write, the role of the LACs from January 2007 is under review. The proposal paper mentions that the new groups (possibly called Local Audience Panels) will be more informal and 'engage with a wider cross section of the population and particularly those whom the BBC finds hard to reach . . . and with the flexibility to consider a wide range of broadcasting matters affecting local licence payers'. There would be fewer members (from 12 to 6–8) who would meet around six times a year.

'We're very lucky to have a very loyal — and honest
— audience. If they don't like something they hear they're
very quick to let you know.
Every year on our birthday we give the listeners a chance
to do just that with our Birthday Phone-In. For an hour we invite
all comments, good and bad, that people may have."
Andrew McEwan, Presenter Radio Borders,
*The Radio Magazine*, 29 January 2005

Several stations have programmes similar to the one that Andrew describes. Listeners call the station manager to comment and question. It's great to give them the chance to do this, but the presenter who's hosting the show needs to be seen to be impartial but at the same time backing up their boss. Perhaps it's an idea for the manager to have some idea of what each comment's going to be about, so they can mentally prepare the arguments as to why there's not more Alma Cogan on the station or why 'that rubbish presenter's still on at breakfast'.

Other stations go further and set up a specific phone line where listeners can leave their comments, good or bad. Sometimes called 'the listener line' or the 'tune up line', they may run for a week to a year, and give listeners a sense of involvement, ownership and empowerment. Like all feedback though, it can't be taken at face value. Some stations have suffered with organised and vocal campaigns to get rid of certain presenters (some led by local papers), which may not be representative of the views of the vast majority of quieter listeners.

If you're new to a station, bear in mind that people will call, criticise and complain. Remember people don't like change. Work hard to win them over by admitting you're new and researching the area — not by trying to pretend that you know it like the back of your hand. (I've even heard of one new presenter who set up her own listener panel on the programme. They called if she got something wrong and suggested the best places to go in the area to get a better feel for it. All this was done on air and made her more relatable, more quickly.)

# PRE-PRODUCTION

What's in this part:

o  I'll look at the different kinds of shows on a local station, their importance and different characteristics and also at music programming.

o  Then about how to put together a programme with clocks, running orders, show prep and getting guests.

o  The excitement of producing and presenting an outside broadcast is outlined . . . and the necessary admin.

o  How to stay out of trouble. All the legal stuff: what you can't say on air and what to do if someone else says it.

o  Plus ideas on coping with daily broadcasts — things like working as part of a team, stress and time management.

o  And advice on interacting with listeners — those who want to meet with you and those who want to sleep with you, and pass on some thoughts on how to protect your privacy.

# 7 The programmes

Radio stations divide each 24-hours of airtime into different slots: the programmes. These may be four-hours long, some are up to six, and contain different elements such as songs, news competitions, guests and phone-ins, or they may be as short as half an hour and be based around just one of those elements (such as those on Radio 4).

Station managers use the target audience as the starting point for deciding not only the overall style of the station, but also the specific items that go to air.

Let's take the style first. This is called the format and some stations deploy theirs very rigidly. Programmers say that whenever someone tunes in to the station they should know the kind of output they'll get. Some call this the hot tap policy (when you turn on a hot tap you know what's going to come out, in the same way when they turn on a particular station a listener should know what they're going to hear). But presenters often believe strict formats are unnecessary and a way of stifling their creativity. Perhaps that's because they misunderstand what the programme controller's trying to do. Think of the format of Channel 4 and that of ITV1. When you see a programme listed on one of those channels you automatically know the kind of show it's going to be, but within that format there's room for individual programmes in individual styles. And that's similar in radio.

A presenter who accepts this and works to format will discover two things. First, who's paying their salary and second, that there's more room for creativity than they might have first realised. It's a bit like being at school and being asked to write an essay on what you did on your holidays. The subject is too broad for you to be creative, interesting and inspired. But if you were asked to write on one aspect, perhaps the journey or the hotel, then it's been narrowed down and you've got focus. You know what's wanted from you and you can work and be creative within that.

## The programmes

Programmes through the day on any station are constructed to mirror the lives of the majority of those who are tuning in. It's one of the basic ways that a programmer can connect with the listener and make the station seem more relevant to them.

The style of these shows remains the same from day to day, although the actual content will change. That will happen to keep it fresh, and as new presenters and programmers take over and as there's a reaction to listening figures, and what other stations in the market are doing.

## Programme names

The three- and four-hour long shows most often heard on local radio (BBC and commercial) often had names, 'The Early Riser', 'Drive Time' or simply 'The Breakfast Show'. Stations are now moving towards calling shows by the name of the presenter 'The Phil Myles Show', for example, or even just 'Phil Myles'. The promotion of presenters' names is to help strengthen the station's brand and the awareness of it by listeners. After all, there are any number of stations that can have a breakfast show but there's only one presenter called, for example, John Warnett. Love him or hate him, it's important for people to know that he can only be heard on one specific station.

> **INFORMATION FOR INSPIRATION:** At a time when the same songs are being played from station to station, it's the personality of the presenters who help make each station unique.

# The breakfast show — c. 06:00—10:00

This is the lynchpin of the station's output and sets the tone and personality for the station as a whole.

> 'It's a dynamic and entertaining start to the day that gets you out of bed and out to work — brimming with great music, stacks of listener interaction, entertainment and all the local and national information you need. Valuable social ammunition.'
>
> *GWR Brand Handbook 2000*

> 'This programme is the flagship, attracting the biggest audiences of the day in most localities and reaching the widest spectrum of age and social class. The most successful of our breakfast programmes combine journalistic impact with wit, warmth and unmistakable local characteristics. The output should be a showcase for our best journalism and led by high profile, popular and respected presenters.'
>
> Connecting England, BBC, 2001

## The facts

In the morning, ten times as many people listen to the radio than watch TV (36 million versus 3.6 million). In fact, more people listen at breakfast than at any other time of the day with the peak audience usually between 7:30 and 8:30; one of the reasons that a station's breakfast show is often referred to by programmers as a 'relationship programme' is because it strives to build a specific link with listeners.

As more people are listening, commercial stations charge more for their airtime during the breakfast show. Local BBC stations are committed to 100% speech output during the peak morning period.

## The audience

By 7:00, there are more people awake than asleep; most people are woken by a clock radio so the first thing they hear could be the sound of your station. It's a busy and highly-structured time for families as they get the kids up, washed, dressed and breakfasted and out of the house for school and themselves to work. The morning commute peaks at around 8:30, and the radio is with most people as they rush around in the bedroom, bath-room, kitchen and car. TV just doesn't fit with our lifestyle at this time of day, as it needs to be watched.

'It's hard-wired into the DNA of the British. People don't have time for a primary medium in the morning. Radio is a secondary medium. It fits into people's lives while they are performing ablutions, picking up their toolbox and making toast.'

Paul Brown, CRCA Chief Executive, *The Radio Magazine*, 7 June 2005

## The programmes

It stands to reason, then, that radio schedulers should put their best and most popular presenters on at this time, to take full advantage of the large potential audience.

'Your breakfast show is your flagship; it defines the entire tone of your station.'

Paul Jackson, Programme Director Virgin Radio, *The Radio Magazine*, 7 June 2005

## The three Fs

A typical breakfast show will have the three Fs — fun, familiarity and format.

Fun, because people want their mood lifted by what the presenter says and the music that's played. The programme might:

o   Be dynamic and fast-paced to get the listeners 'up and out'.
o   Be fun and cheeky (London's Heart 106.2 promoted its breakfast show with the phrase 'get up with a giggle').
o   Play the most instantly liked, recognisable and up beat music (especially on a Friday).
o   Have lots of listener interaction such as texts, e-mails and calls.
o   Have high-profile, big-prize competitions.
o   Have 'talked about' or 'water cooler' factors such as stunts or big name guests.
o   Showbiz or entertainment news.

Familiarity, because at this time of day people are creatures of habit and want comforting consistency on the radio as much as they do in their get-to-work routine. Knowing which programme element comes next (though not the actual content) gives structure to this busy time. The show should include lots of 'the basics', often called 'the need to know' information.

o   The news, so listeners know that, after eight hours out of touch with the world, every-thing's still OK. Also, so they don't feel left out of the loop and know what everyone else is talking about.
o   The right content at the right time. Think of who's listening when. Your bulletin may include more finance-type news at 6 and 7 (for early-rising commuters), a news angle on a road closure at 7, 8 and 9 (as the roads become busier with those driving to work and school) and so on.
o   The travel, so listeners get the kids to school and themselves to work on time (or so they can leave earlier or make other arrangements if it looks as though they'll be late).
o   The time, so they aren't late. People *need* to know what time it is.

- The weather, so they know what to wear.
- Other regular features at regular times.

Format, because the show to the biggest audience should:
- Set the tone of the station. Make every 15 minutes representative of the station as a whole. So, a music station will play two or three songs, have news, weather and travel, have several time checks, an ad break and a few entertaining links during this time.
- Reflect the station's personality to the biggest audience.
- Play trails promoting other programmes on the station to this big audience, to increase the likelihood of them sampling the rest of the output.

> **INFORMATION FOR INSPIRATION:** Think of your breakfast show hours as four 15-minute shows, each containing several of the key programme elements.

## A final word

When presenting breakfast, don't mention how tired *you* are. Your job is to motivate, not moan! (Also see the Appendix: Coping With Killer Breakfast Shifts.)

# Daytime shows — c. 10:00—16:00

'The output should reflect the rhythm and flavours of the day, being bright, original and enjoyable, not grey and cramped. Although predominantly speech-based, music will play a significant role — music for pleasure, to provide punctuation and music for a purpose . . . Long-running strands, in particular, may need to be regularly refreshed before — rather than after — the audience start to lose interest. Generally, the audience ask us to be bright and intelligent, not Radio Glum; often providing background radio, accompanying other activities. Our tone will be conversational, engaging laced with good humour. We will avoid the banal, but at the same time understand that some of the output should be entertaining. The quiz format is still a popular audience attraction and a good vehicle for the creation of a phone dialogue with listeners.'

Connecting England, BBC, 2001

## The facts

Few people watch TV during the day, so radio reigns! Only till around 4pm though, when more people are watching than listening. Before that, over the course of a week, around two-thirds of adults tune in. The BBC's Daily Life Survey (quoted in the *Sunday Times*, 6 November 2005) says that 19% of all British radio listening is done in the workplace, with another 20% in cars. The article goes on to quote statistics from commercial radio, saying that 46% of its female listeners tune in on the way to the shops, that 65% of its audience listens in the kitchen, with 53% in the bedroom, 20% in the garden and 14% in the bathroom.

## The audience

The weekday can be split into two broad groups of listeners: those at work and those at home. For those at work the morning and afternoon shifts are much the same. In an office there may be the opportunity to listen to a station on-line or catch up with the news at lunchtime. In the factory a radio may be on non-stop and workers will enjoy music to help them get through the workday. Speech radio is difficult to follow in this environment, and for these people radio is background.

At home people are usually busy with jobs in the mornings and then relax in the afternoon ahead of picking up children and preparing meals. Radio is a companion.

By 4:30 there are more people at home than out at work or travelling.

## The programmes

Whereas the big name personalities are often on air at breakfast, their lesser-known colleagues are often on mid-morning or mid-afternoon. That's not to say that they're less important, just that their role is different, and inevitably have fewer listeners.

The breakfast host plays less music because there's not much time between the other elements that listeners demand, but once 9 or 10 o'clock comes most people are either in their office or factory, working around home or out in their car. There's less need for time checks and travel news (although these are still provided, there are fewer of them) and news bulletins are short updates.

To help listeners get through the working day the amount of music played is increased (perhaps two or three songs in a row – unheard of at breakfast), there's less interruption from the presenter, and less interaction from the listener. More music, such as with the popular feature the No Repeat Workday (where between 9 and 5 no song is played twice), encourages people to listen longer. As one of the biggest complaints against music radio is the high rotation of songs, this can be a great lure for listeners.

Stations in the BBC local network often use the mid-morning or lunchtime show to create specific listener interaction with a phone-in. The thinking is that, after listeners have heard and considered stories in the breakfast show, there's a chance to put their views on-air and have them tested by the presenter and other listeners. Older people (the usual audience to a BBC local station) also have more time to call and take part in such programmes.

Lunchtime programming often includes a news show (such as the Lunchtime News on BBC Essex) or an extended news bulletin, to update those who tune in over their lunch break.

# Drivetime shows — c. 16:00—19:00

'A vital show linking daytime and evening output covering the key afternoon travelling period.'
*GWR Brand Handbook 2000*

'There are different sensibilities as people's moods are different. At breakfast people are more easily annoyed, but with drive, if they've had a shit day they're on their way home so things aren't as bad. And the audience is constantly changing at breakfast so you're constantly resetting subjects.'
Geoff Lloyd, Virgin Radio, Radio Academy event, October 2005

## The facts

This is the time when children leave school and adults leave work. At home, chores are finished and meals prepared. There are more TV fans than radio fans for the first time in the day.

## The audience

Most people are in a good mood as the strains of the day ebb away and they look forward to their free time.

## The programmes

These shows are often seen as a mirror of breakfast shows, although they have smaller audiences (TV viewing overtakes radio listening at about 4 pm) and so make less money for the commercial stations. However, the breakfast and drive shows are, if you like, the two 'tent poles' of the weekday schedule, holding up the programmes that precede and follow them.

These two day-parts have similar content and style, because getting people to work on time mirrors getting them home. A round-up of the day's news (rather than a reprise of the overnight stories); lots of travel news time checks (so they can get home and get out on time); weather (often looking forward to the following morning); what's on information (often clearly targeted to new films, new clubs to visit, and so on).

## Musical chairs

In the past, afternoon hosts have been used to deputise ('dep') for the breakfast show presenter when they're away, but this is becoming less common. Drive hosts would often aspire to present breakfast, for the larger audience and larger salary, but such depping has often been at the expense of their own show's audience figures, which would invariably go down in their absence. If you consider their absence from their own afternoon show while covering for breakfast, and their own holiday time, they could be away from their own listeners for two or more months a year. Then there was the question of who fills on drive? And who deps for *them*? A kind of musical chairs developed, and all that change caused havoc with so much of the day, and makes Rajar figures difficult to interpret, that nowadays it's common to simply call in a weekend presenter instead.

# Evening shows — c. 19:00—22:00

## The facts

There's little radio listening done in the evening, as most people are out socialising or watching TV (the 'soap zone' is between 7:00 and 8:30), although there's a small rise in the early evening as meals are prepared and the washing up done, and another around 10pm as people go to bed.

## The audience

Those who are listening at this time are more likely to be men, because of the midweek sports coverage such as Sport on Five, and 15–24 year olds tuning into commercial radio music shows, although one of the most popular programmes at this time is The Archers on Radio 4! People are more relaxed than at any other time of day, and are in an especially good mood on a Friday as the weekend kicks in.

## The programmes

From 7pm most of the potential audience is out or watching TV. Because few people are listening you can experiment a little more with your style of presentation, the features you run or music you play. This is safe in the knowledge that those who are listening really do want to hear you or at least the music that you're playing.

BBC stations seek 'ratings by day and reputation by night', so their programmes tend to be more specialised in the evening, catering for smaller, niche audiences. Musically this might include jazz, country, big band, alternative new music and the like. These may be presented by musical aficionados who have no real desire to be full-time broadcasters.

> 'In relevant areas, output for specific ethnic minority groups will have an important and prominent place in the evening schedule. This will often be local in origin and attract specialist audiences.'
> Connecting England, BBC, 2001

Speech programmes might be scheduled here, such as Asian programmes for a minority group in the station's TSA. These are 'appointment to listen' programmes for those who tune in, and seen by BBC stations as part of their remit to extend listener choice.

There's less scheduled information in the evening shows: fewer time checks, news and weather and travel reports. That's because, as you've noticed by now, programming tries to reflect people's lifestyles.

BBC local stations often join together in 'clusters' in the evenings and overnight, to share running costs. Programmes between say 7 and midnight might be shared between perhaps five or six stations. Similarly, commercial music stations also often link together in small networks, for similar reasons.

# Overnight shows — 22:00—06:00

## The audience

By 10pm TV viewing has peaked and many people are at least thinking of going to bed (a third of adults are in bed by 10:30). Commercial music stations are more popular than BBC stations through the evening, night and overnight.

From 11pm until 4 the next afternoon, radio reigns over TV, listened to by those going to bed, those working night shifts, insomniacs, and those getting up for the start of a new day. These listeners tend to be very dedicated, and a club-like atmosphere often grows up around overnight shows and their presenters. Some, like London's LBC presenters Clive Bull and Steve Allen, have worked the night shift for decades and attract the weird and wonderful callers who often know each other and have unwritten 'rules' and in-jokes.

'I do like the extra dimension that the night time seems to add to a phone-based show. Things seem to happen at night that just couldn't happen in daytime. People seem to be more receptive to the idea of joining in and going with the flow.'

Clive Bull, Presenter, LBC 97.3, *The Radio Magazine*, 20 April 2005

# The programmes

This slot, what's commonly called the graveyard shift because so few people are listening, is often the real training ground for new presenters. Overnight audiences are relatively tiny, sometimes too small to measure, so there's room for innovation and little harm can be done to the listening figures or the style of the station.

Overnight shows are valuable in helping recycle listeners from one day to the next. The station that people fall asleep listening to will invariably be the one that they wake up to the next morning. So it's important that you don't see this shift as any less important to the station's figures than any other day part. That's why even the smallest stations try to stay live and/or local overnight. Those in a large group may have a networked show shared between several stations, which is live but not necessarily local. Some BBC local stations have an automated show played off computer, which is local but not live.

Both these ideas are better than the station closing down overnight (which is what happened when I started in radio) or taking a 'sustaining' service (some BBC local stations still take Radio Five Live or the World Service overnight) but both of these ways of programming overnights removes the option of a newcomer practicing their programme when few people are listening.

# The pros and cons of the graveyard shift

The advantage of working overnight is that you have, obviously, so much more time in the day. You can enjoy the sunshine, go shopping, banking and to the doctor, pick the kids up from school and so on: all things that 9–5ers can't do. At work, there's less interference from managers, fewer interruptions in the studio, and much more of a relaxed atmosphere on air.

The drawbacks are that you can't go out at night to concerts or meals with friends. And at work some of the advantages are also some of the disadvantages: you never see the boss for feedback and you miss your colleagues' banter and gossip.

**INFORMATION FOR INSPIRATION:** By the end of your overnight shift, your energy and enthusiasm may be waning, but many of the people who're tuning in will be those who are waking up early for the start of a new day and need to be invigorated. Similarly, the breakfast presenter will come on, all guns blazing for the first hour of their show. So to avoid a massive gear-change, you have to keep energised throughout your programme.

> Make sure that you occasionally stay late or arrive early and meet up with the other on-air presenters. That way you'll feel much more part of the team and they'll be more likely to mention your show during their show.

(Also see the Appendix: Coping With Killer Breakfast Shifts.)

# Saturdays

'Morning output will be more relaxed than on a weekday, recognising a more leisure-based focus to the day. A younger audience is available, adding listeners in some areas, but it's counter-productive to try and attract the under 45s with programming that drives away our heartland and secondary audiences. However, potential heartland listeners, working during the week, will be available and efforts should be made to draw them in. Sport remains a big attraction on Saturday afternoons and whenever possible this should include live match coverage.'

Connecting England, BBC, 2001

## The audience

Saturday mornings are the furthest point from work for most people and they wake up positive and with thoughts of what to do for themselves and their families. Like weekdays, morning radio is popular, but the number of people listening is lower and the breakfast peak lasts longer – often through till lunchtime – as people take longer to get going. Most listening is done at home and in the car as background.

During the afternoon the TV takes over, but radio listening is still strong, especially for sports coverage and sports round-up programmes, for example on Radio Five Live. Between 5 and 8 people wind down from their day and start getting ready for their night out and may have a music station on as they prepare.

## The programmes

Weekend radio shows reflect listeners' increased leisure time. Breakfast shows usually start an hour or so later and are less frenetically paced, with fewer travel bulletins and time checks, and more music. There are inevitably more suggestions on what listeners can do with their free time, extra what's on information and BBC local stations may also broadcast gardening or DIY advice.

During the day most stations will offer mainly music programmes. Then, party music is played on many stations – London's Heart has Club Classics, and Virgin has its Party Classics. Often BBC local stations also play similar feel-good tunes from their own core music list: BBC Radio Kent's Classic Countdown from the '60s and '70s, for example. But it's Saturday afternoons that are most distinctive.

# Sports coverage

'Most stations will continue to produce major local sports output
on Saturday afternoons where we achieve one of our highest
audience shares of the week. Many stations have developed
evening sports programmes (on weekdays) with football phone-ins
proving particularly successful in some areas. We should build on
this "fanzine factor" especially in areas where we have retained
extensive high-profile match coverage.'

Connecting England, BBC, 2001

In the recent past, commercial stations were prepared to pay an increasing amount of money to have the rights to broadcast live match commentaries. They saw them as audience builders and revenue raisers. However, over time the high price was reviewed by most stations who decided not to renew contracts with their local clubs. Now it's BBC local stations that broadcast full sports shows on Saturday afternoon. These are often three or four hours long, with reports and live commentaries at the big matches involving local teams whether home or away. If several local teams are playing, priority is given to ones who are away, and therefore will have fewer local fans travelling to see them. These stay-at-home supporters can follow the match action on the radio along with, increasingly, ex-pat fans from other parts of the country or the world and who listen via the internet. As most BBC local stations have several frequencies, stations can cover two or more matches at the same time.

Commercial radio coverage on a Saturday often amounts to lots of music with flashes of goal news and extra sports bulletins. It's cheaper and is a good halfway house: sports fans are kept up-to-date with the action while non-sporty types don't mind the odd interruption if they also get a good dose of music. London's all-speech station, LBC, covers the goal flashes (concentrating on London teams, or the matches which will affect London teams) as they happen with main presenter John Cushing who's joined by pundit and ex-England player Kenny Sansom in the studio who comments and passes judgement on the developments.

It's understood that real fans may migrate from the local commercial station to the local BBC one for Saturday afternoon's full match action. Commercial radio stations hope that their weekday promotion pays off and that the listeners will return. For the BBC locals the opportunity's on a plate for them to 'sell' their station and programmes to a new audience, and tempt them to stay longer or to retune later in the week (perhaps for a midweek commentary, or longer weekday sports bulletins).

Of course, given the big business of football in particular, sports output can travel across a station's schedule. Obviously there are the midweek matches, but also the kick-off times of matches (on whatever day) are dictated by TV schedulers rather than those in radio.

# The importance of sport

'Sports journalism captures a crucial
audience of younger listeners.'

Connecting England, BBC, 2001

**INFORMATION FOR INSPIRATION:** Sport is a great way for a station to connect with its audience. Presenters are talking about something that's happening locally, something that people know about, care about and are talking about themselves. Sport is about where people live and their emotional involvement. And these emotions help the station bond with its listeners.

It's important to see a match as more than just a 'game of two halves'. Even for those who aren't interested in sports, there's human drama, passion, battles, fitness and even fashion. All topics which can be linked to sport to make it more accessible.

Commercial radio gets very excited about sport when there's a big, headline-grabbing event such as a Euro football tournament, World Cup or Olympics. Then it's a case of demonstrating passion and solidarity with listeners, rather than supplying nitty gritty info. Stations will get behind the national team, present 60-second updates on matches, play stirring trails, and say which local pubs are opening out of hours to screen the matches.

# Sundays

'Breakfast will set the tone of the day and output will be dominated by religious and spiritual concerns, reflecting our local multi-faith communities . . . Religion is an audience winner on Sunday mornings, often achieving the second biggest share of the week . . . Mid-morning is a crucial showcase for our output. It provides a good platform for debating big issues and demonstrating the BBC's commitment to the local community at a time when listeners are available. It needs a high quality presenter able to combine both serious and light-hearted material in an attractive magazine format. At weekends we must be careful not to simply duplicate BBC output elsewhere, or produce specialist music programmes in single localities for small audiences.'

Connecting England, BBC, 2001

## The audience

Sunday is more leisurely, with people sleeping in. After the lie in, there's the long breakfast and the Sunday papers to read. Then there's shopping, errands, meeting friends and doing things with the family, so radio is the top media through till lunchtime when TV takes over. People don't want to think about the week ahead, but by early evening homework's being completed and bags packed. The feeling of freedom fades.

Throughout all this, radio is the secondary activity: background to whatever else people are doing.

## The programmes

Sunday mornings on BBC local stations invariably sees an increase in their religious or ethical obligation. Often this is early, between 6 and 8, for example. Sunday afternoon is traditionally the time when BBC Radio 1 and most commercial stations have their chart show from 5 until 7, the commercial stations either coming together for the Hit 40 UK programme or one of several others (such as the Smash Hits chart) produced by independent production companies. Radio 1's biggest audience of the day is when listeners (mainly 15–34 year olds) tune in to hear what's number one.

# 8 Music programming

'In broad terms, music is used in BBC Local Radio in two ways:
Music for pleasure — as a break from speech, a breathing space;
as an entertaining interlude, much appreciated by many listeners;
as background harmony, acknowledging that many listeners use
the service as an accompaniment to other activities.
Music for a purpose — as production punctuation in idents,
quizzes, trails and other promotional material; as an illustrative
device; as part of programme formats, such as a "Down Your Way"
device; as part of local identity, when the music or musicians
have strong local connections.
Extensive audience feedback across the country tells us that while
some music is appreciated by listeners, it will not in itself attract an
audience to a speech-led service. Those who principally want music
will find it elsewhere. However, inappropriate and badly scheduled
music can repel even our most loyal listeners.'
Connecting England, BBC, 2001

'If the figures go up we're playing the right music.
If they go down, it's the wrong DJ.'
Geoff Lloyd, presenter Virgin Radio, Radio Academy event, October 2005

Most stations in the UK are music-based, and music is perhaps the single most important factor when the choice of station is made.

For listeners:

- Instant gratification. They want to hear songs they love.

For the station:

- It's relatively cheap to play: although stations do have to pay for each track they play, see p. 85.
- The mix of songs instantly identifies the style of the station (its brand): music more than anything else determines the format of the station.
- Music gives a show time to 'breathe', and the presenter and producer time to 'regroup' and consider what's coming next.

Stations need to play music that is well-loved by its target demographic, mixed with a few well-chosen new releases. That way people know the kind of songs they'll hear whenever they turn on the station (the hot tap policy I mentioned earlier; see p. 60).

'I've always described it as being like a chef — when you're tossing a salad, you wouldn't necessarily say that the individual ingredients are your favourite food, but when you put them all together it creates a very pleasing experience!'

Pat Geary, Station Manager, 3C Continuous Cool Country, X-Trax magazine, August 2005

**INFORMATION FOR INSPIRATION:** As far as music goes, familiarity breeds content.

# Music research

To work out which songs are the best ones to play (the 'most-loved'), stations need to do some research. Many use phone-out research, in which hundreds of people in the target demographic are asked about their musical tastes and then to identify their current favourite track from a shortlist of musical 'clusters' played down the phone to them. They may also be asked their opinion on a list of current songs. All this information helps the station to work out what songs they should play and how often.

There's also auditorium research — it's the same process but done en-masse in a room full of people, rather than on the phone individually.

Researchers for BBC local radio play 'the hook' (an instantly-recognisable few seconds, usually featuring the song's title) from individual songs to volunteers, and ask them what they think: do they recognise the track? If they do, do they like it? If they don't, could they tolerate it or would it make them turn the radio off? From their responses it's decided whether the song's scored well enough to be included on stations' core music list.

# The core

The songs that test best are made core tracks of the station and are ones that will be played most often over a long period of time. They're the ones that most clearly reflect the sound of the station, the all-time classic songs that the station plays. The core may be added to and reviewed on an ongoing basis, but won't change much from month to month.

You may also hear people talk about 'core artists', which are the singers or groups that also 'embody' the brand. Core artists for most commercial music stations are likely to be singers like Kylie and Robbie.

# The playlist

The playlist is the tracks that the station plays on a regular basis (its 'active categories'). Commercial stations have a typical core playlist of about 4000–5000 songs, although 'tight' stations may have as few as 200 (and in the States this can be as few as 100). BBC local stations have a core of around 900, considered rather large in commercial terms. The 'running order' is the list of music for an individual show amounting perhaps to ten or so tracks an hour.

In the mid 2000s a format known as 'Jack' became popular in the US and Canada. These stations' formats, often without presenters and with a much larger core of over 1000 songs, are known unofficially as 'random radio' or 'iPod shuffle formats' (even though they pre-dated that device) and often use an anarchic slogan such as 'playing what we want!' Pre-recorded links are updated regularly by the station voice and, like the slogan, also have an 'attitude' which reflects the station's brand values.

Although the Jack format is untested in the long term, critics say that without presenters the stations lose one of the main advantages over an iPod: the sense that a live person is programming the music. Indeed, *Newsday* described the format, with the lack of local programming and personalities, as 'another step towards the McDonaldisation of radio'.

# Scheduling music

Once the overall style of the station has been decided (by considering which tracks tested best with the audience the station wants to target), the songs have to be scheduled.

For each song on the playlist, the head of music will input various data into the computer software system (often Selector or PowerGold, both trade names). The information is so the computer can shuffle the songs, and much of it is basic and obvious:

- The song's title, artist, duration.
- The year of release (so the computer doesn't suggest two or three similar-sounding '70s disco songs in a row).
- Whether the artist is a mixed group, boy group, girl group, male solo or female solo (so you don't get James Blunt followed by Elton John followed by Will Young, for example).
- Additional artist information (so a song by Wings isn't played next to one by Paul McCartney, and one by Destiny's Child doesn't follow one by Beyonce Knowles. If this happens it's called an artist clash).
- The speed of the song (beats per minute).
- Payment details such as who wrote the song, the publisher and distributor (so PRS royalty payments can be made).

Other information is more subjective:

- Its tempo, energy and mood. Although speed can be a good indicator of mood, it's not always. Some fast songs are 'sad', some slow ones are 'happy'.
- Its genre (rock, reggae or rap and so on – you've probably seen the different categories on your iPod).
- How often it should be played (its rotation). Some songs are on low-rotation (played less often than ones on high-rotation) either because they don't research as well, because they're brand new and are being introduced to the listener, or because they're falling down the charts (often, but not always, a good guide to a song's popularity). You want the most popular songs, both the current songs and those from the core, to be played most often. But if you play them *too* often people will get fed up with them, so once every three hours is usually a good rotation.
- When it should be played. Some stations separate their songs into different time zones. We've seen already how stations programme their output to mirror the way their listeners lead their lives day-to-day, so it'll come as no surprise to hear that more lively songs are usually played at breakfast time, slower songs at night and a broader mix during the day. (This isn't always the case. Club Classics on London's Heart 106.2 will play upbeat songs in the evening, notably Friday and Saturday night when its listeners are preparing to go out.)

o  Other reasons may be because of the length of the track, for example, playing a long song in breakfast when there are other elements to fit in would cause problems.

o  It may be because the style or content of the song is more appropriate to play in the evenings rather than to a family audience at breakfast time, or maybe because of the title: *Wake Up Boo* might sound odd if it's played at 10 at night, or *Nightshift* by The Commodores at 9:30am!

o  Ideally, each song should play in a different part of the day over the course of a week before it's repeated. That means that it may play in breakfast on its first outing, then evening, then afternoon, then morning, before being played again in breakfast. That's so listeners in each day-part get to hear the songs evenly. The music scheduling system will ensure this is what happens.

The computer is also programmed with the details of the overall station sound that is required to ensure an even distribution of tracks' style and speed through the hour. The first choice of song will be determined by category (see below), after which the computer will consider the other 'rules' that it's been given. It will then provide a running order for each show that fits with that request.

# The playlist meeting

The choice of what will be added to that week's rotation of songs is usually made at a weekly playlist meeting. At small stations it may be the programme controller who decides what makes it to air, at larger stations a group will listen to the tracks and decide the policy, probably for several stations. Group-wide music policies exist so the sound is consistent across those stations.

# Music categories

Programmers often talk about 'A-list' songs and 'B-list' songs. These are two terms used to define certain groups that are on a similar rotation.

A-listers are playlist songs from the current chart (and so are likely to be on high-rotation) and B-listers are new releases (which are played less often).

These are the most-used music rotation categories on a typical chart hits station in 2006. Some stations and programme controllers use different terms or have slightly different definitions and rotations, but this is a good basis:

| Name | Definition | Typical rotation |
|------|-----------|------------------|
| Introduction | The initial period after a song has been added to the playlist | May be here for two or three weeks before it's familiar to the audience |
| Current | A song doing well in the charts right now, usually stays as a current for 12–14 weeks | |
| • Current heavy | The 9–15 most important songs of the moment, which set the style and sound of the station. Often called the 'A-list' songs. (There's usually an odd number of these to give easy rotation in quarter hours) | One per quarter hour, each played every three to four hours |
| • Current medium | New songs going up and hits on their way down. Also called the 'B-list'. Probably around 6 songs | One of these an hour |
| • Current light | Generally used to introduce new songs to the listener, so they become familiar before being moved to a higher rotation. These could be songs yet to be released. Often called the 'C-list' and played in non-peak hours, perhaps in the evening to a younger audience | Fewer plays than the A and B list, as they're still new to the listener |
| Power oldies | Older, 'classic' songs that are on the station's core from the 1990s and 2000s, possibly numbering around 250 songs | Some all-time favourites may spend many years in maturity. A couple of these may be played each hour |
| Recurrent | One-time A-list songs up to a year old. There may be around 30 in this category | Two of these might be played each hour |
| Gold | The biggest hits from the 1980s numbering around 150 | Two of these might be played each hour |

Every station will have a different rotation policy which determines not only what songs are on what list (the A, B and C lists) but also what their rotation is, and how many from each list gets played each hour. That rotation is all-important: if you play too few from your A-list it'll take you most of the day to play each one of them. By the same token, if you play too many an hour, and the time between each one of them is say three hours (the 'turnover'), the list will need to be longer.

**INFORMATION FOR INSPIRATION:** If there are too many songs overall on the station's playlist, people have to listen longer before they hear one of their favourite (or most-effective) songs. That lowers the overall 'listenability' of the station. So, a greater variety doesn't necessarily mean that people will listen longer.

## The mix in an hour

Some stations have a policy to play a certain number of songs in an hour or a certain 'minuteage' ('another forty-minute music sweep'). Others guarantee the *kind* of music they play ('Your no-repeat work day station – between 9 and 5 you won't hear the same song twice', 'Your hotter, fresher mix', 'The best of the '90s and today . . .').

The choice of music, determined by the criteria given to the music selection computer program, should give the general music show a good mix throughout each hour. The contrast may be between a solo male singer, followed by a female group, followed by a male/female group. Once the computer has also considered the tempo of songs, their genre, year of release and rotation, you can begin to see that there's an infinite combination of songs from hour to hour and day to day.

**INFORMATION FOR INSPIRATION:** Don't just play the right songs. Play them in the right order.

Let's see how this works in practice on a typical chart-based commercial station. Here's an actual running order from a mid morning hour on a station in a well-known radio group in January 2006:

## Kelly Clarkson – *Because Of You*

Not a typical hour opener as it's a ballad, but the listeners love it. Music testing has shown that the audience loves the song, proving that it's not always chart position that counts when considering which song to play. This is currently an A-list song with about a 3 hour rotation.

## EMF – *Unbelievable*

A 1990s' hit that's still cool in 2006, and a target song for people who were in their mid-teens then and are now around 30 – the target demographic for this station at this time of day (a 'music of your life' song). Thought will be needed on how to segue between a slow song and a tune with a hard start, so this order isn't perhaps ideal, but that transition can be done with perhaps a 15" music demonstrator. This song is a Power Oldie.

## No Doubt — *It's My Life*
Gwen Stefani is a very hot artist and this is a classic song remade. What's not to like? A good strong Recurrent.

## Nelly — *Hot in Here*
A very accessible urban song, a 'naughties' classic and another Power Oldie.

## A-ha — *Analogue*
New on the B-list at the time, and although it's not going to be an all-time great, it's still a good song from an '80s' favourite.

## Bangles — *Manic Monday*
A good mid-morning Gold song, sympathetic with the 9–5 worker and exactly 20 years old. (Note how the potential 'weak link', the A-ha song, was sandwiched between two absolute bankers. Remember the 'if-I-don't-like-this-song, I-know-I'll-like-the-next-one' theory.)

## James Blunt — *Goodbye My Lover*
Another A-lister and another ballad, which is very strong with the core female audience. This is a big hit that, if teased correctly before a break, would have held listeners over the ads.

## Madonna — *Beautiful Stranger*
A great Power Oldie song from a core artist – you can't go wrong playing this.

## Gorillaz — *Dare*
Another Recurrent. Remember, these are some of the strongest tools in your music box.

## Westlife — *World Of Our Own*
A 1990s' Power Oldie, and a catchy, in-offensive, well-produced song.

## Coldplay — *Speed Of Sound*
Recurrent. At the time *Talk* from the album *X&Y* was a B-list newcomer, so this very solid performer from the world's biggest earners in 2005 is a dead-cert.

## Christina Aguilera, Lil Kim, Mya & Pink — *Lady Marmalde*
Again, a classic Power Oldie song, well remade by the hottest US female artists, also from the *Moulin Rouge* soundtrack. Ticks all the boxes.

## Scissor Sisters — *Laura*
A long running Recurrent and absolutely spot-on for a target audience of 30-something females.

An hour, chosen at random, not cutting edge (and it doesn't closely follow the 'typical' rotation outlined above) but very, very solid for the station's target demo. There are no weak songs, plenty of variety and that gives the presenter lots of opportunities to give gossip about the artists or be relatable to the Gold music. There's a good mix of tempo and mood, male/female/US & UK artists. A range of genres too from Gold Pop (Bangles) to Alternative (Coldplay).

## Hour-starters

Some programmers say the first song out of the news should be a classic, others that it should be a current hit. Most agree that this is the location for a 'showcase' song, one that represents the sound of the station, and that it should certainly be a strong and generally up-tempo song.

> **INFORMATION FOR INSPIRATION:** Whenever you come out of a speech insert, such as commercials or an interview, play a huge hit. Talk that's long is followed by a song that's strong.

## All the hits?

Remember, just because a song has been number one, doesn't mean that your station will play it. It has to research well with the target audience.

An easy listening station such as Smooth FM or Magic FM in London will not play the Scissor Sisters just because it does well in the charts, but may play a track from that group if it's compatible with the station sound. An oldies station, of course, wouldn't even consider playing a new release. Others may refuse to play a novelty song.

## The role of the computer

It's often a surprise for listeners to discover that most of the music played on a station isn't chosen by the presenter themselves, but having said that, of course it's a human who inputs the details of each track into the computer in the first place.

The head of music will look over each hour's schedule to double check the selection that's been made. That's because the computer is only working to the rules it's been given, and it doesn't have ears! Two rules together may produce a quirk that hadn't been anticipated, and you could end up with two songs together which *you know* won't sound good. Indeed, a scheduler can give the computer so many rules about what songs can't go together, that it provides either a very stilted and limited running order, or can't produce one at all!

Some presenters, for example those on specialist music shows or experienced presenters, may be given a free choice, but this is the exception rather than the rule, and even then the choice would have to be within the station's format. The reason is to stop a music free-for-all, with each presenter playing their own favourites, not necessarily those of the audience. Some songs would be played too often, others not at all, and the whole station sound would be watered down.

# Street-level scheduling strategies

- Remember the basic idea behind music programming is to have a balance of music that flows through each hour, with a variety of styles and artists, and tempos that rise and fall.
- Play more of what people know and love. Stations are rarely hurt by what they don't play, but can be by what they do.
- Playing the *best* songs is better than playing the *most* songs. Quality is better than quantity.
- Playing too many songs which have 'burned' (ones that people are tired of) is as bad as playing too many unfamiliar songs.
- If listeners think there's too much repetition, it may be because there are too many 'borderline'-scoring songs on poor rotation. People don't complain when their favourites come around more often, only when they regularly hear songs they don't like.
- Cut back on playing new and unfamiliar music at breakfast. At this time of day people want to hear their up-tempo favourites.
- Schedule new and unfamiliar music last in a group of songs and next to at least one classic core song.
- Rotate music evenly. In other words, a song should not appear in the same hour from one day to the next because it'll be heard too often by some people and not enough by others
- Every 20–30 minute period should have a mix of music that represents your station.
- To create a slower feel for the station, increase the rotation of the slower songs. To give the feeling of a 'hotter and fresher' station, you do the same with the up-tempo songs on the playlist.
- 'Music of your life' songs help listeners recall their teenage years and are often a big hit. This is because teenage years are our formative years, when, as one presenter put it, 'Having fun was our job . . . before our job was our job!'
- 'New gold' songs are ones which are about six months old, that is two seasons ago. They remind listeners of recent memories. For instance, if it's winter now, it reminds them of last summer.
- Similarly 'anniversary songs' remind people what they were doing this time last year.
- 'Sunshine songs' or 'Friday feeling' songs are classic up-tempo songs that make people feel good.

**INFORMATION FOR INSPIRATION:** People need to know that even if they don't like the song you're playing now, they'll like the next one and love the one after that.

# The playout computer

The playlist computer in the music scheduler's office 'talks' to the playout computer in the studio, so the music running order for each hour is seen on screen, and the tracks are loaded automatically to play from a hard disk.

'Nowadays presenters can spend the time during songs and
ad breaks being creative, rather than, cuing up records
and loading the cart machines.'
Kevin Stewart, Chief Executive Tindle Radio,
*The Radio Magazine*, 7 September 2005

The hard disk also contains all the station's jingles, adverts, news clips and so on, which saves you loading all those elements manually. That means that you have more time in which to think about your verbal links. You can take calls off air (and interact with your listeners), record calls that can be played later (making them tighter and more relevant), or talk to guests when they arrive (and help the image of the station).

On the studio screen the song title and name of the artist is displayed, together with the duration of the track and whether it 'ends' (comes to a dead finish) or fades out. These are usually marked as E or F alongside the track listing. That's handy for a presenter to know, to make it easier to link from one song to the next. Other information that you might find useful to know is also mentioned, such as the chart position of the track or when the artist is next in concert.

Selector and other similar music programming systems will also give presenters easy access to the station's database of songs, for example, for requests and dedications on so-called 'jukebox' shows. As well as showing the song's availability (whether it's one that's suitable for the station and is therefore allowed to be played), it will also show the last time it was played. This ensures that such a 'free choice' by a presenter doesn't cause the same song to be played too regularly. If you're taking requests, simply type in the song's title or artist and you can have it playing on air within seconds.

**INFORMATION FOR INSPIRATION:** At some small stations, where the on-air presenter is a member of management, they often use the valuable seconds saved to do other work — prepare a management report, sales figures, or call a contact. But this isn't advised: when you're on air all your concentration should be on your programme.

# The presenter and the music

I mentioned before that the music-scheduling computer doesn't have ears, so it's down to a human to check whether two songs go well together or not. That human may be the programme controller, or it may be you while you're on-air. Always check that you're allowed to change the order of songs before you do it, even though it may make perfect sense to you at the time. Altering the music policy at a station is no small misdemeanour and may well be a sackable offence. Any discrepancies should be questioned before the programme or after it. The programme controller may see it as the top of a slippery slope when songs are dropped on the whim of individual presenters.

Sometimes there will be exceptional circumstances: you may want to play a song by an artist whose death has just been announced, or a song by a band that's appearing locally. In such cases your own experience of your programme controller will tell you whether altering the playlist is appropriate.

**INFORMATION FOR INSPIRATION:** You'll get fed-up with songs faster than listeners, because you hear songs in concentrated periods of time. A current hit will almost certainly come around once in each of your four-hour shows, possibly twice. The typical listener will spend just eight or so hours a week listening to the station. So you might hear the song six times in a week on your show alone, whereas they may only hear it that many times in a month. That means that after a month or longer on the playlist, it's only just starting to become a strong favourite with many listeners.

One of the arts of music programming is to recognise how listeners perceive a song, and to have the strength of character to keep it on high rotation even though presenters are fed up with it. (A song's airplay and release date can be as much as six weeks apart, and some songs are very 'slow-burners'. The Verve's *Bittersweet Symphony* peaked a year after release.) Indeed, some programmers say that you should never stop playing a hit record completely, just slow down its rotation. So currents are played several times a day, recurrents a couple of times a week, and golds a couple of times a month.

## The importance of music

Arguably, the music played on a BBC local station has to have researched better than that on a commercial station: if I listen to a song on a commercial station and it's not my favourite then I know that within three minutes there will be one that I'll like. Listening to a BBC local station, I may have to wait ten, 15 or 20 minutes for a song (because of the station's increased speech quota). That means every song needs to be the the very best.

'We rotate somewhere in the region of 5500 songs, covering the '60s, '70s, '80s, '90s and 2000s. One minute you can hear a classic Beatles' tune, the next it's Avril Lavigne's brand new hit single. People on the street seem to enjoy it, they tell us that if they don't like one song, they at least know that in a couple of minutes, they'll be hearing something completely different.'

Derek McIntyre, Programme Controller, Your Radio,
Scotland, *X-Trax* magazine, July 2005

## Music features

Music features (such as a Golden Hour, or Classic Top Ten From When) should include tracks that the station plays all the time (in their core) or certainly still be in format. Songs that go on the radio have been carefully chosen and tested to appeal to a target audience. They're part of the station brand and to dilute that by playing your own personal favourites will undermine that hard work.

# Inappropriate music

You may have to adjust your playlist when, usually because of news events, playing a song with a certain title or by a specific artist may not be appropriate. For instance, after the hurricane in the southern United States in 2005 many stations dropped, for obvious reasons *Walking On Sunshine* by Katrina and the Waves. Other songs are effectively banned at hospital radio stations. *I Just Died In Your Arms Tonight* being an obvious example.

Occasionally it may not be obvious that a song needs to be dropped, as the offending words don't appear in the title. It may not occur to you that it may cause offence if you come out of a news bulletin which includes a story of a shooting, with *Bohemian Rhapsody* (think of the opening few lines). However, you can take things too far and be over-sensitive. When you're head over heels in love, every song you hear seems to have been written just for you. In the same way, when a news story is uppermost in your mind, almost every lyric takes on a subtle second meaning.

Songs by individual artists may be banned if that singer's life takes a turn for the worse. Gary Glitter is rarely heard on British radio any more after he was found guilty of child abuse charges. A similar thing happened to Jonathan King. Even though both of them had successful and long-lasting pop careers, few of their songs are now played. In 2005 Michael Jackson appeared in court charged with various offences alleged to have been committed against a young boy who stayed at his Neverland ranch. Some radio stations were said to have dropped all songs from his back-catalogue including those of The Jacksons. Before the verdict was announced, a memo at Radio 2 said:

'It depends if he is found guilty and on what grounds. It's possible it may end up as a charge of supplying alcohol to a minor, which is unlikely to attract a jail sentence given his past record. Under these circumstances there would be no real reason to stop playing his music, however, I would go easy on rotation because reputations will inevitably be harmed and feelings raw. However, if he's found guilty on the more serious charges of child molestation etc then we have a duty as public service broadcasters to take in to account the feelings of our listeners. There'll be an immediate backlash in the media so it would be best to rest the tracks for the time being. The difference between Jacko and King is the sheer volume of the music that Jacko has provided over the years. His status as one of the world's greatest pop artists is unquestionable. Michael's legacy to pop music radio has been immense while King's has been more novelty than substantial. Many of our listeners will always love Michael's music because it's so good, but the whole question of paedophilia is so sensitive and abhorrent that many would not deem it appropriate to listen to his music.'

# Appropriate music

You've got a local biker's club in to talk about their charity run – don't play *Motorbiking*! A similar rule if you're talking to some lottery winners and are tempted to use *Everyone's a Winner*. These are musical clichés and have been used many times before. Try to think of songs that are equally appropriate but used less often.

# Exclusive tracks

By building up contacts with music companies, some stations or groups can get exclusive airplay of new releases. These are often played from a central studio and distributed live to stations via satellite where they're put straight to air, usually in the peak breakfast show.

# Obit songs

All stations have songs which have been highlighted as suitable to be played in the event of a royal death or that of any other VIP (such as the prime minister), or national tragedy. These need to be reviewed regularly with some tracks added and others taken away so, come the event, your appropriate songs are not from a time frame that stopped five years previously. Such a playlist was used for more than a week after the death of Diana, Princess of Wales, and included classical music as well as more modern instrumentals (*Song For Guy*, *Albatross*) and even more recent songs with lyrics (*Everybody Hurts*).

Not only should a list be available (in the Obit Book that is kept in every studio), but it's also wise to have the songs recorded onto a few CDs for immediate access.

# Radio edits

Some songs contain lyrics which are likely to be offensive to listeners and may, if aired, break broadcasting codes. That's why some songs have what's called a 'radio edit', a version of the song with the offensive reference either edited out and replaced with a 'bleep', or by a slightly different lyric (such as James Blunt's *You're Beautiful* with the replaced lyric of '*flying* high'). Be sure you play the right one: there are stories of the wrong versions of Smokey's re-release of *Living Next Door To Alice*, and The Beautiful South's *Don't Marry Her* . . . both being played on air!

Another reason for a radio edit might be because of the length of the original song: *American Pie* has a radio edit version which is about half the duration of the album track.

# Power starts

Other songs have starts which simply don't sound good on radio. Perhaps they make it difficult to cross-fade with other tracks or don't fit in with the style of station, even though the rest of the song does. One station I worked at edited off the start of Belinda Carlisle's *We Want The Same Thing* because of the shouts, another did the same with *Happy Christmas War Is Over* because of the whispers.

# Christmas songs

There are stations in the States which play non-stop Christmas songs from just before Thanksgiving (at the end of November) well in to the new year. In the UK, festive tunes are usually played for about a fortnight before Christmas (with one an hour the week before) and tail off completely by a few days after. Each station is different with the number, type and rotation of songs.

# Christmas countdowns

Many stations fill the awkward week between Christmas and new year with a countdown of listeners' Top 500 of All Time. They're handy because you can easily schedule 100 songs for each of the five daytime periods (the usual station playlist runs overnight) and it gives the impression that you're playing what listeners have chosen.

That's not strictly true for several reasons:

▫ Such countdowns attract very little listener response.

▫ The most-suggested songs are usually those that have been in the charts most recently.

▫ Stations are never going to play some of the songs requested because they simply don't fit with the station format.

These countdowns are difficult to administer accurately, not least because of the low number of votes cast. That means that dozens of songs in the lower reaches of the 500 may only be separated by one vote. Then you're forced to 'falsify' the results – you can't have 30 songs all tying for the same place. In this circumstance, put the songs most representative of your station's core up as high as you can, while also bearing in mind the usual scheduling mix of singers, speed, years and genres.

# PPL, PRS and MCPS

There is another great time-saving device that is built into music scheduling computers and that's the ability to sort out the paperwork for music payments. Radio stations have to pay, via blanket licences negotiated by broadcasters, for each song they play. That money is split between the music publishing company, the distributor, the composer, arranger, lyricist and performer of the song.

Stations are allowed to broadcast music from CDs (and records, etc) because of an agreement with the Phonographic Performance Limited, the main society that represents record companies and performers. Stations pay PPL a sum for the blanket use of their songs, and are obliged to tell them which songs were played and for how long. That's so the money is fairly divided between all of their members.

The Performing Rights Society collects money for its members (composers, lyricists and publishers), the amount being linked to the audience size of the station on which the song was broadcast. The Mechanical Copyright Protection Society collects dues for its publisher and composer members.

There is an argument that by playing songs on the radio, stations are giving free publicity to the artists. The member groups say that playing music attracts listeners, and therefore advertisers, and so stations can well-afford to pay the people who created the music in the first place. PPL, PRS and MCPS have won the argument, but at least send stations free copies of songs as their part of the deal.

The paperwork for the music that's played ('the returns') is down to trust to a large extent. Every piece of music is logged by individual stations and details sent to the copyright societies. The blanket licence money is then split between copyright society members entitled to royalties. Spot checks are made on stations to ensure that returns are accurate, with penalties charged if they're not.

Can you believe that only a few years ago, presenters would have to time the duration of each song they played down to the last second, plus the duration of every jingle and music bed that was used. This was all while they were trying to present a show.

> 'All rights of the manufacturer and the owners of the recorded work reserved — unauthorised copying, public performance and broadcasting of this record prohibited'
>
> Label on CDs

> 'A PRS licence doesn't give you the blessing to use well-known songs in advertisements. PRS covers "public performance and broadcast of musical works", it does not give you the right to use PRS members' music in anything you see fit.'
>
> John Calvert, MD Airforce commercial production,
> *The Radio Magazine*, 17 April 2005

John makes a good point; you can't just use music for whatever you want. In the run-up to the millennium celebrations, the band Pulp banned the use of their song *Year 2000* for any use apart from as a straight track – it couldn't be used for adverts or beds or anything else.

Also be aware that all audible music has to be reported. That includes:

- Traditional or out of copyright music such as *Auld Lang Syne* or *Happy Birthday* (you may not have to pay for using it but it still has to be reported).
- Ice cream van bells or football chants (for example, in a feature you produce).
- Sound effects from a Publisher's Library recording.
- Even one second of a tune – all has to be logged and reported.

# Library music

Some music can be used without additional payment but still needs to be logged so publishers can receive royalties from the PRS. This may be music that's been bought outright by the station and is of the type used for adverts, music beds or theme tunes and is called 'library music'. They're called things like Network News Themes or Comedy Punctuation, but be warned, you have to listen to an awful lot of tracks to find the one that's right for your purpose.

# The spoken word

You can't get around paying for what you use by simply broadcasting plays, poetry or comedy instead of music. That's because the agreements stations have don't extend to the use of the spoken word. That means that a station would normally have to get individual permission from the copyright holder before they could use such items.

# Internet tracks

Some stations play clips of TV programmes or cartoons either as features or mixed with their sweepers. In the mid '90s you were bombarded by Homer's 'Doh!' on almost any station you tuned to, nowadays it's more likely to be clips of the previous night's Big Brother. Again, it's a risky procedure: the actors are entitled to more money if their work is being used in places other than they agreed, and even though Channel 4 may like the extra publicity that you playing clips of the latest goings-on in the BB House would bring, it's probably best to get their agreement in writing.

Taking music off the net (either new releases or theme tunes) is also not advisable, as you don't always know if the recordings are legal in the first place: a pirate copy of a live concert, or an unauthorised remix, for example. Although it's safe to buy from recognised sites (iTunes, for example), you can't be sure that other sites have the right to record, use or sell the track that you're after.

# 9 Speech programming

The previous chapter dealt with what type of music to play, when to play it and in what order. Now I'm going to talk about something similar with more speech-based programmes. Although many elements will be of use if you're in commercial radio, I'm going to focus mainly on the kind of shows that are usually heard on BBC local stations.

You can't just go on air with a list of topics to talk about, phone numbers of interviewees to call and songs to play. Each programme needs to be planned – you need to know when you'll run all those elements.

There has to be structure so:

□ The items go in the most appropriate place.
   □ According to the size and make-up of the audience.
   □ According to what other items are either side of it.
   □ According to what's in the rest of the hour or programme.
□ You know what you're doing from one moment to the next.
   □ So you can schedule space for it.
   □ So you can prepare for it.
   □ So you can promote it.

A lot of the output of BBC local radio is music and speech programming, usually about 40:60 in favour of speech. Producers have to be careful how they balance their items: too much speech and it may sound odd to have a song suddenly appear, or it may sound like a music show with an ill-placed interview intruding.

A lot of the considerations about what to put in a show have to do with the time of day it's on (BBC local stations have a policy of no music at breakfast, and little at drivetime, but more during the day), the style of presenter (whether they're more comfortable doing longer interviews or presenting their own short links) and the resources available (it's more time-consuming to set up speech items than it is to programme another hour's-worth of tracks).

A balance is what's needed, so when putting together your music/speech programme, consider where in the hour you want to place your songs to balance, or compliment, the speech items.

## Planning the running order

It's exciting, but also a little daunting, to be given an hour (or two, or three) to fill with material. Here's how to make it much more manageable.

# The programme clock

Regular features (sometimes called 'furniture') are often shown in an easy-to-follow 'programme clock' (as seen here). This is a clock-face for each hour of the programme showing the location and duration of each item, and makes it much easier to understand what goes where in your empty hour and how you can place other items in their optimum position.

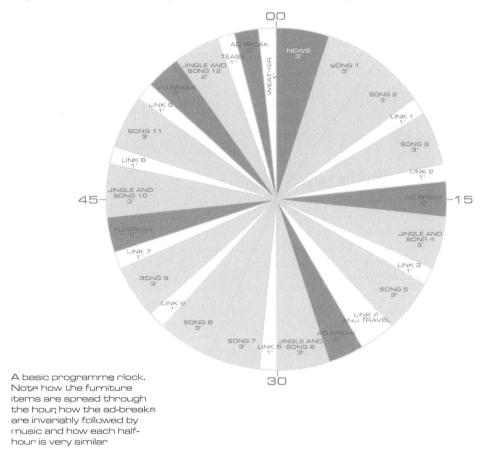

A basic programme clock. Note how the furniture items are spread through the hour; how the ad-breaks are invariably followed by music and how each half-hour is very similar

The clock here is for a very basic music-heavy commercial radio station show, but you can see how it could be adapted for a programme with more speech, or a BBC station with no commercials. One or two of the links shown here could very well be a pre-recorded trail or a what's on diary, or the adverts could be replaced with a guest interview, competition, newspaper review, financial report, TV review, or job spot.

A clock is an easy way to picture the programme, although a list of features and their duration is more practical when you're entering information in a running order on a computer.

This is an alternative running order for the same programme shown above:

| Start time | Content | Duration |
|---|---|---|
| :00 | NEWS | 3' |
| :03 | SONG 1 | 3' |
| :06 | SONG 2 | 3' |
| :09 | Link 1 | 1' |
| :10 | SONG 3 | 3' |
| :13 | Link 2 and tease | 1' |
| :14 | AD BREAK | 2' |
| :16 | JINGLE | 10" |
| :16 | SONG 4 | 3' |
| :19 | Link 3 | 1' |
| :20 | SONG 5 | 3' |
| :23 | Link 4 and TRAVEL and tease | 2' |
| :25 | AD BREAK | 2' |
| :27 | JINGLE | 10" |
| :27 | SONG 6 | 3' |
| :30 | Link 5 | 1' |
| :31 | SONG 7 | 3' |
| :34 | SONG 8 | 3' |
| :37 | Link 6 | 1' |
| :38 | SONG 9 | 3' |
| :41 | Link 7 and tease | 1' |
| :42 | AD BREAK (NB: start calculating back time) | 2' |
| :44 | JINGLE | 10" |
| :44 | SONG 10 | 3' |
| :47 | Link 8 | 1' |
| :48 | SONG 11 | 3' |
| :51 | Link 9 and tease | 1' |
| :52 | AD BREAK | 2' |
| :54 | JINGLE | 10" |
| :54 | SONG 12 | 3' |
|  | SONG 13 (in reserve) | 3' |
| :57 | Tease | 10" |
| :57 | AD BREAK | 2' |
| :59 | WEATHER into NEWS | 1' |

Fixed items – news, ad-breaks

Jingles and songs

Links and speech

## Fill in the blanks

First, place the features that can't be moved, the fixed items or furniture, on your clock or list. These are usually speech items such as news, travel, weather, what's ons and commercials. They are in fixed positions in each hour decided by the programme controller, usually evenly spaced at the top and bottom of the hour and at quarter-past and quarter-to.

That 60-minute block is then broken up into four much more manageable quarter-hours.

If the news is three minutes, headlines another one minute, two travel bulletins a minute each, a minute for weather and another for what's ons (and they're conservative estimates) then that's already eight minutes of the hour gone. Then add the ads (sometimes up to ten minutes' worth) and you can start to see how the original 60 minutes are being eaten away.

## Where to put the music

You'll probably want to put music either side of the fixed items you've just put in. You may even be able to fit in some pairs of songs back-to-back (even if you only play four songs in the hour that's another 12 minutes and almost half the hour has gone).

Scatter your music as evenly as you can through the hour, don't cluster it all together. You can't 'bank' music with the listener before a speech item. If you play several songs in a row and then go to a slab of speech, the listener won't know what kind of programme they're listening to; better to spread out all the different elements as evenly as you can throughout the hour.

When you've placed the music you'll be able to see how much time you've got left, maybe for an interview or competition.

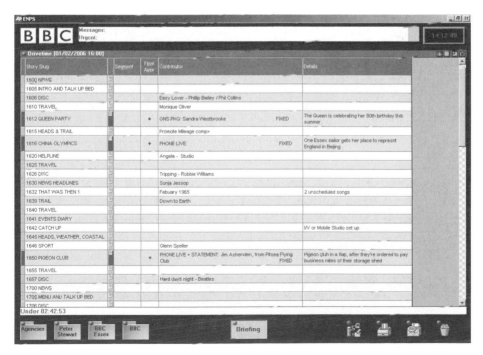

A typical BBC local radio running order on ENPS. Note the instructions and reminders to the presenter; the mix of music, furniture items and guests. Courtesy: Ray Clark at BBC Essex

## Where to put the speech

Many producers still construct a programme as they'd write a news story. In other words, they start the hour with the best item and follow it with items that are progressively less important. The listener almost slides down the interest-scale as the programme continues. After they've done that a few times, listeners will realise that after the first ten minutes there's little of value in the remainder of the programme. So instead of a slide, we need to think of each hour of a programme (and the programme as a whole) as a roller coaster, with a series of peaks and troughs.

We've already seen that music schedulers place songs through the hour so there's a spread of different genres, tempo, male and female singers, groups and eras. You should think in the same way when placing speech items.

> INFORMATION FOR INSPIRATION: Speech items are stronger if they don't last longer than three or four minutes — coincidentally about the same duration of most songs. That could be an individual item lasting that duration or the second part of a longer interview. Always leave 'em wanting more!

Let's take the example of a news-magazine programme, with interviews and music, that you're likely to hear on a BBC local station at drivetime.

First take your running order and fill in what you know you have to do at certain times:

```
00:00
00:15   TRAVEL
00:16
00:30   HEADLINES
00:31   WEATHER
00:32   TRAVEL
00:33   SPORT
00:38
00:45   TRAVEL
00:46
00:58   TRAVEL
```

You can see that there are four travel bulletins evenly spaced through the hour, and there's a news/weather/travel sequence at half past, followed by sport.

Now, put the songs in the running order, considering that it is best to have them
- Evenly spaced through the hour.
- Either side of a speech block.

```
00:00
00:12   SONG
00:15   TRAVEL
00:16
00:27   SONG
00:30   HEADLINES
00:31   WEATHER
00:32   TRAVEL
```

00:33   SPORT
00:38   SONG
00:45   TRAVEL
00:46   SONG
00:58   TRAVEL

That's quite an even spread, songs every 12 minutes or so, and is a good skeleton for the rest of the programme.

After the programme theme and introductions at the top of the hour, it makes sense to have the lead story (the one that's most relevant and interesting to the audience) and probably follow that with the second lead. I mentioned earlier that it's good to keep the speech items no longer than the duration of a song, about three minutes, but I've given these stories four minutes to include the time it'll take to read the cue (the introduction to the piece) and to wrap up the item (bring it to a conclusion) if it's an interview.

Then it's important to play a song as a break from the speech content, so let's bring what we'd scheduled at :12 forward slightly. That will give us a couple of minutes just before the travel news to remind listeners what else is on the programme and read one or two what's on items.

After travel news, there's 11 minutes to fill before the song and the speech block. That gives us time for two more news stories (perhaps a live or pre-recorded interview, or feature), and a little time over. We could do the third lead here, but then we're starting to lead listeners down that slide I mentioned. It's probably better to put *that* item after the half-past speech block to give some weight to the second part of the hour. But you can't have the two top stories followed by the two bottom stories – that would sound unbalanced. Consider taking leads 4 and 6 at quarter past the hour, and having 3 and 5 later. That gives a peak and trough that I mentioned earlier.

We may need the extra time in case we're running late, so we'll keep it in hand but also prepare something to fill with just in case. At :12 we mentioned the rest of the show and the what's ons, so we can't do exactly the same again. Instead consider teasing ahead what's in the next half-hour, and also what's on the station later that day or the next day. It's best to do these mentions before SONG 2, so we don't add to the length of the, already considerable, speech block.

00:00   INTRODUCTION
00:01   STORY 1
00:05   STORY 2
00:09   SONG 1
00:12   Tease and what's ons
00:15   TRAVEL
00:16   STORY 4
00:20   STORY 6
00:24   Tease and trail
00:27   SONG 2
00:30   HEADLINES
00:31   WEATHER
00:32   TRAVEL
00:33   SPORT
00:38   SONG
00:41   STORY 3
00:45   TRAVEL

```
00:46   SONG
00:49   STORY 5
00:53   And finally story . . .
00:58   TRAVEL
```

Above is what our running order looks like, together with the regular 'and finally' item at the end of the show.

## The music/speech mix

There's certainly a balance to be made: after a long period of speech does the listener want a song to lighten the mix? If the answer is yes, then consider playing an up-tempo and well-known (core) song to maintain interest, rather than a relatively unknown track which may alienate the listener. On the other hand, too many songs and the listener may feel hungry for more information.

## Slabs of speech

Commercial broadcasters have an added consideration when they're running a music/speech mix because they may also have up to 9 minutes of adverts an hour. If you put a song either side of an ad-break, then you're fast running out of time to have meaningful speech. In such a situation, interview slots are usually placed just before a break, with music either side of that whole 'speech block'.

## Your best material

Put your best material where your best audience is – it makes sense, doesn't it? So, if your programme is on at breakfast, don't 'waste' your top story, best observation or most interesting guest in the 6–7 hour. Ask your programme controller to tell you when the audience peaks and consider putting the item there instead.

## Your worst material

Sometimes producers are tempted to put an item in the running order even though they know that it's not really strong enough. In other words, they think that 'slot filling' is more important than making an item relevant, interesting and compelling. Don't be seduced if you see other producers do this. Again, the phrase to remember is quality not quantity.

## Drag 'em through

Position items to prolong listening. If you've an item on what to buy your wife for Christmas, consider putting it after the sports news, to keep one audience (possibly mostly men) listening for longer. If you continually chop and change different kinds of content, the show has no flow and listeners may go.

## Life is a roller coaster

It's a song by Ronan Keating and also a good maxim to remember when putting your show together. Make sure that you have various peaks during the programme and that you end on a high. Consider whether, once you start the show, it's a case of downhill all the way.

## It takes two

Even though slots are often best kept at around three minutes, it doesn't mean that you have to then get rid of your guest after that time. They may be worth longer, in which case give them longer, but not in one slot. Spread them over two slots instead.

In a news programme you may consider placing those slots at two different parts of the hour rather than consecutively. You may start with a 'pro' opinion at the top of the programme and then promote that you'll be hearing from the 'anti' view just after the headlines at the bottom. That way you have a balanced show (with both sides of the story), and a balanced hour (with the lead story starting each half-hour segment).

## Phono? Oh, no!

Also consider the kind of audio that you have in each slot. It is best to have a variety of different kinds during the course of a programme. There may be someone on the phone (a phono or phoner), perhaps a guest in the studio with you (what's called 'in quality'), several people recorded on location in a feature (or package). If you can, try to spread out these different kinds of sounds through the hour so it's not phone-interview followed by phone-interview.

Similarly, if you're able to, have a range of different kinds of voices. Often, the temptation on a news programme is to get a councillor talking about an issue. The trouble is that you then get a lot of people of a similar age, and with similar accents, and they're usually quite dull. Try for a range of male and female, young and old, experts and those with experience. In short: light and shade.

## At :58

Don't start a programme item too near to the top of the hour. The news is a fixed junction and can't be late, so starting an item here (or maybe continuing one) may mean that it's rushed, and that'll show that you hadn't planned your programme properly.

Other fixed junctions in the hour are also important, but you can use a live interview to build-in flexibility: you can wrap up a 'liver' so you get to another item on time, but it's more difficult to stop (or 'pot') a pre-recorded item.

## Stay flexible

Things go wrong, of course they do. One guest may bomb but then another may be better than you'd anticipated. Feel free to alter a running order to take these situations into account. Cut the crap and extend the friend.

## Broadcast with flying colours

Print your running order on brightly coloured paper so you can always find it in a hurry among your other scripts and notes.

This chapter has been looking mainly at placing speech items in an hour, which is most appropriate for producers on BBC local radio. How to mix music, do short links, and run competitions is covered later in the Handbook.

# 10 Show prep

'Working with colleagues whether presenters of
producers to make better radio than yesterday's
programme is still the key driver for me.
The best bit is sitting down with a blank piece of
paper and coming up with ideas.'

John Collins, Presenter Forth 2, Edinburgh,
*The Radio Magazine*, 15 January 2005

One of the biggest concerns among new presenters is knowing what to say between the songs. Presenters of magazine shows have got it reasonably lucky as a lot of their links are written in advance in the form of cues (or introductions) to their stories and interviews. But presenters of music shows have to talk off the top of their head. Where do their ideas come from?

In this chapter I'll be talking you through how to prepare (prep) your show. Some of your colleagues will say that they don't prep, and scoff at you with your notebook of ideas. These people say they're experienced enough to wing it, and that preparing material means they can't be reactive and spontaneous. They're also usually the people who do poor shows.

**INFORMATION FOR INSPIRATION:** Preparation is the difference between a presenter who is at the top of the hill and another one who is run of the mill.

## Where links come from

In short: everywhere. You get material from what you've observed and what you've overheard. It is what you would actually talk about even if you weren't on the radio. Your own show prep should be going on all the time. Everything you read, watch, see, hear and do is a potential source of material for your show.

### Fifteen Steps To Prep

If you're stick stuck for sources, follow my Fifteen Steps To Prep. You don't use every step for every link, but you may want to steal a few of them.

#### 1. Keep your eyes and ears open

Read lots, especially what your listeners read (and watch what they watch, and go where they go) so you can reflect their concerns and interests. Speak with your programme controller and ask for a demographic breakdown of who is listening and how they live their lives (all but the very smallest stations will have this kind of information).

- What to read – national and local newspapers, the trade magazines, pop culture magazines, anything on psychology or advertising (to give you insight into how people think and react).
- What to watch – go to the cinema, watch TV, know which celebrities are doing the rounds and why.

All sounds a bit expensive? You can probably get a freebie to the local cinema if you do a review on air, and stations are often sent free press copies of magazines before they hit the newsstands. That means you can be talking about the features and the fashions before they do.

Be one of your own listeners: do what they do.

## 2. Be prepared

You'll get the idea that potential material for bits and links are all around us. But that is only good if you can remember it all. I always have a notebook and pen with me if I'm preparing for a programme. It's by the TV, in my pocket as I walk in the park, and it goes with me on holiday. You never know when inspiration will strike. If it strikes when you're in the car use a Dictaphone, or your mobile to call home and leave a message on your answerphone.

## 3. The emotion quotient

Often the best links are ones which cause a reaction with the listener – that's not necessarily anger, it could be pity, frustration, humour, concern, envy, wonder, recognition, thanks, joy.

Listener reactions are caused when something is relevant to them, so it's good to know what those relevant subjects are. They can be easily divided into four general groups.

### What's personal

For example, stories to do with the family, education, careers, love and relationships, differences between men and women, learning and self-discovery. Stories which are geographically local. (The psychologist Sigmund Freud said that people are only interested in two things: work, out of necessity, and love, for comfort: both of them are contained in this group.)

### What's in their purse

Our hard-earned cash and what it's spent on: savings, mortgages, pensions, bargains, private health and private education, the price of petrol, cigarettes, taxes.

### Skin and bones

Sex, babies, general health, vitamins, diets, cancer, old age, health of parents, cures and treatments, popular psychology, looking good and feeling good.

### Funny bones

Funny stories and anecdotes, overheard conversations, quirks and contradictions, wry personal perspectives, the unexpected, the rare or unusual. The weird and wonderful, the first, last, biggest, smallest, most expensive. Plus gossip about celebrities in sport, entertainment and politics.

Some of these topics merge: for example, choosing private over state education for your children to give them the best start in life is 'personal' and 'purse'. Note also that the examples

I give in each group may not be appropriate for your station's specific target demographic, they're merely illustrative.

So, consider using stories, anecdotes or comments about these kinds of subjects so you can relate more to your audience and their lives.

### 4. Make it personal

The more personal you are, the more your comments will resonate with the audience. That's because a personal connection humanises a story – people connect with people.

Look to your own life for inspiration for links and then tell the story from your personal perspective, showing your thoughts, feelings, attitudes and emotions. Stories from supermarket queuing, coping with the cold, the price of petrol, how to cook a roast, buying a car – I once heard a presenter talk on and off for a whole show about the best way to peel potatoes. One station group suggests their presenters come up with a personal link like this, each hour.

### 5. Gee whizz, McFizz

Is there an excitement factor? Are you passing on new information? Are listeners learning something new that they can use? Is it information that they're going to want to share, so they look clever or well-informed in front of their family, friends and work colleagues? The BBC calls this social ammunition.

### 6. What do they *want* to know?

Information that affects the target listener indirectly.

This could be:

- Information about a song, the memories hearing it evokes, the band's next concert.
- Or your considered, maybe humorous, thoughts on a TV programme or film.

### 7. What do they *need* to know?

Information that affects the target listener directly.

This could be:

- The time, travel and weather information.
- Or suggestions on how to spend their well-earned free time (what's ons).

Of course, one of the easiest ways of knowing what your audience wants and needs to know about is to go out, meet them and ask them.

### 8. The ideas generator

Still can't think of a link? Try these kinds of activities for inspiration:

- Do something different: drive in to work another way or go to an art gallery exhibition you wouldn't normally go to.
- Think about your dreams and thoughts: see where they take you.
- Read a book or magazine that you wouldn't normally choose.
- Randomly pick a word from a dictionary: what thoughts does it prompt?

### 9. An injection of connections

Look for links between your different ideas, clash opposite thoughts together and see the suggestions from other perspectives. Do this because out of similarities and differences comes insight, humour, contradiction and drama, all of which help make potentially great anecdotes.

### 10. Consider these questions

Test whether your idea has on-air potential:

- Who's it for?
- How are they involved?
- How does it touch or relate to them?
- What's the point of interest?
- Is there a 'now' angle?
- How will you get in and out of the idea?
- Is there a punch line or a comment?

### 11. The vol-au-vent advantage

Always over-prep your show, then if there is an expected problem you've still got enough material. Having plenty ready-to-run means you've got a safety net and that you can self-edit as you go along. Many times I prepared for a show with items that seemed great at home but when I came to read them just before using them on air, I had second thoughts. You can't do that if the amount of material and the amount of links are the same. It's like holding a party and having the last person there eat the last vol-au-vent and drink the last glass of wine, and you thinking, 'I planned that well!'. You always over-cater for a party, and on the radio too, you should always be left with a figurative plate of vol-au-vents.

**INFORMATION FOR INSPIRATION:** Never come out of the studio having just used your last piece of material. That's not good timing, it's good luck — and bad preparation.

One rule of thumb is to prepare an hour off air, for every hour on the air. If you have ten links an hour, and each one is a minute long and the show is four hours, that's 40 minutes of material that needs to be prepared for each programme. If you present six shows a week (not unheard of) that is four hours of material you need to find. So, together with prep for a guest and putting together competitions and so on, you need to put aside around a day each week to prepare your weeks' shows.

### 12. Don't over-prep!

*Prepare* but don't *practice* – over-rehearsing loses spontaneity.

### 13. It's everyday life

Make your own life a programme resource.

> **INFORMATION FOR INSPIRATION:** If you're interested in something, the chances are other people will be too. If you aren't — don't use it. Bore them — and you lose them.

### 14. Have a reaction

It's great to read lots and to be able to talk on the radio about what you've read but there's a danger that the process might be a straightforward reading → regurgitation, simply blandly repeating the facts. Instead, make it one that goes reading → assimilation → *reaction*. In other words, discover what's happening, then discover your own feeling towards it and put that reaction on the radio to more powerfully connect with your audience.

### 15. Go mental

Don't just do radio. Develop an interest in another area and become passionate about it. Meet people with other experiences, or read about issues that help you make different connections and discover more about yourself, your personality and reactions.

> **INFORMATION FOR INSPIRATION:** Programme prep for the next day should start with a programme review of *that* day.

Work like this as a matter of routine. After a while it will get to the point where you'll get really frustrated when you're on holiday and not doing the show. You'll be conditioned to look out for stories and material during your every-day life and get really frustrated that you can't use it on air, especially if it's topical material that won't last until you're home. It's a good sign that you're moving in the right direction as a presenter.

## Breakfast show prep

Breakfast shows are a little different as far as prep goes, because they're usually more 'link-heavy', and more interactive. The time of day that these shows broadcast also brings added requirements.

When producing your breakfast show you may want to consider:

- Personal stories – share something with your listeners.
- Phone topics – not necessarily callers 'views on the news', but their own personal stories.
- Interaction – for example, a competition (that they win) or feature (that they take part in, such as choosing the music that fits with the 'theme of the day').
- Guest interviews – either short-form on the phone, or long-form in the studio.
- A production piece – such as a song parody or sketch.
- Promotion stunt idea – to raise the profile of the station, the show and yourself.
- Continuing storyline – medium-term themes develop among the show's team members to encourage personal anecdotes and to keep listeners listening longer. Spread over a few days or a few weeks, these could be subjects such as finding the perfect Christmas gift, moving in with someone, trepidation before a school reunion.

Of course the great thing about producing and presenting breakfast is that everything in the papers is new to your audience. The bad thing is that that means a lot of work for you first thing to scan them and identify the key listener-grabbers. Over time you'll realise that most of the stories are the same from one paper to another (so you can skim past them when you see them a second time). You'll also notice which papers are best for which features (funnies, quirkies, letters, features. Hint: it's not always the 'red tops') and you'll soon be able to spot stories and angles which are appropriate or different.

If your station is in a group, then perhaps one person can be responsible for the clippings. When I was at Essex FM and reading breakfast news, I did just that: went through all the papers, using a blade to cut out the best items and gathering them into rough themes as I did so. Then, I photocopied and faxed the sheets to each of the eight breakfast presenters in the group. It took one person about 20 minutes, but would've taken a total of several hours if every presenter had done the same thing.

If you're working on breakfast as a producer, you may want to talk to the presenter about what's set up the evening before. That way they can mentally prepare for the topics that you have in mind, or be able to suggest a better idea or angle.

I mention elsewhere that it's good for presenters to talk about TV shows that will interest their audience; I also said why it's best to talk about the programmes after they've been on rather than before. But if you do breakfast, it's tricky to watch a night time show, as you have to be up so early the next morning. Here's a trick. Always try to see the first episode of a new show that is likely to appeal to your target audience and read the TV critic's reaction to it. These are the shows which introduce the characters, settings and themes. After that you may only need to watch the first few minutes of each episode (the story so far) together with a quick flick through the TV guide to get an idea about what's happening. Come up with a comment from the first few minutes and it gives the impression you saw the whole thing. Some presenters even set up their videos or TiVos through a cassette recorder and then listen to the soundtrack in the car to work the next day. Others make a feature of the fact that they didn't see the show and invite listeners to call and tell them what happened in the previous day's programme.

If you're on breakfast, don't forget to check out How To Cope With Killer Breakfast Shifts, see p. 366.

## Show prep services

Script-writing companies advertise in the trade press, offering to send subscribers daily information to use on their radio programmes. Such material usually consists of humorous lines, comments on the day's news and topics for phone-ins. There may also be horoscopes, fascinating facts, a web page of the day, celebrity birthdays and 'this day in history' items, too. Others may additionally send you audio pieces: interview clips, song parodies, custom-made jingles and so on.

Such material can certainly help you prepare for your programme, but notice the words 'can' and 'help'. In other words, buying these pages doesn't mean that you don't need to do any other work yourself. And not everyone *needs* to buy show prep. If you're happy writing your own material that's great. It'll be original and totally personal to you and your station. Bought-in prep isn't.

## How to choose one

Enquire about several prep services and ask what they provide, how often, at what cost and about market exclusivity. Ask which other stations or presenters use them (they may not tell you) and whether you can see some examples of their work. Beware those who send you what seems to be a sheet or two of their 'best bits', rather than an actual sheet from a recent day. Also be wary of the quotes from other 'satisfied customers'. Whether or not these testimonials are credited, don't use your hard-earned cash on a service just because a hotshot DJ uses it. If it doesn't work for you it will be a waste of money.

Even when you are happy with your provider, keep an eye on what else is available. It may be worth changing service if someone else is writing material that is more appropriate for your audience or show. You may want to look at buying more than one service. If several fit with your criteria and offer you more material (or different material for different parts of your show) then don't limit yourself to just a single source.

Some show prep services are free but the better ones usually charge a fee, and may offer you some market exclusivity with your subscription. This may be an agreement that no other presenter at your station will be accepted as a subscriber, or that no other presenter in your station's TSA will be accepted. Exclusivity may go further so no-one else from neighbouring (rather than overlapping stations) will be sent the same material, or it may be written solely for you (in which case it will cost really big bucks!)

**INFORMATION FOR INSPIRATION:** In general, the more money you pay the better the material and the greater the exclusivity. If your station won't finance the service then you may want to consider buying it yourself. If you're freelance then it will be tax deductible, but either way it's an investment in you, your programme, and your career.

## How to use one

If you simply go into a studio and read the prep service's lines on air and expect to be an overnight success you're probably fooling yourself. It's the same as someone buying a Jamie Oliver cookbook and thinking they're going to be a master chef. You have to make the material your own, not change yourself to fit the material. That may mean rewriting the item completely. You may think that as you have paid for the items then they should all be radio-ready, but as you'll share the same writer with dozens of other presenters around the country, not every item can be personalised to all of you. If you want a tailor-made script, then you will have to pay a great deal of money!

One of the easiest ways of making the material your own is by making it real to you and your situation. So, instead of saying, 'A woman went to the doctors and . . .' transplant the comment on to yourself, your wife or girlfriend. Use characters you know, and perhaps your audience are familiar with, such as other people who work at the radio station.

Another way to personalise it is to change the location of the anecdote and use local places, streets and landmarks that your audience will recognise and connect with. So, if the comment is about someone stuck on the elevator on the New York subway, make it about how you were stuck in the lift on the London Underground. If it's about a boy's football team in Anytown, put them on the Red Rec around the corner. Certainly rewrite anything to fit your own speech pattern and using the words that you would use. Put it into your own language and that of your audience.

You have to practice reading the items and ensure that you really understand them. Do you know the significance of the item, why it's funny or what the underlying tone is? Have you got the pronunciation correct? (I once heard someone talk several times about a sports message therapist, rather than a *massage* therapist – did he never wonder what one of those was?) Be comfortable with the material and deliver it with confidence. (See more in the section on Celebrity Birthdays, p. 252.)

Decide whether each item is something that your on-air character would be comfortable saying. If you think an item is great (be it funny, sarcastic, outrageous, topical or whatever) but your radio persona would not say it, then you can't use it. Consider giving it to another character on your show or another presenter on the station. Then think about whether you're doing this too often, and paying for material that you just can't use. (See more on on-air characters, p. 318.)

## But the main thing is . . .

Be comfortable with what you say on-air. No prep service is going to be full of radio-ready lines that you can use straight off the page. You have to adapt them to make them work for you. Some may not be useable at all.

> **INFORMATION FOR INSPIRATION:** If you can't rewrite, don't find it funny, or it's something your character wouldn't say on-air, don't use it.

## Other tips and hints

### Liner prep

As well as writing links relating to something in the news or something that happened to you on the way to work, show prep also consists of preparing basic liners for your regular features. Otherwise there's a likelihood that you'll always introduce them the same way. Spend several minutes a week coming up with new ways of saying old things. A new way to introduce the travel, for example (some ideas are mentioned on p. 235) or how to describe your regular competition.

When I presented a Sunday night disco show on Essex FM in the early 2000s I developed several stock phrases that described the show and its content. Instead of always saying, 'It's the Sunday night Carwash on Essex FM' sometimes it was, 'The soundtrack to the movie of your life', 'Songs from the best years of your life', 'Dance heaven from seven, songs from way back when through till ten' . . . and the one which really caught on and is still said to me today 'Your flare-flappin' floor-fillers'. OK, these were (deliberately) cheesy, but they fitted with the kitsch '70s' mood of the show and meant I had a repertoire of positioning phrases to use.

I also made a note of everything that referred to life in the UK in the '70s and '80s. Not just news events, but more relatable facts such as the price of a pint of milk, where people were going on holiday and what food they were eating in restaurants (prawn cocktails and black forest gateau were de rigueur). Then I brainstormed with my friends to come up with relatable stories from our youth that were either personal to us, and that I could pass off as my own, or were universal. These included memories of Chopper bikes, Shiver and Shake comics, sherbet dib-dabs, the terror of asking a girl out on a date, the anguish of opening exam results. I built up dozens of pages of potential links which were much more relatable and personal for that programme and its songs than simply saying, '. . . and here's Barry White with his second number one of the '70s . . .'.

Thinking hard about such lines and saving them for future use saves you from relying on clapped-out clichés that anyone else could come up with.

**INFORMATION FOR INSPIRATION:** To keep yourself ahead of the game, always strive to deliver your idea, link or comment differently from how everyone else would do it. Think 'What's the audience expecting me to do?' and then give it a twist.

## Swap shop

Share ideas that work for you with other presenters and producers in the group, ideally a market or two away from you. Compare guests, contacts, programme suggestions and angles. Steal the idea and then develop them for your own station and with your own spin – you could set up a web-based forum, or have a conference call once a week.

Don't guard your best ideas, sharing makes them even better. You could swap suggestions for up-coming programmes: a colleague could have an insight that'll improve it. If several of you are keen, you could share the workload for writing the script or producing the audio. The more you give the more you will have.

## Stockpile

As you will come up with more ideas than you can use each day, keep track of them in a book or ideas file. If you see an article that could make a feature or a follow-on, put it in the file. An interesting observation which you couldn't use because the planned event didn't happen? Write it in the book. Also make a note of what you, and other media, did on major anniversaries. If the local paper did a feature on the residents of Christmas Road in December, you can do it yourself a couple of years later. What you did at another station one Halloween you can do again at your new station.

Inevitably, there are slow days, perhaps when you've just got back from being unwell, or have to battle through while moving house or soon after the death of a relative, when you simply haven't had the time or attitude to do show prep. Over-prepping by having lots of items in your file or notebook means that this won't be a problem and you'll always be using the very best material.

## Be ruthless

Just because you spent all night crafting that perfect gag or sketch, you don't have to use it. If something better comes in or if the show is going in a different direction, just drop it.

## User-Generated Content — UGC

This, as its name might imply, is show material provided by the listeners, and could include material sent in by e-mail or text. (For the section on phone-ins, see pp. 295–314.)

It is important to remember that just because someone has sent in a contribution to a programme, it doesn't mean that it has to be used. No one has an automatic right to airtime if what they submit isn't relevant, interesting or compelling. So, for example, if someone sends a joke that doesn't work or is as old as the hills, don't use it. Keep the masses entertained, not the individuals. No one else will know what they missed, but they will notice if they have to endure it.

**ACTUAL AUDIO**

PRESENTER  It's good to have lots of reaction, but not too much please or we won't have time to read it out.

*BBC local station, January 2006*

## Websites

'The immediacy of e-mails can greatly enhance the debate within your programme. They also allow our listeners at work or abroad to contact us with ease.'
*BBC Five Live Style Guide*

Almost all radio stations have a presence on the web, to promote themselves and give support to their listeners. Get people 'future-proofed' and in the habit of logging on to listen, download and interact. Trail the website heavily throughout the day. Try to refer to it as much as possible and give out the address every time. Some stations do this as often as once every 15 minutes so it becomes part of the listener's consciousness.

Most presenters know how to read web addresses now (although you still occasionally hear people call them 'numbers' or confuse the web address with the e-mail address). Drop the 'www dot' at the start, and call the 'forward slash' simply 'slash', for brevity and simplicity. Some stations also have a policy that no other URLs should be given out on air, to reduce the number of complex addresses. Simply put other addresses on yours, '. . , and there's loads of information about this year's nominations on the website, go to relevantradio.co.uk and click on the picture of the Oscar statue'.

That mention of the Oscar statue is a good one, as the more specific the reason you give people to go to the site, the more likely they are to do so. A general 'take a look at our website' reference is pretty much a waste of time.

## Ten key reasons for a website

They allow your listeners to get 'added value' from your station, by enabling them to:

1. Listen live on-line.
2. Get audio on-demand, to hear or download items they have missed or want to hear again.
3. Get more information on what has been broadcast: longer versions of the interviews broadcast, background interviews, advertiser links or what's ons.
4. Have access on-demand, such as news, sport, weather and travel.
5. Contribute to the programme output via e-mail links on the site.
6. Communicate with guests in the studio by e-mailing comments and questions, or off-air in a web chat.
7. See what's happening in the studio via the webcam.
8. Find out more about your programmes and presenters.
9. Debate with other listeners through the forums.
10. Keep in touch with home when they're away.

## Five key website features

The station sites themselves are a showcase for the station and carry a great deal of information for the listener. Content could include:

1.  Items which back-up or support on-air programmes, like more information on a topic, other websites of interest, full scores, competition rules, links to advertisers, a live webcam or pictures from this morning's stunt/concert/celebrity visit.

2.  Items that feed back into on-air programmes: anything that sparks a discussion on air or encourages interactivity with the station, and reinforces listeners' relationship with it. E-mails are a direct way for a listener to react almost instantly to what you do. Most shows read out comments sent to the presenter or posted on the station's bulletin board. Listeners should be encouraged to e-mail via the website, rather than to your own personal address. First, it reduces the number of complex addresses that may be have to be read out on-air: all you need to say is, for example, 'e-mail us via the website at relevantradio.co.uk'. And second, if yours is a commercial station, this drives traffic to your site and increases the number of people who see the adverts.

3.  Items which appeal to your target audience, such as what's ons or an online version of a game you're running on air, and give listeners the chance to practise in a safe environment before they call in.

4.  Items which differentiate your station from the others, like web-streaming and podcasts.

5.  Items that can help generate further income, like adverts, downloadable tracks, a shop to buy albums or station merchandise or more information about an advertiser or sponsor.

## Seven key ways producers can use the website

1.  Advertise – booked guests, special programmes, talking topics, competitions.

2.  Trail – to promote, via links to other pages in the website, other programmes, features and presenters.

3.  Poll – interactivity with listeners such as straw polls or voting.

4.  Research – asking for comments, ideas, personal stories or contacts for future programmes. You can use it to gather material for a forthcoming programme: 'Tomorrow we're going to be talking about remodelling Bristol city centre. See the plans at relevantradio.com and then message me from the site to have your views included . . .'. Get them to send you their phone number, and you can chase interesting callers, rather than waiting for them to call you.

5.  Reduce on-air clutter – with information such as competition details, addresses, Snowline school closures or what's ons. The presenter can mention the interesting or exciting angle of an event, and point the listener to the website for the 'boring' information.

6.  E-mail – direct advertising of the programme to the people who ask for it (the next show's guests, topics, features, competitions.) This could be through a VIP club and give away extra prizes and perks: 'Go on the website for extra clues to the competition . . .' or 'Listen to the Mystery Sound as often as you like . . .'.

7.  One-to-one rather than one-to-many – you can only have so many callers on air, but hundreds can send you their views/ideas and feel they have been included through e-mail. Really keen presenters can reply to as many as they like on an individual basis. Many people would be hesitant to pick up the phone to a radio station, but most are happy using e-mail.

**INFORMATION FOR INSPIRATION:** Your website is a fantastic way to connect with your listeners. Your page on line should be an integral part of your show on air.

Be aware that it is against the law to have a message on your station bulletin board/message board which is defamatory, or if a libellous statement sent by text or e-mail is read on air. BBC stations have staff to check postings either before they appear on a site or soon afterwards, and to take down those which are illegal. You as a presenter or producer should always be aware that not every message can be broadcast.

# Texts

'We try to involve our listeners as much as possible — the advent of texting has probably been the biggest boon to this.'
Andrew McEwan, Presenter Radio Borders,
*The Radio Magazine*, 29 January 2005

Texts will appear in the studio either on a screen, or at some smaller stations on a mobile phone. Texts to some stations are free (apart from network charges), or at reduced rate, while many commercial stations charge listeners for texting in (usually around 20 pence on top of network costs). This charge doesn't have to be mentioned every time texts are asked-for, but does have to be said regularly. This is usually done in a produced trail in ad breaks.

Given a choice of phoning or texting, people will often want to text: it's easier, cheaper and anonymous, but calls are more interesting. Save texts for competitions, votes and one-line comments, not for human interaction. For that, ask listeners to phone.

Anonymous comments are less relevant, interesting and compelling than those with names, so think twice about the value of using them on air. And because they're anonymous, you'll suffer from 'textual abuse': 'Crap record', 'Shut up', 'You're boring' (and worse). The advice is just ignore it and don't react to it on air.

If you get a cracking text but don't want to just read it out, try calling the texter back (don't do this live on air as you'll lose the trust of the audience). Ask them if they'd like to make their comment in person. You never need mention the text on air.

Some larger phone systems allow for a text vote. This is generally a way of sorting the incoming texts into separate folders according to content. It can then produce graphs and statistics from the incoming texts. This is a great way to do a quick straw poll and get the audience involved. For more on phone UGC, see p. 289.

# 11 Getting guests

There's certainly a skill in booking guests for shows: knowing who to approach, how to approach them and what to do with them when you've got them. This is information that's not usually taught to up-and-coming producers, it's what you pick up as you go along over several months.

## Choosing guests

On some occasions the opportunity for a specific guest will come your way (perhaps they're on a publicity tour). Other times it's up to you to find them. Obviously every news story is different so I can't tell you who to book for every eventuality, but I can offer some overall advice.

### Variety is the spice

Don't just go for the usual suspects that you usually approach to speak about a certain topic. On council stories these are usually middle-aged office-type men or women, who often sound boring on the radio. Instead, try to go for someone who has actually been affected by the story. Whereas the 'suit' can give you facts, the 'real person' can give you reaction, and when given the choice, 'reax' beats facts (which you can put in the cue for the presenter to read) almost every time.

As well as experience, also consider people's age and accent too: a local station usually thrives on representing people from across the area.

### Book early to avoid disappointment

Unless it's a news story when you have to put in a call for an interview at a moment's notice, the earlier your request goes in the more likely it is to be accepted. Whether it's celebrities or spokesmen, very often only a certain amount of time is put by in which to do interviews and once those slots have been taken, that's it. But, if everyone else has got the same guest do you really want them as well? (When you're booking guests you often put in a 'bid' for them. It's just radio jargon meaning you've put in a request. See p. 372.)

### It's still for the listener

Don't be thrown by the perceived status of the celebrity. If they don't fit the station format and will be of no interest to your target listener, then don't book them. If you do, the likely reaction from your programme controller will be, 'You're having them on? You're having *me* on!' So, you've always wanted to interview the heartthrob soap star and you work for a news programme? Chances are you won't be able to book them.

## Reach for the stars

You're doing a feature on animal rights and you know that a celebrity is a big supporter. Put a bid in. They might just say yes. Aim high. One of my news editors told the story about how, when the American hostages were taken from the embassy in Tehran in the '80s, he found the embassy's number and called it. He had a tape running as the hostage-takers answered the phone and they spoke to him in broken English. You may just get a scoop if you put your natural urge to play it safe, to one side.

> 'The wonderful thing about radio is the spontaneity you can have an idea and five minutes later you are on-air with it. On TV it can take two years.'
> Maggie Philbin, presenter BBC Radio Berkshire,
> Radio Academy event, November 2005

## Number Ten

Tony Blair being interviewed by Danny and Nicky on Southern FM. Courtesy: GCap Media

So many stations have interviewed prime ministers now that it is less of a coup than it was in the past. However, that doesn't mean you shouldn't try. Tony Blair has appeared on a number of commercial radio shows, giving great publicity to the stations concerned.

If you work for the BBC there is protocol to be followed and you have to go through the correct channels within the Corporation if you want to put in a bid. It's to stop Downing Street being besieged by requests all from the same group.

# Making the call

When I started in radio I found it really awkward and embarrassing to make phone calls in front of other people in the office. What if they overheard me and thought I was doing it all wrong? I used to wait until other people were on the phone too, before I went ahead and made my call. Sometimes we all have to make a call that we'd rather not have to. It may be to a local MP at 5am about a breaking story that you'd like a comment on for the breakfast show. It could be to an officious PR person for a big star, or a complaint to an event organiser who went back on arrangements for an outside broadcast.

People rarely explain how to make calls like these. It's quite straightforward really and I learned by trial and error, but it's no such baptism of fire for you.

- Know why you're calling. Have the name of the potential interviewee, when you want to speak to them on the radio, whose programme it's for, the reason for the request, the question areas they'll be asked and so on, and some alternatives in case your first offer isn't convenient. The clearer you are about your objectives, the more successful your call will be.

- Set up some strategies. As well as considering your desired destination, think through possible steps to get there. For example, if the other person turns down your request what comeback will you have, how will you try to persuade them?

- Have your phone number to hand. OK, it's really basic, but if you're a freelance and new to a station you may not remember it in the heat of the moment.

- If you sound awkward and embarrassed when you make the call, the person on the other end will pick up on that and will be less likely to take you seriously. So, take deep breaths, think positively, and rehearse in your head what you're going to say.

- Then comes the call itself. You're not likely to always get straight through to who you want. You may have to go through a 'gatekeeper' first, a receptionist, secretary or PA and it's imperative you get them on side too. Start with a polite and friendly greeting, 'Good morning!' It's better than a straight 'hello' and gives them a second to get used to your voice rather than just blurting out, 'Simon Pieman, MP, please'.

- Make sure you have a smile in your voice. Be polite, introduce yourself and use their name. One of my ex-colleagues, David Whitely, used to work with me as a reporter at Essex FM. One of the many things that impressed me was his approach to calls: he would disarm the press or PR person the other end by chatting to them before he asked for anything. 'Hi Anne. How are you? It's really cold today isn't it? Did you have a good weekend? Now, the reason I'm calling is to ask if it's possible to . . .'.

- Your job as producer is to check the facts and opinions of the person you've called. People do lie! You need to get clarity and see if there's another possibly better angle to the interview than the one you originally thought of.

- You also need to 'audition' the guest and see if they're going to be OK on the radio. This pre-interview will check if they're clear and concise rather than halting and hesitant. Only then do you invite them on the programme. Don't rehearse the interview or give them the questions. Giving questions can stop your presenter being able to follow up lines of enquiry and can also cause the interviewee to over-rehearse, and learn answers off by heart, which will sound awful.

- Never over-promise the duration they'll be on-air. No one has a right to airtime and the guest may be cut short if they're a poor interviewee. It is better to be realistic and then say on the day 'this is great . . . could you possibly stay for another ten minutes?', rather than say they'll have 20 minutes and cut them off after five. The advantages of this are many: the guest is made to feel great, the presenter sounds considerate and the station is seen to be spontaneous.

- Be assertive not tentative, but not cocky and pushy either. Know what you'd like and ask for it politely and pleasantly and give yourself room to be a bit pushy later if the answer's still no. If they're unsure, offer to call them back later when they've had a chance to think it through.

- Don't offer to pay the guest, and if they ask, refer up (although in local radio the answer is usually, 'We don't pay, sorry, but I would be very grateful if you could spare a few minutes . . .').

- Don't forget to say what you want from them (the BBC calls this fairness to contributors). Explain why they're being invited on, who they'll talk to, and at what time. Give some idea of the question areas, if they'll be alone or part of a group, if there's a phone-in involved or if they'll be asked to react to something that's already been broadcast, and whether the interview is live or pre-recorded.

- Sell the opportunity to appear on the radio. Say it'll be great exposure for their cause, book or production. Say you're sure there'll be a lot of interest and that you've run the other side of the story and you want to be fair and broadcast what they've got to say as well.

- Follow up your call with an e-mail. It shows you're efficient and polite, and it clarifies in writing any issues that you think they may go back on or misunderstand on purpose. Don't forget to confirm the details, time, place and directions. Make sure you've got their correct name and title and mobile number in case they don't turn up on time.

## Celebrity guests

Well, let's start at the top of the tree, because if you don't ask you don't get!

You'll probably approach a celeb through their agent or PR company. Be sure that you can sell the reasons for wanting their client on the radio. What's in it for the celebrity? Well, they'll probably be able to promote something, look good and come over as 'normal' to the listening public. Stars don't pay to advertise themselves (and let's face it, their celebrity is their product) and you don't pay to interview them, so it's a win–win situation.

Most really big superstars only do the really big markets and, despite what I just said about the win–win situation, it's clear that you'll get more out of an interview than they will. Smaller names, those on the way up the ladder, are going to be much more likely to speak with you.

Even if you do get a big guest, they may not give you much time. You could consider doing what one station does when they want a big name for the breakfast show, but the big name can only give half an hour. Get the guest in at a time to suit them and record the interview in up to a dozen two or three minute self-contained bursts, which you can then play out over the course of the three hour show. You'll have to plan the bursts well so the conversation progresses logically from one clip to another. Introduce the guest each time, 'With us on Radio Super's breakfast this morning is Hollywood star Harry Heartthrob . . .'. Then it looks as though your station's so big, Harry is with you all morning.

## Interview locations

Interviews with the stars are often pre-recorded at a London hotel, and you're part of a procession of presenters from stations across the country who are granted five minutes each. That's not much by the time you've got in, greeted the star, and turned on and checked your equipment. Alternatively, the interviews may be as part of a press conference-type situation, and frankly they're not much use. First, the sound quality is usually very poor and second, your listeners want to hear their local presenter asking the questions, not different people whose voices they don't recognise.

Another way celebs do an interview with you is by cheating! PR firms distribute promotional CDs of their clients talking about their latest release, with each answer on a different track. The script of the questions is attached and you're invited to ask each one in turn and then play in the appropriate track as the answer.

## The questions

Make them memorable. The celebrity is going to be fed-up with everyone asking the 'same old, same old' questions; here's your chance to stand out and be different. Think of questions that you want to know the answers to and that the celebrity will enjoy answering. Focus more on their human side rather than never-ending questions about the film or their latest album. Remember, you answer to your audience, not the celeb's PR people.

There may be a problem with this. Some stars don't like talking about their lives off set and you may be given strict instructions about what you can and can't talk about. Alternatively, the PR people may ask for your questions in advance. Unfortunately, they rather call the shots in this. You may get away with asking an awkward question once, but you may never be given another celebrity, but do you want to talk to those kinds of people if you're told what to say? Perhaps the trick is to warm up a celebrity with an easy first question and then test the water gradually and see what their reaction is as you approach the fun question that you've got in mind. Only you will be able to judge their likely reaction as the interview progresses. Certainly starting anyone off on an easy question helps relax them, and then they'll loosen up, talk more and hopefully reveal more of themselves in the interview.

There's more about interviewing technique later in the Handbook (see pp. 288–294), but at the moment I'll give you a couple of pointers by way of a tease. First, prepare. Don't think you can wing it. You'll do a much better job of the interview if you've done some basic research or read the notes your producer's given you. That's extensive research, not just from press releases, but also previous interviews which are likely to tell you what drives them, about their own passions, hobbies or charities they support. You could even ask the guest what else *they* want to talk about and put some of that in.

Second, don't always write questions. Make notes of questions, or bullet points, but if you write full questions you'll be tempted to read them word for word. Notes make an interview sound less scripted and more conversational, and that makes radio that is more relatable.

Finally, you're probably going to have the guest for more than the usual three-minute slot, so tempt the audience to keep listening by using this technique as a tease. Ask a surprising question and then, before it's answered say, 'You'll hear the answer to that after the travel . . .'.

## Plugging products

Earlier I mentioned that guests are often able to promote something. How much should someone be allowed to plug their product on the radio? It is, after all, the reason they're doing the interview. It's probably best to speak to the interviewee or their agent about this before they start forcing the name of the product into every answer. Suggest that the presenter will give the book/play/film a mention at the start of the interview (they'll have to do that anyway, to explain why the guest is there), that one of you can mention it again during the interview and the presenter will do it for a third time at the end, together with credits of publishers, release dates or whatever.

I once interviewed live on the radio a famous sports personality who was representing a parcel delivery firm. We were able to talk to him about his sports career as long as we also mentioned the survey (I think it was about Christmas shopping) that he was fronting. The celeb managed to crowbar the name of the parcel company into the first three answers, so I jokingly warned him on air not to do it again. He did. I then said that if he continued, I'd stop the interview. He tried to call my bluff and the very next answer contained the company name again. He was cut off mid-sentence live on air. His reputation and I suspect that of the parcel company was slightly damaged because of the continued and unnecessary references.

## Publicity

Of course, if a star comes in and says something newsworthy or controversial alert your newsroom who may take a clip for their bulletins and the promotions team, who'll alert the media.

# Local appearances

You're much more likely to get a celebrity when they appear in your area, perhaps in a local play or concert. To stand a better chance, you need to do some groundwork. Schmooze the PR person from the local venues and get on their lists. You need to be able to get all the press releases from the area and the advance notification of all the local events (plays and their actors, shows and their stars are booked up months in advance, well before the public gets to hear of them).

Be friendly with the reps from all the local theatres. Send out a mass mailing to venues, book publishers (so you can get an author if they do a local book signing), PR agencies and so on. Sell your show, list the demographic and audience figures and ask to be on their press list.

If a particular celebrity is booked to appear at a local theatre, then the relationship you've already established with the press office may help you get them on your programme. If it's a concert and you play that person's music, again you have a head start. Remember, it's probably part of an actor's or singer's contract with the theatre or the tour company that they'll do publicity.

Local theatres often claim they have little money to spend on advertising: that could cause a problem if you're forever giving what amounts to free publicity for their events. There's usually a deal that can be struck, for example, the station logo printed in the theatre programme for free in return for all the mentions.

# Politicians

Every member of parliament has a press secretary and an office in the House of Commons, as well as an agent and a constituency office, so there's no reason why you shouldn't be able to get hold of them. But bear in mind that some local MPs don't need to do interviews. They're sitting on such strong majorities that they simply don't need the publicity. I've worked at a radio station where the journalists haven't spoken to some local MPs for years, and that's not through the lack of trying! There are laws about talking to politicians in the run up to an election (whether that be local, general or European), see p. 137.

# Actors and musicians

If there's a new TV show coming out soon, with a big star in a lead role, or a singing sensa-tion has just released a new album, it may be that you can bid for an interview. For actors, trace their agent through *Spotlight* (the book and the web page), or via Equity (the actors' union), or through the TV company which made the programme. For singers you'll need to contact their record label's regional plugger. Your programme controller or music scheduler should be able to put you in touch with them.

# The hierarchy of interview locations

Where live is 'high' and recorded is 'low', and when face-to-face is 'high' and down-the-line is 'low', this the hierarchy of interview locations.

Live in the studio
Live on the phone
Live down the line — ISDN
Pre-recorded face to face
Pre-recorded phone
Recorded down the line

## Live in the studio

Main advantage: quality of audio.

Main disadvantage: the guest has to come to you.

Live is always best because of the frisson of not quite knowing what's going to happen. People simply don't react in the same, sharp way when they know that an interview is being pre-recorded.

The studio is usually the preferred option because:

o   You can see the guest, so the interview is more friendly and personal. It's much more natural to see the person you're talking to. Having said that, one presenter I know of puts live guests into another studio to force themselves to listen to the answers they're given, and still have good quality audio.

o   You can see and react to the guest's body language.

o   You can chat to them before the interview and during the ads (although there is the possibility of them saying, 'As I said earlier . . .').  ·

o   You, the presenter, are on home ground, so you're at an advantage if the interviewee is a celebrity.

o   There's good quality sound.

o   You can take live calls from listeners.

o   You or the guest can react to what's happening in the news or to a song played (you could play your guest's favourite song).

o   Listeners can see the interview on the studio webcam.

o   Pictures of you and the guest can be posted immediately on the station's website.

o   You can speak with several guests at once – a bit tricky on the phone.

## Live on the phone

Main advantage: accessibility.

Main disadvantage: poor quality audio.

Well, live is still good, but it's on the phone.

This is sometimes necessary because:

- The phone offers flexibility in location – the interviewee could be anywhere in the world, especially with a mobile.
- The phone offers flexibility in time – the interviewee can give you a quick five minutes and it means they don't have to use time travelling to meet you in a studio.

Unfortunately if they're down a phone line:

- They won't necessarily know the station format or the presenter.
- You won't be able to read their body language and be able to accurately judge if you can ask that personal question.

And there's another hierarchy of phones:

Landlines
Mobiles
Cordless
Speakerphones

Speakerphones are the devil's work when it comes to radio interviews. Frankly, because they sound so echoey you're often better off cancelling the interview altogether.

If you do have a guest on the phone always take their number so you can call them back if you're cut off.

## Live down the line – ISDN

Main advantage: quality of audio.

Main disadvantage: lack of accessibility.

ISDN is a high-quality phone line that makes it sound as though the person on the other end is in the studio with you. However, the audio can sound rather 'thin', with a lot of treble. This option would mean that there's good audio quality, but again there's no eye contact or body language: no 'spark'. And you're reliant on the guest being able to get to where an ISDN is installed. There can also be problems with dialling ISDN numbers, especially if the radio station and the remote studio where your guest is have two different ISDN systems.

Sometimes, celebrities sit in a studio belonging to a PR company and offer interviews to as many stations as want to speak with them over the course of a morning, each with a ten minute 'window'. Inevitably, stations overrun into your allotted time and you find yourself cut-off just as you were about to ask the killer question.

## Pre-recorded interviews

Main advantage: quality of audio.

Main disadvantage: it's not live!

These, face to face, on the phone or down the line, may be worthwhile if you've got a big star. Frankly, the bigger the star the more likely you are to go down the hierarchy of interview locations!

You'd probably agree to a pre-recorded item if the guest simply isn't available during the time your show is on air. Many big-name interviews on the national networks are pre-recorded. It's simply more convenient for the celebrity, the interviewer and the producer who has to book the studios. But be careful if you pretend that an interview is live when it isn't. Some presenters have got into trouble for doing this and misleading listeners who then turned up at the studios to see their idols. Don't say whether the guest is live or not, just play the interview as it is and leave the listeners to draw their own conclusions.

The balance here, then, is that with live you can be sparky and unpredictable but you can edit a pre-recorded interview if the unpredictable doesn't work!

# Briefing sheets

A producer's job is to give the presenter all the information that they will, or might, need to carry out the interview. The producer may give an angle and line of questioning, or merely suggest one — it's down to the way that each producer works with each presenter's idiosyncrasies. The host must be able to make an informed choice from the pre-sifted information they've been given, which should have been checked by the producer in the call to the guest and/or their PA or PR person and then written on a briefing sheet.

Each programme team works in a slightly different way, but this is the kind of information that you'd be expected to include. Let's take as an example, a story about a remake of the shark film *Jaws*, in which your guest is one of the actors.

## Tasters and teasers

At the top of the sheet is a one-line summary or headline on the reason why the guest is on the programme (this may be called the taster). This is so when the presenter looks at the show's running order before going on air, they can see the topic at a glance.

GUEST: *Ray Scheider. Actor in* Jaws *remake, out next month*

This may be followed by a taster. I'll give you some more ideas of what teasers are and how to write them a bit later in the Handbook (see p. 220), but briefly it is a short line about a forthcoming item that tempts people to listen longer. Look back at the taster and you'll see that, as I said, it's a one-line summary. It's not interesting or compelling to read (or hear), it's just the facts. That's great for the presenter, but it's not going to necessarily tempt a listener. So with a teaser, be a little more mysterious.

TEASER: *'Fancy a bite? You won't when you hear what actor Ray Scheider's got to say about his new film . . . he's our guest in twenty minutes . . .'*

I'm sure you'll agree that a teaser is more interesting than a taster, and that's because they do different jobs.

If the item is from a pre-recorded feature, then the teaser may be a short clip from that feature, together with an in-line. An example from a different story might be:

'And find out why this man has spent the night queuing outside Bartholomew's department store'.

Audio: 'I'm cold and wet-through . . . but I know it's going to be worth it.'

## Contact details

After the taster and the teaser, draw a line across the page and then write the contact details for the guest. You may be the producer setting up the show, but not necessarily the one who'll be with the programme when it's on air. Either way, all the information needs to be together in one place. So that's the name and title of the guest, what their contact numbers are, and how and when you're going to contact them, plus any other appropriate details.

You can't have too many contact numbers, home *and* mobile, for example, even if the guest is coming to the station. Always take a second number, and always give them yours too. That could be the number in the production area if they're likely to call while the programme's on air, or your desk number. Many producers give out their mobile number so they can be contacted wherever they are in the station.

Try not to let a guest call you for their interview slot, *always call them*. Some guests say they won't give their numbers for privacy reasons, in which case assure them that it won't be passed on, or that you won't call them again after this interview. If you don't have any number for a guest then you're totally reliant on them calling, and at the right time. They could forget, lose the number, or change their mind. You'd have no way of knowing, and be left with an empty slot that potentially needs to be filled.

So, your contact details for Ray might be:

GUEST: *Ray Scheider, actor in the remake of* Jaws.

*Ray will be arriving at the studio at 11.45 for the interview from 12.10. He'll be driven by Becky Clark, Press Officer for Worldwide Superfilms, who has directions to the station and the car park. Her number is 07777 112233 (m) and office 020 8123 4567.*

*Becky asks that Ray has a cup of herbal tea (any flavour!) during the interview, as he doesn't drink tea or coffee. I've bought a selection pack which is in my desk drawer.*

## Cues and questions

The cue is the introduction to the guest that the presenter reads on air. Make it relevant, interesting and compelling to the audience. In short: make it ear-catching. Decide your angle, keep your sentences short, and don't try to cram too much information into it. You'll need about three or four sentences, followed by the questions.

The producer, will have had time to mull over these questions for several minutes while doing their research into Ray, so they should be good. Look back at some of the ideas I mentioned before: start off with a nice straightforward one, talk about the film but then venture into more personal territory. By 'personal', I don't mean 'private': personal might be, 'You were away filming for six months, I bet you missed your new wife Emily . . . ?' while private might be, 'I bet after six months away, you and Emily couldn't stay out of the bedroom . . .'. See the difference?

Also put down some questions which are more fun, the presenter will gauge how far they can go with these, but if they're written down they've got a choice. The presenter may not use all, or indeed any of your questions. I once produced a breakfast show presenter who usually ignored all the questions that I'd written. That's fine and was his prerogative if he saw a better line of questioning or had some other knowledge to bring to the inter-view, as long as other questions had been prepared as a safety net. However, it made setting guests up pretty tricky: when they asked what questions would be put to them, I'd say, 'Well, these are the areas I'm writing questions on, but he probably won't stick to them. Is that OK . . . ?'.

Sometimes it's a good idea to follow a question with the expected answer in brackets (you'll have got this from your pre-interview chat with the guest). This is so the presenter can see why your line of questioning is going a certain way.

Also on this part of the page, put any production notes that the presenter needs to be made aware of, such as music, sound effects, audio clips and where they can be found. So, the rest of your briefing sheet will be looking something like this:

AUDIO:     Jaws *theme (number 958 in your jingle file).*
CUE:       *That music still sends a shiver down the spine doesn't it? I guess it's up there with the music from the shower scene in* Psycho *as one of the scariest movie scores of all time. And you remember a few years back they remade* Psycho? *Well, now they've remade this film,* Jaws, *too. It's out next month and I'm delighted to welcome actor Ray Scheider as my guest today on Blankshire FM.*

▸ *Welcome*
▸ *I did say RAY Scheider, not ROY . . . he's your dad isn't he and he was in the first edition of the film . . . (Ray was on the original set when his dad made Jaws and has some great stories).*
▸ *How did you get involved? (By chance, casting director didn't know the family link)*
▸ *Where filmed (Hawaii), how long (6 months) etc.*
▸ *[More questions about the film, storyline, decision for remake . . .]*

▸ *You were away filming for six months; I bet you missed your new wife Emily . . . ?*
▸ *[More questions about new marriage]*

▸ *What kind of shark in the film?*
▸ *You got to know more about sharks? (Yes, now a supporter of the Shark Park conservation charity).*

▸ *I wonder how much you really know about marine life? Some fish have some fantastic names don't they? Can I ask you to play Fish or Fishy? (I will check Ray is OK with this before the interview. Shouldn't be a problem).*

▸ *I've got ten names of species of fish, but not all of them are real, some I made up. For each one you mis-identify, you take another step along our plank . . . so if you get more than five wrong you fall into the sea and become shark-bait yourself! (Fish names and answers below. Sailor's Hornpipe music in jingle file number 959).*

▸ *Thanks and goodbyes ( Jaws 2006 in cinemas from next Thursday . . . listeners can win tickets by playing Fish or Fishy on our website radioblankshire.com, and it's reviewed on Film Friday with Dominic at 6.15 Friday night. Ray will pose for pics for the website after the interview).*

I've not put in all the questions, but given you an idea of the kind of areas that you may want to cover. Note that I've not written all the questions as actual questions, some are just in note form so the presenter can add some spontaneity.

The Fish or Fishy feature is to surprise Ray, and make him laugh and show more of his personality. That way the interview stands out for both the listener and for the guest (and makes it more interesting to produce and present).

## Background information

At the bottom of the sheet, or maybe securely attached, give more information on the guest and the background to the story so the presenter can put your questions in context or come up with more of their own. In this case it could be a review of the film from a newspaper or website with a few quotes highlighted, a picture of Roy and Ray on the set, and the Fish or Fishy questions and answers. Make these points concise. The presenter doesn't want to have to plough through lots of information, so just write them up as bullet points. Put the facts in a logical order, highlighting the key points and noting your sources for any quotes, cuttings or extracts. You may also want to write any areas that must be avoided in the interview ('Simon Pieman, MP, can't talk about allegations of an extra-marital affair because of the pending court case'). Never write anything that you wouldn't want the interviewee or members of the public to see – they just might.

## Minutes and seconds

It's worth mentioning here the format for writing the time in radio. A duration of four minutes and 30 seconds is written in shorthand as 4' 30" or possibly 4m 30s. Some people use 4.30 but that can be confusing if it's not obvious whether it means 4 minutes 30 seconds or 4 point 3 seconds or even the time half-past four. Even though you could write $4^{1}/_{2}$ mins, you'd never write a duration of 4' 20 as $4^{1}/_{3}$ mins, so it's probably best to stick to one of those first two suggestions.

## Handover sheets

I mentioned before that you might not necessarily be the only producer working on the show. For example, on a breakfast show there might be a producer who gets in at, say, 5am and works with the presenter while they're on-air and then starts setting up items for the next day before going home at lunchtime. Then another producer who continues with setting up the features through until the evening.

You can see why there's a need for a handover sheet so each one knows what the other's done. It's a 'story so far' explanation and could list information such as items confirmed, what bids are in for who, who's calling back, what production elements still need to be recorded or edited and so on. There may also be a double warning (for example, about Ray's penchant for herbal tea) and feedback on the previous show from the presenter and programme controller. This might be what worked well or not so well, if a guest turned out to be better than expected, if a contact number was incorrect and so on.

## The guest on the day

As a producer you'll need to meet and greet each interviewee. This may be as straightforward as calling them up just before their slot for a phone interview and giving them the usual warnings about having the radio off, listening to output down the phone and so on (see also pp. 295–314).

With a studio guest you need to welcome them, find somewhere for them to wait before they go into the studio (it could be a green room guest area, or with you in the control room) and have something for them to read, perhaps a newspaper. You'll probably have a water cooler that you can point out to them, or offer to make them a coffee (in a station-branded mug, of course).

Talk to the guest about the nature of the show, remind them of the presenter's name and confirm what they're expected to talk about and for how long (that way they can fit their answers into the allotted time and pace themselves). You may also want to remind them not to touch the mic stand (it causes a 'bump' which can be heard on air), or moving too far away from the mic (to the listener it will sound as though the interview is being held in a bathroom) (see also p. 154.).

Some guests may ask for a recording of their appearance. This may be possible if they've brought in a cassette to record it on, and you've got the means to record it as the interview goes out. For these occasions, some stations sell blank cassettes at reception with the money raised going to charity. Otherwise it's a great deal of trouble to find the interview on the logger tape (the automatic recording of the station's output) and re-record it. You may want to do this if the interviewee was particularly helpful, or put themselves out to do the interview, otherwise you need to think of a nice way to say no. (Perhaps, 'Sorry, once it's been broadcast that's it . . . it's gone forever . . . so sorry . . .').

## ROTs

This stands for Recording Of (or Off) Transmission, in other words, a copy of what was broadcast. There are various different kinds of recordings, each with its own name.

## Logger

Every station has to keep an audio copy of everything that's transmitted. It is the law. It allows the regulator (either the BBC and/or Ofcom) to listen in case there's a claim by a listener that something was wrong. It may be that they feel they were misrepresented in an interview or that they were libelled (see pp. 134–136). An advertiser might want to hear that the ads they paid for actually went out (there's a paper ad-log that each presenter has to sign to verify that the commercials were played, but some advertisers may want to hear for themselves).

The racks room at Capital Radio. Courtesy: GCap Media

The logger is usually kept in the racks room, the central nervous system of the radio station where all the computer drives are stored, where the programmes go on their way out to the transmitter and where all the phone-in lines come in. It's usually on slow-recording videotape or, increasingly on a computer hard drive.

As I say, loggers are legal requirements. One station was severely dealt with when regulators asked for a copy of their transmission for a certain date. They wanted to check that the station was sticking to the format that it promised when it won its licence. Programmers knew they hadn't been, so decided to re-broadcast the entire day that the regulator had asked for recordings of, changing the parts that had been wrong, and sending off the tape of *that* day instead! The trouble was, eagle-eared regulators spotted that although everything seemed to be in order the news bulletins contained stories from several days after the date that they had asked for. Either the station knew in advance what was going to happen in the news or the tapes had been doctored – a huge offence. So, the station was asked for some more tapes this time of the day they had broadcast the 're-created' show. They were caught!

## Autorot

Some stations also have an autorot which is the same as the logger, but which staff can edit. It's usually on a hard drive and accessible from your desk. You may want to use this to take a clip of an interview for a news bulletin, take a clip of a guest for a 'drop in' (short voice clip that you drop in over music), for the archives of great guests, or for your review of the week/year show.

## Snoop tape

This is what is produced via the cassette deck in the studio. It is set up so it starts recording every time the mic is on, and pauses when it's turned off. It's used when a programme controller wants to review a show with the presenter. The snooped show stops and starts (it is 'telescoped') so only the links are heard, not the music. This means that one cassette can last for around four hours and that, during the review session, the programme controller doesn't have to continually fast forward through music and ads.

## Dub

This is a recording of a recording. If the programme controller asks for a dub of the programme, they want the whole programme rather than the snoop tape mentioned above. Ofcom may want a dub so they can hear a programme in its entirety, too. A guest might ask for a dub of their interview, and a company that's provided prizes may ask for one to hear how the competition was won and to check that their product got the number of agreed mentions.

## Transcripts

A guest may ask for a transcript of a show, but they're unlikely to get it. That's because of the huge amount of time it takes to listen through a show and provide a written version of every word uttered. There are, though, several independent transcription companies that provide this service for a fee.

Occasionally you may get a call from a solicitor asking for a transcript or a recording of an item that was broadcast, perhaps because they believe their client was libelled on the station. These calls should be passed to the programme controller. They will ask the solicitor to put their request, and the reason for it, in writing.

## Your contacts book

This is the producer's lifeline. You can be judged not only by the number of pages but also whose numbers you've got on those pages. Keep every number you call, but more than that, write them in the book! It's such a temptation to tear off the corner of a press release, or stick in a Post-it note, but when you come to need that number (and you will) you won't be able to find it unless you've written it in.

You'll be able to develop your own system but certainly there's a problem deciding whether to list say, the PR woman from the local theatre under her first name or surname: will you be able to remember either to be able to look it up? You could list her under the name of the theatre, or under T where you list all your theatre contacts. Either way, create a system and stick to it or put it in several times, otherwise it could take you a while to find who you want.

Perhaps better than paper and pen is an electronic organiser. Pick one that has a ready-made contacts template, and also one that you can search by various criteria at the same time. That way, you only need to put in 'theatre' and all the theatres come up, wherever the word is mentioned in each contact.

Whether you have your information available by paper or screen, always make regular copies. You can lose your book or machine, the organiser can crash or a jealous colleague can steal it (yes, it has happened). Photocopy pages regularly and back up electronically, too.

Some stations have a contacts file on computer to which you might be contractually obliged to add. There may be an issue about what contacts are for everyone and which ones are your personal contacts, because you found them and promised not to share their number but essentially any work you do in work time belongs to the company that's paying you.

# 12 Outside broadcasts

Let's start with a couple of terms.

An outside broadcast (usually called an OB for short, although they're also called a remote) is a broadcast from a site other than the studio. This would usually consist of some kind of transmitter, either on a radio car, full rig, or a backpack. The station may decide to present an OB from a county show, for example, and have presenters interviewing the organisers on stage, and have a roving reporter interviewing stallholders or passers-by.

A roadshow is when a station is at an event and puts on special entertainment for that audience, usually on a stage attached to the side of a large rig or OB unit. A roadshow may involve games and competitions on stage with the presenters and the public, interviews with people at the event, singers or dancers performing, and lots of station giveaways thrown into the crowd. These elements of a roadshow are not usually broadcast because, as the presenters are playing to the crowd and not to the at-home audience, they don't make for very good radio. A roadshow may be the sole reason that the station is at, say, the county show (that is, there's no OB element), or there may be a roadshow before or after the station goes live on air. A client of a commercial station may pay for a roadshows, to draw crowds to an event, for example at the opening of a new car dealership.

A personal appearance could refer to a number of things. They're commonly called a PA, not to be confused with public address system, or personal assistant which share the same initials.

In this chapter I'm going to outline some of the basic considerations when producing and presenting an outside broadcast, although many elements are also appropriate for roadshows and personal appearances too. A lot of the advice consists of what to remember to do before the event and take along with you, so I've written much of it in the form of tick-lists. I've not gone into detail of what to do because each event is different, but most of the points below will be applicable whether it's a three-day appearance at the county show or a ten-minute insert from a Remembrance Sunday service.

## Why an OB?

'Our presence in the community, whether it's at events, with sponsorship, holding stunts, whatever, is about so much more than being seen by x thousand people.
It's a vital part of establishing our brand positioning within the local area.'
*GWR Brand Handbook 2000*

Outside broadcasts:
- Help the station get involved in the local community, so it's not perceived as being detached and broadcasting from an ivory tower. Some events are goodwill gestures for local charities.
- Help you meet people – listeners and *potential* listeners – face-to-face, help make new fans and solidify relationships with existing ones.
- Help *them* meet *you*, so they can put a face to the voice.
- Create interest in the station's output.
- Create and strengthen brand awareness of the station.
- Could bring in some income if it's paid for by a client.

It is easy for someone to suggest doing an OB, but that kind usually comes from someone who doesn't have to put it together. Among the considerations before you start organising what is an expensive and time-consuming production are:
- Does this event add to your portfolio? A station needs to be at a variety of events, not only the big mainstream events (with a full OB unit and main presenter) but also the smaller and more unusual ones (maybe an exhibition, sporting event or public meeting), simply with a radio car and reporter doing inserts into the programme.
- Is it appropriate to your brand? All station promotions should project and protect the station's image as well as the actual station: an outside broadcast at the opening of a new old-people's centre would not be appropriate for a Top 40 station, however much the sponsors are paying for your attendance.
- Is there publicity your PR potential with this event? If you can meet a variety of people, lots of them and get your message in other media, then an OB looks more likely.
- Can you maximise the visual presence? What will the station look like? Consider the OB unit, publicity material and whether you can hire other elements to help you put on a show and create impact. Maybe a bigger rig, a stage, dancers, celebrities.
- Will your presence exceed expectations? Many listeners and potential listeners will be seeing you and meeting you for the first time. Will you live up to, or surpass, the picture they've got of you in their head? That's both on an individual presenter basis, and when they experience the overall station brand.

With those basic questions answered you can start planning.

# Before an OB

The first thing you need to do is get some more information about the event and what editorial justification there is for being there. In other words, is it going to sound good on the radio? Speak with the organiser, or anyone from the station who was at the event the previous year, or the sales person who wants you there this year:
- Will there be enough to talk about, people to talk to, and things to do, see and hear?
- Will the at-home audience be interested in it?
- Will your presenter be interested?

Does the whole show have to be broadcast live, or could there simply be short inserts? If it's the latter, what happens on your stage for the rest of the time? Perhaps you need to arrange some giveaways or games for the visitors so your station stand looks exciting and inviting.

# The recce

Then go and recce the site (a reconnaissance) to visualise and anticipate where you'll be at the event and what you'll need to be able to perform there (either on or off air). Take the station engineer and someone from the sales team/promotions department with you. It always helps if those people are the same ones who'll be there on the day of the event, the conditions are realistic and you meet the right people on site (for example, the organiser).

Editorial questions might include:

- Does your position have a good vantage point? Will there be crowds? Some atmosphere is good, but you don't want to be right beside the toilets or the beer tent.

And technically:

- Will you be able to get access and permission to broadcast from the site or the event?
- Is the signal strong enough for an OB? Or will an ISDN line need to be booked? When by?
- What about signals for the radio car, backpack and mobile phones?
- Will there be a PA system at the event that the station can use, or should one be taken?
- What about other noise perhaps from generators, air conditioning or fluorescent lights, the event's PA system or the nearby warm-up area for the marching band?
- Are you able to use radio mics without causing or picking up interference?
- What's the layout of the building, grounds and the event itself?
- Consider the room needed for any or all of the following: a mobile studio, stage and equipment, commentary position, the crowd.
- Take your OB truck on the recce so you can check that it can get through the gate or under the barrier and that there's enough room for it to turn.
- Where's the car park? When can you have access to the site? Where is the refreshment tent and the toilets?
- How will you be able to get an electrical supply and how reliable will it be?
- Will anything be different on the actual day?

Now you need a meeting for anyone else who will have a part in the OB. That could be other producers and presenters, the engineer, marketing and promotions people and sales staff. Check with them:

- The date of the event.
- The location of and directions to the venue.
- The location of and directions to the pitch the station has been allocated.
- Arrival time for the OB staff.
- The start time of the event.
- Who will be there from the station (presenters, producers, sales staff, promotions staff).
- Their names and mobile numbers.
- Draw up a schedule and running order to outline everyone's responsibilities.
- Decide what the on-air commitment will be.
- Will there be access to a computer, fax and/or e-mail for scripts, headlines, weather, callers' details and so on which will be sent from the studio?
- What facilities will there be for pre-recording items and then editing them for later playout?

On that last point, organisers of large events (such as the Ideal Home Show, Boat Show and Chelsea Flower Show) often provide studio facilities for stations to broadcast their programmes, but because of the sheer size of such events (and because interviewees may not be available when you need them live) a presenter and producer arrive several hours early to pre-record interviews. These are self-contained so they sound live when they go to air. That means the interview may start with a back-anno of the song that will have just ended, or even a predicted time-check. These are then played out from the event as live, giving listeners plenty of guests and lots of flavour of what's going on.

By now you should be building up a good picture of what more needs to be done to make the OB a success, but there are more considerations:

□ Get any necessary permission. This could be from the organiser of the event who gave their verbal agreement to you having an OB truck when you spoke on your recce, but didn't have the authority to do so. It may also be the police, council or traffic wardens. You may also need access passes, tickets or, for a royal visit, a COI Rota Pass. (The Central Office of Information distributes limited passes to local media on the understanding that audio and pictures are pooled, or shared, with those media who did not go.) Shopping centres, railway stations and so on are private property and you will need authorisation to be there (a programme at a railway station may need the agreement of the British Transport Police. To be able to use a radio mike from a hot air balloon you'll need permission from the CAA.) Always get permissions in writing – never trust anyone.

□ Start putting together a programme running order and briefs for each item/interview. What's going to happen, who the guests will be and so on. Make sure these people know what is expected of them.

□ Prepare some background information on the event, so its history, organisers, timetable of events and so on are all to hand for the presenter.

□ Consider what will be done in the event of wet weather. Could the event be changed or cancelled altogether? How will the event organiser contact you if it is?

□ Security and/or crowd control. Is it necessary? Where will it come from? Is the station appropriately insured?

## Publicity

Whether you are broadcasting from an event or not, it is worth telling people about your presence: talk-ups and on-air trails before the day, banners and posters on site, together with giveaways and competition prizes. If yours is a commercial station you may be able to negotiate a deal with another company to supply the freebies. For example, a company with a new chocolate bar would love to organise its taste tests at your stand as you would both be attracting a similar audience. Work with them or better still, get them to pay you for the publicity they will get at the event and on air!

Make sure the station looks as good as it sounds. The stage should be well-dressed with banners and posters. Make it look as though you own the event. Publicity material should be available (stickers, presenter photos, bugs and paper hats and so on; you may also consider some careers advice material, too), together with paid-for merchandise such as T-shirts and mugs. You will need people to staff the stand and to hand out the freebies, and rota them so they don't work longer than they should and have rest breaks (staff shouldn't work for longer hours just because it's an OB).

If you don't have a large events stage you may be able to hire one through an event management company, which may also advise on the rest of the stand: such as an inflatable. Many stations own one of these, often in the shape of a radio. You can let children have a session for free and attract more people to the stand. Again you'll need to be able to staff the inflatable, and check your insurance company is aware. Make sure the blow-up remains clean and in a good state of repair.

Any station vehicles used should be washed and polished with the logos up-to-date and not fading or peeling.

Could you get extra coverage from your appearance at the event? Think of an imaginative way to draw the public, and the press, to your stand. Maybe you can get a local celebrity, or a national star to appear, perhaps the local majorettes, a school gym display or karaoke.

All staff, on stage or off, should be dressed appropriately: although staff at a Christmas carol service in station-branded sweatshirts may look out of place. It should go without saying that everyone should be neat and clean, be on good behaviour and not be seen lolling around the stand or smoking anywhere near it.

## The day before

Everyone involved in the OB should meet up again before the event. Everyone needs to be sure of their roles and responsibilities, and you need to know that nothing's been forgotten. Consider a second recce, to reassure yourself that nothing has changed.

# What to take on an OB

There are lots of items that I've outlined above; these are some additional ones that you might need to have in your OB Kit Box and take with you. This standard kit should be checked out and in again for every event.

## Essential kit

☐ Gaffer tape, string, sticky tape and cable ties – to stick down cables, or hold up banners.

☐ Station mobile phone – with emergency contact numbers for the programme controller, engineer, head of sales, promotions manager, etc.

☐ Pen and paper – for scripts, notes and requests.

☐ Money – for car parks, petrol, tickets and stalls.

☐ First aid kit and accident book.

☐ Passes and permissions – so you can get in!

## To help the programme

☐ Radio-controlled clock – so the OB and the studio are both working to the same time.

☐ Clipboards – to hold together scripts, programme of events, questions.

☐ Plastic sheeting – to cover the clipboard and sales table in the event of rain.

☐ Paperwork – scripts, running orders, music and ad logs.

☐ Security/crowd control.

## Promotions material

- ☐ Banners – to publicise the station.
- ☐ Barriers – to keep the crowds back, or away from the transmission mast or generator.
- ☐ Freebies – stickers, programme schedules, presenter pictures.
- ☐ Business cards – to give to possible clients or contacts.
- ☐ Camera – to take pictures for the website.
- ☐ Audio recorder – to record vox-pops or interviews for the OB or another show.
- ☐ Radio – so the visitors can sample the sound of the station.

## For comfort

- ☐ Tables, chairs – your staff can't stand up all day.
- ☐ Refreshments.

## Technical items

- ☐ Personal radios – so staff away from the stand can monitor output.
- ☐ Walkie talkies – so staff at the stand can keep in contact with reporters at the stalls.
- ☐ Mic flags – to help promote the station and look 'corporate'.
- ☐ Batteries – for the clock, the radio mics, walkie talkies, personal radios.
- ☐ ISDN kit/backpack (portable transmitter).
- ☐ Wet weather clothes.

# On the day

On the day, check all the equipment again to make sure that you have got everything, and arrive at the site early. Meet your contact and go over your plans with them; do the same with the rest of the team when they arrive.

Do another signal check and risk assessment once your equipment is set up, and before the public arrives.

# The broadcast bit of an OB

So far we've talked about the O of the phrase outside broadcast, now here's what's involved in the B!

Years ago mobile studios were all the rage. Songs, jingles and commercials were all duplicated so the entire programme could come live from an event. Then came a period when the presenter was on location with a mic and a mixing desk, and a technical operator played in all the other inserts from the studio back at base. Now we're moving back to square one – with a difference. Increased ISDN bandwidth means data and audio can use the same line, so a presenter on the road has remote access to the station's studio computer. This puts them back in control of the programme rather than relying on a TO (technical operator).

The next couple of paragraphs are for the many stations which still rely on a TO, on whom a lot of the success of the OB will depend. They will need to know:

- The programme back to front.
- All the junctions and regular features, and where the jingles and themes are.
- Whether they need to play in any audio or pre-recorded interviews.
- The in and out cues to all the links (or crosses, if you are contributing to someone else's programme, rather than presenting the entire show from the event).
- What to do if it goes wrong, the line goes dead (goes down) or the signal starts distorting.

When you are on an OB you need to make sure that you are able to talk to the studio TO down the OB mic while a song is playing, without your voice going to air. That way you can be in constant contact with them. See if the engineer can rig up a way for them to be able to talk back to you too. If not you will have to give the TO clear and specific instructions and hope that they understand and follow them. Alternatively, have the TO call you on your mobile studio to your mobile, every ten minutes or so, just so you are reassured that everything is running smoothly as the programme goes to air.

Your aim as a producer is to make the OB sound as seamless as a studio-based show. You will still have produced a running order and done your show prep, and balanced items of interest through the hour (see earlier).

The trouble is that there are not always loads of people to talk to and things to describe at an event. That is why it will pay dividends to prepare material in advance if you can. Pre-record some interviews and either play them out from the event or send them down the line (over the air, but not on-air) back to the studio before the programme starts and explain to the TO when they are to be played in.

Another advantage of doing this is that in places like a county showground, where stalls are scattered over large areas, you need some material to fill time while you and your presenter race to another interviewee with a radio mic and back-pack.

When you are putting an OB programme together do not make it too tight or too loose: build in an item each hour that you can move or drop if you need to. It may take you longer than you had anticipated getting from the display of Shire horses to the majorettes' arena! Also, don't change the product: keep some regular programme elements (benchmark features), so the three hour OB doesn't sound as though it is on a completely different station.

## Unobtrusive cues

To avoid the obvious and grating 'now over to you' and 'now back to the studio' cues, devise some other signals which won't be so intrusive to the listener. Perhaps your colleague will know you well enough to identify when you are finishing your link by your tone of voice. More likely you will use an SOC, a time check, or a mention of the station name. An SOC is a Standard Out Cue, you hear them giving these on the TV at the end of news reports, and in radio we have them too: 'Peter Porter, Radio X News, at the town hall'. Obviously we don't want something as formal as that at the end of each cross so consider something shorter and more informal: 'And that's what's happening at the big charity carwash . . . at 11.25' or '. . . it's Radio X' or 'I'm Peter Porter' and so on. Just make sure the TO knows!

## The live audience

Do not play just to the people gathered around the stage, remember those at home. It is a balancing act to keep the live audience involved and entertained but to also give a flavour of the sounds and sights to those who aren't at the location (by far your biggest audience).

**INFORMATION FOR INSPIRATION:** Remember the listeners *and* the location:
Don't let what's happening on location compromise what's on air.
Don't let what's on air compromise what's happening on location.

Consider taking some pictures on a digital camera and posting them on your website so those at home get to see what's going on.

## Two more things

Always have a backup plan for the backup plan: you cannot control what is happening in the control room at the radio station or indeed at the event itself.

Don't forget your team. Make sure they have food and a break.

## After the event

- When you leave, help tidy up. The way you leave the site or event also reflects on the radio station.
- Thank the organiser. Personally on the day if you can, if not, then later by phone or letter.
- Consider a review meeting. What worked well in the lead up to the day and on the day itself? What could have worked better? Can it be fixed for next time? Who will make sure it is? Write this down so it is available for the next time.

## Risk assessment

As you can imagine there are lots of legal and Health and Safety implications in running an OB. You may need to consider these points so you can complete a risk assessment form which helps you to realise your obligations to the safety of yourself, your colleagues and the public. You should really go on a proper H&S course, but in the meantime here are some main considerations for a radio OB.

- Be aware of cables that are lying on the ground around your stand that people could trip over, or other items that they could collide with. All leads should be taped down or secured over doorways.
- Gangways and fire exits should always be kept clear.
- You may need to consider the security of the public, especially if you have organised the event yourself.
- Consider the volume and height of speakers so deafness isn't caused.
- What about the effect of light or chemicals at the event? You may want to use strobes or dry ice and there are health implications for both.
- Make sure that any transmitting aerial and other live equipment is well guarded from the public.
- Ensure that you are not causing a nuisance. For example, drivers looking to see what you are doing, or staff at their place of work (say a factory) who may be distracted.
- Do not cause an obstruction to passengers or passers-by. For example, if a crowd forms on the pavement outside a shop, which causes other people to walk into the road.

- Are there any outside dangers? (It is forbidden to broadcast from a petrol station or near overhead wires.)
- Will you be near any machines, for example at a factory or on a farm, which could cause a danger to staff or the public?
- Does the station need extra insurance to be at the event or does the organiser have public liability insurance which covers you? (NB: if you sign an indemnity form to clear an event organiser from any blame should there be an accident, you may negate all the rights of your station's own insurance.)
- Does the OB crew need to wear any special clothing or need to hire particular equipment? On a boat you will need soft-soled shoes, in a factory you may need to wear masks, overalls, reflective jackets, ear defenders, hard hats or goggles.
- If you are thinking of travelling during the outside broadcast (perhaps a boat ride or pleasure train) is the operator trained and licensed? Do they have safety equipment?
- Is your own outside broadcast vehicle roadworthy and recently serviced? A reminder that the radio car or OB vehicle must not be driven with the mast up, or carry any passengers (other than station staff).
- Do you need weather protection for the staff or crew? Wet weather clothes, or wind or sun protection?
- Do you have emergency money and first aid equipment?
- Are animals involved? (Quite likely at a county show event or farm open day.) Will the animals have trainers or handlers with them? Do any of your crew have allergies or are pregnant? Animals may resent intrusion into their territory and there is a risk of bites and scratches.
- If cooking is involved, consider whether the cook is experienced and using equipment which to safe.
- Does the weather forecast change any of the above? Are strong winds, driving rain, ice or fog forecast?
- Lifting equipment: is there any to help carry OB speakers and help put up the stage?
- Where will the radio car or OB unit be parked, and is there enough room to erect its mast?
- Are there barriers to protect the equipment from the audience – and vice versa!

# Personal appearances

If you are the only person going to open a fair or fête you have a slightly different role than on an OB where you have the whole station behind you.

Call the organisers personally and check that what you have been told is what they are expecting. Check the time you are wanted, the location of the event, where you can park and (if appropriate) how much you will be paid, and who will give you the money. Several times I've had to find an elusive fête organiser, who then tried to negotiate a lower fee than the one I was expecting!

Double-check what equipment you need from them and what you need to take. If you feel it necessary, ask for the brochure or programme of the event to be sent to you in advance, that way you can prepare notes for any speech, announcement, or introduction that you have been asked for, and double-check the station logo and your name and spelling: I've seen Capital Radio billed as Capitol Radio before now.

Speak to your promotions department. You will need a station sweatshirt or jacket to wear and some giveaway promotional items. Will you take them with you or will they be delivered to the event? What about a mileage fee for driving to the engagement and a few pounds from the kitty to spend on the stalls? Again, on some occasions I've ended up out-of-pocket, after paying for petrol, parking, entrance, and then being encouraged to have a go on most of the stalls. And that's despite being paid for the appearance!

## Charity events

As a local personality you will often be asked to open or compere charity events *for free*. This puts you in an awkward position: it is difficult to say no to worthy causes which don't have much money, but you can't say yes to everyone and be out of pocket yourself. Going to these events is work as you are on display and meeting listeners and clients. It isn't really enjoyable because you can't relax. You are working and not getting paid, although other people such as the catering staff, are working and getting paid. Choose a couple of charities that mean something to you, and agree to appear for free at two or three of their events each year. Then when others approach you, you can explain politely that you help these other causes and don't have time to take on any more.

# The presenter's role

> **INFORMATION FOR INSPIRATION:** You are the station — the brand is reflected in you; how you look, dress and interact with the public. Everything.

Your behaviour at the event should be impeccable. It is fine having fun, that's what you are there for, but make sure it doesn't appear to be too juvenile. Be aware that some of the crowd won't be listeners and may try to disrupt the event with catcalling. Work out in advance how you will handle this. Some people have the ability to deal with hecklers but unless that is you it is probably best to avoid trying. A clever-dick put-down may backfire on you.

Image is also about not smoking. A group of staff wearing logo-ed jackets and smoking, either in front of the stage, on it, or around the back of the rig, looks awful. If you need to smoke, remove your branding and walk some distance from your stand. It is unlikely there will ever be an occasion when it is OK to drink alcohol on your stand (indeed to do this while on duty may be breaking your contract).

When you are at the event, however bad it gets, keep smiling, and keep up professional appearances. You don't want to let down yourself or the station. Back up the station and its policies on music or adverts even if you don't agree with them. Criticising your station or another one should not be done in public.

Always stay in character. If you are the grumpy old git on the radio then that is what the general public is expecting, so don't disappoint by laughing and joking.

If you have to make an announcement, such as opening the event, start off by saying who you are, the station and what show you present. You may have a couple of funny lines relating to life on the radio that you can tell both at this event and every other one. Thank the event organisers for their hard work and highlight some of the major attractions, and finally thank everyone for attending and ask that they listen to your station on the way home.

Then, meet and motivate. Shake hands, have a chat with stallholders and visitors and keep moving: don't wait for people to come to you. Smile and thank people for listening. Be polite. If you are assured without being cocky, courteous without being sycophantic and competent without being over-confident, you will form a strong bond with them. Because they will have met you, you will become *real* and they will have a greater loyalty to you.

To the organisers, the event is the culmination of months of hard work and sleepless nights. To you, let's be fair, it is another couple of hours of gym displays, dodgy homemade cakes, and conversations with the vicar's wife. You will be encouraged to stay beyond your booked time but be firm. The best way to do this is to drop into the conversation as early as possible, 'I wish I could stay but I have to rush off to another event after yours and I really can't be late . . .'.

# Finally

PAs and OBs are great ways of reinforcing the station brand directly with the public. Never miss an opportunity to get involved in one: they are great ways of converting non-listeners into listeners and listeners into loyal listeners. Be friendly, pose for photos and sign T-shirts. Ask people what they like about the station and your show and get instant feedback that will help you do a better job and increase your fan base even more.

I was once booked to present a concert in front of 30,000 people at an outdoor event in Essex. I was asked to play some CDs as people arrived and put down their groundsheets and tucked into their hampers. I turned up to find that not only were there no CDs to play, but that the sound desk was mid-audience 50 yards from the stage. I managed to retrieve some CDs from my car, and hand them to the concert's sound engineer to play in. When I wanted to talk to the audience I had to wave at him to turn my mic on!

Later I had to MC a fancy dress competition on stage. The organisers had expected a dozen entries and put aside ten minutes but 30 people wanted to take part. That meant that the second half of the show overran and so, when the crowd asked for an encore at the end of the night, I was asked to go on stage and tell them that the event's licence had expired and 'thank you and goodnight'. I was pelted with coins and fluorescent light-sticks for my trouble. Then I had to get out of the car park at the same time as 30,000 disgruntled concert-goers, and because my car was logoed, it was spat upon!

Not all personal appearances are as bad as that, but they can get close. After reading through this Handbook you'll be better prepared to stop such a nightmare happening to you!

# 13 The law and guidelines

This is just a guide to some of the main aspects of the law for broadcasters.

My advice is to invest in proper legal training to save your skin, your career and a whole lot of money. There have been very high profile cases where presenters have commented on on-going trials (those of the mass-murderer Dr Harold Shipman and child-killer Ian Huntley), and have lost their jobs as a result. Ask and cajole your manager for a media law session. Certainly get your hands on *Essential Law For Journalists* (Butterworths) and ask your head of news what sections you should read. You should also download Ofcom's Broadcast Code and read the BBC's Editorial Guidelines too, both of which give more information on what you can and can't say and why (and in the case of the BBC, what their complaints procedure is).

Remember, ignorance is no excuse. Saying 'I didn't know I couldn't say that . . .' will not let you off the hook.

## Libel

Committing libel is a serious offence.

Libel is anything which:

□ Holds somebody up to hatred, ridicule or contempt.
□ Causes them to be shunned or avoided.
□ Lowers them in the eyes of right-thinking people.
□ Damages them in their office, trade or profession.

Libelling someone attacks their reputation. Think: 'Would I like it if someone said the same thing about me?' Calling someone a cheat, liar, homosexual, drug addict and so on could all be libellous . . . unless you can prove that it is true.

Watch out for these potential traps:

□ Libel by innuendo – you don't have to say the libel specifically, the implication's enough. For example, dropping regular hints that someone is gay which, when added together, give the implication that they are.
□ Nameless libel – not actually naming the person is no defence if it is quite clear who you mean. If you described them or revealed where they worked and they could be identified from that information, you could be sued.
□ Unintentional libel – ignorance is generally no excuse. If you made the comments about Mr A, and the clues you gave to his identity were too vague for him to be identified then you may still not be safe. What if the clues pointed to Mr B? He could then sue, even though you hadn't actually meant him at all.
□ Libelling somebody just because everybody else is. Each repetition is a fresh libel, so stay clear of the more salacious stories you may read or hear.

There are a few defences that you may be able to rely on: one is if the comment is actually true, but you would have to prove that what you said was true, rather than the other person having to prove that what you said was not. And that could be pretty difficult, and expensive.

The station is responsible for any libel that is broadcast; it does not matter if the person who made it was a presenter, a guest or a caller. You are even more culpable if you knew that they might have been going to say it. That is why it is important for you, or your producer, to take the number of callers you intend to put to air and to screen them, consider recording them or putting the programme into delay.

If you are discussing a contentious subject you should be listening out for guests libelling each other and be ready to take down their fader and distance you and the station from the comment. 'Well, that's *your* opinion and not the view of the Radio X . . .'. *Do not* repeat what they just said: 'When you said that Charlie Farnsbarnes stole your song lyrics, you were giving your view not that of the station . . .'.

Then take a break or play a song and speak with the guest and explain what the problem was, and consider whether they should still be a part of the programme. If the libel happens with a listener on a phone-in show, get rid of the caller immediately.

Libel can happen almost before you realise it, in the most innocuous of circumstances. For example, the Radio X Roadshow at an OB. A presenter's on stage, running some fun and games and has asked for a contestant from the crowd which has gathered around the rig. A young boy is chosen from the audience and makes his way up the steps.

PRESENTER:  Hi! Who are you?
JAMES:  *James.*
PRESENTER:  Hi James. How old are you?
JAMES:  *Thirteen.*
PRESENTER:  And what school do you go to, James?
JAMES:  *Blankstown Secondary.*
PRESENTER:  OK, and what's your favourite subject?
JAMES:  *English.*

Up to this point all is going swimmingly (apart from the fact that the presenter keeps asking closed questions which are eliciting short answers) and there is no legal problem. You will probably agree this is just the kind of conversation that you have heard many times.

PRESENTER:  And what's your *worst* subject?
JAMES:  *History, because Mr Cromwell smells of drink and can't control the class.*

You have just allowed James to potentially libel Mr Cromwell (if it is true, remember, there is no libel). Mr Cromwell has been identified by name, school and position, and what James has said will have held him up 'to hatred, ridicule or contempt', will 'cause them to be shunned or avoided' and will 'lower them in the eyes of right-thinking people' and 'damage them in their office, trade or profession'.

Do not insult people even as a joke, do not talk with heavy innuendo, cast doubt on whether someone can do their job, or suggest they are lying. Don't rubbish a product on air (there are some ways to get out of such a situation, such as 'fair comment', but a good rule of thumb is not to do it in the first place). Do not let any of your contributors do any of these things either.

Those who feel that they have been libelled have a year in which to bring a case against the radio station (three years in Scotland), so if the incident happens on your programme you have potentially a lot of sleepless nights ahead of you.

Just because they make these kind of comments on the TV show *Have I Got News For You* and follow them with the word 'allegedly' does not mean that you can. That show is recorded and heavily 'legalled' (checked by lawyers) before transmission. You probably don't have the benefit of either of those. Saying 'allegedly' after a libel does not cover you one tiny little bit.

Defamation is material that damages the reputation of an individual or an organisation. Defamation is an umbrella term and covers libel (defamation in permanent form: what's 'published' either in print, online or *what's broadcast*), and slander (what is said out loud).

There can be serious financial consequences if you publish anything that you cannot legally defend. Take particular care to avoid publishing defamatory material through your user generated content such as material posted on message boards. One option is to moderate the high risk sites but this will not be suitable for all sites.

# Contempt of Court

The Contempt of Court Act 1981 states that a person is in contempt if they create a substantial risk of serious impediment or prejudice to active proceedings. As soon as an arrest has been made (or a warrant has been issued for an arrest), anything you say could influence the mind of potential jurors who may be listening to your programme. It is they who decide if someone is guilty or not, after hearing all the evidence put by both sides, not you.

You could be in contempt without realising it, but again, not knowing the law is no excuse. So, you can't say, 'I see they've arrested the man who attacked the woman in Blankstown', although you may be able to say, 'I see they've arrested a man over the attack on the woman in Blankstown' (note: '*a* man' rather than '*the* man'). The first comment presumes that the person arrested and the attacker are the same person, the second one (which is safer, but also ill advised) does not.

---

 **ACTUAL AUDIO**

NEWSREADER   A woman from (town) is due in court today accused of stabbing a 72-year-old man on Saturday evening. 27 year old (name) will appear at the town's magistrates this morning. Her victim was found in his home on (street).

*BBC local station, June 2005*

---

Here the use of the phrase 'her victim' implies that she (the woman named) is the culprit.

Never say anything about current court cases. Leave it to the journalists who should have had proper training (although that example above came from a news bulletin).

When the case is not current then you are able to say more. That is when:

o   The arrested person is released without charge.
o   No arrest has been made within a year of the issue of a warrant.
o   The case is discontinued.
o   The defendant (the person charged) is acquitted (found not guilty) or sentenced.
o   The defendant is found unfit to be tried, unfit to plead, or the court orders the charge to remain on file.

But that does not mean you can say whatever you want, or allow others to, because you could still be found guilty of defaming them.

There have been serious and well-highlighted cases in the past, where radio presenters have passed comment on the serial-killer Manchester GP Harold Shipman, and the Soham child-murderer Ian Huntley while those trials were actually going on. In those and similar situations, the accused could have been released and the presenters jailed instead, for contempt.

# Elections

There are also rules covering elections. If you break them you could cost the station thousands of pounds. Like the laws covering defamation and contempt, they exist to ensure fairness: in this case so each party has the same opportunities to persuade the public to vote for them.

Play safe as soon as any election is called. That could be:

- A general election.
- A by-election.
- A local government election.
- Mayoral elections.
- Scottish Parliament election.
- Welsh, Northern Ireland and London Assembly elections.
- A European parliamentary election.

The law says that equal coverage must be given to each of the major parties during the election period (usually around five weeks), and that the smaller parties must be given coverage appropriate to their support. The start of the election period is always publicised: it may be the dissolution of parliament or the publication of the notice for the election.

If a candidate takes part in an item about their constituency (the area that they are trying to represent) then other candidates must also be given the chance to take part. Although the item can still go ahead without them, they must have been invited to participate in the programme. You can see how tricky things could become if a caller to a phone-in show starts giving their views on the council tax during an election period, only for a producer to discover subsequently that they are one of the candidates. So do not mention elections. Leave it to the news people. Here's a reminder why: in 2000, Virgin Radio was fined £75,000 for Chris Evans' on air support of Ken Livingstone in the run-up to the London mayoral elections during his breakfast show.

# Other legal issues

## Children and young people

Briefly, children in court cases (those under 18) cannot usually be identified, that means by their name (or that of their parents) or school or even cub pack. It also means that if you inadvertently gave some information about the child (so small that they could not be identified) and another presenter, station or newspaper gave some more (also, by itself, not identifying them), the child may be able to be identified when both clues are put together. This is called the 'jigsaw effect'. Do not talk about children involved in court cases.

## Sexual offences

The jigsaw effect can also work with victims of sex crimes. You cannot identify anyone who claims they have been raped (either a man or a woman), even if a court throws out the case as unproven. You can, though, name the person accused, whether they are found guilty or not. The victim can agree to waive their anonymity, but to cover yourself, they must put this agreement in writing.

## Rehabilitation of offenders

The Rehabilitation of Offenders Act 1974 was passed so anyone who has been convicted of a relatively minor offence can live it down and get on with their life, without the incident being dragged up in the years to come. The length of time which has to pass before a conviction is spent depends on how long the sentence was in the first place. Generally speaking, do not comment on spent convictions.

## The nations

Note that laws vary in different parts of the UK (that is, Scotland and to a lesser extent in Northern Ireland), and abroad. So if you are on holiday in the States and watch the TV news or hear a radio presenter commenting on an ongoing trial, remember: their laws allow them to, ours do not.

## Finally

Remember, ignorance is no excuse and the purpose of training is not necessarily to find out how far you can push a comment or discussion, but to realise when you're heading for dodgy ground. Many radio groups have access to lawyers 24-hours a day, so check any problem or potential problem with them before it becomes larger. Do not try to handle it yourself or put a correction or apology on air without speaking to them, or at the very least to a senior producer or manager.

# 14 Your health and safety

## The presenter/producer relationship

No one gets on with everyone all of the time and that is as true in radio as in other walks of life. In a live and fast-paced environment such as broadcasting, where things can change just before transmission or a deadline, things can become fraught. An understanding of other people's problems will help oil the wheels of radio. That is why producers *and* presenters should read this Handbook, to learn and understand each other's role.

### How a producer can help a presenter

A radio producer is like a psychologist. You may have to deal with childish behaviour, work with someone's ego, give praise, sometimes give marriage guidance, and work within bounds of confidentiality. Some presenters are particularly demanding and have special requests: they only work in one particular studio, only have a certain set of headphones, like their chair at a certain height, their coffee brewed in a certain way and delivered at a certain time in the show. Work with them! They will perform better if you do and they will love you more (although they may not show it).

You will certainly need to be confident when you are working with your presenter on a live show. They may be older, more famous and paid more money than you, but you still have to get the best out of them. Make sure they know this: that you are working as a team for the benefit of you both and the station.

- **Keep them on track.** As you put together the running order of the show, you will know how much time is allocated to each item or guest. When the programme is on, make sure the presenter is on schedule, only let them overrun on one feature if it is worth it and if you know you will be able to shorten another item or drop it completely to make up the time. As you know, some items such as travel, news and weather cannot be moved, so you should be very aware of the knock-on effect if something overruns.
- **Move them on.** You will be listening to the show in a different way than the presenter. In fact, the way you hear it will be much more like a listener does. You may have to indicate to the host when to change topics during a phone-in show, for example, as you will be able to gauge how popular the subject is by the number *and* quality of calls.
- **Remind them of the basics.** Messages to the on-air host via verbal or visual talkback may range from telling them that a break is due, to start a backtime jingle or to promote upcoming topics to increase the time spent listening. You need to be aware of basic radio 'formatics' (the way a station works on air).
- **The visible audience.** Many presenters like to direct their comments to someone they can actually see rather than the invisible listener. That is why they may look at you as they talk or as they pose a question. By reacting normally, as a listener would

if they were part of a conversation, you will help the host sound, well, conversational, which can only be good.

- **Be a cheerleader**. On a bad day, the producer helps change the mood of the presenter by concentrating them on the programme in hand. They shield the host from the station politics, making their job easy and enjoyable, so they shine on air.
- **After the show**. You and the presenter, together with the programme controller, should review the show and discuss what worked well, what didn't, and why.
- **The extra mile**. I once heard of a producer who was so determined to work hard for her host, she would give callers details of when he was going to be appearing in their town so they could be groupies and help add to his fan-base. That reflects well on the producer, the presenter, the station, and the organiser or sponsor of the event in question.
- **Make them sound good**. All of these considerations will help the show and help the host to be much more interesting and entertaining to the listener, with forward momentum that benefits the whole show team and the station.
- **Realise**. If the show goes well it will be because of the presenter. If it goes badly it will be seen as the producer's fault. Read the rest of this chapter to help you be assertive in explaining why it's not.

## How a presenter can help a producer

- **Understand their problems**. Presenters get cash and kudos; producers get the complaints and the crap. Appreciate that a good producer is trying to make you sound your best. Do not put additional problems in their way, or if you really have to, make sure you do it in good time and in the best way.
- **Look after them**. It is unlikely a presenter will be able to arrange more money for their producer, but perhaps there is something you can do: perhaps you can buy them a coffee every so often. Small gestures go a long way. I once worked with a well-known presenter on a national station who often came in boasting about what he had been sent by some PR company or other (in return for a mention on the station). Meals, tickets to sporting events, golf clubs the list was almost endless. It riled the production staff no end, as you can imagine. Many of them considered reporting such 'payments' to the taxman by way of revenge.
- **Praise them**. Thank them as often as you can, especially when they go the extra mile or have to do a load of drudge work such as logging or dealing with complaints. And praising them in public is worth much more than praising them in private.

'I feel as though I'm swimming in treacle when my producer Maxie Allen is off so he would be first pick in any dream team. I don't want to give him too much ammunition for his next round of pay negotiations but he's helped me learn things about myself, let alone just radio.'
James O'Brien, presenter LBC 97.3, *The Radio Magazine*, 14 September 2005

- **Bounce ideas**. Use your producer as a source of story ideas or thoughts for links or topical comedy. If you are a middle-aged female presenter and they are a twenty-something male, they will undoubtedly have different experiences and see things from different perspectives to you. Tap into this resource to give your listeners a more rounded picture of life in the area.

- **Give them a try out**. Get to know your producer, try them out before they are given the full-time role, and ask to have a say on whether they get the job of working with you (note: 'with you' not 'for you').

- **When you've got a good 'un**. When you find an ace producer whether by chance, hard work or nurturing, make sure you do everything you can to keep them. Perhaps you can build their contract into the negotiations for *yours!* Some presenters take their producers with them from station to station. They obviously have a close working relationship and know what the other is thinking, which can be invaluable.

## The C-word

We're in the communications business, but in general we're very poor at communicating with each other! Maybe productive on-air conflict in a zoo programme spills over to off-air and becomes destructive. One is friction, the other is fighting.

Healthy conflict can be good. It can be a time-saver: in a live show things sometimes go wrong or become confused, and often the quickest way to resolve it at the time is a direct question or order: 'I've got ten seconds', 'I need it now', 'Shut up!'. Make sure that each part of the partnership knows that such communication isn't rudeness, it is simply necessary in a fraught, intense and live situation. Remember, volume has limited effect and shows that you are not in control. People look to producers for leadership and if you shout, that is not what you are showing.

> **INFORMATION FOR INSPIRATION:** Many people in high pressured production areas think that noise + directness + regularity = strength. And yet they actually = little communication.

Conflict can lead to creativity, but make sure you apologise as soon after the outburst as possible and see whether there was a reason for the situation developing so you can try to avoid it another time.

Alternatively, maybe there is more of a long-term problem. Maybe you are a presenter who hates the kind of interviews you are getting, or maybe you are a producer who is getting angry at the way the presenter blames you on-air for technical mistakes they make. You've driven home gnashing teeth and complained to your partner more times than you can remember. And yet you know the only way to sort out the problem is to talk.

That, of course, is easy to write but not so easy to do. Here are some easy steps to take when you are about to have one of those difficult conversations!

## Communications made easy

- Work out in advance what you want to say and why, and how you are going to say it. You want to resolve a problem for the benefit of the show and the station, not win a fight.

- Make your comment about what happened as soon as possible after it. There is no point talking about an occasion when the presenter ignored you, the producer, three weeks later when the incident has been forgotten. Don't let several nags build up over time. However, you may have to wait until a moment of high pressure has blown over.

- Be specific in what you say about an incident. What was it that you did or didn't like and why — facts rather than opinions. There is no point in making a general comment, 'You sometimes don't put through the best callers . . .' if you cannot think of a particular incident. So, avoid phrases like 'you always' or 'that kind of thing'.
- Mention items one at a time. Coming out with a whole list of comments and/or complaints is no good to anyone. Pick a specific behaviour or observation and stick to it.
- Ask as well as tell. What did the other person think and feel about the programme or incident? Give them an opportunity to talk and make sure that you listen.
- Be constructive — not destructive. There is a subtle but important difference between saying, 'That went wrong' rather than, 'Maybe this might have worked better'. The second is rather more positive. Make what you say, point the way.
- Only talk about what you saw yourself, not what other people say happened.
- Describe the impact of what happened rather than speculating on why it *may* have happened. For example: 'I had to fill for a couple of minutes when the guest wasn't on the phone on time . . .' is better than continuing '. . . because you weren't concentrating, as usual'.
- Put yourself in their shoes. Imagine how you would feel if someone was criticising your work. And also consider what kind of language and approach would be acceptable to you in that situation, and maybe use it. For instance, butter them up: 'I think you'd sound even better if . . .', or 'It could be really funny if you . . .'

## How to take it — good feedback

A lot of people feel quite awkward when someone praises them, perhaps on a great outside broadcast or a well-constructed interview. They may feel a little boastful if they agree with the congratulations that are being offered. Don't do yourself down! Thank the person that's giving it (then they are more likely to do it again), and accept it with good grace.

## How to take it – bad feedback

This does happen occasionally. If it happens to you, remember you can learn from it.

- Hear — listen to what is being said. Ask for examples if you are not sure.
- Avoid — don't slip back into your old ways by sulking or getting into a row!
- Decide — how much of what is being said is true and accurate? If it is completely true, say so: 'Yes, you're right it was badly organised and I feel really bad about it'. If it is only partly true agree with those parts but deny the others: 'Yes, some of it was badly produced . . . but I think most of the rest went really well'. If you think what is being said is completely unfair then say so, politely and firmly, and ask for a reason for the comment. 'No, I don't agree the show was badly produced at all. What makes you think that?'
- Understand — what have you learnt from the conversation? Do you want to change your behaviour as a result of it, and if so, how?
- Pack up and go — do not keep thinking over the conversation. Move on!

## Assertiveness

## Different characters

Whether you are a presenter working with a producer, or a producer working with a presenter, your relationship, your programme and your life will all be much better if you get on with each other. In this section I will offer some basic relationship advice; show you how to recognise your character, and that of your colleague, and then share the secrets of dealing with them effectively, so you're more likely to get on with them.

If you find it difficult to speak your mind, or are apologetic and falsely polite when you do, you are showing classic signs of passive behaviour. You may avoid conflict by having a mousey voice and hesitate when you ask for something (probably starting, 'I wonder if it'd be OK if you . . .') This behaviour gives the impression that you are inferior and makes other people feel as though they have to make all the decisions. In effect, this is a Lose/Win situation.

Aggressive behaviour is shown if you ignore the opinions of other people, perhaps by talking over them or being sarcastic towards them. Using the words 'you' and 'I' a lot in these circumstances may make others feel hurt or angry and possibly less likely to make suggestions in the future. Perhaps this could be referred to as a Win/Lose situation.

Some people try to get their own way by making others feel guilty. You know the kind of things: 'OK, well, I don't think it'll work, but if that's what you want to do despite my advice then off you go . . .'. In this passive aggressive behaviour someone plays the hero, so the other feels guilty and gives in.

## Being assertive

Being assertive is different from being aggressive. Someone with assertive behaviour is clear about their needs, wants and feelings. They're direct and honest and expect others to be direct and honest too. This is a Win/Win situation.

Being assertive means you get heard, respected and therefore have more confidence and less stress, and other people know where they stand with you. Remember, assertiveness can also be used to give you the power to say no.

But even though you are being *assertive*, the person you are talking to – a producer, presenter or other team member – may think you're being *aggressive*. In other words, communication is a two-way process, so consider not just how you *say* something but also how it is being *received*. If necessary, change your communication.

## How to talk assertively

Use lots of open questions to help you get as much information as you need. If you use closed questions you will be much more likely to show your *own* thoughts. That means instead of saying something like, 'Don't you think we should move this guest to the second hour?' say, 'What do you think is the best way to re-structure the running order?'

Also, use short specific sentences. Doing this helps focus your thoughts and clarify them to who you are talking with. Being fluent with your thoughts portrays confidence in your beliefs.

## How to look assertive

It is not just *what* you say and *how* you say something, it's also what you *don't* say – how you *look* – that can portray you as being aggressive (or passive) rather than assertive. So, when you're being assertive, remember SOLER which I mention on p. 291.

## How to say no

As well as other people having the right to assertively ask *you* to do something, *you* have the right to assertively refuse. Make your comment clear and concise and explain your reason honestly. It may make it easier if you say that it is the request you are saying no to, not the person who is asking. Be assertive, but not aggressive.

# Your personal safety

'If you get too close you break the illusion.'
*Radio Investments Station Style Guide 2002*

As you go out and about (for roadshows, outside broadcasts, celebrity appearances, or even while shopping with your family), you may well be recognised and stopped by listeners. Some presenters love every approach by a fan, most only enjoy meeting listeners when they are 'on duty', others shun the limelight completely and prefer the safety of a studio where they perform best without being watched.

Whatever your character, you have to remember that meeting the audience is part of your job. Anyone who has taken the time and trouble to come and meet you (and perhaps pay an entrance fee for the event at which you are appearing) deserves to be treated politely. A quick conversation and a handshake is a small price to pay for the people who help pay your salary and those of your colleagues. Remember that most contracts have a line in them about not bringing the company into disrepute. So, being rude or offhand to a member of the public (or saying something that they perceive as rude or offhand) could land you in trouble. Most listeners will be friendly and chatty and will want nothing more than to meet you, get an autograph or picture and say, 'You look nothing like I imagined'. Some listeners are a little different.

## Awkward listeners

There are some people who will watch you present your show from the other side of the studio window that looks out onto the shopping centre. They will turn up to every outside event. They may bring you presents or remind you of some small remark you made on air months previously. The kind word for these people is 'fans', other less kind words are 'anoraks' or 'weirdos'. (Indeed, presenters in studios that look out on to streets or shopping centres so listeners can watch them work, often refer to the 'weirdo window'.)

Anoraks keep every piece of radio station merchandise and listen all day every day. (You've got to hope that they get a Rajar diary!) Treat them professionally and courteously, and even though they may simply stand and watch you for an hour at a time, try to put them out of your mind.

Despite what I say later about revealing a little bit about yourself in your links (so the audience can relate to you), do be careful about how *much* you say and the nature of it. Personal information helps you connect with your audience – *private* information is not for public consumption.Comment on your life but do not identify where you live or where your children go to school and so on: remember how the jigsaw effect can work – listeners piece together what you say over months and years. Perhaps change the name of your children when you mention them on air, talk about where you *used* to live (giving the impression you're still there) and so on. There is plenty you can talk about, revealing your thoughts and emotions, without putting yourself or family in danger.

## Being aware of your safety

Some safety information is especially pertinent to radio presenters who may be recognised because of their celebrity.

Before putting together the following advice, I spoke with experts on personal safety to get their support and endorsement and to ensure that what I was suggesting was accurate and up-to-date. That's why I am proud to say that the following information was written using safety guidance and tips from the Suzy Lamplugh Trust.

- Take care where you shop locally. If you are asked to put your address on the back of a cheque, think twice about shopping there – who exactly will see those details? If you need to develop a camera flash-card, do it yourself or send it off to a printer – do you want to be recognised in the pictures of you and your family on the beach? Ensure your credit card has an initial rather than your full, and more instantly recognisable, first name. Do you want to pay by cash instead?

- Be careful what colleagues say about you on-air or off: 'June is covering for Jane today, as she's off on holiday for two-weeks'. Station receptionists meet the public face-to-face and may easily let something slip: 'Jim does do a great show, doesn't he? Who would have thought his wife left him last month . . . ?' I once worked at a station where one of the female presenters was, quite rightly, angry that news of her pregnancy had been broadcast by one of her colleagues. She felt that it was *her* news to tell if she wanted too, and didn't want listeners to know that much about her.

- Do not reveal too much on your personal website or the station's.

- If you move stations, consider whether that is a good time to change your on-air name, go ex-directory, or have post directed to a PO box.

- Do not give your full or your real name when calling for a cab and make sure you cannot be overheard by people who already know who you are, when you give your address to the cab company.

- Only put your last name on your doorbell label, or do not put it on at all.

- Take off your ID badge as soon as you leave work so it can't be seen in public.

- Branded cars are all very well, but ask that although the station logo is included, your name is not.

- Consider pulling the blinds on the studio 'weirdo window' so passers by can't see you.

- Ask for the studio webcam and the CCTV camera which shows the studio to guests waiting in the reception to be turned off when you're on air.

If someone seems to be following you on a regular basis, or you get the feeling that you are being watched, then you need to take particular care. Take a note of what happens and when, and pass it on to the police immediately, letting your manager at work know too. (BBC security has staff who are well used to working with the police and dealing with such people.)

---

 **ACTUAL AUDIO**

PRESENTER  . . . and now he knows who I am and where I live.
*Female commercial radio co-host January 2006, after telling how a plumber at her house had asked her about her job and who she subsequently turned down a date with.*

---

## Presents to presenters

Gifts from listeners should not be asked for or anticipated. It's great to get Christmas cards or holiday postcards from listeners, but some send more. I have known many packages containing biscuits, others with leather wallets and on occasion envelopes with money inside! Your station may have a policy on such presents. Certainly the BBC says any gift should be refused (that makes it less likely that a presenter may endorse a product on-air after having been sent a free sample). It is unlikely that any station management team would get upset about you handing around a tin of biscuits, although other views may be taken about you taking advantage of leather goods as described above, and certainly hard cash.

The most usual gift is food, usually homemade cake. It is up to you what you do with this, although it may not surprise you to learn that most station staff will turn down the opportunity to have even the smallest slice of Battenburg that has been sent in. Who knows the hygiene of the person or the kitchen where the delicacy was baked? Most people decide not to risk eating the un-asked for gift, and it is a sorry fact that such items usually end up in the bin.

## Dating listeners

Despite the maxim 'never date a listener' it does happen quite often. It is inevitable: you will date people who live in the area and a lot of those people will listen to the station, or at least have heard of it, and therefore have heard of you. Every situation is different, of course, and you will have to weigh up whether someone is interested in you as a person, or because of your celebrity. You could be another notch on their bedpost, or become the subject of a kiss and tell (if not to the papers then to their friends).

When meeting someone for the first time, take the usual precautions: let someone else know where you are going, who you will be with and what time you are expected back. Make that first meeting in a public place. Safety is paramount, but don not get paranoid. More information is available from the Suzy Lamplugh Trust (suzylamplugh.org) and from your station's own safety procedures. Legally, every company should have these and they should be made known to employees.

# Your health

## Broadcasting under pressure

Radio is a fantastic business to work in, but like any other company it is not going to be a barrel of laughs 24/7. There are going to be the staffing problems, issues over pay, office politics and so on, plus the issues that are unique to radio.

Radio's strength of immediacy can cause pressure. News flashes, rolling news, Snowlines and so on can be exhilarating, but also potentially stressful. And that is even more the case if you cannot rely on colleagues:

> 'Sometimes in radio one dodgy person can make a difference and destroy the show in one go, simply because the teams are smaller . . . if there's no back up there's an accident waiting to happen.'
> Roger Mosey, Head of BBC Sport, ex-Controller BBC Radio Five Live,
> Radio Academy event, November 2005

To be better able to cope, look after yourself physically and mentally: you know the physical stuff (more exercise, fruit and veg; less alcohol, caffeine and nicotine) but what about mentally?

Don't eat, drink, sleep and breathe radio. Do other stimulating things (especially artistic ones such as theatre, reading and so on) that help you relax and give you a sense of perspective and balance. Challenges will also make you more creative and give you something else to talk about on the radio.

> 'Our presenters tend to have had a life outside broadcasting:
> Stephen Rhodes was a hairdresser; Rob Perrone had an
> import/export business; our drive presenter Ian Pearce was a
> teacher and the afternoon show's Martyn Coote was a builder.'
> Mark Norman, former Managing Editor, BBC Three Counties Radio,
> *Ariel* magazine, June 7 2005

Other short-term tricks:
- Try be positive and upbeat.
- Don't complain.
- Offer solutions.
- Stay calm.

If the pressure drags you down long term, remind yourself what it is all about – why did you get into this business in the first place? Is that fire or goal still there? Ask yourself if, in reality, there is something else that you would rather be doing now (see also p. 366).

## Off days

Don't dwell on your weaker programmes (there will be some), as that will only drag you down. Certainly don't refer to them on air. Once you have realised why something went wrong (that you hadn't checked a guest's title properly, you hadn't set the desk in the correct way, or that it really was a technical failure that wasn't your fault), you are halfway to overcoming the problem.

Work out what you would do differently so you learn from the mistake, then go and do another show. All presenters occasionally do what they consider to be a duff show, although listeners rarely notice. We can be our own worst critics, although that is no excuse for not striving for excellence.

If you have too many poor shows then consider if there is a reason outside the station. If you have just split with your partner or it has been months since your last holiday, then you may need some time off to reinvigorate your relationship and your love of radio, and remember why you got into both.

> **INFORMATION FOR INSPIRATION:** Most shows will be OK, some will be stinkers, but there is nothing to beat the buzz of having done a great one. That high is worth working for every day.

## Time management

Time – the one thing that we can't buy more of, yet it can cause anxiety, frustration, guilt, health problems and mistakes.

**Strategies to save serious seconds**

- Write down what you need to do in a notebook so you can cross them off and have a sense of achievement. List who to call and who to get back to, the cues that need writing and questions to ask.
- Categorise what's important and what's urgent. Some things are one but not the other, other things are both important *and* urgent.
- Rank them: 1 – what's urgent and important; 2 – important not urgent; 3 – urgent and not important; 4 – not urgent or important.
- Allocate time next to each task to set a goal and increase your planning skills in the future.
- Start with tasks in 1.
- Then do some smaller things so you feel accomplishment.
- Review the list often so you know what is still left to do.
- Backtime each day to get what needs to be done, by the time it needs to be done.
- Have a day-to-day file so paperwork is in order, in one place.
- Have a future file, to stockpile ideas so you are never scrabbling around.
- Have a pocket notebook, to write down flashes of inspiration.
- Keep contacts up to date.
- Put your phone on answerphone and return all your calls in one particular hour, to save constant interruptions.
- Have a signal to stop colleagues dropping by for chat when you are busy, maybe a closed door, a pulled blind or headphones on.
- Get two things done for the price of one: read and make notes on the bus or train; read while you watch TV; make mental notes as you shower.
- Realise that it is OK to say no.
- Remember that starting a job is far easier than agonising over it.
- Keep things in perspective, few things are urgent or important.
- Work out whether you're not getting something done because it's dull or difficult, and ask for help.
- Cluster similar tasks together to avoid wasted start-up time.
- Is it your job? Helping someone is great, as long as you don't end up *doing* it.
- Consider whether you really have to be at all those meetings?
- Break tasks into small sections to make them more manageable, and you will be better able to monitor your progress.
- An impossible deadline? Get it extended, get more resources, redefine what is needed or at least give your boss a warning it might be late.
- Use a diary to monitor progress by others to avoid last minute cock-ups. Chase things before it is too late.
- Optimise your work environment, keep it tidy, organised, and if possible, quiet.
- Perfectionism can be procrastination: does what you are doing have to be 100% perfect?
- Organise your e-mail inbox.
- Reward yourself!

# INSIDE THE STUDIO

What's in this part:

o  Learn what the knobs, buttons and switches do in a studio.

o  Find out what initials like EQ, PFL and TBU stand for and the
   difference between red, green and white lights.

o  Then there's an explanation of different audio imaging
   elements — what they're called and when they're used.

# 15 Knobs, buttons and switches

Let's get some of the lingo out of the way to begin with. Is it a studio, a booth, an NPA, NCA or a cubicle or workshop? Some of those mean different things to different people and at different stations or in different situations.

A studio can be the self-operated room in which the main desk is based and where the presenter is (a self-op studio). However, it may also be the room with the studio desk, from where the programme is operated (by a tech-op or panellist) with the presenter speaking in another room (which may itself be called a studio or a cubicle), separated by soundproofed glass and linked by a talkback system. Granted the NPA is always the BBC term for the news studio from where bulletins are read (News Production Area) and the NCA is where contributors speak to other stations in the BBC network, from your station (Network Contribution Area), although both of these may be referred to by the generic term studio!

The area where a producer may sit (setting up guests, answering phones and so on) and from where they may also go on air, is rarely called a studio (unless it also happens to be one), although it may be called a booth, a production area or more usually an MCA (Master Control Area – known colloquially as a Mission Control Area).

Areas where audio production is done may additionally be called a workshop or an edit suite although this latter term is usually used in TV rather than radio.

Having said all that, for the purposes of clarity and brevity, I will call the place where the self-op presenter works from the studio!

Below is virtually everything you need to know about all the bits of kit in a radio studio. I have tried to put them in the most logical order, but because a studio is a sum of its parts you will probably need to read everything through a few times so you can see how it all works together.

## The studio

Studios can look complicated and daunting, but, like driving a car, with practice and training operating the controls should all become second nature (in fact, it's often referred to as 'driving a desk'). It doesn't matter how witty or incisive your comments or how creative your competitions are, if you can't press the right button at the right time, it's all going to sound very messy.

# Studio at BBC London 94.9

1 Anglepoise microphone and logoed mic flag.

2 The RadioMan audio playout screen used by BBC local stations and its operating keyboard used to cue and play songs, jingles and interview clips.

3 The Calrec screen used to assign sources to specific faders (you can see the Calrec hard drive just under the desk to the right of the headphones).

4 The faders. There's no big panel of knobs here – just little more than basic fader, cue and gain controls.

5 The visual talkback screen is used by production staff to tell the presenter information such as the name of the travel presenter and which caller is on which line.

6 This phone can be used by the presenter to patch or route phone-in calls through the studio desk, or to dial out on a line which can then be put to air via the TBU.

7 Studio headphones are usually stored this way. Note the personal volume control.

8 This hotline phone is used to call within the building or for colleagues to phone the studio. It will flash rather than ring. Calls through this phone cannot be put to air.

9 The talkback system. Note the microphone and the 24 keys for the location of talkback receivers. The silver knobs can be rotated to assign other locations to those individual keys.

10 A professional CD machine.

11 TV, whiteboard and station logo. You may make out the station's phone-in number and website address which have been stuck to the whiteboard. The window to the left of the TV looks through to another studio.

A typical BBC local radio studio. Courtesy: BBC London 94.9

**INFORMATION FOR INSPIRATION:** You will get better at operating a studio the more 'flying hours' you put in: increase the hours and you will increase your skill and confidence.

## Acoustics

The studio is usually a small room, which may not even have a window. If the station is on a busy street the architects may have decided to put the studio in the centre of the building so that noise or vibration from the traffic won't be heard on-air. If there *is* a window, make sure you use it: telling people in your town that it is bright and sunny when it is pouring down with rain will simply make you look daft and disconnected with them.

Most hard surfaces in a studio will be covered with material to stop sound echoing off them: the floor will be carpeted, the ceiling covered in sound-absorbent tiles and the walls covered in wadding and material. Some of the desk surfaces will also be covered in material, to stop sound bouncing around (sound reflection).

You can test the acoustics of a radio studio, or any other room in which you are going to do some recording work, with nothing more technical than your two hands. Simply clap and listen for the sound that is made. If it sounds flat and dead then it is a well-treated room with little sound reflection. If there is an echo effect when you clap then it is not such a good room for recording in or broadcasting from: microphones pick up sound slightly differently from the way our ears do, and that 'echo-ness' will be exaggerated.

Everything that the self-op presenter is going to use regularly should be within easy reach. Obviously that includes the controls on the desk (or panel), but also the talkback controls, the outside source switcher (in the BBC this is a BNCS screen), phone pad (to switch between lines when taking calls to air) and so on. Explanations of all these terms will be given later.

## Line of sight

There should preferably be line of sight to your studio guest (obviously), the producer (if you have one), as well as to any other studio, including the one where the news comes from. The latter issue is sometimes overcome with a CCTV camera set up in the news booth and a screen in the main on-air studio so the presenter can see that the newsreader is in position and ready to read.

Some stations also set up a camera in the studio with the pictures sent to a screen in reception so guests can see what is going on. Be sure to be on your best behaviour: rowing with your co-host or picking your nose will all be seen (see also p. 173).

## The other studios

There are usually at least two studios at a station. As well as the main on-air studio, a second doubles as a production area for making commercials or trails, or for recording interviews or links for an automated show. It may also be used for reading news bulletins from, and that means that other production staff may be asked to leave for a few minutes either side of the top and bottom of the hour, to allow that to happen.

If there is only one main studio, presenters have to perform a hot-seat changeover, when one presenter is tidying up at the end of their show and the next one is setting up theirs in the same studio.

The producer will probably be sitting in the control room (or ops room – operations room) separated from the main studio by a heavy door and thick double-paned glass, which keeps out extraneous sound. The visual contact with the producer allows the use of gestures and hand signals (see p. 187) and for the presenter to use them as an 'audience' while they're talking to the unseen audience.

## Your place of work

The studio is the place that everything goes through before it goes to air. All the station's work is channelled through this small room: the work of the sales and advertising copywriting teams, the promotions staff and the news, production music scheduling departments. Without a studio from which to broadcast, all the other departments are pointless. It is (arguably) the single most important part of the building.

That is not to say that a presenter should feel self-important and full of ego. Far from it. The presenter's job is to link together all the material provided by their colleagues in a relevant, interesting and compelling way – to make *their* work worthwhile. Indeed, the presenter should really be humble because the contribution made by other people makes them sound better, which leads to more fans and adoration, more money, fast cars and holidays in the sun.

## New technology

There are pros and cons of the increasing amount of computers in a radio studio.

- An easier life – presenters don't have to spend time cueing up records and then putting them back in their sleeves and filing them away.
- Timesaving – any piece of audio is played instantly at a touch of a button. That should mean that the presenter has more time to spend preparing what they are going to say, which makes for a more relevant, interesting and compelling show.
- Digital audio – the quality of the audio sounds better on air.
- Accessible audio – an item edited in one place can be played out in a studio, perhaps miles away, without physically taking it there.
- Archiving – saving audio is easy, cheap and takes up a small amount of room.

On the other hand:

- Different makes and models – there is more kit to learn, each with a slightly different way of editing, saving or playing audio.
- Increased speed – technology has made more things possible, but increased the pressure on getting things done.

In practice, each system is based on similar concepts and it does not usually take long to learn a new system. Indeed, any presenter makes themselves much more employable the more expert they become in the different makes and models.

## The basics

### Microphones – mics

There are various types of microphone for different situations, usually used when recording drama, concerts or when you are outside.

Omni-directional mics pick up sound from a wide area around the mic head, and directional mics pick up the sound that is right in front of them and so are the usual ones used in a studio.

The main presenter microphone is one of the single most expensive pieces of equipment in the studio: a good one can cost many hundred pounds. It gets a lot of use, though! Whereas guest mics tend to be quite basic and on a stand on the table, the main desk mic may be held in place on an anglepoise arm that can be positioned wherever is comfortable for each presenter. Alternatively, it may hang from the ceiling with a complicated-looking system of wires and weights. With this suspension method there is no anglepoise arm to be knocked, which should it happen, would be heard clearly on air.

Although it is best to sit about 15–20 centimetres away from a microphone when you are speaking into it, presenters vary in the height and distance that they sit away from the desk and of course they all have a different volume of voice, so it is essential that the position of the mic can be altered. Check your levels off air before you start your show. With some mics it is not easy to see if they have been turned around the wrong way, and if you talk in to the wrong side then your voice will sound distant. There is usually a logo on the correct side to talk in to!

If you talk too closely into a microphone you will get a strange popping sound when you say words beginning with letters such as P and B. Put your hand in front of your mouth and say, 'Polly baked a piece of brown pitta bread' and you will notice the rush of air that comes from your mouth as you say the Ps and Bs. These are called plosives as they explode from your mouth. (Say 'Tony toasted a wholemeal loaf' to notice the difference.) If you are too close to the mic when you say plosive sounds, the rush of air will be picked up and momentarily distort what you are saying.

On-air mics will, therefore, have a pop-shield attached to them. This is the foam covering which helps disperse the air before it reaches the sensitive mic head. If your plosives can still be heard, alter the angle of the mic so you are not speaking directly into it, but at more of a 45-degree angle. That way the airbursts pass over, and not into the mic.

When you go into a studio you should be aware of anything on you that could make a noise that may put off or confuse listeners. That means that mobile phones are turned off, not just put on silent as the signal will still be picked up by studio equipment (another reason is that you need to concentrate on your show and not be sending or receiving personal texts). Also, take off bangles, bracelets or pendulous earrings that may make a noise. Bear this in mind if you are presenting an outside broadcast: the continued rustling of a nylon-textured raincoat every few seconds will drive your listeners mad!

Similarly advise any guests about phones, jewellery and coats. It is also an idea to warn them against touching the microphone itself, knocking the stand, banging the table or drumming their fingers on it. All these sounds will be picked up and magnified by the mic.

Some guests move away from their mic during the course of an interview. If you turn up the level on their mic, it will also pick up some of what you say too, as well as the hum of the computers and studio air-conditioning system. Before you start an interview, always ask a guest to stay about 20 centimetres away from the microphone.

The mics are controlled by a fader on the main desk, which I'll come to in a moment, but some older studios also have an additional button for the presenters or guests to use. The cough button simply lets you turn off the mic momentarily so you can clear your throat.

Some presenters use mic/headphone-headsets powered by a pocket-pack, the kind singers wear on stage. A lack of wires means they have the freedom to move around the studio or the station and use their hands.

Presenter Euan McIlwraith wearing a microphone headset as he broadcasts his show from the reception and production area at BBC Radio Scotland. Courtesy: Dawn Baxter and Flora Clark at BBC Radio Scotland

## Station logo and mic flags

It always looks good when you see a presenter interviewed for the TV sitting in their radio studio, with a huge station logo as a backdrop. That may cost a lot of money, but at least have a poster or two showing the logo and frequency, or the logo on a mic flag (the box that is attached to the mic). It reminds guests where they are and makes the station look corporate.

## Headphones – cans

When a song is being played, the presenter can hear it in the studio through the speakers, but when the mic is turned on, the sound from the speakers is cut. This happens to avoid feedback or howl round (a sudden, loud and high-pitched tone) as the noise from the speakers is picked up by the mic, which is then played out through the speakers, which is picked up by the mic. Feedback is very serious, and even one exposure to it can do long-term damage to your ears.

So, one reason why presenters need headphones is so they can hear what they are playing on air when their microphone is open.

There are other reasons too:

- When a song is playing on air, the presenter needs to be able to hear how the next song starts. By flicking a pre-fade button (more of which in a short while) they can listen to this other source in their headphones, without it being broadcast.
- It is similar when a guest comes in to the studio and the level of their voice on their microphone needs to be set. You cannot turn their mic on, as it would go to air, so you listen on pre-fade through your headphones instead.
- The enclosed nature of headphones makes it much easier and clearer to hear what is actually going to air than listening via the studio speakers.

o   Your producer can speak to you when you have the microphone open, by using the
    talkback system. Their voice will be heard in your headphones, but not go to air.

Most presenters like to sound big and butch as they present their show and perhaps move
the various settings on the mic channel on the desk until they think they sound just right
in their headphones. The truth is, though, that by the time their voice has gone through
various bits of kit in the desk, racks room compressor and transmitter and into someone's
stereo it probably won't sound anything like they intended; your headphones can give you
a false impression of what you actually sound like. That is why many presenters like to work
with one side of the headphones on an ear and the other side off. That way they can hear
themselves as they *actually* sound, as well as what the studio desk is making them sound *like*.
    But there are problems using this technique:

o   There is an increased chance of feedback, as the sound from the off-the-ear half of
    the headphones may be picked up by the mic. The same problem can be caused by
    open-backed headphones that don't fully encase the ear, which is why I personally
    prefer models such as the Beyer DT-100.
o   You can't properly assess the mix of sound that is being broadcast.

When you are on-air, don't get too hung up on your voice. Concentrate on *communicating*. When you are doing a show the most important thing is what you say, not what you
sound like.

> 'I've got to use my own headphones. Since the health
> and safety thing went mental, the engineering staff have
> put limiters on the headphones so you can't turn them up
> too loud, and if you do they distort. I like to use my own
> headphones because I like it nice and loud . . .'
> Gareth Brooks, presenter Xfm, *X-Trax* magazine, September 2005

Gareth's right: limiters on cans are set to 93dBA for H&S reasons. It is also true that many
presenters like to use their own headphones. Whether they are fitted with limiters or not, it
is much more pleasant to know whose ears have been up against that piece of foam!
    Proper working headphones in a radio station are like gold dust. Cans are not always as
robust as they were years ago and the electrical connections crack and break very easily. That
causes sound to cut out in one ear either totally or intermittently, which is annoying when
you are presenting a programme.

**INFORMATION FOR INSPIRATION:** Not all headphones
are the same. Even same model-types may sound slightly
different or sit better on your head, so find a type that suits
you and hold on to them.

The main volume controls for the presenter and guest headphones are usually on the
mixing desk, but an additional personal control may also be found next to where the cans
plug into the desk or table.
    Incidentally, guests rarely need to wear headphones. They often don't need to hear other sources

being prepared or to hear what the producer is telling the presenter (especially if it is 'They're boring, get them off!'), and may be put off by hearing the sound of their own voice. They will, of course, need headphones if they are asked to take calls from listeners in a phone-in.

Some studios have foldback which means you don't have to use headphones. Foldback allows the studio speakers to be kept on, even when the mic is on, but you have to be careful to set the level so that foldback does not cause feedback (see below).

## Monitoring

You are wearing headphones to hear what is going out on the radio, but there are slightly different mixes of that signal that you can listen to.

If you monitor (listen to) the *desk output* (as a button on the monitor panel on the desk will probably be labelled) then you will hear what you are *sending to* the transmitter *from that studio*, but this isn't necessarily what is being heard by the listener at home. Another studio may be live (either inadvertently or on purpose) and also sending audio to the transmitter, or the transmitter may be broken and not transmitting anything. If you are only hearing what only you are sending, you would not be aware of either of these scenarios. So, if you are in an off-air studio, to record a trail or a pre-recorded interview, monitor desk output so you can hear what you are doing (and not what is going to air).

If you are on-air, monitor the (perhaps confusingly named) *off-air output* to hear exactly what the listener is hearing. The quality of your voice will be slightly different as it will have been through a processor to make it sound more resonant, and there may be some slight static, but you will be aware of any problems that develop. See p. 186 to see on which occasions you *have* to listen to the desk output.

## Monitor speakers

These are the main speakers in the studio, which are usually of very high quality. They are used to hear the output of the mixing desk, but cut out when a microphone is opened, to avoid feedback.

## The chair

The chair is an important part of the studio. Although some presenters do their show standing up (so they feel as though they are performing in a club to give the show more energy), most present sitting down, so it is probably going to be the most-used chair in the station! That makes it essential that everyone is going to find it comfortable. Not so that they fall asleep, but so they can sit upright and not get a bad back after a four-hour show. The height and tilt of the chair should be adjustable, as should the back. The chair may be armless so it can be pulled in close to the desk. It should have wheels so the presenter can turn easily from one piece of equipment to another. Many stations have a plastic mat under the presenter's chair to stop a build-up of static.

## Mixing desk — panel, board or console

This is the piece of equipment that, as its name suggests, mixes the different sounds (or sources) as they go to air. A source could be a piece of equipment in the studio (the mic, a CD machine), or an outside source, or OS (from an OB, another studio, a phone call and so on). Even for the simplest mix, you need at least two sources which are controlled by the various knobs, faders and switches on the desk. For example, one to control the CD player and another to operate the microphone.

There is a series of faders along the bottom of the desk and above each of them is a row of buttons. Desks can look very daunting but are really quite straightforward: when you know what one channel does (one vertical line of knobs) then you will realise the same principal is replicated across all the other channels. There are many makes on the market, but just like a car dashboard, they all operate in much the same way – they just look a little different.

> 'Driving your own desk and talking at the same
> time is incredibly difficult to pull off.'
> Katie Hill, presenter Capital FM, Radio Academy event, November 2005

By clicking the icons at the top of the screen and dragging and dropping them on to the virtual faders, a presenter can easily personalise their on-air desk. Courtesy: BBC London 94.9

To make things easier, many desks now have assignable channels. In the past each channel would only do what it was wired-up to do: one channel for the main mic, another for the CD machine, and so on. Now, each presenter can decide which sources they will be using for their show and which fader they would like to control that source, by simply dragging and dropping icons on a screen. So, if you have got a discussion programme with no music, you can easily change the CD channel to a mic channel instead. This is also handy if you are left handed. For me as a 'righty', I like to have the most-used fader (the one for the main mic) as the one closest to me on the right hand side, but that may be awkward for other presenters who can set up the desk in the way that is most convenient for them. And that means they make fewer mistakes.

Each assigned channel may have an electronic display saying what its role is, but not every make of desk has these. That is when I find a useful memory-jogger is nothing more technical than a corner of a Post-it note, with mic or CD written on it, and stuck at the top of the appropriate channel.

Finally, separating the different sets of channels is a space for your scripts – the script space.

A close-up of the lower half of typical fader channels. Note the main (unlabelled) remote start button, PFL and fader start buttons, and the buttons to enable different sources to be assigned to the fader

# Faders

I mentioned this a moment ago, but it's worth repeating: on the desk, each vertical row comprising a fader and series of buttons or knobs is known as a 'channel' and each channel controls one particular source at a time.

It is called a fader because you use it to fade the sound up or down, by moving the button along a vertical track. Each fader's control will be a different colour. This makes it easy for the presenter to see at a glance what each fader operates. Although different stations assign different coloured controls (white, blue, green, etc) to different sources, red buttons are always used for mic channels.

Think of a fader as a volume control, the further away from you it is, the louder the source on that particular channel (and the closer, the quieter). There was a time when all BBC desks worked the other way around (you brought a fader towards you to make it louder and pushed it away to get quieter). That meant that if you were asked to put the mic up, you moved the fader down, and vice versa. Very complicated! There are various anecdotes as to why the BBC made desks this way, but suffice to say the new generation of desks used in the Corporation's studios are more traditional in their design.

Let's take an example of a simple mix using two channels, say one for a CD and another for a mic, and you will see how varying the position of each fader gives a different effect. To talk over the start of a track you would start the song with its appropriate fader at a low position and start speaking through the mic channel, the fader for which would be at the top. Assuming that you had pre-set your levels correctly, the listener would hear you talking at a normal volume with the music quietly playing in the background.

The effect can be altered by moving each fader – you may want the music louder than at half-level so move that channel's fader further from you. There will come a moment when the mix of voice and music will be optimum, beyond which the song drowns out what is being said. Those two levels are reached from experience, what sounds good on other stations you have heard, and what sounds good with the combination of your voice and that particular song on that particular occasion.

There are three ways to put a source, such as a CD, to air.

- You can put the correct fader up to the desired level, and then reach to the piece of equipment and press 'go' or 'start'. The disadvantage of this is that the machine may be some distance from you and you may have to turn away from the mic to be able to reach it. If the song is played off a touch screen in front of you though, it is quite straightforward.

- You can put the correct fader up to the desired level and then press the on button below that fader on the desk. This is called a remote start and saves you stretching across, but it may be a split second between you using the remote and the source actually starting. Always gently press, or preferably squeeze, a remote start. Some presenters punch them, and the resulting click (or sometimes a thump), can be heard on air.

- Or, you can use a 'fader start'. Activate the fader start for that channel on the desk (by pressing a small button alongside the fader). Then when you raise the fader by even the slightest amount from its 'home' position (the end-stop) the track will start playing. This can be convenient but it means the item will start quietly for a split second and you can't set the channel's level in advance.

All of these starts are quite acceptable; different presenters use whichever method they feel happiest with.

Be aware that on some desks, as well as putting the fader up to allow sound from that source to go to air, you may also have to make sure that the channel is on. You can do this at the start of the show and then it should stay on throughout.

## PFL – cue

This is the pre fade listen switch (or cue switch, pre-hear or audition) but it is usually called the prefade, which does as its name suggests. It allows you to listen to the source of that channel before you put the fader up. That means you can check the track, how it starts and so on without going to it blind on air. In other words, you have cued it up.

You are also able to use PFL to talk to other people; for example, to check that a travel news presenter is at the end of an ISDN line before you introduce them on air. You do that by using the PFL together with the talkback system (see p. 167). By pressing the talk-back button on that channel you'll be able to speak to them (off air) down the mic (either the main studio mic or one connected to the talkback unit). Your voice will cut across their feed of what's going out on air (it won't be heard on air, unless you've inadvertently opened your mic channel) and you'll hear their response in your headphones or on the studio speakers.

Using PFL and the mic channel is also how presenters record phone calls with listeners off air, while a song is playing on air through the same studio desk.

Some desks have a switch for the headphones, so you can alternate between listening to the output in both ears, listening to the PFL in both ears, or having output in one ear and PFL in the other. This latter combination is useful so you can prefade a track at the same time as you are broadcasting.

## Levels

The level of your voice should peak at 6 on the PPM (Peak Programme Meter, which goes from 0–7), and music at around 5.5. Obviously, the meter will quite often show a level below this and occasionally above, but these are the average peak readings that you should aim for. You'll see what level you're peaking at by looking at the meters on the top of the desk. These are traditionally shown with needles that move according to the volume of the output, but are often replaced by a series of LED lights that flash (but can be less easy to read).

Levels are important for several reasons.

If you've got a channel that is peaking too high for more than a few seconds, the sound will start to distort (sound 'mushy' and 'squashed') which will be unpleasant to listen to. If you have a song that's too quiet the listener will struggle to hear it and may turn up their radio, only to have another source, at the correct level, boom out and surprise them. So, having standard levels at the studio end of the process means that only one person (you) has to alter levels of everything that's being heard rather than lots of people having to do it at home.

> **INFORMATION FOR INSPIRATION:** Use your ears! Some music can sound loud even though it's not peaking very high. This may be the case where there is a 'full' sound perhaps an orchestra playing, or when you are mixing several sources. So, use your discretion.

Other factors to consider when mixing music with other music or with speech:

- AM radio, also called medium wave, processes the mix of sound differently, so if you're broadcasting on one of these wavelengths make sure that the music is dropped significantly before you start introducing another input.

'Remember Five Live is on AM and the sound is therefore heavily processed at the transmitters. Music has to be carefully balanced to avoid swamping speech or disappearing completely . . . As a rough guide, if you're working on Sadie, Cooledit, or in the studio — balance the track under the speech so it sounds punchy and well-mixed, then reduce the music level by about 3dB for broadcast.'

*BBC Radio Five Live Style Guide*

o  In general, older listeners find it difficult to distinguish what is being said if the music level is too high.

o  A music programme will be mixed differently from a news programme where the speech is more important than other sounds.

o  It's also down to experience – make sure you use your ears! If it sounds wrong, it probably is.

## Processing

Pieces of equipment called compressors are based in the racks room. These act like a super-expensive graphic equaliser on your home stereo, changing the bass and treble on everything. In other words, they 'process' the sound. In a complicated process, they can be set to give the impression of a louder volume without actually altering the volume of the output at all. (Ever wondered why TV adverts sound louder than the programmes around them? It's often because the sound on them has been compressed to *appear* louder, not because it actually is.) To a certain extent, a compressor will be able to boost the quiet parts of a song and 'damp down' the louder parts – but it can only work with what it's given. By sending it the best possible mix of levels it will work hard to make them sound even better, but by sending levels all over the place it will struggle to cope.

Some radio aficionados hate compressors and say they make all the output sound the same with quieter parts boosted and louder parts quietened to fit into a small volume range. It is down to each station how theirs is set, but it is certainly true that to hear everything with so little variety in level can be quite tiring to listen to for any length of time.

Some stations have their own house rules on levels and require you to, for example, peak music at one level, speech at another and commercials at another. It is worth checking your station what the guidelines are.

**INFORMATION FOR INSPIRATION:** Keep an eye on all levels that go through your desk. That's not just your mic and the guest mic and the songs, but also the callers, adverts and trails, the news and travel bulletins and radio car inserts. Everything.

'In general, it can be said that as processing is increased the total number of people listening to the station at least once within a given time period (typically one week) tends to rise, while average time spent listening falls due to long-term listing fatigue. On average, males are less likely to be irritated by certain types of processing-induced distortion than females. And the level of irritation also changes with the age of the listener: adolescents tend to be much less irritated by distortion than 40 year-olds. A canny programmer will use all of this information to adjust a station's processing to complement the target demographic of the station. The correct processing is the processing that maximises the station's share of its target audience, not the processing that satisfies purists. For several decades, all Optimod instruction manuals have contained the following text: Never lose sight of the fact that, while the listener can easily control the loudness, he or she cannot make a distorted signal clean again. If such excessive processing is permitted to audibly degrade the sound of the original program material, the signal is irrevocably contaminated and the original quality can never be recovered.'

Robert Orban, Vice President, Chief Engineer Orban/CRL,
*The Radio Magazine,* June 15 2005

A close-up of the top half of typical fader channels. Note the balance, EQ and gain controls

## Gains

Gain controls are usually at the top of each fader channel. The faders control the overall volume of the source; the gain control adds extra volume. The reason for using them is when you 'set your levels', you are ensuring that when each source is broadcast and its fader fully opened, the PPM is 5.5 (see above). However, on some quiet tracks you may have your fader right at the top and yet the level is still not peaking at 5.5. So, you turn up the gain slightly until it does.

Similarly, if you are playing a loud track, or have someone on a mic with a booming voice, put the fader all the way up, and then fine-adjust the volume by turning down the gain.

The rule of thumb is, when the fader is fully open the channel's audio has to peak at 5.5 and you should adjust the gain until it is. Use the fader to do just that: to fade something in and out; do not use it for setting your 'standard' volume, for example, by playing a song all the way through with the fader only half open because the song is peaking too high.

## EQ – equalisation

These buttons control different sound ranges for each source, through each fader. Acting like the graphic equaliser on your home stereo, by turning each one you can boost or cut the bass and treble sound to alter the tonal quality of what's broadcast.

## Pan controls

Pan controls can alter the perception of the location of the sound to the listener at home. The rotary control's 'home' position is at the equivalent of 12 on a clock face. The further it is turned to the left the more the sound of that particular source will appear from a stereo's left speaker. The further to the right, the more it will come from the right speaker.

Consider a situation where you are interviewing two guests. Ordinarily, you would all appear to come equally from both left and right speakers of a stereo, but if you turn the pan of Guest 1's mic slightly to the left of the home position, and that of Guest 2 slightly to the right, they could appear to be separated in the listener's room – just as they would sound if the listener were sitting in the room with you. That gives the programme a much more live and dramatic feel.

Care must be taken when using pans. A subtle use is invariably best. Someone listening at home will become confused or annoyed if different sounds appear to come from widely different parts of the room.

## Sources

Potentially there are a number of sources that are needed on even a basic studio desk. Two mic sources and another two or three for the audio playout system. Other sources might include a CD player, news studio and various ISDNs and phone lines.

You make different sources appear on different faders by re-patching the desk (plugging wires from equipment to different sockets on the mixer) or doing it electronically via a screen like the one on p. 158

## ISDNs

This is short for Integrated Services Digital Network. It's a high-quality phone line used for carrying audio to and from radio stations, for example, from a remote studio such as a travel

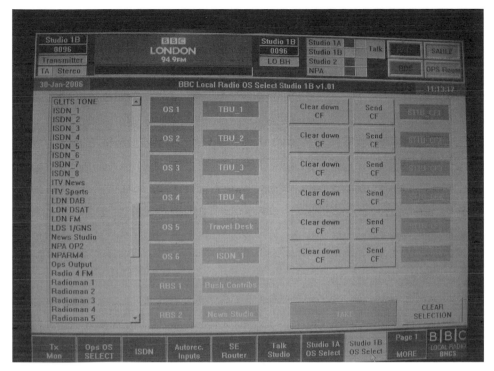

A BBC Radio touch screen BNCS system. Through this, the producer can assign any source (some of which you can see on the left) to any of the outside source channels (OS1—6), send clean feeds, put different studios to air on different transmitters and dial up ISDN numbers. Courtesy: BBC London 94.9

centre or district office. It's got a similar connection to a phone line and is usually routed through the desk and comes up on a fader.

If you're dialling a contributor you will need their ISDN number (just like a phone number), which you usually key in on a phone-like pad. Be aware that there are several systems available and they're not all compatible with each other, so check before you rely on the link working.

## Line-up tones and clean feeds

You may have a guest in another studio, maybe one owned by a PR company, and be dialling them on the ISDN. The line-up tone is the signal sent back down the ISDN line to you, to show two things: that a connection has been made and (because the single tone is of a set frequency) what level has been set for the microphone in the other studio. You will then have to send the remote studio the sound of your programme (the feed – the actual output), so the guest can hear your introduction and questions.

There's a difference between a 'cue feed' and a 'clean feed' that you may send down the line. A cue feed is the actual programme as it goes to air: the music and presenter mixed with the contribution from the guest in the remote studio. In other words, the guest will hear themselves in their headphones as they talk (albeit with a slight delay after their voice has travelled to the main studio and then been fed back to them). Contrast that with a clean feed, in which the remote contributor hears the programme *without* their own voice. This may be to avoid feedback, for example if the guest is hearing the presenter on a loudspeaker rather than through headphones.

# The lights

## Studio lights

It is very important that the lighting is right for the programme and the presenter. They have to be able to read their scripts and screens, but also use lighting to create an appropriate mood for their show: lights full on might be appropriate to give an intensity to a chart show, low lights will help create a 'love songs' environment. A dimmer switch on the light switch is a good idea.

## Red light

A red light usually means that a mic is live, although it can mean that the studio is on air (which, of course, aren't necessarily the same thing). A flashing red light (which is rarely used) usually means 'stand by', that the studio is about to go to air.

Never enter a studio with a red mic-live light unless you are beckoned in by the presenter on air, or if your need is urgent. Then, open the door quietly and close it manually behind you (don't let it 'click' shut with the closer).

If waiting in a studio to collect or give something to the presenter, wait patiently until the red light has gone off (not just until they have stopped speaking, they may be playing a jingle and talk again when it has finished), and until they have taken off their headphones. This is not just so they can hear what you say but also as this signifies the end of their current link.

## Blue light

This light, not in common use, signifies that that studio is being used, possibly for rehearsal. The rules of entry are similar to those for a red light, wait for permission to enter the studio. To barge in or creep in quietly may disrupt the proceedings; for example, a dry run of a complicated link or timing of a programme insert.

## Green light

Well, if a red light means 'stop . . . mic live', green means 'go!'.

In a situation where a presenter is being driven by somebody else, a producer may make the decision when they want them to read the next link. (When a programme is 'self-opped', that choice is of course solely down to the presenter.) So, a red light would show that their mic was live, but a green light (which would follow a few seconds later) means 'start talking now'. For this reason a green light only stays on for a few seconds.

An alternative to a green light is for the producer to physically point at a presenter through the glass from the production studio to the talks studio: this is a 'manual cue' or 'visual cue'.

## White light

This may be on the desk or may be on the wall of the studio alongside other lights. When it flashes, it signifies to the presenter when a phone is 'ringing', probably the studio XD line which should be answered as soon as is practically possible.

## Orange light

This is usually the fire alarm light, which flashes. An alarm in a small, enclosed studio may cause considerable problems if it rang while the mic was on. If the presenter was speaking on air at the time and wearing headphones, it could cause considerable damage to their ears. If this light is activated, put on a pre-recorded emergency CD or put the playout computer into automatic mode and leave the studio.

## Obit light – obituary light

There is no set colour for these but they are usually labelled as 'obit alarm' or similar. They're activated by the station's national news provider such as IRN or GNS and signify that a VIP (such as a major royal or the prime minister) has died. See p. 332 for obit procedure, but in short, the activation of this light means for the next few hours or days the output of the programme could change considerably.

# Talkback unit — squawk box

This is the internal communication system through which you can talk to people in different parts of the radio station and to outside sources, see picture on p. 151. The unit has different buttons for different locations. Simply press and hold the button for the location you want to speak to (for example, another studio or the newsroom) and talk about ten or twelve centimetres away from the mic. The mic you use may be one connected to the talkback unit (sometimes called the squawk box as it can suddenly squawk at you like a parrot without warning) or a small condenser mic built into the desk, or may be routed through the main on-air mic. After speaking you need to release the button to be able to hear the reply, through a speaker in the talkback box, the main studio speakers and/or your headphones. Your conversation will not be heard on air (unless you have the mic channel open at the same time.)

There is certain etiquette in using talkbacks:

- There's the problem that you can't always actually see the person you are talking to. Many times, people at radio stations have wanted to criticise, say, an engineer to a colleague in another studio and pressed the button labelled engineers by mistake! Check you are about to press the correct location button.
- There is no warning that the talkback box is about to burst into life. As the unit is often on someone's desk, to suddenly speak in a loud voice can make them jump. Press the button and keep it held for a second before you speak so they hear the background sound of your location and are ready to hear what you have to say.
- Start your message with the courtesy of saying who you are and where you are: 'Hi, it's John in the newsroom . . .'. It's basic: that way the person you have contacted knows which button to press to be able to reply.
- Of course, you don't know whether someone has heard your message until you hear a response. Is there anyone actually in the area that you've called? Have you pressed the right button? There may be no one there, in which case, try your message a minute later. On the other hand the person may be on the phone and unable to reply, so don't just keep repeating the message.
- It's protocol to always answer a talkback message, especially one from an on-air presenter who may need assistance urgently (a piece of equipment may have failed or they may need someone to play in the next song while they go to the toilet).

Therefore never turn the volume down on a talkback unit and never ever turn it off. To do either of these is almost a sackable offence: the needs of the on-air presenter always come first.

o    Remember that your message is being heard loud and clear to whichever area in the station you've selected on the unit. So be careful what you say. You don't know (because you can't see) that the managing director or editor is showing a local dignitary around the newsroom just as you launch into a tirade about another presenter.

So much for using a talkback to another area of the station. What if you are using it to talk to someone during their on-air shift? The talkback audio comes into the studio, either through the talkback speakers, the main studio speakers and/or the headphones, but when the microphone channel is open (as it would be if the presenter is speaking or about to speak) the speakers (main and talkback) are automatically shut off. So, when the mic is open, talkback can only be heard through the presenter's headphones, not even the guest's. This is great because a presenter can be given direction by their producer without anyone else hearing: 'Mary is on line 4 with the correct answer', 'You've forgotten to go to the travel news' or 'Your guest is starting to get boring, can you wind up the interview, please?'

However, if someone on the talkback speaks too suddenly, it may make the presenter jump and possibly let out an oath on air. If they speak too loudly the same thing might happen plus, the message may 'bleed out' (or leak) from the presenter's headphones and be heard on air through the mic. Last, but not least, it can be very confusing for someone to be talking on air and suddenly have another voice telling them something at the same time. It's not too bad if you are doing a straightforward link, but much more annoying if you are in the middle of a penetrating and serious question and suddenly, without warning, you can't hear yourself, but instead hear a (possibly inane) comment from a colleague.

If you need to use talkback to speak to a presenter while they are on air, first check they are not actually speaking at that moment. If they are and the comment can wait, hold fire until they play a song. If they're in an interview and it's urgent, wait until the *guest* is speaking. Then, double check you're about to press the correct location button, squeeze it and hold it for a second to give the presenter time to register that someone is about to speak to them. Then, without shouting, give a succinct message and clear the line. Remember, they may not be able to reply to you on the talkback if they are actually live at that moment, so don't keep repeating the message thinking that they didn't hear you.

A presenter's temper can go from placid to furious if, while conducting an in-depth interview in the studio, they suddenly have someone shout, 'How many sugars in your tea, Sue?' several times by someone wondering why Sue (in the newsroom) isn't replying to their message being sent to the studio.

On occasion it *is* necessary to talk to a presenter while they are talking themselves, for example to help them with a question for a guest if they are floundering or to correct an important inaccuracy. At these times, as I have said, hold the button for a second, then speak slowly and succinctly in a normal voice and release the button.

# Other equipment

## CD machines

Most professional stations, and many hospital and university stations, nowadays use a computerised playout system, with songs played off a hard disc, rather than having the presenters cue up CDs individually. However, CD machines are often kept in studios for backup in case the playout computer crashes and also for music features when certain non-core songs aren't on the system.

There are obvious advantages for CDs over vinyl; one of them is that if you need to cue a song past a quiet start you can do it with ease. With a record, you stand a chance of the song 'wowing' in as the turntable picks up speed, but with the forward and back buttons on a CD player you can start from the exact millisecond. Indeed, you can rehearse the point at which you have cued the song to ensure it's exactly correct.

Why would you want to cut off the quiet start of a song anyway? Well, it may help you on a loud to soft mix (a segue, pronounced seg-way) if your 'soft' song can start later, where more is going on. Of course, if the playout system has been programmed correctly there are unlikely to be many such music clashes.

Always set the timer on the CD player to count *down* rather than *up* – you need to know how many seconds are left on the track, not how many there have been. And it is always wise to PFL 'end play' on each track (not every CD machine has this facility). First, to familiarise yourself with it for the forthcoming segue, as once the track starts there won't be another chance. And second, to check the timing on the track. Some CDs have poor duration information and you could have several seconds left on the track even once the display shows 00:00. Alternatively, it may end 15 seconds 'early' or, after a period of silence, there may be extra noise recorded on the end of the song or the song may restart, which is what happens with the Beach Boy's song *Barbara Ann*, of course.

## Turntables, carts, DATs, MDs and cassettes

It is possible that you may also find these pieces of equipment in your studio, most usually used as standby kit. Let's have a quick look at each of them in turn.

The use of turntables was dying out towards the late '90s as more and more recordings came out on CD. However, they are making a re-appearance for a few reasons. First, because not every song has been released on CD, so if a request programme wants to play an obscure track then it may be that the only recording available in the station library or from the BBC's central gram library, is on disc. That is just as true for specialist music shows of the type heard on many BBC local stations, such as a big band programme or a show-tunes programme. In these instances the discs are usually copied onto minidisk or CD before being played out on air. And of course other specialist programmes, for example featuring imports or new releases, may only have their material released on vinyl. Finally, some presenters just prefer playing songs from a record rather than a CD, especially if they are doing a dance mix show, as a turntable allows them to mix beats and to scratch the songs much more easily. Remember, if you're using a turntable, it will take a second or two for it to pick up speed. So find the start of the track and then take the needle back half a rotation of the disc before you start it playing on air.

Cartridge machines, or carts, have probably died out from studios completely but in their day they were incredibly useful. Inside a plastic box (about the size of two packets of cigarettes side by side) was an endless loop of tape, of various durations between 20 seconds and five minutes. Jingles, sound effects, signature tunes, commercials and sometimes songs were recorded on the tape. Once a cart was played in a special machine, it automatically re-cued to the start by detecting an electronic pulse that was put on as it was originally recorded. Carts were bulky and despite being re-recordable they had to be wiped clean with a de-magnetiser before each use. The main reason for their decline though is that computerised playout systems now hold all the audio one needs at the touch of a screen.

DAT, or Digital Audio Tape, was hailed as a huge step forward in technology in the '90s. The small cassette-sized tape worked like a video recorder with slowly rotating heads. The sound quality, being digital, was very clear, but DAT had its drawbacks. The tapes were very difficult to cue accurately and they were very prone to being chewed up by the machines. They therefore fell out of favour and are now mainly used to archive long recordings.

Minidisks are good because they are robust, reliable, high quality, they can record in mono or stereo and are re-recordable, editable and you can move tracks around, and they're cheap. However, some audio aficionados say the compression on a MD can be too overbearing.

Cassette players, remarkably, still have a place in even the most advanced studios. It's because they are cheap, rarely go wrong, are easy to use and because most people have a cassette player at home. That means that if a guest comes for an interview and wants a recording of their contribution, it takes little effort or expense to run off a cassette copy as the programme is being broadcast. Cassettes are also used for presenter snoop sessions, where a telescoped recording of the programme is made without the songs or adverts. The cassette player is linked to the mic channel, and it starts recording every time the mic is opened, and goes into pause when it's closed.

# The screens

## Playout systems

As you're becoming to realise virtually all of the audio that is played on the radio comes from a single playout system. That's the songs, the jingles, the pre-recorded interviews or news stories, the competition sound effects and the ad breaks. Once recorded onto the system, the songs and ads are loaded on to the studio playout system automatically, taking direction from the music scheduling computer and the ad log computer.

Other audio, such as jingles that the presenter has a free choice in using, can usually be accessed through another screen on the same system. Some pages of these may be open to all presenters, others may require a log-in so each host can have their own personal bank of effects or personalised jingles which only they have access to.

Audio is usually played out either by using a keyboard or touching the screen.

## Text screens

As well as a talkback system described earlier, messages can also be sent from the produc-tion area to the presenter on screen, for example, saying who has won a competition or who the next caller is to a phone-in. This system may be as basic as two screens linked together or may be part of an ENPS-type system, and is usually called a 'visual talkback'. (ENPS is the Electronic News Production System used throughout BBC news as well as in many programme production departments. The sophisticated network allows the easy sharing of news stories and messages between staff.) There may also be a screen showing text messages and e-mails that have been received.

## TV monitor

It is quite usual for a radio studio to have a TV in it, so you can keep abreast of the news, so keep the channel tuned to BBC News, Sky News or a text page.

Be careful how you refer to the use of the TV screen. Certainly never say that you are watching it. Even if it's a news item just make an oblique reference, 'I understand that the prime minister has just left Downing Street . . .' or at the very least use the term monitor, rather than TV. 'I can see from our studio monitors that another plane has just crashed into . . .'.

The reason? Why tell your listeners that you are watching TV when you are supposed to be working? It gives them the signal that something is more interesting to you than keeping them entertained. Additionally, they may pick up on what you say and turn on the TV and turn off your programme.

---

### ACTUAL AUDIO

PRESENTER  We're not supposed to watch TV in the studio, but on GMTV this morning . . .

*Commercial station, January 2006*

---

As I mentioned earlier there might be another TV screen linked to another studio (so you can see that the newsreader is ready to present a bulletin) or the front door, via CCTV.

# The phones

## Phone lines and TBU

Stations usually have half a dozen lines from which they can put callers to air. This is usually done through a computerised switchboard and a TBU, the call then appearing on one of the channels on the desk. The TBU is the Telephone Balancing Unit, which increases the quality of the phone signal so it sounds better on air.

Presenters can talk to a caller off air once they have been put through the desk and are ready to go to air. It is usually done by pressing the PFL for the phone line channel (to hear them) and then the PFL for your mic. Some stations then route that mix through to a recorder, so calls can edited before they are played out as though they were live ('as-live').

By pressing just the PFL on the phone channel you will be able to eavesdrop on the caller as they wait on the line, which can be quite amusing as they rehearse what they are going to say to you. Be careful though: I was once on air in a new studio and thought that for the caller to be able to hear me I had to PFL my mic. That wasn't the case, PFL-ing the phone channel made my mic live, and the caller heard everything I said to a colleague in the studio.

## Phone delay

Delay equipment is used so if a caller makes an obscene or legally dubious comment while through to the studio it never actually goes to air – even though they think it has. In delay, the caller and presenter talk 'live' but the rest of the audience hears the conversation around seven seconds later.

Years ago, when a station went 'into delay', the station output was re-routed through a machine which had a replay head seven seconds back from a record head. Nowadays, a different type of digital machine is likely to stretch out what is being broadcast until a desired delay is reached over the course of a few minutes. Only then can a presenter safely take calls.

In order not to confuse everybody taking part in a delayed programme, the presenter must listen to the desk output rather than the off-air output that would normally be monitored. If they don't they too, will hear themselves seven seconds after they have started speaking! And it must be stressed to callers that they must turn off their radio and only listen for the presenter to introduce them down the phone, for the same reason (see monitoring, p. 157).

Here's what happens in a delay situation:

PRESENTER:  And now here's Sue on the line from Northport. Hi Sue, what are your thoughts on the rise in local bus fares?
SUE:  The people who run the buses should f★★★ off!

Immediately you, the presenter, hear the obscenity:
- Whack down the phone fader.
- Switch the monitor from 'desk' to 'off-air', where you'll hear what went out seven seconds ago.
- When you hear yourself say 'local bus fares?', press the 'dump' button connected to the delay machine. That will switch the station output back from the *delay* (seven seconds ago) to the *desk* (what you're putting out right now).
- You carry on talking making no reference to what has happened: 'Sue, Sue? We seem to have lost Sue but if you want to call us then our number is . . .'.
- Start the procedure for going back into delay before you take another call, and then return to listening to off-air output.

Sue is left thinking she's shocked the world with her comments but in fact the only person to hear it was you! The rest of the listeners are none the wiser that anything's gone wrong.

Although talk radio stations such as LBC 97.3 and talkSPORT have output delay systems, they're rarely fitted, or used, at BBC local or small commercial stations.

## The studio XD – Batphone or boss line

This is the phone line that strikes fear into the heart of presenters everywhere. It's an XD phone line in the studio which you need to answer as soon as you can. For that reason it is often referred to as the Batphone! It may be used (but shouldn't be) by a colleague who doesn't want to call on the usual number, but is more likely to be the police asking you to put out an appeal for a missing person or your programme controller congratulating you on your last link.

You may find that your PC may also use the line to call you in the middle of your programme to criticise or complain. Unless you've made a basic error or said something that needs to be rectified immediately (perhaps you allowed a caller to defame someone), I believe that most managers' feedback (especially negative) should be given *face-to-face after* the show, not *on the phone during* it. Otherwise your concentration is thrown while you deal with the call and the conversation could affect the rest of your performance. Not everyone agrees with me: I know of one station manager who, fond of strong drinks, once called a presenter more than a dozen times in an hour. This affected the presenter's performance, who stopped thinking creatively and understandably felt intimidated. It may also have stopped a real emergency call getting through to the studio.

# Don't forget!

## Studio clock

Some studios have digital clocks but most have ones with traditional faces and hands, and that all-important second hand for accurate timings. That second hand may either move second-by-second or 'sweep' around the face.

The clocks are radio-controlled so all of them in the building, and indeed the country, tell the same time. They're not without their faults though. I have introduced a news bulletin because the clock told me it was 3 o'clock, only to be greeted by silence. The clock was ten minutes fast.

## Whiteboard

One of these is often on the studio wall so that the presenter can easily read from it. Written on it is basic information such as the phone-in number, updated information such as the current rollover total for the Mystery Voice competition, which presenter is filling in for who, the closing date for the Christmas card competition and so on.

## Webcam

These are increasingly common in radio studios so listeners can *see* what is happening as well as hearing it. Such cameras should be visible to you as a presenter, rather than hidden, and there should be a notice near the camera warning people (such as guests) that the camera is operating.

There may be another CCTV camera, as I already mentioned, which shows what is happening in the studio on a screen in reception so guests can see what is going on. These two cameras are likely to be live all the time, so be careful how you behave!

Some BBC local radio studios are on the same site as a regional TV studio and the two services cross-promote each other. This happens at BBC London 94.9 where there is a TV camera in one of the radio studios so, in the 08.55 regional news bulletin, Vanessa Feltz can appear on TV explaining what's going to be in her radio show later that morning.

# Studio etiquette

**INFORMATION FOR INSPIRATION:** The studio is an office — your place of work. It is not somewhere your friends can visit or phone for a chat. Neither is it a glorified meeting room for colleagues to discuss last night's TV or this weekend's on-air give-away. It's your office and you need to concentrate in it.

## Studio socialising

Friends and guests will rarely be allowed to sit in the studio with you as you present your programme. That is usually a blanket rule at stations to help protect the presenter who doesn't like to say no to friends who are always asking. It's a rule for a reason: without the distraction of people watching and asking questions, the presenter is better able to concentrate on what they are doing and present a better programme.

If you let this rule slip then before you know it you will be joined by the head of news who wants to borrow a newspaper and stays for a chat, the silent work experience person who hovers over your shoulder, a sales exec wanting to book you for a personal appearance at the weekend, your producer asking about tomorrow's guest and the 3rd Great Blankstown Cubs on a station tour. When you slip up and play the wrong song, who'll look stupid? You.

If a tour is hovering just outside the studio door, and you think that it is going to come in, look busy. Put your headphones on to give the impression you are about to speak on air. Some presenters will also nudge the mic fader open slightly so the 'mic live' light goes on outside the studio, and that deters visitors further. Alternatively, or additionally, look busy on the computer or go searching for a CD in the racks, or fill out an important looking form. Or turn the speakers up really loud.

If the tour still ventures in, keep your answers polite but short and then explain that you will gladly do the tour or explain the workings of the desk *after* the show, but not right now.

It is very likely that at a small station, the manager also has an on-air shift. It is also likely that colleagues will treat the studio as an extension of that person's office, coming in during the programme to as various questions. The way to get rid of them? 'Sorry, I'm the DJ. The station manager is back at 12'.

## Keep it clean

Your studio should be as clean and tidy as possible during your shift. All presenters have their own way of working, a place for scripts, somewhere else for newspaper cuttings and so on and the more organised you are, the faster you will be able to find what you want, when you want it. Having said that, clear up as you go. When you have used a script or clipping then either throw it away or put it in another pile to be filed. (Some presenters keep good stories or observational links to recycle and use again either in another year or at another station.)

You may like a can of Coke or a hot milky coffee, but the desk won't. The water and sugar will gradually rust and corrode the elements inside, resulting in expensive and time-consuming repairs. Some stations ban all food and drinks in studios, others say that only water is allowed and that cups have to be placed well away from the desk.

## When to arrive at the station

Turn up at least an hour before your on-air shift. It shows professionalism and also gives you time (although arguably not enough) to ensure all of the elements of your show are prepared. You can read your e-mails, post and memos, and acquaint yourself with any changes. Arriving on time regularly also means that if you fail to appear, the programme controller (or at a weekend, the presenter of the show before yours) can call your mobile to check what's happened, and if necessary arrange cover.

## When to arrive at the studio

Turn up in the *studio* at least ten minutes before your programme starts. This gives you time to log in to the computer, set the mic level, assign sources to the faders and cue your first few songs. At some stations you are obliged to talk to the current presenter about what is in your show (a 'handover'), as well as taking control of the output ('putting your desk to air') and playing in the news bed. All that means that you can't bumble in to the studio while the news is on.

Additionally, it means that you should listen to the presenter who is on before you so you can comment on a song, feature or a comment they have made. That way the station sounds more 'joined up' and fluid, giving listeners fewer opportunities to tune out.

Walk, don't run, to the studio. Running may mean you are out of breath when you arrive or you trip and fall and end up on a stretcher, not in the studio.

# Studio fault log

Studio faults, such as a piece of equipment not working, should be logged in this studio book together with your name and the date. This is so the equipment can be repaired and other presenters be made aware of the problem. The station engineers will date the comment when they read it, add the progress of the repair, and then the date once the item's been mended.

This fault log is also the place where you will write non-urgent messages to other members of the station team. This may be a song clash, wrong song or intro duration on the playout screen, an ad-break featuring two car garages, and so on. The programme controller will look at the Log daily and bring any problems to the attention of the appropriate department.

You should refer to the Log before you start your programme to note, for example, if the CD player is skipping, the studio chair has lost a wheel or one of the phone lines is faulty.

Obviously if there is an urgent problem, such as a complete transmission failure or an ad for a sale today that still says 'starts tomorrow' then you should call the relevant manager immediately to alert them.

# Competition log

This is the place to log all the winners to every competition run on air. It is what the promotions team will go to before they can send out the prizes from a competition. It's what you should go to before you run any competition to double check the 'mechanic' and to make sure that the same person isn't winning again and again. More on competitions, see pp. 274–287.

# Studio bible

Every station should have one of these, but like the logs mentioned above, not every one does.

It is the place where all the important memos and procedures are kept for every eventuality on the station such as:

- Staff office, mobile and home numbers – personal numbers should never be given out on air, but you may need to contact the head of sales one weekend if a disgruntled advertiser calls you, or the head of music in the middle of the night if a major artist dies and you want to know if you can schedule some of their songs.

o  Other emergency numbers – local police stations, your national news provider, the on-call lawyer, the local councils'/electricity/gas/water press officers, Floodwatch and so on. One presenter at a station I used to work for added the number of the Samaritans: a good idea. Callers in the middle of the night may contact the station because they're desperate and you can pass the number on. On a rather more cheery note, a presenter at Essex FM added the number of the local pizza delivery service.

o  Snowline and Stormline procedures – this will outline what to do when winter weather strikes: who to call, the changes to the programmes and so on.

o  Bomb threat forms – these can be downloaded from the Home Office website and are used if a caller to the station makes a threat (either against the station or anywhere else). Yes, it may be a hoax, but that's for the police and the courts to decide. Your job will be to complete the form while the caller is on the line, or soon after, with details such as their likely age, accent, location and what they actually said.

o  Complaints forms – most people who call to complain just want to let off steam and, if you deal with them correctly there and then, don't want to take it any further. Some want blood, and this is where you note down the details so you can pass it all on to the programme controller: the complaint, the complainant's name, address and phone number.

o  Pronunciation guide – how do you pronounce those odd little villages in the back of beyond in your area? Or foreign or difficult names? People expect you to know, and you will do by looking them up here.

## Obit procedure

I cover this in rather more detail later, see p. 332 but briefly the obit procedure ('obit' is short for 'obituary') will tell you what to do when a VIP (for example a royal or top politician) dies. It may be that the death is announced during the day, in which case there will be plenty of staff at the station who will help out and advise, but it may happen overnight (such as that of Diana, Princess of Wales) or at a weekend when you'll be on your own.

The procedure will tell you how you will be likely to hear officially about the death, who on the station staff to call, the songs to play and the changes to the schedule. Included in this file will be a few CDs of appropriate music (I mentioned this on p. 83).

You should read this Procedure regularly. Being on air and coping with a royal death is not when you should be going through the plan for the first time. In the past, stations and presenters who have broadcast inappropriate material at a sensitive time like this have been criticised by the newspapers and their listeners. Don't let it happen to you.

## House style guide

I wrote earlier about the importance of a station brand and how everything that goes out on air reflects the ethos of the station. A lot of this will be laid out in the house style guide. Some stations are very disciplined and have very tight styles, even down to what presenters say out of songs, or what jingles are played and when.

A brand-enforcing style is necessary, especially in such competitive markets as today's. When was the last time you went into McDonalds and were greeted with the phrase 'Welcome to Mickey D's, would you like a large burger'? Never! It's always referred to as 'McDonalds' and a 'Big Mac'.

**INFORMATION FOR INSPIRATION:** You too have to ensure that what you do is distinctive and consistent, and that your product is always sold in the same way.

The house style guide may list how to say the time (some stations specify whether it's 'ten twenty' or 'twenty past ten'), the date ('February the fourteenth' or 'the fourteenth of February'), the name of the station ('Radio X, across Blankshire' or 'this is X the sound of Blankshire'), the frequency, the station strapline, the temperature, what you call the what's ons and so on. It may also give presenters information such as the target audience, TSA, and programmes' pace and style.

Be sure to ask for a copy at each station you work at so you're not caught out when someone says 'I thought I mentioned that . . .'. Such guides may be only a few sheets of a Word document, or they may be professionally printed and bound. The layout isn't the issue as much as the content, and its very existence.

# 16 Audio imaging

Jingle is the generic term for a short piece of music, maybe with a sung strapline, station name or frequency. As well as (or, instead of) jingles, some stations have other audio brand imaging such as 'sweepers' (spoken announcements over a 'whoosh' bed).

Such on-air branding:

o Helps the flow . . .
o . . . and the sound of the station.
o Exists because a musical message may be more memorable than a spoken one.
o Can help punctuate or provide a bridge between items.
o Lets listeners know when a certain item is going to appear.

The choice of jingle or imaging package, like the choice of music, adds to the overall style of the station – the tune and tempo should reflect its image. Many stations don't have music jingles at all and rely on verbal announcements (not strictly jingles), either by the presenters or pre-recorded, to get the station's name, frequency and strapline across. These are said in a way that reflects the format of the station they're on: soft, slow and smooth, or fast, urban and cool, for example.

Many stations make on-air brand imaging (such as spoken sweepers or liners) in-house, and have sung jingles produced by a specialist company. The jingle package will contain cuts of various type and duration around a common theme. That's usually based on a series of notes which reflect the number of syllables in the station name or strapline.

Heard every few minutes on air, jingles/sweepers are vital to reinforce the station name and its values, by what is said or sung and how. They're the station's audio trademark or audio logo and reinforce the station's name and frequency through constant repetition.

Other generic jingles are available on 'library music' (see p. 86 on music programming).

## A few rules

o Use jingles/sweepers that are appropriate for what you're doing. Don't play one that sings or says 'fun at the weekend' on a Wednesday, don't play one that refers to 'much more music' before an ad break or an interview.
o Never play musical jingles over a song. They'll be in different keys and will clash horribly.
o Don't just play your favourite cuts, get to know others in the package and experiment with them. Ones that you don't like will be liked by many listeners.
o If you create your own, check with your programme controller before you use them on air as they may 'water down' the brand or message.

Although this Handbook has a huge glossary of new radio words and terms at the back, all the ones about jingles and sweepers are collected right here.

# Jingle jargon and terms for other on-air brand imaging

*Acappellas* are jingles that are sung 'dry', that is, without music. It's rare that you'd use one of these over the top of another piece of music, whether it was a bed or a song, as they would both be in different keys. As well as giving variety to your jingle package, acappellas are particularly effective if played into a song which starts with a vocal, but only if the tone fits. For example, to play a soft acappella into The Beatles *Help* would grate, as would a hard acappella into Celine Dion's *Because You Loved Me*.

*Beds* can mean two things in jingle jargon, but both definitions derive from a bed being music that you can talk over.

A bed may be a small music-only section of an individual jingle. Some jingles have singing at the beginning followed by music: that music part is the bed. The most common occurrence of this is what you hear going into the travel news: there is a sung or spoken announcement, followed by a couple of minutes of music, over which the travel news is read.

A bed may be a complete music track, with no sung or spoken part at all.

By their very nature, beds are usually 'backing tracks' rather than the full 'orchestral' theme, as the less instrumentation there is the easier it is for a voice to be heard and understood. A listener could be distracted by a full 'theme' playing underneath your voice, for example. (A full orchestral version is more likely to be a signature tune, see below.)

Having a music bed under your voice on a long speech item may make it *appear* more interesting, but it is the content of the link that matters more.

Don't play a music bed too loud, many people find them intensely annoying.

*Custom packages* are jingles that are written and performed to the radio station's requirements. The music may reflect the format of the station and so the strapline fits when it's sung. Alternatively, some stations use a cheaper 'off the peg' (or syndicated) package. It is still a collection of beds, transitions, acappellas and so on, but written in a generic style. That may mean that your station phrase may sound a bit garbled if it doesn't quite fit with the beats of the jingle. And there's always the chance that a neighbouring station may have the same package.

*Demo CDs* are provided free by jingle production companies to show what kind of packages they provide.

*Donut* is the term used for a jingle which has a sung section each end and a music-only 'hole' in the middle (hence 'donut'). Presenters can talk over this middle bed, or play a dry drop in.

*Drone*. Think of the questions asked in the later stages of *Who Wants To Be A Millionaire* on TV. The long, low single note that you can hear in the background is a 'drone'. In the same way, a drone is used during radio competitions to add tension to what's going on.

*Dry drop in* is a spoken phrase (it may be the station name, frequency, phone number or the presenter's name), with no music underneath. You can, as the name suggests, drop one of these into a donut, or onto the start of a song, or use one 'solus', by itself, perhaps between two songs.

Drop-ins come in a variety of styles, 'soft', 'medium' and 'hard', and read by a male or female voice-over. These are the 'station voices', artists who will appear on all of your spoken 'on-air station imaging' (the trails, announcements, drop-ins and so on). The 'voice' will also help embody the format and brand of the station, in their perceived age, accent and attitude. Some stations use one of their own presenters to record the drop-ins, which sounds really cheap. At the very least get a presenter from another station in the group to record them, and then return the favour. I was once the voice for the station where I was also reading the news. At the end of the bulletin listeners got me, live, saying, 'It's five minutes past four' and then me, recorded, saying, 'It's the Afternoon Show on Radio. . .'.

You can use drop-ins in a variety of ways. Use a 'hard drop' going into (or over the intro to) a loud and lively song, a 'soft drop' over a slower song. Try to drop the drop over music to fit with the musical phrasing: perhaps mid-way in a short musical break, or backtimed just before the vocals or a key change. See p. 268 onwards for other ways of doing this.

*Instrumental* jingles are usually quite short (like most jingles, up to about ten seconds) and so a little different from longer beds. Where they are similar is in the fact that neither of them contain either sung or spoken messages.

*jx* is the abbreviation for jingle.

*Liner* is what some stations tell their presenters to say at certain points of the programme. It's not a jingle as such, as it's said live by the presenter, and certainly not sung. However, it does include elements such as the station's name, frequency, area, slogan and so on, and is often used in place of a jingle.

*Loop* is what you can do to a short musical phrase or instrumental break from a song when you want to increase its duration to use as a bed. Take the short section and edit it together several times. But be warned, editing music is easier said than done, and if done badly can sound horrific.

*Music demonstrator* is the name given to the sequence of clips from songs that are representative of the ones played on a station. There's a short 'hook' from three or four hits, together with a voice-over saying, 'We play songs like this . . . and this . . . and this . . . that's why we're Blankshire's number one hit music station . . . Radio X'.

*News jingles* are also called TOTHs or 'top of the hour' jingles. They usually reflect the drama and urgency of the news and invariably include the station name, frequency and coverage area, read by the 'station voice'. 'Across north and south Blankshire, on 99.9 FM, this . . . is Radio X.'

Stations often re-record this jingle to include important station information, because it is probably the most-heard ident (identification) on the station. 'With more listeners than ever before/the home of the Martin Knight breakfast show/the place where you can win a grand-a-day, this . . . is Radio X'.

Jingles can be of any duration, but they are usually (beds excepting) around ten seconds. News jingles are different. They can be short ten-seconders played at ten seconds to the hour, or have that ten-second start and then continue as a bed. But they can also start with a bed, say of 50 seconds, and then *end* with the announcement. If this news jingle is started at :59 minutes past the hour then it gives the presenter 50 seconds to tease what's happening later in the show, before the station name and frequency kicks in. This kind of jingle can help with backtiming (see p. 272).

Some news jingles have time signal 'pips' on the end, the last one of which signifies the exact top of the hour. These pips are either recorded onto the jingle, or at BBC stations, are played in live. Only BBC stations are allowed to use the traditional tone and sequence of pips (five short ones, followed by a sixth long one), commercial stations have to make up their own variation.

*Out of news jingles and hour openers* are as important as the 'in to news' jingles. That is because so many people listen to the radio at the top of the hour to hear a bulletin and then what comes after it. I mentioned earlier in Music Programming how important the first song out of the news is, to re-set the format of the station, and the same goes for the jingle. An up-tempo, loud-and-proud jingle with the station name included, is a great way to start the next hour of songs on a typical chart music station.

*Power intros* are the specially-produced sung jingles pre-mixed with the introduction of a current chart song. They sound as though they're part of the song itself, but the vocalist sings the station name and strapline (in the style of the artist on the track), just before the lyrics start properly.

*Ramp* is the musical part of the jingle over which you can talk before the vocals come in. (Compare with donut above.)

*Shotgun* is the term used for a short, fast-paced instrumental.

*Shout* is a sung fast-paced, short acappella.

*Signature tune.* You will be familiar with this term, also known as a theme tune. The best ones are those that reflect the content of the programme and the tone of the station as a whole. Usually the brighter, catchier ones are the best. Also consider those which are easy to fade and that have a strong ending so you can backtime their start. But sig tunes can be a barrier between you and the audience. Some themes have become memorable for all the wrong reasons – because they're disliked with a passion. Indeed, many Radio 4 programmes don't have a theme tune at all and its news programme PM was forced to drop its short theme tune because of listener complaints. Not every theme tune is as well loved and memorable as that to Jonathan Ross' TV film programme.

*Slogan* refers to your radio station's 'positioning phrase', which may be used in your jingles either spoken or sung. An early example is 'Radio One is wonderful' or 'it's just for you – Radio Two.'

*Stabs* are, like 'shotguns' short, fast-paced jingles. A stab is used in conjunction with a bed. The travel jingle may start with a said or sung announcement, 'Travel news on Radio X', followed by the bed which is dipped for the presenter to read their bulletin over. When the bulletin is finished, the separate stab is played at 'standard' volume. The effect is one of completeness for the listener.

*Station theme* is a long and orchestrated theme tune for the station (heard less and less on stations nowadays). As well as reflecting the format of the station, it has at its core the main musical phrase that is repeated in all the jingles in the package.

*Sting* is a short jingle, maybe as short as 2 seconds, used as a punctuation or exclamation mark between two items.

*Sweeper* A spoken announcement over a sound effect 'whoosh' to help transitions between songs. These are increasingly common, especially on commercial music stations.

*Transitional jingles* are really handy as they help you move from one tempo of music to another. Transitionals are sung, instrumental, dry or sweeper jingles which start off slow and finish faster or vice versa. So if you are going from a slow song to a faster one, you can fade song A, play the slow-to-fast jingle/sweeper, and when it's finished, play song B. They can also be used between music and speech (or vice versa).

*Verbal idents* (also see liner) are when the presenter says the elements of a jingle themselves. They don't sing but may include all or some of the following:
- The name of the station.
- The frequency.
- The strapline.
- The area it broadcasts to.
- The name of the presenter.
- The programme title.

*Vox IDs* are the sweepers which contain clips of listeners commenting on the station or its mix of music, in the style of a vox pop.

*Whisper* is exactly that, a whispered voice-only drop-in, which is useful to play into a soft love song for example.

# GOING LIVE!

What's in this part:

- The basics of being a radio presenter.

- What buttons to press and what to say.

- I'll show you how to talk, how to tell the time and how to be a big tease.

- There's advice on presenting music, running a competition, interviewing and being a presenter and producer on a phone-in.

- What to do when it all goes wrong — I'll explain why silence on the radio is often a good thing — and tell you what to do at the end of your show.

- We look at show reviews, by other people and yourself.

- And we'll still have time to go to the zoo!

# 17 Stand by studio

'The level of creativity in radio in this country is unique in the world and we can look forward to understanding our audiences more deeply and using different distribution platforms to build stronger relationships with our listeners. The future is bright for talented presenters and programme management talent — there's never been a better time for great programmers!'

Dirk Anthony, GCap Media Content Director,
*The Radio Magazine*, 7 September 2005

## Arriving on time

The alarm clock doesn't go off, the car breaks down, you're held-up by a bank raid as you wait to speak to the manager about your overdraft. These types of things will inevitably happen. When they do, make sure you call the programme controller and/or the current on-air presenter.

It sounds bad to hear a presenter end their show, only to appear again after the news because the incoming presenter hasn't arrived. If this happens to you, start the show with two or thee songs back-to-back, to give them another ten minutes or so to burn up.

## Checking the studio

Just like a pilot won't take off without first checking all the plane's controls are working, you shouldn't embark on your trip without giving the studio the once-over.

- Check the equipment – that the headphones are there and that they work, the same for the mics. Adjust the height of the chair and the level of the air-con. Check the mic levels and put the faders on or off fader or remote start. Set up the channels so they are assigned in the way that you'll need them.
- Read the Fault Log, Competition Log and whiteboard to check for any broken equipment, a new competition or changes to the programme schedule.
- Tidy up – chuck the rubbish away, pile up the papers, put away CDs and put guest chairs under the desk.
- Set yourself up – make sure that you've got your scripts, spare paper, pens and show prep. Check that your scripts are in the same order as the running order, and that both of those tally with the playout screen. Cue up as much as you can before the show starts.
- Go to the toilet and get a drink, you don't know when you'll get another chance, but walk, don't run, back to the studio.
- Listen to the output, so you can comment if necessary on something said by the previous presenter. Get ready to take control. Prepare for take-off.

# Operating the desk

This can seem quite daunting at first as there's so much that has to be done at the same time. It's referred to as 'driving a desk'. Remember how tricky it was to learn how to drive a *car*? And yet now you get in and go without a thought. The same will be true of driving a desk and even though there may be the odd 'crash', no one will get hurt.

It all looks really complex doesn't it? But if you can drive a car and hold a conversation at the same time then there's no reason why you can't drive a studio desk. It's all down to practice. Grab every opportunity you can to sit in a studio and watch other people present their programmes. When you do, wear headphones to hear how what they do in the studio changes the sound on-air. When it's convenient, ask questions: why they chose a particular jingle at a certain time, why they cued a song past its start, or why they talked over the end of one song and not another.

Then ask if you can sit in a studio after the show and see how it all feels: what happens when you alter faders, what it's like to hear your own voice in your headphones and how to talk out loud and PFL a song at the same time.

One of the tricks is to think one or more steps in advance. Know what you are going to do next, and after that and, in case something goes wrong, the step after that as well! Bear in mind that, even though it's easy to set up the next item while a song is playing, it is rather trickier to do it as you are talking to a live guest.

I've already been through all of the controls on the desk and later I will explain how to do some basic mixing. So read the advice, then go and practice, practice, practice.

# Automation or voice-tracking

This is worth a quick mention here, as it is when a programme goes to air without a live presenter.

The computer playout system broadcasts different programme elements (pre-recorded links, music, commercials, jingles) in sequence giving the impression that it is live. It usually happens on smaller stations and overnight and at weekends. Previously, pre-recorded programmes had to be put together in 'real time'. In other words, an hour's show took an hour to produce, because the presenter had to sit through each song as it was recorded onto tape.

With automation, a presenter needs only to record the links and put them in the right order on the playout system (in between the songs, ads and jingles which can be dragged across from the hard-disk), for a programme to be ready for transmission.

## For automation:

- Costs are lower – a presenter can record a show, even from home, in less time than it takes to present a live one.
- The programme can still sound live with links over song introductions.
- Links can be carefully considered and rehearsed before recording, so the best possible programme is produced. Fluffed links can be re-recorded.
- On daytime shows, elements of automation can be used to segue a few songs in a row while you go to the toilet, let a guest into the studio or when a presenter has to attend a public appearance before the show is finished.
- Even small stations can broadcast 24 hours a day and on difficult-to-fill occasions such as Bank Holidays, Christmas or New Year.
- Different links of the same duration can be sent to different transmitters, and those

links could include content local to those areas. So automation could mean that listeners are better served. Indeed, automation can be used with syndication (when a live programme is simultaneously broadcast on several stations in the same group). Station-specific commercials, jingles, drop-ins or song introductions can be played from a central computer giving the impression of being live and local.

- News, weather or travel can be played in automatically. The system fades the last song in an hour and opens the satellite feed from the news provider for a clock start and clock end, which is followed by a pre-recorded weather bulletin. The travel news provider can remotely record bulletins into the playout system.
- The 'feel' for the music is achieved by allowing the presenter to pre-fade the song as they record the intro for it. That way they can also still hit the 'music post'.

## Against automation:

- Interaction with the listener is not possible; for example, phone calls and competitions.
- The station can't react to breaking news (although extra links can be recorded at home and placed in the running order remotely).
- If there's a computer fault and the playlist stops running or repeats itself, for example on an overnight programme, there's probably no member of staff to hear it, let alone fix it.
- It is sometimes difficult for a presenter to get the right feeling when they have to record a Sunday night show the previous Monday morning.

Incidentally there is 'no restriction on the amount of automation — voice tracking — that a station may use', so says the regulator Ofcom.

## Automation tricks

- Imagine you are actually live on air as you record your links to get the mood and feel right.
- Occasionally listen to the programme as it is broadcast to see how 'live' it sounds and what you can do with your future recordings to make the programme sound better still.

# Answering the phone

So you have a producer or phone op (phone operator) to do it for you? Fine, sit back and watch them work while you relax. Some teamwork! One of the benefits of computerised playout systems which automatically cue songs and ad breaks for you is that you have more time to do other things. That includes preparing each link thoroughly, but also helping your colleagues and talking to your listeners on the phone.

Always answer your studio line. It is one of the basic jobs for a presenter and it is important for several reasons. First you don't know what you might be told. It could be anything from information that is valuable to you: 'You just said this song is by Kylie Minogue and actually it's her sister, Danni.' Or it might be something of use to another department at the station: 'I'd like to buy some advertising space . . .', 'There's a huge fire right opposite where I live', 'Did you know you don't seem to be on the air on your 99.9 frequency?'). Perhaps it's going to be something for your listeners 'Police have closed the motorway at junction six . . .'.

The second reason is that it's a chance for you to talk directly to your listeners. It's your chance to sell yourself to them on a one-to-one basis that you just can't do on the radio.

Use callers for instant feedback: greet them by name, ask where they are calling from, what they like about the show and so on. Chat them up, get them on side – it's polite and you never know who is going to get a Rajar diary next time around. While you do this, it is important to stay in character. If your on-air persona is 'boy next door' and you are dismissive of the caller, you will have probably lost them for life.

Some calls may be from listeners wanting help or a chat, so be prepared for this. People see the station as the fount of all knowledge, and to a large extent this is what we want them to think. But they don't necessarily call the newsroom to comment on a news story or the travel hotline to pass on details of a road hold up. They call the number they know – the studio phone-in number. It means you may get questions, comments and complaints while you're on air, most of which have nothing to do with you directly. Be polite to all callers. Tell them the correct number to call. It may be that they need more specialised help (perhaps to speak to a councillor about a broken paving stone, or even a counsellor about a broken heart). Ensure that appropriate numbers are in the studio.

Other calls maybe kids' pranks, someone asking for a song that you have only just played, or someone who can't string two words together. These people only make up some of the calls – most will be from your listeners, the ones you are there to serve. Answering calls is not beneath even the most high-flying presenter. Indeed, it'll mean more to the listener to have the 'celebrity presenter' take their call than someone in the control room.

# Non-verbal communication

Hand signals in other words! I have already mentioned the talkback system between the studio and production area, but sometimes it's not convenient to use that verbal system. A producer can speak to the presenter while they're on-air, but it's impossible for the presenter to reply! That's why hand signals have developed instead. Some of them are ones that you'll use in everyday life. For example, creating the shape of a phone to signify there's a call waiting; as though you're holding a mug which means 'Do you want a drink?' and so on.

Other possible gestures:

- Holding up an index finger and making a wide circular motion with your arm means 'Start finishing the item now'.
- Drawing a finger across the throat: 'Stop the item as soon as possible'.
- Holding two clenched fists side by side as though holding a stick and then snapping it: 'Time to play the commercials' (break).
- A similar action but then pulling the fists apart horizontally means 'Carry on talking, extend this item'.

# 18 How to talk

'Be yourself. Keep your style natural, conversational, lively and engaging. Try to help the listener feel they're part of the discussion. Address the listener in the first person — this is more intimate and encourages a sense of belonging. Use the present tense wherever possible — it gives a sense of immediacy. Five Live vocabulary should be accessible, jargon-free, simple, clear and intelligent. Be careful not to overcomplicate things and don't be unnecessarily formal in your delivery. Try to avoid becoming too predictable or repetitive, particularly at regular junctions. It's easy to get into habits such as repeating the same expressions e.g.: "to be fair", "you know", "I have to say", "I mean" or starting your programme, strand or bulletin with exactly the same phrase every day.'
*BBC Radio Five Live Style Guide*

Radio is intimate and personal in a way that television is not. People often listen to the radio alone – in the bathroom, bedroom, kitchen or in the car and it is the skill of talking to people singly while actually speaking to an audience of thousands that the presenter has to master.

'TV at its best is an amazing medium of pizzazz and excitement. But radio is fantastically intimate: one person a microphone and a relationship.'
*Roger Mosey, Head of BBC Sport, ex-Controller BBC Radio Five Live, Radio Academy event, November 2005*

Talking to everyone, one at a time, is something that many newcomers to radio have trouble grasping – especially those who have previously been television presenters where the style is different. You're still *broad*casting, so you would think it natural to refer to listeners as a group, a crowd. But where most TV viewers tend to watch in a group, most radio listening is done alone.

**INFORMATION FOR INSPIRATION:** Always keep in mind the first eight letters of the word 'personality'. Each listener should feel as though you're having a personal conversation with them. Include them, don't exclude them.

So how do you talk to someone on a one-to-one basis, when you are actually talking to thousands? Read my 'One to nine on being one-to-one' list below to know what approach or 'attitude' you should have for being on-air. Then read how to make the most of your voice with my short guide on how to sound good. Only once you have got those two important elements sorted, we can start to look at the issue of what to say in the next chapter.

# One to nine on being one-to-one

### 1. Be conversational
Your listeners are your friends so talk to them in the same way that you do with your friends: conversationally. That's not only *what* you say, but also *how* you say it.

### 2. Use your usual speech pattern
If something is given to you to read out on the radio, read it out loud to yourself first. If it doesn't sound right to you, maybe it doesn't flow, sounds confused, or there are too many long words, then rewrite it. Keep the message, but change the style: use *your* words and *your* speech pattern. Usually, the thought is the important thing, not the exact words that someone else has chosen, and the message will be much more effective if you are communicating it in *your* language, not theirs. Note that sponsorship credits or competition rules often have to be read as they are written because of contractual or legal requirements.

Identify strange pronunciations or unusual words, such as people's names – for local place names refer to the studio bible, which should have a list of them. If you do not know how to say something, ask. It is better to be thought a fool in front of one person in the office, than thousands of people on air.

We rarely trip over ourselves when we ad-lib – we're more likely to do it if we're reading a script that someone else has written and that we're not familiar with.

In summary: always read it out loud first – or don't read it at all.

---

 **ACTUAL AUDIO**

NEWSREADER There have been more protests in Bethlehem's Manger Square . . .
*('Manger' rhymed with 'panda'.) Commercial radio station, November 2004*

---

### 3. Use everyday words
Don't get caught up with using phrases that are trendy, police-speak or radio jargon: 'The hot, top sporting stories', 'Up and coming between now and the top of the hour', 'There's been an RTA on the by-pass', 'I can't find my weather stab', and so on. Just speak naturally and straightforwardly without using DJ clichés.

The example about a weather stab is a good one. Although some programme controllers may say using some technical terms helps break down barriers between the station and the audience and demystifies broadcasting, using radio jargon on air is mostly confusing for people outside the business.

### 4. Use contractions

When you are talking with a friend you will automatically shorten words, so make sure that you talk the same way on the radio. And, if you are writing something to be read on air, use the same style to make it friendly on the ear. That means instead of 'it is' you write 'it's' and 'you have' becomes 'you've' and so on.

### 5. Keep a single listener in mind

Radio people often talk in terms of 'the listener' rather than 'the listeners', because we speak to them on an individual basis. So it's never 'all our listeners', it's 'you'; it's never 'all of you', it's 'you'; it's never 'some of you', it's 'you'; it's never 'everybody', it's 'you', etc. Don't talk about 'our listeners', or ask if 'anybody heard what happened . . .' (especially not, 'anybody *out there* . . .') or refer to 'you all'. Like a confirmed bachelor, keep yourself single.

To help remind them to speak to one single person, some new presenters find it helpful to have a picture of someone they know on the other side of the desk or pinned to the wall of the studio.

 **ACTUAL AUDIO**

NEWSREADER (to another presenter)  What we want the listeners to do is to call us with their experiences of . . .

*BBC local station, June 2005*

### 6. Show genuine emotion

Think about what you are saying and the listener's likely reaction to it, just as you would if you were speaking with a friend who was right in front of you.

I once trained a TV newsreader who had a story in her bulletin about a missing girl who was thought to have been murdered. She almost sang the story, with no feeling for the story or the victim's family who may have been watching. The reader and I worked out that because she had read the story so many times, she had forgotten its significance.

Don't be over dramatic, but don't always be 'light and bright' either. Be real. If you are always 'up' you'll come across as phoney, cheesey and possibly a little deranged!

### 7. Make the information personal

From telling the time, reading the weather and relaying the travel news, it all has to be done in an everyday way (see separate sections on time, weather and travel presenting). For example, is your listener going to get wet on the way to work, will they arrive on time? Tell them that information, not about the 'chance of precipitation', or about 'a driver shortage on the Blankshire branch line'.

### 8. It's the message not your voice

When you are on air you should no longer be thinking about how you *sound*, but instead about the *message* that you're trying to get over. Having that thought in your mind will help you focus on what you are doing with your link.

### 9. Talk about relatable experiences

You become more conversational when you drop the façade of being Mr Personality who is trying to impress with stories of their DJ lifestyle, and instead talk from the heart about issues that matter to you and to your listeners – the stories that are relatable, interesting and compelling.

The more you reveal just a little glimpse of your personal life, the more you will connect with the audience and get them to trust you. Personal stories – not personality stories.

'I can honestly say that I am true to myself on air . . .
if I had to maintain some kind of act it would be impossible.'
Stephen Nolan, BBC Radio Five Live,
*The Radio Magazine*, 16 November 2005

**INFORMATION FOR INSPIRATION:** You should be talking *with* the listener, not *to* them.

## Your voice

I once read that the quality of your voice, its pitch, tone and inflection, counts for 84% of its message. In the next chapter I'll look at what to say, but right now will focus on how to say it.

'Good radio speech should be:
Warm but not smarmy
Friendly but not intrusive or too cosy
Clear, but not over-elocuted or precise
Natural but not undisciplined, authoritative but not aggressive
Fluent but not unbelievable
Sympathetic but not patronising
Understandable but without obvious or unpleasant
speech impediments'
*BBC Local Radio Training Manual*, 1987

We noticed before that one of the unique things you can bring to the role of presenter is your voice. What you say will only cut through to the listener if they like your voice, its quality and your style, and if they feel you are warm, friendly, sympathetic, easy to under-stand, positive, enthusiastic and believable. They won't listen if you sound boring, lack interest, are too complicated, too fast or sound confused. Remember, radio is a single-sense medium. The entire concentration of the listener is focussed on the voice.

Your accent may not matter as long as it is not too broad — in fact, a local and relatable accent may be a positive advantage. What matters most of all is that your voice is clear, well rounded and easily understood.

Do not rely on changing the EQ controls on the microphone channel or altering the compressor to make you sound more 'butch' or 'punchy'. If you're not careful, such changes can have the effect of making you sound muffled. Far better to change your voice in your body instead.

You may be fortunate enough to work at a station that values its staff enough to employ a voice coach on an occasional basis to work with all on-air staff. This does happen at some BBC and commercial stations, but isn't done nearly often enough. Students on radio journalism courses sometimes have as little as half an hour's tuition on how to use their voice in their entire year. Unfortunately, it shows on air. Surely this is a false economy. You will know yourself which radio voices you love and which ones you immediately turn off. Surely a station manager wants the best possible sound coming from the radio — the best possible voices?

Is it worth paying for voice coaching yourself? It may be, but there are several companies that promise you the earth and only give you mud. Poor advice about your voice can literally do more harm than good. Certainly go to a voice coach who is used to working with broadcasters. It is difficult to communicate voice techniques in the written word, especially when every person has different needs, so if you really want to develop a strong voice with a wide range drop me a line at my e-mail address at the front of the book and I'll pass on some recommendations.

One secret is to be yourself. Do not try to copy someone else because you will sound obviously false. Another is not to force your voice into something that it cannot be. Instead, learn to enhance the voice that nature gave you, to enhance the message that you want to give to others.

Here are some things to bear in mind.

## Breathing

This should be done from the stomach — if your shoulders rise when you breathe you're doing it wrong. Stomach breathing is deeper breathing and when you have more air getting into your lungs it will also steady your nerves, which is really useful before you go on air. But don't be so relaxed that you mumble.

Your chest is one of three places in your body that can help add resonance to your voice, to give it a fuller sound (see below). So, if you breathe properly you will relax, trip over fewer words, and also sound more resonant. Then, because you are making fewer mistakes and sound good, you will build up more confidence and so be more relaxed and sound better, and so on.

So, breathe from your stomach and then let it out gradually while you are talking.

Breathe *from* your stomach, but *through* your nose. Filters in your nostrils clean the air, warm it and help add moisture. If your breathe through your mouth you are letting bugs and cold air in, which will make your vocal cords dry and you will start to lose your voice. So, in through the nose and out through the mouth.

## Resonance

You've seen those diagrams showing you how to sit at a computer. Well, it is similar for presenting a radio show. Feet flat on the floor, upper legs in contact with the chair, a straight back (but not so straight that you are tense) carefully supported by the chair, shoulders back (again, not so you are strained), and head up. You can afford to relax a little, but not too much: I call it 'informal formality' and here's why. The more you sit up, the more air you can get into your lungs. This will reduce tension, keep you alert, and increase the resonance of your voice. That is because a lot of the sound of your voice rattles around your ribs (put a finger on your breastbone as you speak and you will feel it).

But there is no point in increasing resonance in your chest if the sound gets caught up in a 'U-bend'. That will be what is created in your throat if, despite sitting up straight, your head is angled towards the desk. So, hold your head up and have a clear flow of sound from your chest, up your throat to your mouth. This is the third place that can add resonance to your voice. Look in a mirror and say your name and address naturally. Watch how much you open your mouth. If it is not enough the sound that comes out can be rather muffled, and it also means that your tongue has to work harder to make the shapes that cause the sounds to become words. And if there's not much room for it to move, there's a big chance that you'll trip over your words. If that happens on air, your voice will rise (because that is what happens when you are tense), you'll hear that difference in your headphones, which will cause you to become more tense.

So, open your mouth wide enough. How wide is 'wide enough'? Put your thumb up, and bend it at the joint by 90 degrees. Put the joint of your thumb in between your top and bottom teeth: that is how much experts say you should open your mouth to give the tongue room to move and to give your voice space to resonate.

## Clarity

However resonant your voice is won't matter if you speak too quickly to be understood, or if your diction isn't clear, or if you run words or sentences into each other. TV presenters usually have an easier time as viewers can subconsciously lip-read, watch facial expressions or even put on the subtitles. There is no such help for your listeners, so you have to help them as much as you can. This means speaking clearly and being careful technically. For example, do not play music beds so loud that your voice is battling against or being lost in the music. Another potential problem with using music beds is that the paccy background can encourage you to talk too fast. Although your delivery should mirror the bed, do not let it force you into speeding up so much that you sound garbled. Do not let the music bed 'chase you'. Radio listeners only have one chance to hear and understand what you say.

## Warming up

Sing something silly. Play with your voice. Don't push it and hurt it, but do see where it can go. Play Elvis's *Way Down* in the car on the way to work and see if you can reach his tone (but don't *force* your voice down). Do something similar with Bronski Beat's *Tell Me Why*. Make silly sounds and do imitations. Swoop your voice high and low. Do not do any of these if they hurt or if you feel dizzy but use them as a way of finding what else you can do with your instrument. Some presenters warm up by chewing gum before they go on air to relax their jaw muscles.

## During the show

It is very easy to stay still in a studio and only at the end of a programme realise that you have been in the same seat for three or four hours. Sitting still will make you sound dull and lifeless. Get re-invigorated by walking around the studio whenever you have a chance.

It will get some air into your lungs and help you sound more alert the next time you open the mic.

Many presenters stand up to present their programmes saying that it gives them a more energetic performance. That would certainly make sense. Standing up gives you better control of your breathing, helps you stay alert and means you can move around much more freely as you gesture. It also makes you feel more as though you're are in a club where you may feel more at home. Stations which have presenters who 'stand to deliver', have studio desks which are raised slightly so they don't have to slouch to operate the faders and some even have microphone head-sets so their presenters can walk around the studio as they talk.

## Nerves

Nerves and tension will affect the muscles across your jaw, throat and chest making your voice sound a little thin and weedy. There are lots of relaxation methods you can try both before you go into the studio and while you are on air. The easiest and most effective one is to take three deep breaths to steady your nerves.

If you do make a mistake, don't panic. It's not a crime. You will be forgiven if you do not do it too often and do not draw attention to it. Jokes about putting your teeth in are passé in the extreme. Don't keep thinking about the mistake, it will distract you and make another mistake more likely.

## Be your own critic

You will improve your voice when you start to listen to it. Record and listen to your programme on a regular basis and be aware of any vocal mannerisms you may have. It could be that you hesitate too much, or that you use verbal crutches such as 'kind of', 'sort of thing', 'good old', 'the hour of' or 'to be fair'. But do not listen to each show too soon after you do it, leave it a week or more. You need to have a certain distance so you can hear the content with a fresh pair of ears and be more objective — almost as though you're listening to someone else rather than yourself. A good way of doing this is to listen in the same way as other people listen to you, perhaps in the car or in the kitchen preparing a meal rather than sitting down with a notebook and pen ready to dissect each link.

## Six strong speaking strategies

1   Are you speaking too fast? If you are, your words will be unclear, you may stumble and your message will be lost. The average talking-speed is three-words a minute.
2   Or too slowly?
3   Maybe you are too 'sing-songy' (going unnecessarily up-and-down in tone, the 'sea-sick syndrome'). 'Singing' and speaking slowly can both come over as patronising.
4   Are you sounding too nasal? Are you breathing properly? Perhaps you are too tense or eating/drinking the wrong foods.
5   Do you sound as though you have a permanent smile on your face? Although a smile is good to sound warm and friendly, it is not appropriate for every single link, because of the change in content. Do not sound as though you are putting on a fake smile of sincerity.
6   Speaking too loudly will alter your pitch and put a strain on your voice.

# Body language

Talk with your whole body to help you explain things and get a message across – it is only natural! After all, in evolution, gestures came well before speech. Think about how you give directions to someone: you don't stand with your hands in your pockets, you use them as you explain about traffic lights, bridges, roundabouts and turnings. Use the same techniques on air to help you communicate. As well as making your sentiments stronger, gestures such as a clenched fist or a smile will also help you change your voice to fit the mood.

When you present, be interesting and interested. Interesting – so if you say you are angry about something make your voice *sound* angry! If you are excited make sure that is how you sound. Interested – so you sound as though you are enjoying your programme and are interested in your own material.

# Vocal variety

Have texture in your voice as you present different items. Travel news, headlines and a birthday request will all be said in a slightly different tone: straight, serious and happy in these examples. There is more to variety in the spoken word than just tone. There is also volume and speed. A change of speed, for example, can be within a sentence – you pause before or after significant words or phrases to add emphasis. Sometimes it is more effective to use a voice that is unexpected for a certain situation, to carry more weight. I am not suggesting putting on silly cartoon voices, but in the right circumstance a whisper may be more dramatic than a shout. Think how threatening a whisper in a horror film is.

# Your projection

Think how far away you stand from someone if you are enquiring about the price of an item in a shop. It's about a metre. Further away and we feel distant and disconnected from them. The situation feels 'rude' and your voice will change as a result and become louder. If you stand closer to them both of you feel awkward (think what happens when you get into a crowded lift) and because you are so close your voice will change again and become quieter and more intimate. The best distance is about metre; it is the natural distance we stand away from someone who we have a basic relationship with. Translate that into the studio situation. Imagine someone sitting the other side of the desk to you and talk to them in that 'one metre' voice, don't talk to the microphone or to the other side of the room, and you should get the projection of your voice about right.

# Health tips

Drink loads of water! The best way to keep your vocal cords in shape is to down a couple of litres a day through constant sipping. But do not think that the water you drink will immediately relieve any tension in your throat by lubricating it, it won't. You need to have enough water in your whole body, so that the blood stream is healthier and lubricates the cords from the 'inside'. There is an old maxim that says 'If your pee's all white, you'll sound all right', which does make a certain amount of sense.

Drink the right kind of water – drinks from the machine (cold and fizzy or hot and caffeinated) do not count towards your two litres. You need plain, ordinary $H_2O$ at room temperature – cold water can give your throat a bit of a shock. Hot drinks make your vocal cords swell, caffeine speeds up the production of extra-thick phlegm and that will mean you spend more time swallowing hard or coughing.

How to cough – if you have a tickle, don't 'hack' as that will inflame your vocal cords even more. Simply swallow hard, preferably with some warm water.

Don't whisper — whispering when you have a sore throat only makes it more red and angry. Try it right now and feel the strain your vocal cords are under. What you are doing is pushing them into an unusual shape and then passing extra air over them that only adds to their dryness. Instead, if you are going hoarse, just speak really softly.

# Reading out loud

Finally in this chapter, a few words on reading words out loud. That's not ad-libbing, but reading scripts or the travel news.

It is difficult to explain how to do this in print which is why not many people have tried it, but there are some basic pointers. I can give you.

## Six secrets for speaking the written word

1. If it sounds as though you are reading an item, you are doing it wrong. You should sound as though you are telling a friend something of interest.
2. Make sure you understand the sense of the story, why it is relevant and interesting, and then you stand a better chance of making it compelling.
3. Lift gently, rather than 'stress' or 'emphasise', which we rarely do in normal conversation.
4. Consider what is really happening in the cue. It is often a case of 'while this is happening over here, that's happening over there . . .'. In your head you probably just read that sentence, slightly lifting the words 'this', 'here', 'that', and 'there'. That is because they are the 'balancing words'. Look for balancing words in your scripts and lift them too.
5. Also lift people's names, places and titles.
6. Also lift new information, and subdue old information. So, in the sentences 'Mary had a lamb. The lamb's name was Larry', you lift 'Mary', 'lamb' and 'Larry' because they are names or new information, but subdue the second reference to the lamb, because that's old information.

Increasingly, presenters are reading their scripts straight from a computer screen and that causes several problems. It means that it's difficult to sight read a few lines ahead of what you are currently reading. It also means that you can't mark your script with which words to lift or drop in emphasis. It is, I'm afraid, technology overtaking practicality: 'we've got the technology, so we should use it' seems to be the argument, despite the problems which it causes the presenter.

If you are reading from paper, take a pen into the studio so you can scribble on your cue (mark it as suggested above, rewrite sections if necessary, add extra notes) and of course separate any pages that are stapled or held together with paperclips. Just as pages on a screen can freeze or go missing, so can their paper alternatives. Check before you start reading an item that you have all the pages you need.

**INFORMATION FOR INSPIRATION:** Your presentation is about what you say and how you say it: Entice, engage, inform and be warm.

# 19 Links

Listeners tune in to a radio station for items such as good music, an entertaining and informed presenter, local and travel news, weather and so on. They tune out when they hear an incompetent or bumbling presenter, long and boring interviews, content which has no relevance to them, too many adverts and uninspiring music.

It is one of the jobs of a presenter and producer to increase the 'tune in' factors and reduce the 'tune out' ones.

You have to play listeners' favourite songs and talk about things that interest them – hardly rocket science, is it?

A link is a short, spoken comment between two programme items, usually songs. A 'bit' is a longer link, perhaps a few minutes long and is more likely to be a conversation between co-hosts, a competition, a pre-recorded windup phone call, or a spoof song. Together, they are the glue that holds the rest of the structure of the programme together, so it's important that they're not 'tune outs'.

The similarity with both of these is that preparation is the key to making them work. Know what message you want to get across and work out how you going to do it.

**INFORMATION FOR INSPIRATION:** Don't become one of those presenters who talks until they've got something to say.

Ask yourself these questions before you start a link
- Is it relevant? Have I localised it? (See below for what I mean by local.)
- Is it interesting? Will everybody understand it?
- Is it compelling? Will this add excitement or enhance the station?

In this chapter I am going to give you essential advice on what you can talk about, and how to make it relevant, interesting and compelling for your listeners. (There were even more ideas and suggestions in the chapter on show prep, see pp. 96–107.)

**INFORMATION FOR INSPIRATION:** Entertain informatively and inform entertainingly.

## Playing the piano badly

It may be frustrating to read the advice in this section and realise that it goes against what many radio presenters do on their shows, particularly some of the famous names who may inspire you.

Sometimes you see musicians who comedically play their instruments badly. However, in order for that to be funny and not just a noise, the musician has to be able to play the instrument very well. The same is true of radio presenting. You have to know how to do it properly before you can start doing it 'wrong'.

> 'I was producing a very high-profile DJ at the time of 9/11. The planes hit minutes before we went on air. There was no way we could have done our normal show. However, despite his normal irreverent style he was able to fall back on the 'right' way to do it and presented a sensitive and informative show that received praise from listeners and the media.'
>
> Will Kinder, producer, Radio 1, in conversation with the author

So learn the rules, use them, be professional and then as your personal style develops you might feel you can begin to bend or even break some!

# Basic advice

## Are links scripted?

Most radio seems spontaneous and conversational – a lot of that is down to the skill of the presenter who has done their show prep. They know the features and the topics that they want to talk about, as well as having a lot of background knowledge about local and national events to 'fall back on' if it's needed.

Apart from the cues and introductions to interviews or rules for competitions, scripting links is unusual. (Having said that scripted 'liner cards' were used on some stations in the '90s to concentrate the presenters into broadcasting in the station's style.) What is more likely is a presenter referring to some notes they made earlier and mentally rehearsing the flow and duration of the link while a previous feature is going to air. However, the exact words will be ad-libbed live.

This ad-libbing takes experience and those who have been on radio for a while may tell you that they don't know what they are going to say even as they open the mike. This may well be true for them after years of broadcasting, but do not let their comments fool you into thinking that you can get away without planning at an early stage of your career.

## How often should you do a link?

I don't know. Every station and circumstance is different. However, as a guideline, if it's a mainly music programme then talk after every other song, or four voice links for every six songs (link, song, song; link song; link, song, song; link, song, etc), not after every *single* one. Some stations demand that you segue three songs before you open the mic, but the main rule of thumb is, on music radio, to let the music flow.

> **INFORMATION FOR INSPIRATION:** Even if you aren't voicing a link yourself, it is still good practice to ident the station between every song with a jingle, drop-in or sweeper.

# The length of a link

How long should a link be? As long as it needs to be to create and keep interest and/or evoke emotion. That emotion could be humour, interest, empathy and so on, but as soon as it's boredom or offence then you've failed.

A link could be two minutes long, if that is what it takes to grab the audience, tell the story, stir passions, and build up to a climax. A link could be five seconds if all you need to do is ID the station and trail the next song.

**INFORMATION FOR INSPIRATION:** A link is exactly the same duration as a piece of string is long. Say what you need to say (not what you *want* to say) and then stop. Don't keep going long after you reach the peak of the link.

Some stations will have rules about how often you should talk, and for how long, and this will change depending not only on the station but also the kind of programme. For example, a breakfast presenter will talk more than a mid-morning show host.

Some stations set limits, but most don't – it depends on your house style. At Radio Mercury in the early '90s, weekend presenters had a digital clock in the studio that started each time they opened the mic. If the presenter was still talking after 15 seconds, a caller to the station could win a prize. And the programme controller didn't want to give away any prizes.

Bear in mind the phrase 'bin it after a minute', or 'shrink your link': however long it is, it could probably have been shorter.

# Think before you link

Never open the mic unless you know what you are going to say.

**INFORMATION FOR INSPIRATION:** DJ waffle wastes your time and that of the listeners. If you've got nothing to say, say nothing!

Avoid waffle by planning your links so they have a beginning (what occurred to you, the 'headline' of your link), a middle (the main content, the facts, story or observation) and an end (the phone number, pay off line, station ID). Do not open the mic just for the sake of it.

Always have a spare sheet of paper or a pad in the studio with you so before you open the mic you can jot down a few bullet points on what you are about to say. That way you will be fluent, will only say what you need to, and will know when you've said it.

If you are opening the mic just because you haven't said anything for four songs and feel as though you should, you are probably in the wrong job!

# Know where you're going

Always know what you want to accomplish before you open the mic: what you are going say and where you are going with it. In other words: know the point and the pay-off.

Let's take an example of a link about poor driving – you were cut up on the way into work. That's a good angle (or 'peg to hang it on') and will be a good way to get in to the link – 'I was driving into work this morning and had just passed the Red Lion on East Street (note the relatable reference) when a blue Fiesta (don't mention the registration) cut me up . . .'.

In the office earlier you and some colleagues came up with a few more examples of what annoys you about people's driving habits and you intend to do a 'mock rant' on these and ask listeners to call in with their stories of motoring mayhem. You've decided to call the bit 'Drivers From Hell' and have produced a bed with a voice-over and a clap of thunder going into *The Ride of the Valkyries* music. It's going to be the main topic of the show. But even though you know what you are going to say to get in to the piece (you were cut up), what you will say when you are in it (other examples of bad driving) and what you want next (more examples from listeners), do you know how you are going to get out of that introduction? You have got the beginning and the middle but what about your end? What is your denouement, your 'out', your punch line going to be? It might be something like, 'So many people ignore the Highway Code, it might as well be called the My-Way Code!' Straight into a song.

> **INFORMATION FOR INSPIRATION:** When planning a link know what you want out of it *and* how you'll get out of it.

## Know when you've got there

Many presenters don't know when to get out of a link, whether it is a conversation with a caller or even when they are talking by themselves! They just do not have the confidence or speed to realise that what's just been said is the funniest, most poignant or ironic point.

The climax is sometimes tricky to see, especially when there are several presenters all vying for 'the last word' and it's someone else, rather than you who comes up with the best line! Get ready to seize the moment at the optimum point and go straight to the jingle or the song. Identify the impact point to leave listeners on a high with something strong and memorable. Don't leave the bit to lose momentum, wither and die . . . and fade away . . . like this . . .

## Know what happens next

Many new presenters can plan one step at a time, but not what happens after that. So, they might know what they are going to say, and how to wrap it up, but won't have considered what follows it, leaving a moment of dead air. (See p. 329 for the difference between 'dead air' and 'silence'.)

Know the next thing you must do when you have finished your link so you don't just stop. Are you going into an ad break, another song, introduce a guest? Think it through, and get it ready.

## One thought, one link

A rule of radio is 'one thought, one link'; in other words do not cram in too much information. If you do, your message will be lost. That doesn't mean that you can only give the name of the station or only give the title and artist of the song you have just played, it means you do those and then one on an item of substance.

Do a snoop of one of your shows and hear how many topics you cover in each link.

You could even transcribe each link and then cross out every word and phrase that didn't add anything.

Follow the two steps:

- Consider what your single core message is that you want the audience to hear, understand and remember.
- Say it clearly, powerfully and memorably.

So no 'laundry lists' of songs in the next hour or of next week's guests.

> **INFORMATION FOR INSPIRATION:** Act like the SAS — do what you need to do and then get out.

## The station name

Radio is free and therefore usually taken for granted. So to get the credit you deserve, say the station name often.

This is so listeners:

- Know what station to find in the future, especially if they're listening on line.
- Can tell their friends their station of choice.
- Know what box to mark in the Rajar diary — regular mentions should help increase listening figures.
- For commercial stations: so listeners can tell advertisers they subsequently shop with, where they heard about them.
- For BBC stations: to remind listeners where the licence fee is being spent.

Most stations have a policy of mentioning the name of the station (sometimes together with some other piece of information such as a frequency or strapline) *every single link.* You may think that this gets to be rather repetitive and formulaic, but it is down to you as a presenter to ensure that it doesn't. If people listen to your station for an average of an hour a day, and you only mention the station name every 20 minutes they may only hear it two or three times.

The programme controller may tell you that you have to say the station name as the *first element* in every link but this doesn't sound very conversational and also means there is a chance that the station name (perhaps the most important part of the link) may be subconsciously 'thrown away' and garbled by a presenter wanting to get to the 'meat' of their link.

Others maintain the station name has to be the *last element* in every link: that way it is reinforced as the last thing the listener hears you say.

Most say that it can be anywhere in the link, as long as it is in there somewhere.

You can, of course, vary the way you identify the station, either by simple verbal mentions: 'You're listening to Radio X' or weave the mentions into a script or conversation.

- **Radio X** playing Coldplay's new single, where we're giving away £1000 in our Secret Sound Competition . . .
- That's Coldplay's latest on the station which is giving away £1000 in the **Radio X** Secret Sound Competition . . . (details) . . . so make sure you're listening at 4.30 this afternoon and you could be a winner on the Secret Sound, only here on **Radio X**.
- That's Coldplay's latest on the station which is giving away £1000 in the **Radio X** Secret Sound Competition . . .
- Simon's on the line now to **Radio X** . . .
- Tara, thanks for joining us on **Radio X**.

- Later here on **Radio X** . . .
- Peter Porter reports for **Radio X**.

There is more to identifying your station than simply saying its name. Keep saying *where* you are as well as *who* you are. '. . . here in Leeds . . .' or '. . . here in West Sussex . . .'. These informal mentions remind people they are listening to their own local service not one from miles away. This is especially important when many stations have 'generic' names that are not linked to their location.

## Your name

Mention your name often, about every second or third link, although some stations may like you to do this every time you open the mic. Remember, not everyone will know your name or recognise your voice. If the listener doesn't know who you are, they can't build a relationship with you. Mentioning your name humanises the show.

When you tell them your name, tell them in a conversational way: '*I'm* Peter Stewart' is much more friendly, natural and relatable than '*This is* Peter Stewart', and certainly avoid 'My name is . . .'.

You should also identify and re-identify your guests, and always back-anno interviews – listeners often find it difficult to recognise a voice if they start listening in mid-conversation.

Also read the section on 'zoo programmes' on pp. 315–326 to see how to identify your on-air colleagues.

## One to one-ness

As I mentioned before, it is best for you to talk on a one-to-one basis. That means talking in the singular and referring to 'you' not 'you all' or 'everybody'. So, if you set a competition question, for example, say 'If *you* know call *me*' rather than 'if *anyone* knows call *us*'. If you use 'you', you engage.

## Format jocks

> 'There has to be light and shade. Yes, you have to have big
> personalities on your station and allow them to express
> themselves, but you also have to have great music jocks on the
> air to complement. Too much either way can be damaging.'
> Steve Penk, Presenter Key 103, *The Radio Magazine*, 16 March 2005

A presenter (usually during the daytime), whose main job is to keep the music flowing, is called a format jock. They stick to format (or 'the formatics') and links may consist of little more than what's called the basics:

- The time and temperature.
- The name and the numbers (station name and frequency).
- The slogan and the song.

These presenters (called time and temp jocks in the States), usually have a low profile on the station, but they are confident and competent in what they do, and are hired specifically because they are a safe pair of hands. Although perhaps not Mr Personality in the same way as their drivetime colleagues, they are not going to do long links and they are not going to say anything offensive. Their very job is to be unobtrusive.

> **INFORMATION FOR INSPIRATION:** The bits between the songs, the presentation, is more important than ever, because the songs you play aren't exclusive to you and the market any more.

## The basic link

Bearing in mind what I have said so far about 'one thought, one link', and naming the station and so on, what you need to get over in a basic link are three firm facts.

- The name/frequency of the station.
- What you have just played.
- A tease to something coming up.

'Radio X 99.9 FM playing Supergrass and Charlotte Church . . . where there's your chance to win our weekend in west Wales in the next hour . . .'

'Supergrass and Charlotte Church on Radio X 99.9 FM . . . where there's your chance to win our weekend in west Wales in the next hour . . .'

'That was Supergrass and Charlotte Church . . . on the station where in the next hour, there's your chance to win our weekend in west Wales . . . that's here on Radio X 99.9FM . . .'.

This is also known as the 'that was, this is' link as, essentially that is what you do: just giving the briefest of details in what song was just played, what is coming up and the station ID.

## Hellos and menus

### Your show sheet

Many presenters have a standard programme sheet that they complete before each show, giving changeable information such as their guests, who's presenting travel news, the current total on the roll-over competition and so on. Also on the sheet is static information such as the Ceefax weather page number, the XD phone number for the travel news service, often-used web-addresses or backtimes. This sheet gives all the basics they need for each show all in one place. Some presenters who use a 'stage name' even put that the top of the sheet so they don't forget it.

### The programme run down

At the start of your show, either straight after the news or after the first song, it is customary to 'set out your stall' and tell listeners what they can hear over the next few hours. This is called a programme menu or a programme run down, but it has to be used with care. Very few people will tune in to the start of your show with the intention of following it three or four hours, all the way through – however much we wish they would! So at the start of the show give people an *idea* of what is ahead, your strongest two or three features, but don't mention everything in a laundry list style. And certainly don't promote items giving specific times that they will go to air. If you do, you are giving listeners the opportunity to turn off and only come back to hear that specific feature at that specific time. This will not, of course, dramatically increase your listening hours.

Also avoid giving a list of songs or artists:

- It's boring.
- People will know what they don't want to listen to.
- You may not be able to fit in the last scheduled song in the hour, disappointing the listener who's waited 55 minutes to hear it.

> **INFORMATION FOR INSPIRATION:** A programme run-down is for run-down programmes.

## A pointless plea

A start-of-show plea to 'stay with us for the next three hours' is pretty pointless — people have busy lives. But you may just get them to listen for another 15 or 20 minutes, and that's the key. Keep your intro short and succinct, and then remember to mention various programme elements during the rest of the programme either in the form of teasers or trails (see pp. 221–228 in the next chapter for more on this).

## In a packed programme . . .

'We've got a busy/full/packed programme': it may be busy for you but saying this sounds as though you are desperate for the sympathy vote. It also sounds that the other shows aren't busy — does that mean they're not as good as yours?

'We've got a lot to get through' gives the signal to the listener that they are going to have to concentrate and work hard to follow everything that is happening. How many do you think will be bothered? From the listener's point of view the programme has 'lots of great things' in it, which you will then promote (although not all at once). If it truly is packed, then perhaps you have got too much in it, or it has been poorly produced with too much speech or too many songs.

## A name change

Avoid saying something like, 'I'm Peter Presenter, through till 12 . . .' as it prompts the question, who you will be *after* 12 o'clock!

## The localiser generator

The word local can be defined in two ways. Geographically local to the station and its listeners: the places they live in, go to and are familiar with.

According to the *British Attitudes Survey*, nine out of ten people take part in voluntary activities or belong to local clubs, societies or churches. And in the report *Britain 2010* there is a suggestion that, in an increasingly uncertain world with less job security and more un-predictability affecting issues as diverse as the weather and terrorism, the local community is becoming increasingly important to people.

'I think that it's a great advantage for a presenter to be able to talk to a caller and know their patch, know the places they're talking about. Most of the time they're places I've been to, places that I've had nights out at. I find it so irritating when presenters move into an area they know nothing about and try and hijack the local football team, pretending they're supporters.'
Paul Gough, presenter, Metro FM, *The Radio Magazine*, 25 May 2005

One station group used to have a '4-1 Rule' which required the presenters to mention four local place names in the first hour of their show, three in the second, two in the third and one in the fourth.

Secondly, local to your listeners' 'sphere of interest': the subjects and issues which are of relevance to them. Just because something has happened geographically locally, does not make it interesting. For example, if yours is a chart station in the Midlands, you could still talk about Britney Spears getting married, a new jet that can fly to Australia in record time or an unusual delicacy in Japan. None of them are geographically local to the Midlands, but each are local to your listeners' 'sphere of interest'. The 2004 tsunami wasn't geographically local to UK listeners, neither was Hurricane Katrina the following year, but people were talking about them. The 2005 hurricane that destroyed oil terminals in the Gulf of Mexico wasn't local but it was relevant (because it affected how much I had to pay for petrol) and because it was an interesting story (happening now), and told in a compelling way (with stories of human emotion).

'Always live and local, for the simple reason that the guys appreciate that we're in this with them and not sitting in comfy studios thousands of miles away. We live on a military base, we eat in the same Mess and we share the same highs and lows.'
Damian Watson, British Forces Broadcasting Service,
*The Radio Magazine*, 27 November 2004

In radio you need to use both these definitions to try to keep your audience.

You will notice that there is a crossover between the two types of local. What's ons could be local in both senses, for example, a station targeting over-55s may mention flower shows happening in the area, a chart station may mention a club event happening in the area. These are events happening locally, and also local (of relevance) to their audience.

'Local' could include news, information, comment, observation, what's ons, travel news, interviews, charity involvement, weather, local artists, local arts and culture, sport, phone-ins and so on.

'Content that is drawn from and/or relevant to the area . . . output specific to their area . . . the feel for an area a listener should get by tuning in . . . confidence that matters of importance, relevance or interest to the target audience will be accessible by air . . . programming likely to give listeners a feeling of ownership and/or kinship particularly at the time of a crisis (snow, floods etc).'

Localness is:

- The issues that interest, annoy or concern local people and businesses.
- Having your finger on the pulse, being 'one of us'.
- Adding to as well as reflecting local life.
- What happens on air — the news, competitions, phone-ins and even adverts . . .
- . . . and off air — event sponsorship and charity activities.

'Connecting with your target audience emotionally is crucial. It's also about broadcasting "inclusive content" that makes listeners feel part of the station. Gone are the days of providing "so what?" radio. Every link matters — audiences have so much entertainment choice now that if you don't include them they'll quickly leave you. You have to make your brand compelling so the listener wants more, day in and day out.'

Lisa Higgins, Brand Marketing Director, Century Network,
*The Radio Magazine*, 3 August 2005

## The list to make links local

### Strategy one

Talking about the area (people, places and activities) in a modern, outward-looking, rather than an insular, parochial way, reinforces your connection with the community. Just by adding a local place-name into the story, localises it. Even though the place has no direct relevance to the event, you have made more of a connection with your listener.

Almost any story can be localised, even if it is as basic as saying, 'I was driving through Blanksville yesterday and saw a bald man and that got me wondering: how do they make Maltesers perfectly smooth and round . . .'. Similarly, don't just say, 'When I was shopping . . .' mention the name of the town, or the shopping centre.

### Strategy two

Know the local area — be the expert, understand who's who and what's what. When telling anecdotes about somewhere local, make it even more relatable and memorable by mentioning a landmark. This automatically makes listeners picture the scene and you've made a stronger and clearer connection with them. 'Have you noticed the new paving stones in Blankstown High Street? They're just near the clock tower . . .'.

### Strategy three

Of course not everything that happens to you, happens in your TSA, so presenters bend the truth a little. If something happens to you in another part of the country (or even if a friend tells you something that happened to them), when you tell it, change the location to your area.

### Strategy four

When you have a caller on the air, don't just say which town they are in, ask them to tell you the *part* of town they are in. So it's 'the St John's area of Tunbridge Wells' rather than simply 'Tunbridge Wells'. Or ask them off air, what is near where they live, such as a landmark, a major shop, pub or park. Then when they get on air include the information they gave you in *your* comments:

> PRESENTER: Next up it's Andy in Blankstown. Hi Andy, where in Blankstown are you?
> ANDY: Westcliff Road . . .
> PRESENTER: Oh right, that's near the rec, isn't it? I remember playing football there with the kids last summer . . .

Using this technique sparingly, adds to the feel of connection to the area.

**INFORMATION FOR INSPIRATION:** Localising something makes it more relatable. Specifics make it more memorable.

### Strategy five

Actually *being* local is a distinct advantage: that means having a local accent, understanding the significance of local events, knowing how to pronounce local place names, being able to refer to local landmarks. But newcomers can also talk about what strikes them as unique about the area. The things that only happen there: 'That fantastic view from the top of the Blankshire Tower . . .', 'The feeling of the sand between your toes as you walk down the beach from Northend Pier to Golden Bay, with a bag of chips . . .', 'The sound of the church bells on the Little Blanks village green as you sip a pint of Blanks' Bitter . . .'.

Help people feel good about their local area – celebrate and be proud of local success.

These types of link give what the GWR radio group called a 'love of life round here' factor. This was particularly clever as it had a double meaning: 'love of life' (listeners who were 'up for it') and 'life round here' (in other words, local).

### Strategy six

Represent the whole of your area, not just the part where your studios are based. Be careful of using phrases such as, 'Up there in Chelmsford' or 'Over in Vange'. Similarly, avoid, for example, 'Traffic's heavy coming into Southend' and say instead 'Going into Southend', if that's the town in which you're sitting.

**INFORMATION FOR INSPIRATION:** Reinforce where you are broadcasting to but not where you are based.

You will of course have in your studio bible a list of how to pronounce all those awkward local place names. A quick way for any presenter to slide down the credibility scale (taking the station with them) is if they don't know how to say a town in their patch. Remember, there are many local quirks! Tonbridge and Tunbridge Wells (both in Kent) are both pronounced 'tunbridge' despite the different spelling. Leigh can be pronounced as 'lee' or 'lie' depending on whether you are talking about the place in Essex or the one in Surrey. Then there are the really awkward ones such as Towcester (toaster), or the ones that may get you lynched in the streets (pronouncing Edinburgh as 'edin-burra', for example).

To get a local place name wrong is insulting; being new to the area is no excuse, so make yourself aware of the name traps. Don't ever say on air something like, 'I've had a text from

Simon in the Vale of Belvoir . . . I think that's how you pronounce it . . .'. If you haven't taken the trouble to find out how the local place names are pronounced, why should locals listen to you?

# Further advice

## Personal connection

I mentioned this in the section on show prep (see pp. 96–107) but it is important to make some sort of personal connection every few links. 'Personal' is one thing, 'private' is another.

> **INFORMATION FOR INSPIRATION:** Revealing something of yourself means saying something that no other presenter could possibly say. It makes you unique and memorable. It makes you real and someone the audience can relate to, and that helps build a powerful connection.

## Your own station

Many times presenters do not even have the most basic knowledge of other programmes on their own station. They sound ill-informed and the station, which tries to foster an on-air family feel, suffers as a result. You must have a thorough knowledge of your station's output at all times. Check your pigeonhole and e-mail for the latest memos on station promotions or changes to the schedule (for example, that the presenter who is following you is off today). This information may be repeated on the studio whiteboard, so check all of these places to cover yourself.

Actually *listen* to your own station! That way you can comment on the rest of the output to create more of a bond with your audience. Notice the difference between a link that runs '. . . and Dave Matthews is back tomorrow from ten' and one that goes, 'I was listening to Dave Matthews on the way in this morning and heard the Secret Sound. It's been running for, what, six weeks now and is so infuriating! Dave's told me that the guesses are getting closer now, but he won't tell me what it is. So, I'm just going to listen tomorrow from ten to find out what it is . . .'. The second one is *longer*, but it works *better*.

> **INFORMATION FOR INSPIRATION:** Spending five seconds saying something that *doesn't work* is not saving time over a twenty-second link *that does*. It's wasting five seconds.

If your station is trying to get people to listen for, say, ten hours a week, then that's at least as long as you should be listening too (on top of your actual show). Know your schedules and features back to front. Listeners should not know more about the station than you do.

## Local news

Know what is in the news, especially in the bulletins on your own station. Obviously, you will not want to comment on every story (especially the political ones) but you may be able to give a comment about a new local shopping development, or a local celeb. Remember: newspapers contain 'yesterday's news'. You can be ahead of the game if you comment on stories in your bulletins in your show, not when they appear in print the next day.

If soon after a news bulletin which mentioned that a missing girl had been found, you say, 'I wonder whether that toddler's been found yet', you're showing your audience that you haven't been listening to your own output. If you don't care enough about your own output in your own show, why should they? There is really no excuse not to listen to your own station and catch at least one news bulletin as you drive into work.

## Their PoV

Another way to show inclusivity with the audience is to see things from their point of view (PoV).

Think of the advantages to *the listener* of what you are doing. So, instead of 'I've got lots of things to give away on the OB tomorrow', it's 'Come along and see what *you* can win . . .'. Talking from a listener's perspective makes the information you are trying to get over more relatable and easy to use.

## Incestuous links

These are links about the family at the radio station. Apart from the fact that they are usually not funny and may invade the privacy of your colleague, these links exclude the listener, are discourteous and bad mannered. So, in-jokes, references to things only you can see, problems at the station, a broken piece of machinery in the studio are all incestuous.

---

 **ACTUAL AUDIO**

PRESENTER: Well, it's been a pretty bad day here at the radio station, Several of our friends and colleagues have lost their jobs, so forgive me if the show has sounded a little different today, it's just that we're all really shocked with what's been going on.

*Commercial radio station, October 2005*

---

Don't continually comment on physical appearances, attributes, or lack of attributes of fellow presenters, as it usually sounds insulting.

---

 **ACTUAL AUDIO**

PRESENTER 1:  Where's (fellow presenter) today?
PRESENTER 2:  Dunno. Probably off doing something, like getting his hair cut.
PRESENTER 1:  Or transplanted . . . or re-glued.
PRESENTER 2:  He does look odd doesn't he?
PRESENTER 1:  Do you think he has different hair for each season?
PRESENTER 2:  Seriously, is that a wig?

*Commercial radio station, December 2005*

---

Asking your producer on air to get you a coffee is pointless. Making a joke about the food in the BBC canteen is old and tired. And comments such as, 'Tina's cracking up at a joke I've just told her, but I can't repeat it on air' is one of the things that some presenters still do, and then wonder why listeners who feel left out, tune out.

Another problem with an on-air conversation that should be off air is that one comment, 'See you've had a haircut, Dave!' encourages a reply. 'Yes, I had a fight with a lawnmower!' and then another, 'I know – you have a haircut once a year whether you need it or not!' and so on . . . 'At least I've got hair to cut . . . err . . . baldy!' Excruciating.

Don't put yourself down on air. It maybe self-deprecating in a Jack Dee-style but makes it sound as though you lack authority. Avoid saying your age. If your audience is much older than you, they may question your credibility. Let them keep the picture they have in their mind – the age you are in that, is always 'real'.

Also crass is mention of technical words and phrases that mean nothing to listeners (see also the section When Things Go Wrong on pp. 327–334). 'Argh, I can't find my bed', 'Sorry, I couldn't give you the pips', 'I remember the days when we had carts in the studio' and 'Tina Travel has gone down on me' will have completely different connotations to your listeners.

---

 **ACTUAL AUDIO**

PRESENTER:  Sorry for the bleed through on that ISDN line . . .

*Commercial radio station, August 2005*

---

As far as the listener is concerned, you go into a studio with a boxful of CDs you want to share with the audience. They don't know that the songs have been chosen by a computer after information was entered into a database in Bristol and neither should you tell them.

**INFORMATION FOR INSPIRATION:** Saying something incestuous is usually a sign that you have not done enough show prep, or do not understand what is entertaining.

## Never be negative

Sell the station and sell the music. If you do not like the song you have just played, and you feel as though you can't lie and say it was great, then just do a straight outro (mentioning the title and artist). The song *must* be great, otherwise why would you be playing it?

If you feel as though the same song is on too high a rotation then have a word with the music scheduler. There may be a reason, there may have been a mistake when the song was entered on the database, or it may be your perception of repetition. After all, you listen to the station far more than an 'ordinary' listener so you will notice it more (especially if it is a track that you are not very fond of).

If a competition 'mechanic' (the way a contest is run) seems too complicated, do not make a meal of it on air. Work out a way to make it simpler and speak to the promotions department. They may not realise that what looked good on paper, is in fact complicated to explain, making it difficult to attract contestants.

Problems with music and management, commercials and colleagues, promotions and prizes are all dealt with in the office and not the studio. Why criticise your employer on air? It shows the utmost unprofessionalism, not to mention possible suicidal tendencies for your career. It also gives the message to listeners that, if the presenter doesn't enjoy the station, why should they?

## Happy Radio

This title of an Edwin Starr hit could be the philosophy of those who say it should always be a sunny day on their station.

In other words, almost everything can be given a positive spin:

- Only ever take people to air who you know have the correct competition answer.
- Peter Presenter isn't ill, he's 'off on an exciting holiday'.
- It may be windy – but 'what a great day to put the washing out' and so on.

> 'Doing a breakfast show from war-torn Kosovo was quite a challenge. When you go away with BFBS, you live with the troops so it's nothing glamorous. You might regularly wake up to find your bed's soaked because the snow has got through the air-conditioning unit, and then there'll be no hot water for a shower. But you have to be chirpy on the radio, so the troops have something to take their minds off the fact that there's no hot water! That was a bit of an eye opener and having to keep your spirits up because you're out there to entertain the troops was quite a challenge.'
>
> Gareth Brooks, presenter Xfm, *X-Trax* magazine, September 2005

You may sound false if you always accentuate the positives and are bitter about the negatives. The trick is to turn the situation around: 'What a rubbish day – rain again. It's totally ruined my plans for a kick-about in the park with the kids . . . so we'll have to stay in and play that new Xbox game I got for Christmas. Boy, I really didn't want to do that!' Or, if there has been unseasonably hot weather, don't just moan about the studio air-conditioning but laugh about bathing with a friend and offer practical advice on how to keep cool.

**INFORMATION FOR INSPIRATION:** Putting yourself on the same emotional level as your listeners may mean you communicate with them better. The trick is to realise what gets you down, without sounding negative yourself. See humour in the situation, or a positive side, do not just carp and complain.

Some people call this the 'glass is half full' philosophy, John Ryan, the Managing Editor of BBC Radio Manchester calls it, 'Looking up and looking forward: today and the future, not yesterday and the past'.

## Family friendly

Sexual innuendo and crudity are unlikely to be part of your station's output at any time (unless it is as part of your late night sex and relationship show). Yours is likely to be a family station with a family audience, especially at breakfast, so keep comments clean.

**ACTUAL AUDIO**

BREAKFAST PRESENTER:    I don't smoke after sex, I smoke during sex. At
least I tried to but the ashtray kept falling off my girlfriend's back
*Commercial station, October 2005*

## Don't always be honest — 1

Do not lose the common touch. If your listeners are those who holiday in Spain and you
talk about taking your yacht out to the Maldives, then figuratively you are going to become
rather more distant to them. If they are struggling single parents, do not talk about how difficult it is to find a nanny. In other words, do not make it hard for them to relate to you, do
not alienate yourself. Do not build a wall between you and the listener that they have got
to climb over. Some won't even bother.

## Don't always be honest — 2

If you really feel strongly about an issue there may be certain occasions when you should *not*
speak your mind. It is like the old dinner party convention: don't talk about politics or religion.
Now, politics in the general sense is allowed if you have a point to make about, say, car park
charges or how often the bins are emptied. Much more than that — 'there are yet more asylum
seekers in the town, they should all be kicked out . . .' is going too far, unless you are a talk
show host who is experienced, both in terms of years' service and also in the laws of libel.

   You should not usually have an editorial standpoint. To do so could land you in trouble
with the radio regulator Ofcom and also with a large proportion of listeners who may say
that you are politically biased, something radio in the UK is not allowed to be. Make sure
that you read the section on the law around election time, and speak to someone in the
newsroom if you want it explained further.

## Name checks

If you're talking *about* another presenter, use their full name, 'Simon Jones is on after the
news, with another chance to win . . .'. The image and recall of the station (the brand) is
down to a number of factors, the station name, logo, strapline, and (although admittedly down
the list) the names of the presenters.

   If you are actually talking to another presenter, by all means use their first name (to use
both in this situation would sound ridiculous). But do use a name.

   If you are introducing yourself, use your full name, 'Radio X, I'm Barnaby Rudd', rather
than, 'I'm Barnaby'. The exception to this is if you're only known by one name. Incidentally,
'I'm . . .' is usually more correct and less formal than, 'This is . . .' when you're introducing
yourself. Think about it: you're at a party and someone asks for some introductions, you say,
'I'm Broughton Crangrove and this (introducing *someone else*) is India Fernando-Grey.'

## Stories from newspapers

Do not read these out word for word; in fact do not read them out at all. Instead, read the
story, note what is funny, sad, unusual or whatever about it, then put the paper to one side
and *tell the story* to your listeners. That way the best bits (the facts and emotions that resonated
with you) will come to the top of the tale and the boring, unimportant bits (the man's name,

age, job that kind of thing) will be self-edited out. Of course, you will have prepared all this in advance, so you can add your own comment, observation or punch line off the back of it. When you simply read a story out from the paper you are not interpreting the story or adding anything to it. In other words, you are not communicating as you would in real life.

Certainly do not say, 'It says in the paper that . . .'. If you say that, they might as well stop listening to you and just pick up the paper themselves. Just talk about papers in general or say, 'Have you *heard* that . . . ?'.

## Talking about TV

'Newsworthy stories about rival broadcasters should definitely be reported, but try not to mention the actual brand more than once. Remember that Five Live is part of a competitive world and every mention of a competitor is a free plug for their brand. Find other ways of describing the station — e.g.: Sky = the satellite broadcaster; talkSPORT = the sports station, Virgin = the independent music station.'
*BBC Radio Five Live Style Guide*

Some stations do a run-down of what is on TV each evening, which to me seems mad. There is enough competition for your radio station without promoting it and encouraging people to go elsewhere. Added to that, what does it say about your own station if you are suggesting people try another media? How does your evening show presenter feel about it? Instead, why not tease and trail what is on your station at the same time as the latest soap or reality show is on TV?

I admit that television shows do create 'water cooler moments' – subjects about which office colleagues can chat. A link about *Big Brother* (if that is appropriate to your demographic) will have an instant recognition with your audience who will understand the format, the key players and know the latest events. But instead of *promoting* TV programmes, talk about them *after they've happened*. After all, doing this will actually give you something to talk *about*! Instead of saying, 'This *may be* interesting', you can say, 'That *was* interesting *because* . . .'.

## Talking about other radio stations

'We never worry about the competition, we worry more about getting it right.'
John Myers, Chief Executive, Guardian Media Group,
*The Radio Magazine*, 23 March 2005

It is not so bad talking about the other stations if you are the underdog, perhaps you have got nothing to lose, but why raise their profile or alert your listeners to their existence and prompt your audience to sample them?

There are occasions when BBC local stations are asked to trail a show on Radio 4 or Radio Five Live; in which case those trails and talk-ups must be run. But I can't think of any reason why you would otherwise want to talk about another station, even to criticise it, especially if it is in your area.

## Handovers

Of course, if your station allows, talk to the next presenter and ask them what is in their show and so on, but remember there is a fine line between fun conversations that listeners enjoy and annoying banter that excludes them and encourages them to turn off. The point of such a conversation is to have a seamless transition from your show to theirs, without an obvious 'exit point'. That encourages people to listen longer and makes the show and station 'stickier'.

Don't make the end of your programme sound as though it is the end of the day's broadcasting, but promote positively the next presenter. Indeed, on some stations the next presenter takes over just before the 'watershed' news bulletin to ease this transition.

Don't let your colleagues down by putting them on the spot during a handover. If it makes them appear to lack knowledge or authority on air, you're not only being incestuous but also you're also letting down yourself, your colleague and the station.

> **INFORMATION FOR INSPIRATION:** Do not have incestuous jokes that exclude the listener. Leave 'inside humour', outside.

## The cart and horse

You're probably thinking, 'Strange, surely it's horse and cart?' Well, horse and cart is how most presenters deliver their information: they give the facts and then a comment. With the cart and horse set-up you make your comment first, then give the information.

A quick example:

- Horse and cart – 'It's raining later, so take your umbrella' (information → comment).
- Cart and horse – 'Better get your umbrella, it's going to rain later' (comment → information).
- Horse and cart – 'Tickets for the Elton John concert in Blankstown are going fast. If you want to be there on 15 July, you'd better book now' (information → comment).
- Cart and horse – 'You'd better be quick if you want to be at the Elton John concert in Blankstown in the summer. Tickets for his 15th of July gig are selling fast' (comment → information).

By putting the cart before the horse, you use a comment to hook people into listening to the rest of the link. Listeners ask themselves, 'Why?'. By putting the horse before the cart, the listener knows all the information in the first sentence and they can mentally switch off. You've failed to make the link compelling.

## Ask a question

Another way of involving the listener when you do a link is to ask them a question. They cannot help but respond in their own mind to what you are saying, and in doing that they have continued the interaction with you. For example: instead of saying, 'Now let's see what's happening in the area this weekend . . .' it's, 'Are you just hanging around this weekend with nothing to do? If so, let's see what's on . . .' Instead of saying, 'The news is next . . .' it's, 'Have you been wondering what's happened to those people caught up in the floodwaters in New Orleans? We've got the latest on that horrendous situation for you next.' Instead of saying, 'Now the weather with Anne Enometer . . .' it's, 'Doesn't it make you feel so much better towards everything and everyone when the sun is shining? Let's see if it's going to last . . . here's Anne Enometer . . .'.

I'm not suggesting you start every link with a question. Like all these techniques, it's another blade in your Swiss Army knife of ideas. Asking questions is a great way to hook and engage the listener. It draws them in and they find themselves subconsciously answering it, but be careful not to overuse it as a device.

> **INFORMATION FOR INSPIRATION:** If people do not understand what you are trying to tell them, why should they work hard to listen? They won't. It's what is called the 'Shit/Click Factor'. The listener thinks, 'That's shit!' and clicks off the radio. If you turn them off, they'll turn you off.

# Humour on the radio

Most of the time, people warm to someone who is funny. If a listener laughs at something you have said, it builds up a bond between you. You have evoked an emotion and you will come over as someone they want to get to know.

Humour also reflects on the tone of the station: that it's a fun one to listen to. Some listeners may 'steal' your line to tell their friends, and when their friends laugh they will return to your show to get another one: laughter increases loyalty.

But do not try to be something that you're not. There is nothing more embarrassing than someone who just can't tell a joke, but never gives up trying. If you feel the need to be funny all the time, it will sound forced and unnatural.

'Funny' can often come from being 'fun' – is Dermot O'Leary funny? Perhaps not, but he's certainly fun and entertaining. Many listeners will remember how you make them *feel* not exactly what you *say*. So, relax and your humour will come through naturally.

## Comedy conditions

The situation must be right before someone will laugh at what you are saying, or as I say, find it FUN.

- **F**reedom to laugh. Someone has got to have permission to find it funny, according to the time and place and who they are with. A rude joke may be funny but not if it is told on the breakfast show.
- **U**ninvolved feeling. Most events are funnier if you are not personally involved: someone falling over, for example.
- **N**onsensical atmosphere. The tone of the show has got to be set up. Black humour occurs in unusual situations, but people will laugh more readily if they are already relaxed and expectant.

## The laws of laughter

Comedy is often in response to a situation:

- Abruptness. The best humour comes from something that's unexpected. Say something original and say it well, so the audience can't guess the punch line before you give it to them. Humour of surprise is also when something happens at the wrong time, or the wrong place, or to the wrong person.
- Recognition. Laughter often comes when people recognise what is being described, so draw common experiences to their attention. There is also humour from the

recognition (of a character or situation) that comes with using a catchphrase, although bear in mind that the best catchphrases are usually ones that develop naturally or spontaneously rather than ones which are created deliberately.

- **Superiority.** We naturally laugh at those worse off than ourselves: a social icon or institution, someone in power, someone with bad luck. But sometimes people feel uncomfortable laughing at others, so make yourself the target of the joke and allow listeners to laugh at you. If there's no target, it's just conversation.
- **Enjoyment.** This happens when a climax has been resolved and people laugh out of sheer delight for themselves or someone else. Think of the resolution of a station competition when, after speculation and tension, someone laughs when they win a huge prize.

Considering these elements will help you develop your own more-humorous take on the world. Once you've got the concept, write it down and turn it around. Does the idea work better another way (perhaps the funny observation and *then* the explanation?). Can you push the idea even further (if this is what's funny in an everyday situation, how would the Queen cope with it, or a spaceman? Did the same thing happen in Stone Age times?). Change the words — some are intrinsically more amusing than others (negligee is potentially funnier than underwear. A banana is a funnier fruit than an apple. A guava or a paw-paw may be funnier still . . . or not). Play with the form until it's as funny and fast as possible.

## The comedy clauses

Only use the material if:

- You understand it.
- You find it funny.
- It fits with your on-air personality.
- It's not illegal (for example, defamatory).
- It's not offensive.

## Is it funny?

If you're going to use a line or humorous story written by someone else, first consider whether you understand it and if *you* think it funny or fun. You may have been a best man at a wedding and bought a book of one-liners, and ploughed through it trying to find what you consider to be a funny line for your speech. It's tough! Only use a line that someone else says is funny, if you personally agree with them. If you don't, try and work out *why* it doesn't appeal to you. Can you at least see why it is *supposed* to be funny? In which case, consider whether you can rewrite it so it's better. There's no harm in that, in fact it's the best thing to do. You've paid for the material, so you can do what you want with it to make it work for you. Maybe the characters in the scene are unbelievable, or they have names that are ridiculous — or maybe not ridiculous enough. Perhaps the pay-off is great, but the situation has to be changed to fit better with your target audience. Maybe move it from a hairdressers to a rock concert, for example. Perhaps you've missed the punch line completely. If so, look again to see what the writer was trying to do. Can you develop the idea further or use the set-up for a gag of your own? Perhaps the line just doesn't fit with your own speech pattern; in which case re-write it so that it does.

When you re-write, don't do it word for word. Humorous comments always work better if they're ad-libbed to a certain extent. Jot down bullet points on what to say in the set-up but write down the punch line in full in case your mind goes blank. Reading someone else's lines word for word sounds stilted and false.

Remember, if you don't find it funny, then neither will anyone else. Or they may be laughing *at* you, rather than *with* you, and for all the wrong reasons.

## Would you say it?

Also consider whether the on air 'you' would make such a comment. If it's a humorous dig at a reality show celebrity, but your persona is one that loves watching such shows, then probably not. If it's a clever comment about a politician but you're portrayed as the 'dumbo' on air, again, probably not. If the gag doesn't fit with the personality you're trying to build, then either drop the gag or give it to someone else whose personality *does* fit with the content. Don't break the on-air spell.

## Could you say it?

There are laws about the kinds of things that you can say about people, see p. 134–136.

## Don't tell a joke

When telling a joke, don't tell a joke! Set it up so it's not in the traditional, 'I say, I say, I say' form, but incorporate it into a normal link so it sounds more spontaneous. This'll catch the listener off guard and surprise them more. So, instead of saying, 'Did I tell you about the boy who wanted to be a baker?' link the line in to something else, maybe a song you've just played, or something that happened (or *could have* happened) to you. '. . . with their latest, *The Transatlantic Astronaut*. You know, most little boys want to be an astronaut when they grow up . . . I didn't. I wanted to be a baker, so I could make more dough. This is Radio X at nearly 20 past 12 . . .'.

OK, a pretty weak joke, but I'm sure you agree that the audience will forgive more because it sounds spontaneous and conversational as it's linked with the song, rather than shoe-horned in for no apparent reason.

## The funniest part

This comes at the end of a joke, yet some people wonder why their material isn't funny when they move the payoff so it's two or three words earlier!

For example, 'Last Christmas I ordered a turkey and when I got home and opened up the packaging, it was two legs and a breast all in pieces in the box. I had to put it together myself. I'm telling you, that's that last time I get my turkey at Ikea.' That's funny(ish) but it'd be less funny if the punch line 'Ikea' (the joke simply doesn't work without it), appeared elsewhere: 'I ordered a turkey from Ikea . . .', 'the last time I go to Ikea for . . .'. No. The funniest bit has to be the last bit.

## A punch after the punch line

Notice what happened at the end of the baker gag; the presenter moved straight on. You may want to use a 'boing' effect, or a crowd applauding after a punch line, but I personally think these draw too much attention to it and sounds rather 'music hall'. Also, the listener can feel treated like an idiot: that was the punch line, and I'm going to draw attention to it by using a silly sound. It also makes it sound as though the gag was set up and scripted rather than amusingly ad-libbed.

Instead, play a 'musical exclamation mark' such as a jingle stab (not a slow lead-up one, which will spoil the effect of your pay-off) or go straight into an ad-break or song. They will all have the same effect.

Don't laugh at your own joke, it sounds even worse than having a sound effect of other people doing it. Paul Merton, Jack Dee and Jimmy Carr — a deadpan delivery is common to all three of them, and they're funnier to watch because they give the impression that they don't know what they said was amusing. Instead, move on to say something else but be careful that you don't go into something that really jolts: '. . . so I could make more dough. Cancer charities are collecting in the High Street this weekend . . .' Also, make sure that the next thing you say isn't really important as the listener may still be musing or chuckling at the pay-off and miss it: '. . . so I could make more dough. 01234 567 890 is the number to call for free tickets to . . .'.

## It's also *how* you say it

Look what I say about silence on p. 329; how you can use it to emphasise a point. In links such as these, a slight pause before you say the pay-off will add to the expectation and humour.

## What's not so good

How good is your sense of humour? If it can come over as sarcastic rather than dry you may lose more listeners than you gain. How good are you at making humorous comments? If you get tongue-tied when you think on your feet or find it difficult to make connections between events, then trying to be funny may not be for you.

Also remember the audience, format of the station and time of day: the files of Ofcom and the BBC are full of complaints made against presenters who said something that was (arguably) funny, but said it at the wrong time of day. That could be an 'adult-themed' joke, said in the breakfast show and heard by kids being driven to school. If you present yourself on the radio as a funny person, always ready with a quick quip with lines from a prep service, but in real life when you meet your listeners you're not actually that funny, your credibility takes a knock.

## Humour in topical material

If you are setting up a punch line about a story in the news, make sure the listener knows enough about the event so they can understand the gag. It may just need to be as quick as, 'So, we're using credit cards more than ever before . . .' or 'I'll never forget the first time I saw . . .'.

The listener has to have a framework, before they can find a joke funny.

## April Fool jokes

Most stations will do an April Fool joke, but these are notoriously difficult to do success-fully. Perhaps it is because most of the really good ones have already been done, perhaps it is because people aren't as gullible any more. More likely it is because they take an awful lot of time and hard work to sound convincing. Bad ones are embarrassing.

If you do have a fantastic idea, make sure that it is cleared with the programme controller before it goes to air, and do this well in advance. Many bosses have a serious humour by-pass if they come across a Fool that they didn't know about, especially if listeners are complaining about it. And people *will* complain if they have been seriously misled, if the joke has caused them to be late for work, or cost them money. Sometimes they can seriously disappoint children who believe them to be true. Those who complain may be your listeners who will find it hard to trust you again (especially if the spoof ran in the news bulletins – how will they perceive your news output from then on?) or non-listeners who won't want to even sample your station. You could get a lot of positive publicity if it all goes well, but a lot of negative publicity if it goes badly.

Then you have to make sure *you're* not duped. There are groups of students and even professionals who try to dupe the media as often as they can. At one station I was at, the news editor ran a story about two teenagers who had been locked in their loft over a weekend, when the hatch slammed shut. They couldn't get out so spent two days playing Monopoly. The story turned out to be a hoax.

Perhaps the best trick is to pretend you have done an April Fool joke but actually not to have done one at all!

## Wind-up calls

These can be hugely entertaining, but following a series of complaints in the '90s, regulators decided that the permission of the 'victim' has to be given before the item can be broadcast. It is a quirk that it is within guidelines to record the call, but not to then transmit it without that permission. So make sure you get permission either on tape or, preferably, in writing.

# 20 Teasing and trailing

As a radio presenter or producer your main job, I think, is a maintenance person. By that I mean you are a 'Quarter Hour Maintenance Person'. It is a skilled job and involves you keeping listeners listening longer.

When someone indicates on a Rajar diary how long they have heard a station for, they tick boxes which are divided into quarter-hour segments. It is your job to get them to tick as many boxes as possible. That is done by teasing and trailing (T&T). Teasing and trailing both promote what's still to come. Trails simply explain what's happening and when, whereas teasers tempt by revealing only some of that information.

> **INFORMATION FOR INSPIRATION:** If something's worth doing on the radio, then surely it's worth letting people know you're going to do it.
> Why plan to do something that is relevant, interesting or compelling without giving people a chance to anticipate it and keep listening for it?

Teasing and trailing may:
- Get someone to hear your show for longer, ideally for 16 consecutive 15-minutes = your four-hour show.
- Persuade them to tune in at a different time and sample more of the output (recycling listeners).
- Give forward momentum to the station by providing anticipation of programmes or features yet to be broadcast.
- Reinforce the central station slogan or message helping to strengthen your brand, even if the listener doesn't actually listen to the item that's being promoted.
- Reflect the station style.

People hearing more of one show, or turning on at another time for another, can affect your Rajar results in three ways.

1. It increases the time spent listening to the station, which is reflected in the 'average hours' and 'total hours' stats. This can only be a good thing. (See p. 53 for details of Rajar.) Put another way, the easiest way to increase these figures is to talk-up other shows to people who're already listening.

2. By not teasing and trailing, listeners don't know that there's something of interest coming up, so may turn off early. Over time it's likely they'll conclude that there's nothing on the station of relevance to them, and go to another station and that will cause a reduction in your reach as well as your hours.

3. If you tempt someone to sample an item in another time, they may well tune in early to be sure to catch it, thereby adding to your TSL (time spent listening).

# A few definitions

## Teasers

The teaser (or tease) is like foreplay. Just as kisses and caresses arouse, excite and create interest in what is to follow, so too should your verbal teasers for your programme content. You'll give just enough information to the listener to let them have an idea of the kind of thing that will happen, but not exactly how, when, what way or in what order. Teasers tempt them and create interest.

> 'Teases should arouse curiosity and anticipation.
> Successful teases will hint at information that
> the (listener) will find useful.'
> BBC Nations and Regions document 2000

For example: 'Is work driving you mad? Are the kids running you ragged? They are – I can tell! Well, as Doctor Jock I'm prescribing a fortnight in the sun for you all. Full details soon . . . here on Radio X!'

## Trails

A trail (either verbal or pre-recorded) on the other hand is, to continue the sex analogy, more like talking dirty: 'This is what I'm going to give you, when and how'. You are promoting your item with a short-term specific selling point.

For example: 'In ten minutes I'll give you the qualifying question for the Holiday of a Lifetime Competition here on Radio X. If you think you know the answer, call me on 01234 567 999, and if you're first through on the phone you can play for a two-week stay on the Florida coast.' It promotes, but doesn't tease.

Teasers tempt, trails tell.

## Headlines

Many stations ask news presenters to give two or three story teasers to the main presenter, which can be read at about ten minutes to each hour. Note that I'm saying 'teasers' not 'head-lines'. Headlines are a shortened version of the whole story, whereas teasers merely hint at the topic. A teaser might be, 'We have the result in the Michael Jackson trial . . .' whereas a headline will be, 'Michael Jackson's been found not guilty on all ten counts at his trial . . .'. One cajoles the listener to listen longer (makes the show and the station 'stickier'), the other, because it has told the story already, gives them a reason *not* to.

## Teasing and trailing basics

Listening to some stations' presentation is like watching the prize conveyor belt on TV's Generation Game. Let me explain.

On New Year's Eve 2004 I drove to a friend's house for a party. I heard an hour of a local radio station during which time the presenter didn't give one clue or hint about any programme element other than the one he was doing right then. On New Year's Day 2005 I drove home, and listened to the same station but a different presenter. The same thing happened: her only interest was what was right in front of her (on her 'conveyor belt') at that precise time.

Total listening hours for that station have dropped by more than 30% in the last two years, with weekly reach down 26%. I wonder if there is a connection?

## When do you T&T?

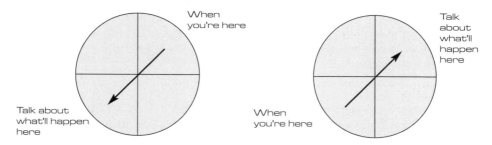

As you can see from the above clock-faces, it is best to talk about what is planned for the opposite quarter hour segment. Note: that's not the *next* 15-minute segment, but on a clock-face the one which is diagonally opposite the quarter in which you are in currently.

That is because a promotion any further ahead than that is 'out of reach' of the average listener, whereas they are much more likely to stay for another 20–30 minutes, and that could see another two ticks in your Rajar column.

## T&T every link?

Teasing or trailing too much or too often, can cause the presenter to be a 'plate spinner' with too much to handle all at the same time. It can also cause the listener to become confused and unable to identify the key messages. Identify *one* item which needs to be T&T-ed in the opposite quarter, not everything.

## Exit points

As much as we strive to broadcast relevant, interesting and compelling items all of the time, we have to face facts that for some people, some of those items will not hit home. An 'exit point' is just such an occasion – when the listener is being given an opportunity to leave the programme. That could be an ad break, a song they don't like, an interview they are not interested in, the news at the top of the hour and so on.

The trick is to hide that exit point: to act like a museum tour guide to the rest of the show, and usher them past that exit door by promoting 'something you'll really like just down this corridor'. We 'promote' (a generic term for teasing and trailing), so people do not notice that there is an opportunity to leave.

## What's for afters?

That is what children say when they are faced with a main course they don't much fancy and want the anticipation of dessert. In a similar way you have to tempt the audience. So, before you say what you're doing *now*, say what you're going to do the *other side*.

Before the commercials sell sofas and double-glazing, make sure *you* sell the song that you will be playing on your station in three minutes' time. 'In a moment A, but first B . . .', 'Music on the way from X, after this from Y . . .'. Do this, and you hide an exit point.

## The porridge pot principle

Remember that fairy tale about the pot that wouldn't stop producing porridge? Consider that in terms of radio, because programmes never end either. (A programme that ends is another 'exit point' – that change of gear gives the opportunity for someone to tune out.)

So, when promoting other shows, say what time they start but not what time they end: '. . . that's the breakfast show, back tomorrow morning from 6 . . .'. If you continue '. . .'til 10 . . .' it shows up the exit sign in big green letters.

## Back-selling

Some programmers also suggest that you 'back-promote' or 'back-sell' items, and tell those who have just tuned in what they have missed. If you say what you are going to do, do it, then say what you have done, you multiply the experience.

The idea is that if a newcomer is intrigued by the back-sell they may well tune in earlier the next day to hear the actual feature. So, extending listening time is not just about getting people to keep listening longer, it is also about getting them to turn on earlier. Therefore, when you back-sell don't give the specific time of an item:

'At ten past nine we had a great interview with Simon Showman and he revealed the most intimate details of his holiday . . . that's all part of our Celeb A Day, Every Day item just after nine every weekday . . .'.

To someone who isn't able to listen just after nine, that link is wasted. However, if you say, 'Earlier we had . . .' then that same person may subsequently tune in as early as they can in an attempt to hear the feature.

Having said that, generally, forward sell (saying what is coming up) rather than back sell (saying what you have done). Back-selling may help set the tone of the station or help people tune in earlier the next day and as such is an effective blade to have in your Swiss Army knife of ideas, but it is teasing that is more effective at helping people listen longer.

## What you're going to do next

Nothing. That's right, you never 'do' anything on the radio. Many times you hear someone say something like, 'Later we'll be doing the school's news . . .' or 'Later Jenny will be doing the sport . . .'.

Just saying that you will be 'doing' something sounds mechanical, and as though you *have* to do it because there's a slot for it, or that is what you have been told to do. It doesn't persuade people to keep listening.

> **INFORMATION FOR INSPIRATION:** Give people *reason* to stay tuned, say what is in it for them. Make the relevance obvious.

So, 'Is your school mentioned in the schools' news this morning? If it is, you could win a Radio Super goody bag for everyone in your class . . . find out if you're a winner in ten minutes'. Or, 'There's an amazing comeback from one of England's greatest football legends. Kevin Keegan's been called up to play for the national side in Tuesday's match against France . . . details with Jenny Wren at half past'.

## The selfish syndrome

You slog your hardest to put together a three-hour show, and then no-one sits through it all. How rude! That's because listeners are selfish, they want to know what they are going to get out of the experience. They want to know how their investment of time is going to be rewarded, by asking themselves:

- o How will I be entertained?
- o How will I be informed?
- o How will you surprise me?
- o What will you give me that I can use?

So, make it really easy for them. Instead of saying, 'The latest report from the government says that . . .' say, 'I'll tell you how you can save money . . .'.

Pre-empt their 'what's in it for me?' question.

## Promote breakfast

Promoting the breakfast show is very important: it is the most listened-to and therefore the most important programme of the day so talk about it often and sell its strong features. But don't do this to the detriment of other programmes: breakfast is important, but so too are other shows.

Remember, the station is more than a series of presenters and certainly more important than just one. Work with your colleagues to promote each other. Always talk about other shows in your show. You will all benefit

## Promote specifics

It is simple and quick to say, 'Toby's here with Drivetime after the news', but it is also pretty pointless. However, if you say, 'On Toby's Drivetime after 4, your chance to get in the Life's a Beach draw for a holiday of a lifetime' or even, 'Toby's first song on Drivetime after 4 is the only one I can think of where the title is not actually included in the lyrics . . .'. It sounds more enticing. Yes, it takes more time to think up and to say, but it is also more creative and has more impact.

# Cross promotion

Do not forget to talk about other stations in your group if that's permitted. Cross promotion to your AM service, which is carrying the football commentary, is imperative to stop people experimenting with other stations' services.

**INFORMATION FOR INSPIRATION:** Throw ahead, don't throw it away.

# Teasing

## The rules of teasing

- Teasers don't tell: a tease intrigues. So don't tell the whole story in one of them.
- Involve the listener. Make it sound as though they will miss out if they don't listen longer. Hint at a reason to stay.
- Create minor suspense: 'In a moment I'm going to play you a hit song that mentions the man's name Ian . . .'. Say that a few minutes before you play Paul McCartney and *Let 'em In* and you have created listener involvement and suspense as they actually want to hear the answer.
- Hook them with an angle – then make them d-a-n-g-l-e.

## Teasing vocab

Many programme controllers hate presenters using the phrase 'coming up' as it says it reminds them of vomiting. There are other useful words and phrases to use instead such as:

- soon
- in a bit
- just around the corner
- next
- later
- in a moment
- before X o'clock
- in a short while
- remind me to tell you about . . .
- don't let me forget to tell you . . .

## Don't lie

Don't suggest that an item, say a competition, is 'just around the corner' when in fact it is an hour or so away. That is deceiving the listener who will be wary of placing their trust in you again. If an item is happening in the next 30 minutes then it is OK to use the general terms outlined above, but if it is in the next 60, say so.

## A wind-up

Saying that you will tell listeners something 'in the next 15 minutes' is not a tease, it's a wind up: you're *telling* people you're teasing them. Listeners want to know *why* you can't tell them *right now*. So explain that it'll be 'after this from Charlotte Church . . .'. Indicate you'd *like* to tell them now, but can't because you've got to do this other thing first.

# When not to tease

If you have got important or breaking news that will affect a lot of people, then you should not play with their emotions and annoy them by only hinting at what is to come. To do that will lose you listeners.

---

 **ACTUAL AUDIO**

PRESENTER:  and big problems on the M25 this morning, which has been closed in both directions. I'll tell you where and bring you the latest in ten minutes . . .

*Commercial radio station, November 2005*

---

In a situation like this, when you have got important or time-sensitive information, don't play games.

# A tease that misleads

You should also not lie in a tease and worry listeners unnecessarily or tempt them to listen by giving them an out-and-out untruth. They will find out what you have done and may not trust you again. For example, if you said that an EastEnders' actor has been found taking drugs on set and booted off the show '. . . I'll tell you who, next . . .' and it turns out to be a bit-part actor on one of the market stalls that no-one has ever heard of, then listeners will feel cheated of their investment of time in your programme.

Look after your listeners – don't abuse their trust or waste their time.

# Trails or promos

These are either:

- Straightforward, live, presenter-read mentions of future programmes or features, which tell (rather than tease).
- Or pre-produced (built) short 'adverts' for these items.

Both kinds of trails may be scheduled to run at a certain time (although that is most likely to happen with the produced trail) and are used to tempt listeners to listen longer.

In this section, I am going to give you a few ideas about the second type of trail, which are usually produced by the presenter or by a specialist producer at the station. They are not usually made by independent companies because they have got a short shelf life and so many are needed.

The style of these trails, the music used, the presentation, the content, all have to be carefully considered to reflect the station brand.

# Scheduling trails

It is most effective to schedule trails to play at a time when the person listening is likely to be interested in what you are trailing. For example, in a Saturday afternoon sports show it would be obvious to promote weekday breakfast-time sports bulletins and the midweek evening match coverage. The kind of caller to a gardening phone-in might enjoy the big band programme later that night – so tell them about it!

# Horizontal and vertical scheduling

It is also a good idea to think of promoting other programmes horizontally and vertically. A *vertical* schedule would place a trail in the breakfast show that told listeners what was happening later that day (think of the vertical programme listings in the newspapers). The thinking is that someone listening now may be available to listen during the day perhaps because of a day off work. (If you are specifically targeting workers then you will want to tell them about your station's drivetime show, of course.) So, vertical is down the hour, show or day.

*Horizontal* promotion is again best thought of in relation to newspaper listings. Each day the programme details go down the page, and each day is presented the same way on a page-by-page (that is horizontal) basis. In radio terms, someone who is listening to the breakfast show *today* will probably be interested in what is happening at the same time *tomorrow*. So, horizontal is across the week at this time.

# Promoting weekends

Think of trailing in terms of looking ahead to:

- The next hour.
- The next show.
- Later today.
- The next day.
- The weekend.

Promoting the weekend is all-important as weekday shows are essentially the same format day to day and because people's availability to listen (and to listen for longer) increases at weekends. TV stations start promoting their weekend coverage from the previous Tuesday as it gives the viewer something to anticipate.

You should certainly be talking about the weekend shows, the what's on events, the weather and what you are going to be doing from Thursday onwards. Then, over the weekend, certainly on Sunday, talk about reasons to stay listening for Monday's programmes.

# The right length

In constructing a music bed for a trail make sure that it is the correct length for the speech. In other words do not have a promo that lasts musically for 30 seconds if the speech ends after 25, or indeed have the music end before the speech. They should both end at the same time – faded music should do so under the speech content. The exception might be if you have a music stab or crescendo at the end of the promo. The item should be accurately timed. Not only is this professional, but will also help your colleagues with their backtimes and help an automated computer playout system that may be scheduling trails.

To explain, some stations have split ad-breaks (different sets of commercials that play on different transmitters on the same station, or on different stations in the same group). The computer will schedule the ads for each break depending on the 'rules' which have been set for each ad (how often it's to be played, and what time of day, as well as avoiding clashes with similar products in the same break), so each break is the same duration. 'Fillers' such as trails may be used by the computer to balance a break on one transmitter, but if yours has an 'awkward' duration such as 27, 33 or 41 seconds then it is less likely to be used than if it is 30, 35 or 40.

## A basic trail

Your own promos can be as basic as taking a magic moment from today's show and wrapping it with a top and tail announcement to promote tomorrow's show:

'On Wednesday's Chris P. Bacon's Breakfast Show we called film sensation Holly Wood and asked her about her new movie (clip). On Thursday's show Mr Nasty from TV's The Z Factor is with us. With news, travel and weather every 15 minutes, that's Breakfast, from 6 on Radio X.'

Note that the promo can be played for the rest of Wednesday and Thursday, because of the use of those day-names — it doesn't say 'today' and 'tomorrow' which would have dated it and made it unusable in the early hours of Thursday.

## Another basic trail

An alternative way to promote your own show is to record a short, dry trail and leave it on the playout system for other presenters to use. Then, when they have a ten second intro to a song, they can play your dry drop-in over the top, which idents the station and promotes your programme:

'Hi Sammy here, from Sammy and Vicki in the Morning — y'know I've got a thousand pounds burning a hole in my pocket for the winner of our Trivia Challenge . . . and that could be you! Listen from 7am tomorrow for more clues, here on Radio X.'

## Personal recommendation

Cross promote, highlight and talk up other parts of the station's output. Support your colleagues and encourage your listener to sample other dayparts. Personal recommendation is very effective. An ad-libbed line after a trail such as, 'Did you hear Chris with Holly this morning? It was great, especially when she sang him Happy Birthday . . . don't miss tomorrow, it's gonna be fantastic . . .', adds to the impact of the pre-produced bit. That's because it is you who said it rather than an unknown voice-over on a trail. Your listeners like you, that is why they are listening to your programme, so what you recommend to them will carry more weight.

**INFORMATION FOR INSPIRATION:** Devise one link for each of your shows that promotes a strong 'reason to listen' to another show.

# 21 Presenting programme items

So far we have looked at show prep, finding and booking guests, scheduling music, what to put in links, and teasing and trailing.

There are a few more elements that make up the programme, though. The next chapter is all about introducing music, but for the next few pages I'm going to share with you some dos and don'ts about presenting regular programme items, such as news, travel and weather. These items are usually scheduled at a specific time, and are called 'furniture features'.

You may devise other features, of course, and I'll give you a few ideas on how to do that too.

## The basics

### Furniture features

You will know where in the programme your 'permanently formatted junctions' or 'furniture' is: the regularly scheduled features which cannot be moved. These may be items which are the same on most programmes on the station, each hour, each day, such as news at the top of each hour, for three minutes, with travel news for two minutes at :15 and :45 past each hour, and what's on information every hour at :45. There may also be set times for commercial breaks.

> 'At the start I found it all very hair-raising, all these junctions kept coming up and they were really frightening. Talking to people was fine, just making it all knit together was the difficult thing.'
> Maggie Philbin, presenter BBC Radio Berkshire,
> Radio Academy event, November 2005

There may also be furniture specific to your programme, set items at set times in your show. These may be things like a Top Ten At Ten chart rundown feature at, unsurprisingly 10:00 each day or a shorter item like a Secret Sound competition each morning at 11:30. It is important to keep these features in the same place each day so listeners know where to find them.

Having said that, you may promote and schedule an item for, say, 11:30, even though it is not on air until 11:33. That's often OK − the listener will stay tuned for a few more minutes (indeed it is one of the main jobs of a presenter to get them to do just that), but never go to a feature *early*. The listener will, quite rightly, feel cheated if they keep listening for an item that you did before you said you would. And as I mentioned in the chapter on teasing and trailing, if you know an item won't be played within a certain period, don't say it will be: stay honest with the listener.

## Benchmark features

These are the regular items such as a particular competition or music feature, which are specific to your show or station, and are what you are known for.

Your station might be known as the one that has the daily Mystery Voice competition (such as Southern FM), the Birthday Bong game (a benchmark for Capital FM), PopMaster or Factoids (Ken Bruce and Steve Wright on Radio 2). Alternatively your benchmarks may be how you schedule your music (the No Repeat Work Day on Virgin), or even something as straightforward as 'double gold' (two classic songs) out of every news bulletin, or a 'then and now' artists feature.

> **INFORMATION FOR INSPIRATION:** Benchmarks are at the same time each day to help give a foundation and familiarity to the format.

## Stranded and branded

Some of the features in your programme won't be specifically yours, but station features also aired by other presenters. For example, the what's ons or a station promotion. That doesn't make them any less important, in fact it makes them more so as they are key identifiers of what the station does and how it sounds through the day.

> **INFORMATION FOR INSPIRATION:** If it's stranded then it's probably branded and you should give the item your full backing.

## Throw ahead

When you introduce a feature, also tease or trail something the other side of it. If you say, 'Now here's the travel news' you are giving an 'exit sign' to all those stay-at-homes for whom the travel news is of no interest or relevance. It is better to say, 'A classic song by Maroon 5 after the latest road news . . .' in an effort to keep them listening.

## Recorded annos

Incidentally, be careful how you introduce features that have their own drop-in introductions. It sounds awful and is a waste of time to say, 'Now here's the Mystery Voice on Radio X' and then play the recorded announcement (anno) that announces 'Radio X . . . the Mystery Voice'.

## News

Listeners to a music station do not tune in primarily for the news. They mainly want music, entertainment and companionship, but they *do* also want to be kept in touch with what is important to them.

If news is done well it can help make a music station sound local, immediate and in touch with listeners' lives. (See the definition of local on pp. 204–209.) If it is done badly then not only can it be a waste of time, but also a potential exit point.

**INFORMATION FOR INSPIRATION:** Many listeners may not turn on for the news, but may turn off because of it if it's not relevant, interesting or compelling.

Your station's news journalists have a difficult job. They have to provide enough information of the right type to satisfy listeners' demands, without getting too much in the way of the music that the listener has tuned in for in the first place.

News should be informing and, on the right occasion, entertaining. It is not supposed to be boring, and just a little thought and training will help your station's news team learn how to make it relatable and accessible.

## Timings into the news

During the day most of your news bulletins will be 'in-house', provided by your station's own team of journalists. At other times, usually evenings, overnights and weekend afternoons, they may come from an external provider such as IRN (Independent Radio News) or SNR (Sky News Radio). At the time of writing, BBC local stations' national news provider GNS (General News Service) provides a clips-only service and no self-contained bulletins.

Those 'networked' news bulletins will be 'clock start' and 'clock end'; that is, they will begin and stop exactly at a pre-set time. Usually that will be a clock-start of :00 (on the top of the hour exactly) and a clock end of :03 (exactly three minutes past). This is so all stations can 'opt-in' (take the feed from the outside source) safe in the knowledge that it'll be there and how long it'll last. This is especially important for automated shows: the playout system will automatically opt-in to that networked news channel between :00 and :03 each hour. The presenter of a pre-recorded show needs to know the duration of a bulletin so they can work out the running order and timings for the rest of their hour.

With in-house bulletins, timings are less important. Many BBC stations play the time signal 'pips' going into the top-of-the-hour news, so the jingle and the reader have to be ready. There is usually no reason (apart from professionalism) for a live bulletin into a live show to *finish* at an exact time, unless stations are joining up for a networked programme after local bulletins.

Commercial stations are no less professional than BBC ones, but their attitude is often more relaxed when it comes to getting into the news bulletins. At one commercial radio I read at, I was often kept waiting for anything up to three or four minutes before I could start the bulletin. This may be understandable if the delay is because the nail-biting final to a huge station competition overruns, but if it is simply because of a verbose presenter or one who has miscalculated their backtime, it is less acceptable. Journalists are busy people, and often have more than one service to produce and read a bulletin for.

As we saw earlier, listeners depend on the radio to schedule their routine, especially in the morning rush. They do this by not only listening to the actual time-checks, but also by when furniture features are on. So if you broadcast an 8 o'clock news bulletin at 8:04, you mislead the audience, upset the newsreader and look unprofessional.

**INFORMATION FOR INSPIRATION:** Getting into the news on time is important for the listener and a courtesy to the reader.

It also makes the station sound amateurish: if the news jingle says, 'News on the hour . . . this is Super FM . . .', does the reader come on and say 'It's 8:04 . . .' or do they lie to the listener and say, 'It's 8 o'clock . . .'?

> 'Bulletins on the hour should always be on time;
> the only exceptions are during live sport, or important
> breaking news. If in doubt, refer upwards.
> You can be slightly more relaxed about timings on the half hour
> but the bulletin should be no more than 2 minutes
> late — otherwise we're not providing a dependable
> service for the listener.'
> *BBC Radio Five Live Style Guide*

I'm not sure that I agree with that guideline: I don't think that being up to two minutes late is being 'slightly more relaxed'. Unless it is unavoidable, perhaps because of breaking news, maybe an important interview or news conference, I think it is showing a poor attitude to your job, your listeners and your colleague the newsreader. (For more on back-timing see p. 272.)

## News jingles

News jingles may be a few seconds long or they may consist of a bed of up to a minute. Either way, they often incorporate a list of towns in the station's transmission area, the name of the station and its frequency.

Longer beds can be tricky as you have to remember to start them, off air, at the correct time. There is little room for manoeuvre with these long news lead-ins, although some stations have a 'get out of jail' jingle — a shorter one to use in emergencies when you forget to start your usual jingle on time.

Longer jingles, usually with a music bed for 30 seconds followed by ten seconds of 'station ID' and pips (coming in from a separate source) will give you the opportunity to promote the next hour of your show.

## What not to say

Don't say, 'I'll be back after the news . . .', 'Let's cross over/hand you over to the newsroom', 'Join us when we return . . .', 'Come back after . . .' for three reasons.

First, you're not going anywhere, so you can't come back (you won't be on air, but then you don't say, 'I'll be back after this song from Madonna', do you?). As far as the listener is concerned, the news and music is all from the same studio and certainly from the same station. (Obviously, the same goes for 'Welcome back', 'Hello again . . .', after the news). The programme team may feel they are having a break, but the output is continuous — the bulletin should be perceived as a part of the programme, as it is by the audience.

Second, you should be promoting what is after the bulletin. So: 'I've got the Number One from this day, exactly a year ago, right after we've heard the latest on the hunt for the missing Blankshire businessman . . .' does two promotions in one.

Third, saying 'I'll be back after the news . . .' suggests to the audience that if you are going away then the news is of no importance, and gives them an exit point.

Everything the station does has value and the bulletin should be an integral part of your programme and the station's output.

# Credibility

Never ask a news presenter (or for that matter, any other presenter), a question *on air* that you haven't asked them *off air* and that *you know they know the answer to*. The news person's role is to know everything, and if they do not it damages their credibility and authority and that of the station.

Get credibility to work positively: when there is a big or complicated news story a presenter can quiz the prepared journalist, who has researched the subject and given the host the questions to ask. The reporter then 'miraculously' knows everything about everything!

 **ACTUAL AUDIO**

(After the sports bulletin presenter had run a story about Chelsea being fined £300,000 by the Premier League for 'tapping-up' Arsenal defender Ashley Cole.)

PRESENTER: Where does that money go? What's it spent on?
SPORTS READER: Err . . . I don't know. I can try and find out if you like . . .

*BBC station, June 2005*

---

'Comedian Sean Hughes startled listeners to the BBC's London radio station GLR yesterday morning when he interrupted newscaster Jason Kay to argue over the nationality of Formula One driver Eddie Irvine. Rounding off the 10am bulletin, Kay described Irvine — second in the Japanese Grand Prix — as a "British driver". "No, he's not," interjected Dublin-born Hughes who was preparing for his regular Sunday morning show on the station. "Eddie is Irish." With remarkable aplomb, Kay retorted: "He is Northern Irish." Sean and Jason are technically both correct. Irvine was born in Newtownards but lives in Dublin.'

*Daily Express, November 1998*

---

The news person is the voice of authority on the station. That is why some stations shy away from having a 'zoo' of characters, where the news person is encouraged to be silly or the butt of jokes. Their credibility suffers if they then have to talk about '200 dead in an air crash' moments later. Of course the news reader can be funny, react to something in the show or be a 'personality' reader (we are a long way past the days of a boring guy in a bow tie), but presenters should think twice before making them the subject of a jibe, or asking them a question that they may not know the answer to.

# News teasers

Presenters often fail to realise that by promoting the news in their show, they're dragging their listeners through another quarter-hour, and keeping up the figures for themselves (news isn't surveyed separately in a Rajar diary, as bulletins are too short).

A few other points:

- News teasers have got to be strong. Never promote a soft story – it's pointless. Indeed, it could have a detrimental affect on your attempt to pull listeners through.

o  It's not teasing the news to give a minute by minute rundown of when the next
bulletin will be: 'It's 20 to 12, so the latest news just twenty minutes away . . .', '. . .
and Jerry Journalist will be here in 14 minutes with the news . . .', 'Don't forget, all
the latest news with Jerry just 8 minutes away . . .'.

## Back teasers

These are also important. Most stations will insist that the presenter comes out of the news
with a sweeper and then two songs back to back. Fine, but later you could say something
that relates to the previous bulletin. It is part of your show after all. What about a straightforward line such as, 'Sounds like the police have got some interesting clues into where that
missing man might be . . . it must be awful when a relative just disappears like that . . .'. This
will mean you have got to listen to the bulletin, or talk to the newsreader, but a personal
thought creates a link between you and your audience.

In November 1998, a three-year-old girl disappeared from her front garden in Cheshire, when
her mother went inside to start cooking tea. A huge police hunt got underway, with officers from
three forces, the army, helicopters, dogs and local people. The whole country was talking about
how terrible it was. On Capital FM, presenter Neil Fox spoke from the heart when he vocalised
the same thoughts as everyone else around the country. 'Where is she? Has someone taken her,
or did she just wander off? How will she cope if she is out in this weather alone?'. Charlotte
was found the next day alone in the woods two miles from her home. Her mother subsequently
faced various charges (see pp. 96–107 Show Prep and pp. 134–138 The Law).

## Tip-offs

Any information that is called into you in the studio that may be a news story should be
checked with the duty reporter. They are better placed to confirm its accuracy before it goes
to air. Indeed, they may have had the same information and already dismissed it as untrue
or unreliable (or been asked by the police not to broadcast it for operational reasons).

One such possibility is details of a bomb warning. It may be that you are called on the
phone-in number with this information, because that is the one (rather than the newsroom's)
which is more often publicised. Imagine the scare and panic that you could cause by using
the phrase 'bomb warning' on air – that would be part of the aim of the caller who could
be a real terrorist or a disgruntled office worker or bored teenager.

Your station should have a form to be completed for these types of calls in the studio
bible (see p. 175). Remember as much as you can about the accent of the caller, their likely
age, what exactly they said and so on. Then pass the information to the newsroom. Bomb
scares will not usually be mentioned on air as they only encourage copycat calls and cause
distress. However, mention would be made about the knock-on effect of such incidents such
as railway station closures, or shopping centre evacuations.

Mention of road accidents and fires, if reported irresponsibly ('. . . so don't go shopping
in the High Street today . . .') could cause a loss of business for local traders, losing your
station money, as these businesses may be advertisers. Better to report the ' . . . accident that
has closed the High Street . . .' (a fact) and not give further comment.

## And finally . . .

Ask your newsreader to always tell you if they are going to include a funny 'kicker' story at
the end of the bulletin. Ask them what it is about so that you can prepare a comment or
reaction, or maybe play an appropriate song. Also ask them to always tell you if there is a

breaking serious story that they are going to include (especially if they intend to repeat it at the end of the bulletin) so you can avoid a music clash. (I mentioned this in the chapter, Music Scheduling, see p. 74. See also the chapter When It All Goes Wrong, pp. 327–344 and p. 332 for obituary procedure).

# Travel news

First, a reminder of some terminology. Traffic is the name given to the department at a commercial station which schedules the advertisements: they 'traffic' the ads. Understandably this can cause some confusion with those people who collate and present the traffic and travel news. 'Traffic' may also be used to describe the department at the BBC which books studios and lines to other remote studios! It's always safer then, to refer to 'travel news'. Some stations refer to 'traffic and travel news' in reference to their coverage of public transport information and possibly flight delays or ferry cancellations as well as road news.

> **INFORMATION FOR INSPIRATION:** Travel bulletins should be relevant, informative and accurate.

## Why we do it

Travel news is more than reading lists of road works and locations of accidents. It's another important link you have with the local community.

- The information is immediately relevant to them (it will take them longer to get to work or to get the children to school). Together with the weather, travel news is one of the key reasons why people listen to the radio. In the morning and afternoon drivetime around 50% of your listeners could be in cars.
- The information is about places that your listeners know, so news of a crash that has closed the high street is of interest to people even if they are not intending to use that road.
- Bulletins often complement the rest of the output. For example, sports fixtures can be affected by delays and traffic can be affected by weather, security scares, etc.
- You become a trusted source of local information which reflects your brand.

## How long and when it's on

Many stations will have bulletins every 15 minutes at peak drive times and every half or one-hour during the rest of the day. They are often 'balanced' in the hour, for example at quarter to and quarter past the hour; however, this is not always possible because of how the bulletins are produced (see below). LBC 1152 in London has travel bulletins every ten minutes, through the day, every day, at 11, 21, 31 and so on past the hour.

You shouldn't drop the travel if it is scheduled in your programme: 'reliability' refers to the scheduling as well as the content of bulletins. Bulletins should not be longer than necessary and rarely longer than a minute or so. If there is little or nothing to report, then the travel presenter should say so.

Travel presenters from remote sites may have a quick turnaround between you and another station (as explained below), so as well as being courteous to your listeners, it is also a courtesy to them to hit the travel junction on time.

## Information sources

The information is often collated and presented not at the station, but by a national company such as Trafficlink. This saves money and time for individual local stations. Trafficlink gets the information from sources such as the police (who can tell of accidents, or severe weather), councils and utility companies (who pass on details of long term road works for resurfacing or pipe-laying). Additionally they may have access to motorbike or car-based reporters (the AA used its network of staff in emergency call out vehicles to pass on news of delays for its travel news service) or access to CCTV cameras. Because so many stations now overlap, the information gathered from a few calls can be broadcast on several stations. You can see how this saves a duplication of effort by the travel news collators and those providing the information, for example those at police motorway control. Travel information from sources such as rail, air and ferry news may be collated and presented by the same provider, or the radio station may set up individual arrangements with staff at those separate companies.

## Jambusters

Another valuable source of road news is the listeners. A phone number (often called something like a 'Jambuster hotline') is given in each bulletin for listeners to call on their mobile phone, often together with the phrase 'as long as it's safe and legal to do so' (in other words, using a hands-free), and pass on details of tailbacks or the exact location of an accident. That information can then be double-checked with the authorities. Doing this encourages a high level of interactivity and provides a valuable source of information.

The problem with using a caller's contribution is that you don't know how accurate they are. Some information may be from people who deliberately want to mislead. Others may report a 'serious crash', which *looks* bad but is soon cleared up, or 'long tailbacks' (how long is 'long'?), or refer to 'heavy traffic' on a route that they don't usually use and so have nothing to compare it with.

Often the callers use a nickname, which can add colour to your bulletin, but beware of double-meanings.

Use callers' names regularly to:
o   Add credibility to the report.
o   Help personalise the bulletin.
o   Encourage a sense of belonging.

Some stations go a step further. Faye Hatcher at BBC Radio Gloucestershire records callers' contributions and then plays them out as part of the bulletin.

## Flying eyes

Some stations have access to a plane or helicopter to give travel reports from the best vantage point possible. The trouble is that even though queues can be spotted, the airborne reporter is unlikely to be able to know what caused it. That is why information is often collated on the ground and then relayed to a 'spy in the sky' reporter to read on air, together with their up-to-date view of the congestion that's been caused.

## Getting the news on air

As far as listeners are concerned, the traffic news broadcast by the station was collated *at* the station. So, Trafficlink reporters present their bulletins via an ISDN line which makes it sound as though they are in the station rather than in a regional centre. Reporters present bulletins

Radio Broadland's Black Thunders and Black Thunder Helicopter (sponsored by Sterling Aviation, Norwich). Courtesy: GCap Media and Barratt and Cole Photography, Norwich.

on several stations around the region during each hour and care is taken not to have one presenter on two which overlap, so the image of individuality isn't broken. Additionally, the hotline numbers for neighbouring stations are different, to further the effect.

BBC local stations that take a service such as this have to pay for it, but it still often works out cheaper than having travel presenters of their own. Commercial stations get the service for free, but in return give up some of their airtime to the travel company who sells it to an advertiser. It can be a great inducement for say, a car insurance company to have their advert heard on stations across the country at peak listening time and played right next to travel news when drivers are paying most attention.

Such an arrangement between a station and service provider is called a 'barter deal'. One where other goods are exchanged in return for airtime would be called a 'contra deal'. For example a hotel might provide a venue for a commercial station's Christmas party for free. That cost would then be written off against a certain amount of adverts for the hotel on the station. Remember, the only thing a commercial station can bargain with is its airtime.

Smaller commercial stations may be forced to make their own arrangements for their travel news because a central supplier may not consider it economically viable to collate and broadcast information, because of the small amount of money it'll make from selling the airtime.

## Getting into the bulletin

Do not play a travel jingle that says 'Travel News on Radio X' and then say, 'That's right, it's time for the travel news . . .'. Try to be a bit more creative. Listen to the previous bulletin and make a note of what is going on, or ask the travel presenter off air, what they are going to lead with on air. Then you can say something like, 'Well half an hour ago Tina, we heard that the M99 was down to 40 miles an hour northbound at Blankstown's exit . . . has that eased at all?' which provides a much smoother flow into the bulletin.

**INFORMATION FOR INSPIRATION:** Saying 'up next, travel' is not a tease. Telling listeners that they'll find out *where* something has happened, or *why* it has happened, is. Give them a *reason* to listen.

## Travel jingles

Travel jingles are distinctive so that they can cut through the mayhem that is the morning or afternoon rush, and 'signpost' the travel news to the listener. If you use a music bed remember to keep it low under the voice so you don't distract the listener.

RDS (Radio Data Service) tones are either an audible 'diddle-dee' tone, or an inaudible one. They may be used as part of the travel jingle, or be played in manually by the presenter. Either way, the RDS automatically retunes a car radio to the nearest station that is playing a traffic bulletin.

You can use the time between the end of your report and the 'out tone' of the RDS to promote:

o   Your station name and frequency – as new listeners may not otherwise be aware of you.

o   Your next song or competition – in the hope that some new arrivals may stay listening to you.

You should not deliberately leave the RDS on for any longer than this, say for several minutes at a time.

## The order of the info

It is important to prioritise the order of the information presented. The general rule is: motorways first, followed by A-roads, then public transport. Usually public transport would always get a mention even if it is just 'no reported problems', to reassure people. In exceptional circumstances, this order may be changed, for example, if your local airport is closed because of fog or the rail network is disrupted because of a crash. Then, work through the roads in a logical order – do not keep jumping back and forth across the area, or up and down the motorway in different directions.

Within that framework, always mention the location before the situation. This was brought home to me when I was travelling on the London Underground just before Christmas 2005. An announcement as I walked through Waterloo station gave some dates and times of a closure to add extra carriages to trains on the Jubilee line.

Can you spot a problem? The announcer had given all the information, but not in a 'user-friendly' way. They told me *when* something was happening and then *why* . . . and only then *where*. By the time I pricked up my ears when I heard something of relevance to me as a Jubilee line traveller, I'd missed the other details.

**INFORMATION FOR INSPIRATION:** Say *where* the problem is — then *what* the problem is.

## The result and the reason

Adding colour to a travel bulletin occasionally can help its 'interest factor'. Try to explain what is causing the tailbacks – people get less annoyed if they have the reason rather than just the result. So if a lorry has shed its load, try to find out what it is that's all over the road. Painting a picture makes the situation more vividly relatable.

## ACTUAL AUDIO

TRAVEL PRESENTER:  . . . because an escalator's fallen off the back of a lorry . . .
PRESENTER:  And we've had an e-mail, apparently police are taking steps to find out how it happened . . .

*BBC Radio Five Live, June 2005*

## Relatable words

Notice I say 'road' rather than 'carriageway' and avoided using 'incident'. These are boring technical words which make your bulletin less relatable. Use ordinary terms that your listener uses. Another to strike from your word-list is RTA (road traffic accident) which you call merely an 'accident'. Additionally avoid confusing the listener with phrases which make no sense: how many of your listeners know immediately what a 'fender bender' is?

## Correct words

Be careful about apportioning blame in the travel news. If you say, for example, '. . . delays on the A99 where a car has hit a lorry . . .' you've suggested that the car driver was at fault. Instead, say 'have hit each other', 'have collided', 'a collision between . . .'

You only need to use collide when both objects were moving or could have moved (for example two cars or a car and a pedestrian). But it's ridiculous and unnecessary to say, 'a car collided with a tree'. Say simply: 'the car hit a tree'. And certainly never use 'the cars collided *into each other*' as 'collided' means just that!

## Twenty travel tricks

1. Your travel news area – The vast majority of the travel information you broadcast will be within your TSA, however you'll sometimes stray outside it. For example, if there is a large accident 'over the border' which causes the closure of a major road that runs through your 'patch'. The tip is to think logically where are your listeners are travelling to. (KLFM in Kings Lynn, Norfolk, provided extensive coverage of the 2005 London bombings to its listeners, even though the station is 125 miles away. Why? Because train lines from their area go to Kings Cross, the scene of one of the attacks and they knew listeners would be concerned for their relatives.)

2. Say it once, say it twice – Just use the word 'shut' or 'closed', you don't need to say, for example that the train services are 'shut down' or a road is 'closed off'. If the story is affecting a lot of people then give the information again. 'Traffic is slow between Anyville and Anytown on the A999. An accident at Blanksville is making things slow in both directions . . . that's the A999, an accident at Blanksville, slowing things to a crawl both ways'. This makes it easier for those affected to register the details.

3. Mispronunciation – If the bulletin is being read by someone outside the area they may get the name of a town wrong, which is almost unforgivable. Make sure they only do it once. Tell them off air what the correct way to say it is, do not draw attention to it on air. In their defence, the travel presenter may be broadcasting on different stations

every few minutes so may not have had a chance to read their script beforehand. Alternatively, there may be a town covered by another of their stations which has the same spelling but is pronounced another way. Even though they should have a list of town and village pronunciations for your area in front of them, they may be forgiven for being thrown by some unusual road names!

4.  Routes and directions – If referring to the main road between, say Anytown and Blankstown, the 'Anytown road' is certainly appropriate to those listening in Blankstown, but to those in Anytown it's the 'Blankstown road'. It is probably better to talk about 'the road between Anytown and Blankstown', or 'between Blankstown and Anytown'.

5.  North and south – You can't 'head northbound' so don't say it! Drivers are either 'heading north' or 'northbound' – not a combination of the two. In fact, it is probably better to say, 'If you're heading to Charlottesville . . .' as more drivers will know that, rather than the actual compass direction. Alternatively, you may consider it clearer to say, 'Heading to Anytown on the A999 at Blanksville', for example, rather than 'westbound on the A999 at Blanksville'.

6.  Motorways – When talking about motorways, make sure you use 'northbound' and 'southbound' (or 'east' and 'west', whatever is appropriate), together with the junction number and name. First because most people know junctions by their name or number, and secondly because it helps reinforce what you are saying. The exception is where the road is commonly known by another name. For example, 'Where the M111 meets the M222' is probably preferable to 'the Redbury Interchange' if most people have never heard of it. Also cut out the verbiage. 'Between junction 7 and junction 8' can be edited to 'between seven and eight'.

7.  Road numbers – These are traditionally read as splits of two numbers, i.e., the A-twelve, or the A-twenty-two. However, roads of three digits are usually read separately: A one-two-seven, for example. You will, of course, find situations where this is not the case!

8.  How big is big? – With increasingly busy roads, a cut-off point has to be drawn with the kind of information that is broadcast. It is likely the station won't want news of minor crashes to be broadcast, especially if it covers a large 'patch', but *would* cover fatal accidents. That is because, with the attendance of fire crews and their cutting gear, ambulances and police, and possible road closures, these inevitably cause bigger hold ups and longer tailbacks. In short, a station will broadcast any traffic problem that's causing major delays or diversions and is going to affect a lot of people.

9.  Report good news – It can be just as useful to know that an accident is cleared and the situation's back to normal. This is so someone who heard about the initial problem and who's planning a diversion can be reassured that it's OK to stick to their original route. It is probably not enough to simply not mention the incident.

10. Don't cause upset – When presenting a news story about town centre delays, or problems on the way to a major shopping centre, avoid putting listeners off travelling to those places. For example, it is fine to say, 'Avoid the A99 London-bound at Adamstown because of a crash', but not to say, 'Avoid Lakewater shopping centre because it's gridlocked.' Obviously, report the congestion, but stick to the facts and do not take an angle that will concern shopkeepers who could be advertisers, listeners or both! Similarly, avoid overtly publicising an event. 'The (competitor station) Roadshow is on at the Blankstown Showground, so there's lots of traffic going there . . .'.

11. Local quirks – Every area will have these. For example, drivers from Essex into Kent cross the River Thames on the Dartford Bridge, but those going the other way use the Dartford Tunnel. It is all part of your local knowledge, on a local station, to be aware of these.

12. Local landmarks – Make your bulletin easy to follow and easy to picture by talking about local landmarks. For example, 'An accident on London Road near the Cross In

Hand pub . . .' or '. . . opposite the superstore . . .'. It is another way you can make the information relatable, even to those listeners who aren't drivers.

13. Rewriting – If you are presenting the travel news, try to rewrite your script to avoid the same phrases every single bulletin. It is inevitable that some lines will come round day after day, so think up some new ones to use. Instead of using the word 'queue', for example, you could use 'jam', 'nose to tail', 'congestion', 'tailbacks', 'bumper to bumper', 'stationary', 'choca-block', 'like a car park', 'crowded', 'struggling', 'slow-moving', 'stacked up', 'inching forward', 'driving in first gear', 'stop-start', 'trickling' and so on. (Another of my books, the *Find-A-Line* thesaurus (Findaline.co.uk) has dozens more alternative phrases for everyday travel news expressions.)

14. One-to-one – Remember that radio is one-to-one. Never say, 'Motorists are advised' or 'If you're all going to the county show then . . .'. Use language that is simple and relatable.

15. Weather and travel – Include bad weather in a travel bulletin if the problems are severe, because the two are so closely linked. But be careful not to patronise the listener and talk about shovels, blankets and flasks of warm tea as soon as the first flakes of winter start falling.

16. Cross promotion – Most stations have travel details on their website too, so mention this (and Ceefax, if necessary) so those without a radio later in the day (perhaps in an office) can check information on-line before they head for home. Point people to other bulletins on your station, for example the evening travel news if they are going to the big local match (and if they are not, a reminder to listen to your station's commentary.)

17. Banter – From time to time, there will be opportunities to banter with the travel presenter, but only do this at the end of a bulletin, and then only if both of you have something worth saying! Drivers get understandably annoyed when they miss their last possible exit to avoid a jam, because of studio wittering. If you have a comment to make after the bulletin, then prepare the travel reader off air beforehand: 'Tina, I've been talking about last night's *EastEnders*, did you see it? Good. Can I ask you what you thought about Dirty Den's ghost haunting the Queen Vic?'

18. Sign-offs – Bulletins usually end with the Hotline number and an SOC. This is necessary so if the bulletin is coming from a remote studio, the presenter knows when the reporter's finished.

19. Tip-offs – If a listener calls the studio with news of an accident make sure you get as much information as possible, and if appropriate pass it on to those who collate and present the travel news. When your bulletin comes around, listen to it carefully; do not use it as an opportunity for a daydream. There may be a story in there that you can pass on to the news room (for example about a major accident that has closed the local motorway). Journalists can be pretty unforgiving, quite rightly, if an obvious story was broadcast on your programme and you did not tell them about it.

20. Faster than the speed of travel – A problem with travel news is that a tailback can start within minutes of an accident but by the time the information reaches the collator (whether they are based with you or elsewhere), the accident and the queues may have been cleared. Be prepared to explain this if a listener calls, irate that a queue you mentioned does not exist.

## The weather

As with the travel, the forecasts you broadcast are a vital service which listeners should be able to rely on. Indeed, it is perhaps the single most-useful item that you give, as it affects every single listener. For those with pre-school children especially, the weather is an important part of their decision-making process.

## Where it comes from

It is usually from PA or the Met Office via the stations' news suppliers. Some smaller stations take forecasts from a TV text page. A few still have their own weather forecasters, and BBC stations often use weather presenters linked with their local TV news output, or via ISDN from a regional weather centre.

## When to do the weather

The majority of stations have the weather either going up to or following the news bulletin at the top and bottom of the hour. Some may also have a more detailed forecast at other times of the hour.

Some stations do things a little differently, to be distinctive. One presents the bulletin at ten-past each hour (a benchmark feature), and names it the 'Ten-Past Forecast', which helps the station sound distinctively different.

## What weather to do

In principle:

- At breakfast – say what it's going to be like today.
- In the morning – say what's going to happen this afternoon and tonight.
- In the afternoon – say what's going to happen tonight and tomorrow.
- On Thursdays – start looking ahead to the weekend.
- On Fridays – do the forecast for Friday, Saturday and Sunday to help people plan their weekend.

## Not a filler

One of the most important elements on a radio programme is the weather, especially in local radio as the forecasts are more specific. That is why forecasts are scheduled so regularly.
Just because you read it so often does not mean you can go into auto-pilot and throw it away. It needs to be presented clearly and read with significance (see below). Always make it count for those who have not heard it before.

Do not race through the weather because you are running late going up to the news, or so you can get to the next 'hot hit' – most people are genuinely interested in it.

## Weather as news

When the weather is making the news, you need to check that your script corresponds with what your colleagues have got. Sometimes weather stories are exaggerated to make good news reports, but you need to ensure the station's facts are consistent. It sounds unprofessional if the newsreader is saying 'the coldest winter in history', but the out-of-news forecast contradicts that.

## Relatable weather

As I keep saying, as a presenter you have to make everything relatable to your audience and easy for them to follow, and that includes the weather. Present it so it has relevance to how your listeners live their lives.

Ask yourself the following questions:

- On any given day, are you able to say with any degree of accuracy, what the temperature is?
- When was the last time you said the word 'precipitation'?

◻ Given that there's a big local outside concert tonight and you are on air now, how are you going to talk about the wet weather that is forecast?

Here are your probable answers.

◻ No. You'll probably say that it's 'pretty hot' or 'quite cold' or 'a bit warmer than yesterday'. So surely it makes sense to give a temperature in relation to something that Larry Listener already knows: yesterday's temperature! '16 Celsius, 61 Fahrenheit today . . . so that's a bit colder than the past couple of days . . .' is relatable and conversational.

◻ You probably never have. So why do some presenters say it? 'There's a chance of rain . . .' is better than, 'There is a probability of precipitation . . .'.

◻ 'So, if you're going to see Ray Dio and The Transistors tonight, better take a coat . . .' Again, this is more relatable and connects with the audience more than, 'It's going to rain . . .'. It takes a fraction of a second to make a great difference to basic and potentially boring content.

So, do not just make the weather a list of facts, make it relatable. Do not use Met Office-speak or read straight from Teletext. Make it friendly, conversational, and one-to-one. Like everything you read on air, read it through off air first and make the item your own.

> **INFORMATION FOR INSPIRATION:** People don't want to know about isobars, they want to know about the wind and the rain. They want to know whether it is going to be frosty and whether or not to put the heating on. They want to know whether to take an umbrella or a coat, leave early for work, or plan a weekend barbecue.

Think what events your listeners could be doing that will be affected by the weather and use those to prompt the angle for your forecast. These events could be washing the car, having a barbecue or mowing the lawn. Or, more relatably and specifically: walking down the beach (at Blankshire Bay), flying a kite with the kids (on Blankshire Downs) and walking the dog (in the Blankshire Country Park).

## 'Right now in Yourtown . . .'

Many stations give a local location when they read the weather: 'And right now in Yourtown it's 10 degrees'. Although this mentions a local place name, it is all a bit vague. When Thames Radio in south west London existed, its policy was to make the locations much more specific and relatable: 'Right now on Epsom Downs . . .', '. . . at centre court at Wimbledon', '. . . at the boat shed at Mortlake' and so on, which sounded much more in touch with the local community than merely mentioning local towns.

Now a little secret: the temperatures listed for such locations are usually fake! I worked for one large radio group where I was asked to merely pick any town I wanted from a list in the studio and then using the day's highest and lowest temperature and the time of the bulletin as a guide, simply make up the 'current' temperature for that location! I would suggest that your credibility can be lost if you do this too often.

There may be a station policy on whether you use Celsius and/or Fahrenheit and/or the word 'degrees' so make sure you know what it is. It should be in the House Style Guide.

# The forecast broadcast dirty dozen

1. Remember earlier I wrote about happy radio? Consider the effect of changing your weather language to be more positive. So 'mostly cloudy' becomes 'partly sunny', 'increasing cloudiness' becomes 'becoming cloudy'.

2. Forget percentages. It is not necessary to throw more numbers at listeners, so if the chance of rain is 30% say 'a slight chance', or if it is greater 'a good chance'.

3. Similarly, drop wind speeds. How many people know what a 15–20 mph wind feels like? Instead use the descriptions from the Beaufort Scale: 4–7 mph, 'a light breeze'; 8–12, 'a gentle breeze'; 13–18, 'a moderate wind'; 19–24, 'a fresh wind'; 25–31, 'a strong wind'; 32–38 'a very strong wind'; 39–46, 'a gale' and so on.

4. Do not say something like, 'Rain's expected *in the towns in the north of our area . . .*'. Listeners don't necessarily know where *your* area is! Make it relatable by naming towns or landmarks ('north of the M99').

5. Do not push people away. Do not say, 'It's going to be sunny *over* in Petersfield . . .' just simply say 'in Petersfield'. Reinforce where you are broadcasting to but not where you're based.

6. Consider that the word 'mild' means two different things depending on the time of year. In summer, a 'mild night' means it is chilly, and in winter a 'mild night' means it is relatively warm, so use this term with care. It sounds strange to say in autumn, winter or spring that it is 'warm' when it's say, 6 degrees. That's not warm, it's 'mild'.

7. Remember it is incorrect to say that the temperature is 'colder' or 'hotter'. The temperature is a number on a scale so it can only be higher or lower – it is the weather that's colder or hotter.

8. Some presenters will also make light of the phrase 'top temperature' when it is say 6 degrees in winter. 'If you can call that a top temperature!' they'll say. Well, yes, you can. If that is the most you can expect, it is the 'top'.

9. Confusion happens in March when the clocks go forward. It is the first day of British Summer Time, not the first day of summer. It can't be the first day of summer; spring only starts a few days before! Yet every year presenters get confused.

10. 'It's 16 degrees outside . . .'. The outside temperature is what you usually give! Drop the word 'outside'.

11. 'The rain's coming down . . .'. What direction were you expecting?

12. If the forecast's wrong, don't draw attention to it, as you will lose credibility and listeners. Most weather bulletins outside breakfast are only once an hour, that means that you have 59 minutes in which to keep an eye out for what is happening and update your script accordingly. That way you will avoid saying, 'Well, my forecast says it is sunny and dry but it's teeming down outside . . . what a load of rubbish . . . !'

# Weather updates

Refresh your weather bulletin often and look out of the window to see if it makes sense 'in the real world'. Mark Twain once said 'if you don't like the weather in England, just wait a minute'!

Drop mention of the day's 'high' or 'low' as soon as it has been reached. At the very least put it into the past tense: 'Today's high was . . .' is perhaps of some interest, but saying 'today's high is . . .' at four in the afternoon is pointless and ridiculous.

Try not to use the same terminology all the time. There are other ways of saying 'hot and sunny'! You may want to consider 'Sunday roast', 'a thirsty Thursday', 'hot and humid', 'things can only get wetter', 'scorcher torture', 'complete heat', 'like toast on the coast' and so on (more ideas via Findaline.co.uk). Be creative, but only if the information is still clear.

> **INFORMATION FOR INSPIRATION:** If something is in your programme presumably it's because you believe it has value for the listener. And if it's worth *doing*, it's worth *promoting*.

## Weather T&T

If you can, promote that you are going to be telling people what the weather is going to be like. Notice I didn't say 'that you are going to be doing the weather forecast' – see all information strands from the point of view of what value the item is to the listener, not what you are going to give them. Even a basic throw-ahead such as, 'It's umbrella weather this weekend, I'll tell you when you're going to need it after this from Atomic Kitten . . .' or 'What's the best day of the weekend to have a barbecue? I'll let you know after this . . .' or 'My grass needs its first cut of the year, but I keep putting it off. I may have the perfect excuse this weekend . . . the forecast follows this from . . .' are all better than suddenly reading the weather. Or saying that 'the weather's next', or worse, 'It's *time for* the weather . . .'. That phrase tells the listener that the only reason you are doing the forecast is because it's the next item on the running order, not because it has interest or value.

## Tides and inshores

Presenters at coastal stations may have to read tide times and inshore waters forecasts. Fishermen and sailors use these, and they can certainly take a bit of practice to present properly.

Tides give the name of a beach, the highest tide height, and the time that it will happen: 'South Point, 4.3 metres at 17.36', for example. There could be half a dozen of these, which you read as a list, although you can turn some of the information around; '. . . and finally at White Sands the high tide is at 17.39 and the height there, 3.9 metres'. You have to say them carefully, and always read what is written, for example, using the 24-hour clock rather than the 12-hour.

Inshore waters bulletins report the state of the sea. Here is an example of how a report may be given to you to read. Read it word-for-word, including my additions in brackets.

(This is the Inshore Waters report) Issued by the Met Office at 0500 (today) Monday 02 January, from Golden Bay to Splash Head.
Wind: southwest 4 or 5, backing south 5 to 7 then veering west.
Weather: rain spreading in, clearing to showers later.
Visibility: good or moderate.
Sea state: slight to moderate becoming moderate to rough, locally very rough in the north.
Outlook for the following 24 hours:
Wind: west 5 to 7, backing southwest 4 or 5, occasionally 6 in west.
Weather: showers dying out.
Visibility: good or moderate.
Sea state: moderate to rough, locally very rough in north.

Again, use the 24-hour clock (so say 'oh five hundred', for example), and say the date as simply 'the second of January'.

The tides and the inshores are two of the few occasions where you *don't* change the content or the words of something that you read on the radio to make it more relatable to the average listener. The scripts are written specifically for those at sea and are vital for their safety.

## Snowlines

At times of severe weather, stations often set up a Snowline service. Regular music and guests are replaced with rolling news, travel and weather information, details of school closures and cancelled events. Your job is to keep your listeners in touch with the information as it comes in and the problems they face.

Websites can play a huge role when it snows: get the details on line in an easy to read format, to reduce the deluge of phone calls, and the on-air clutter. Presenters can then point listeners to the website rather than reading out long lists of schools.

Snowlines (or similar services set up in the event of flood, hurricane, power failure, fire, major accident and so on) are:

o   A great public service in the truest form.
o   A way for the community to focus on the situation.
o   A local morale-booster.
o   A way to increase the listening hours.
o   A way to add new listeners (through unexpected sampling).
o   A way to make money (commercial stations may get their Snowlines sponsored).

All programme staff are expected to be available to broadcast. Backroom staff such as managers, sales and promotions executives are called upon to help collate information. If you live a long way from the studio and will have problems getting in, then arrange, with plenty of time, to stay locally. Leave may be cancelled and shifts altered as the situation develops.

If severe weather is forecast you owe it to your listener and employer to be ready to implement the plan of action, whatever the inconvenience to you (although avoiding putting yourself in danger).

Do not forget it is important to tell your listeners what you are doing as you do it. Reinforce the message of when the information will be given and why yours is the best station to hear it on. Do not be thrown by the excitement of the moment — remember to keep mentioning the name of the station. There will be lots of people who will be tuning to their local station for the first time.

During severe weather or disaster, simulcasting with your sister-station makes perfect sense. It saves duplicating your effort and maximises your audience. For example, during the terrrorist attacks in London in July 2005, Capital Radio joined with other London stations in their group, Xfm and Choice FM to give Londoners the full coverage of what was unfolding.

## Telling the time

There are few things that people want on a radio station more than time checks.

## How often

This is especially true at time-critical parts of the day such as weekday breakfast and afternoon drive times when a time check, or even two, each link may not be too much. But for other shows in the daytime, for whose listeners the time is less likely to be an issue, a time check about every 20 minutes is probably a good average (this is a suggested average, not a rule.)

Some programmers like their breakfast presenters to say the time in two different ways immediately after each other in each link. Their point is that because the information is so crucial for people getting the kids to school or themselves to work, once is not enough. They say listeners may hear that you have given a time check but have not registered exactly what it was so do it twice and they can't fail to get it! For example: 'Gwen Stefani's latest on Radio X breakfast . . . 8:20 . . . twenty past eight . . . and your chance to win a Porsche for the weekend in Porsche Or Pull in five minutes . . .'.

## How to say it
Give the time to the listener as you would give it to a friend.

So:

- Out go DJ clichés such as 'Coming up on 8:20', 'It's 20 after 8', 'It's 11 past 8', 'It's 40 before 9', and so on.
- Drop other time-related DJ clichés: 'Here's a time check', 'The top of the hour', 'The bottom of the hour', 'Minutes past the hour of', 'It's 4:35 *right now*'.
- In the second half of an hour, it's more relatable to say '20 to 9' than '8:40' as people work in relation to what's still to come, not what's been and gone.
- Super-precise time checks are also unnecessary ('It's five and three quarter minutes past ten'). Instead make use of words such as 'nearly', 'just after' and so on.
- Drop the phrase 'It's *time for* . . .'. 'It's time for the news', 'It's competition time' – just say, 'Here's the news' or simply ask the competition question.
- Avoid tautology: 'The doors open tomorrow morning at 9:30 am'. AM means in the morning so either say 'tomorrow morning at 9.30' or 'tomorrow at 9.30 am', not both.

## Time in teasers
Always tease and trail what is coming up in the show, especially what is the other side of a potential exit point. In these circumstances, time references are quite acceptable ('In the next half an hour', 'Before 12 o'clock') – but do not be either too specific or lie.

'Coming soon', 'in the next few minutes', 'later this hour' are all handy phrases, but think of what your listener's perception of these phrases will be. 'Coming soon' would mean, I would suggest, in the next ten minutes, whereas 'in the next few minutes' would give the impression of the next five. 'Later this hour' could mean different things depending on when you say it. So, if you say, 'Coming soon, the grand draw for our hot air balloon flight over the Pyrenees . . .' and you hold off doing that draw for half an hour your listeners will be rightly annoyed with you for misleading them.

## Afternoons and evenings
Be careful when saying 'good afternoon' or 'good evening'. In the summer, 5 o'clock is probably still regarded by many as the afternoon. In the winter, when it is cold and dark, it is certainly perceived as the evening.

## The verbal crutch
Here is another example from my experience. A presenter on a Sunday show gave a time-check in three of her four links: 'It's 6 and a half minutes past 1', 'It's 12 minutes past 1', 'it's 22 minutes past 1'. Arggghhh! I suspect she was using the timecheck to give her space to think of what else to say, an issue that would come out (I hope) in a feedback session with her

programme controller, or even a self snoop. Regular and super-accurate time checks such as these are simply not necessary on a Sunday afternoon, when time isn't critical for your listeners and gives the impression that you haven't prepped properly.

# Ad breaks

## Going in to a break

Never draw attention to your ads. Do not say, 'I'll be back after the break', you aren't going anywhere and you hope your audience isn't either! Saying this gives an exit point, an opportunity to leave the station. Similarly, 'welcome back' after a break should also be a banned phrase!

---

 **ACTUAL AUDIO**

PRESENTER: We're going off on a commercial break — back in a sec.

*National commercial station, January 2006*

---

Also consigned to the DJ dustbin are 'after these messages', 'after the commercial break' or the cliché 'after we've paid the rent'. Instead, promote what's happening the other side of the ads by saying 'soon', 'next', 'in two minutes' and so on.

Perhaps the one time when you can refer to the ad break is when its short duration is a selling point. Most station's breaks are around three minutes, but if you have one that's only *one* minute, it may be something to occasionally mention to stop the listener reaching for the dial. 'Blink 182 are just sixty seconds away . . .', 'The Foo Fighters in two ads' time . . .'.

Some stations say that a link into an ad break should be limited to 20 seconds, so the duration of a presenter's talking doesn't significantly add to the speech block that follows.

## In the middle of a break

Some stations have a policy of stopping an ad-break halfway through to tease the next song. Check if you are allowed to do this. If you are, interrupt the break between commercials, and about two-thirds through a break, to make a short comment such as 'Radio X, where The Prodigy are next . . .' and then resume the break. Doing this re-establishes the station name and is an opportunity to throw ahead.

## Coming out of a break

Most commercial stations have a policy of always playing a jingle and then a song out of an ad-break. This is to re-establish the identity of the station and get back to the music. As listeners will have just heard two or three minutes of talking they will not want another minute or so from the presenter.

Be careful playing a jingle out of a break though: most stations' trails are scheduled at the end of breaks and often end with a station ID, so it may not be necessary for you to play another one straight afterwards.

Come out of breaks the same way as you come out of the news, with an upbeat, strong song that's representative of your station.

# The what's on diary

These are variously called Community Events, the Information Exchange, Public Service Announcements (PSAs) and so on but the point of them is the same:

- You mention charity events on the station to stay connected to the area you broadcast to, even if no listener actually goes along.
- By saying the names of local people and places you continue to have relevance to your listeners and the way they lead their lives, by giving them ideas of what to do with their hard-earned free-time.
- You give the impression of doing good work by publicising charity events for free.
- It is information listeners can't get from a national station.

'We do the usual thing you'd expect from local radio — we cover jobs and what's going on in the local area — but we also run programmes every weekend specifically geared towards local events. If local people are holding tea dances, jamborees, jumble sales and things like that, they generally can't afford to advertise. So we cherry pick five or six events and call the organisers or get them into the studio to represent themselves live on air, to give an idea of what's going on at their event. We're getting local voices on the radio and hopefully helping to push more people along to local events.'

Derek McIntyre, Programme Controller, Your Radio, Scotland,
X-Trax magazine, July 2005

On some stations' details of events, the jumble sales, blood donor sessions and clubs wanting new members, are pre-recorded and played out at certain times each hour. On others it is up to each presenter to read what they fancy from a file of items left in the studio. Many presenters read a tease from a couple of the most interesting items, and then direct listeners to the station website for more information on those and other events.

## But they're boring

So you think that reading information about another jumble sale is boring? Perhaps you had better get a different job. First, such announcements are the life-blood of local radio stations as the events relate your station to the area you serve (note the use of the word 'serve'). Second, it is up to you to present the information so it's *not* boring!

Presenters have traditionally seen reading what's ons as fillers – something to do when they are waiting for the travel presenter or to pad with up to the news. This should not be the case. Every moment on air should count.

It is true that each item is only important to a very limited number of people, that is why you have to work to make it of interest to many more. And if you do that, and speak to those who are interested personally and help make the event a success, you've strengthened the station's bond with that person and their organisation.

**INFORMATION FOR INSPIRATION:** Use what's ons to your advantage.

## How to choose an item

Choose your items to reflect your target listener. The events you mention say as much about the station as the music you play, so even though the local flower group has sent in event details to a rock station, does not mean it has to go on air.

## How to read an item

There is a skill in presenting the sometimes tedious information. Just as I have mentioned before, the way is to add something of yourself to these items to make them relevant and interesting to your target audience.

Often each pre-written what's on script will be in the same format, such as the date and time of the event, then what it is, where it is and a contact number, all on a pro-forma sheet. And that is where the main problem lies. It makes it very tempting for the presenter to read out each item by simply working their way down each sheet, so you get 'On the 22nd of June at 2:30 in the afternoon, there's a jumble sale at St Peter's Church Hall, on London Road, Blankstown. There'll be refreshments and a bouncy castle and admission is 50 pence . . . On the 19th of June at 7:30 pm there's a meeting of the Blankstown Neighbourhood Watch at the secondary school on Freemantle Lane. Tea and biscuits will be available . . . On the 23rd of June . . .'. You get the idea.

So if Rule One for reading what's ons is to make them relatable to your audience (so details of a tea dance aren't given out on a chart station, for example), Rule Two is to vary your order of delivery within a certain format. In the example above, anyone who was interested in the jumble sale would have missed when it was on because that information was given first. So if the date comes first, repeat it after you've given the other information.

The next point is to approach the items with a bit more creativity and relatability. This does not have to be convoluted, but will help draw people in to what you are telling them, rather than merely broadcasting a list of facts: 'I was clearing up the other day and realised that I just couldn't fit any more clobber into the cupboard under the stairs. What started off as a clear up turned into a clear out and I've now got a boot-full of jumble that I really must take down to St Peter's on Saturday for their jumble sale . . .'.

Alternatively: 'I always love a good bargain, and if you do too . . .', 'Here's a chance for you to help St Anthony's Hospital – just in case one day they have to help you . . .', 'If you've been spring cleaning but are loathed to just throw things in the bin . . .'. Just four ways of introducing a straightforward jumble sale notice in a slightly more creative way. Each one took about ten seconds to think of, and you're in the creative business.

Read items conversationally and sincerely. Never make fun of them because if you do that, you risk losing the organisers of the event and other listeners too.

Never refer to 'the public' ('. . . and it's open to the public' and so on). People don't see themselves as the 'public', instead say '*you* can get in for two pounds fifty . . .' or whatever.

## How to read dates

Do not give the listener extra work!

If you simply give a date, say for the neighbourhood watch meeting mentioned above, this is the thought process that everyone listening has to go through:

- What's today's date, I think it's the 13th, let's have a look at my watch, yes, the 13th.
- So the neighbourhood watch meeting is on the, what did they say, the 19th?
- OK, so if today's the 13th and it's Thursday that means that the 19th is . . .
- Hold on . . .
- OK that makes it next Wednesday.

Why don't you, the presenter just say 'it's next Wednesday'?

## ACTUAL AUDIO

TRAVEL PRESENTER: (Saturday night 8th January) And that line will be closed on the 14th and 15th of January for engineering works . . .

*BBC local station*

## How long should each item be?

Despite adding the relatable angle at the top of the listing, try to keep the rest of the what's on short and clear. Occasionally repeat the time and place of an event for those who are only half awake, but don't do this for every item or it will get very tedious.

Remember the what's on is a headline, not a report. Give the 5Ws (who, what, where, when and why) and then move on.

## The extra mile

If you want to make your what's on more creative but are lacking a piece of information to give it that extra 'something', then call the organiser and ask them for some more details about the event, the cause or the stalls. An easy two-minute task.

## Beware the cheapskate!

Plugs are usually for charity and non-profit making events, so be careful if you are sent information for moneymaking businesses (such as tours around the local stately home) or commercial ventures (an open day at the local car showroom). This would be against BBC policy and a commercial station's sales team would understandably be cross with you for giving a free mention to a company that should have paid!

## Action Desks

BBC local stations run Action Desks in partnership with the Community Service Volunteers (CSV) and help local charities and organisations by getting them featured on the radio promoting them to an audience of thousands.

Action Desks can be used to:
- produce an on-air appeal – perhaps for volunteers to drive a community minibus or to give a make-over to a hospice garden.
- running on-air features to publicise things as crime prevention or adult education.
- providing a confidential off-air helpline service for listeners, giving contact numbers for charities and agencies who can help them.
- running events in support of local campaigns.

Again, such work by stations' Action Desks provides strong links with the community and enhances its reputation.

# Other programme items

## Fascinating facts

In these days of the internet, most fascinating facts aren't fascinating. Your listeners are likely to have been sent them from friends already, so you will have to do something pretty special with them before using the same material on air.

Again the trick is to make the feature your own by adding something of your personality to the list of information. Steve Wright's 'Factoids' on Radio 2 are presented in a tongue in cheek way, and the presenters add their own spin on each item as they try and outdo each other with increasingly bizarre facts. Often an item leads one of the presenters off on another direction completely, before being brought back to the feature.

So you could:

o   make the feature a challange to find X facts in X minutes.
o   link the facts with a current news story.
o   play on-air true/false competition with the facts.
o   have listeners give marks out of ten for how fascinating each fact is.
o   check out the facts with an expert who can explain or disprove them.

With some time and creativity you can make such a feature your own.

## Celebrity birthdays

 **ACTUAL AUDIO**

> PRESENTER: The Russian author Dostoevsky [pronounced: dos, dostovskee], who wrote *The Brothers Karamazov* [said falteringly], was born today in 1821
>
> *Commercial radio station, November 2005*

First ask yourself if you have heard of the 'famous' person whose birthday it is. If not, then it is pretty certain that your audience hasn't heard of them either, and therefore won't care.

Second, does the person whose birthday it is have any kind of link with your target audience? To tell an audience of teenagers that it is the birthday of the first BBC television newsreader, will mean nothing to them. Indeed it may alienate them. The above Actual Audio was on a breakfast show to a station targeting 15–34 year olds. The presenter obviously hadn't heard of the writer (he couldn't pronounce his name) but still read it out. That was probably simply because it was the next item on the show prep sheet he'd bought.

The first two rules then: do they know them? and do they care?

Third, do not say when someone famous was born. If you tell me they were 'born today in 1969 . . .'. I have to stop and work out how old that makes them today. If you ask someone in the office how old they are, they will give you their age, not their year of birth! Do the maths for the audience, make it easy for them. Say how old they are now.

Fourth, linking with the point above, if someone is dead (as well as thinking about the relevance of mentioning them at all), say what age they would have been had they still been alive, not the year of their birth.

Too many birthdays on such a list gets boring. Limit yourself to three or four of the most interesting and relevant people, about whom you have got something personal to say.

**ACTUAL AUDIO**

PRESENTER: Guess who's 41 today . . .

*Commercial radio station, November 2005*

Where do I start . . . ?

# This Day In History

These features are very popular with presenters because they can simply read out a list of dates and events from a prep sheet. They can get away with doing as little work as possible. Like every item you do though, it has to be interesting to your audience. Preferably that means that it is local, but remember, being local does not automatically make an item interesting! 'Today in 1981, the mayor of Blankstown died at the age of 75.' That is completely local and completely boring! 'Today in 1981, the mayor of Blankstown, Indiana, USA, died when his ceremonial chain got caught in his kitchen's waste disposal unit . . .'. That is *not* local, but *is* interesting.

Look for what is local to people's sphere of interest: if that is geographically local, fantastic! If it's not, it's still great. Just make sure it *is* interesting!

Does the event have to have been in *recent* history, to make it interesting? No. Some of the biggest selling genres of books are westerns and historical novels. Some of the largest grossing box office films are sci-fi. Just because something did not happen in our lifetime, it does not mean it is not of interest.

So, are This Day in History features popular with listeners? Yes, if they are interesting, they can be.

The item may:

o Be amusing (like the mayoral story above).

o Be ironic ('This day in history was the day the EMI record executive turned down the Beatles, because he said that guitar based groups were on the way out').

o Make listeners think a little about where they were when they heard the story the first time around . . .

o . . . or the changes that have happened since.

But only if the item is interesting.

Once you have mentioned the event, you can make it more relevant still by adding a comment of your own, either for listeners or for your co-host to react to. For example, you could make a humorous comment: 'It was today 35 years ago that the London Marathon was first run. I've never entered: it's not the 26 miles that bother me, it's the lap of honour if I won . . .'.

Or set up a phone-in topic: 'It's this time of year that thousands of birds fly back to Britain after spending the summer in Spain. Why do you reckon they go back there every year? Is it because they have no imagination for better holiday locations, or they want to hook up with young Spanish waiter-birds? Call me with your suggestions . . .'.

Or use the item as a springboard to a trivia question: '. . . the anniversary of the TV prison sitcom *Porridge*. But can you tell me, what linked *that* show with *Only Fools and Horses*? Call me on . . .'.

So, add something of your own to the information: something that no one else can give. What is your own take on the story? What makes you laugh about it? Why? Share that with your audience.

One more thing: it is usually best not to use items that are too serious, or about death: 'Today in 1975 an airliner crashed in the Himalayas, killing all 330 people on board'. Not much fun is it?

## Lists

Items such as the Top 10 DVD Rentals This Week or Last Week's Most Watched TV Shows are, frankly pointless, unless you can add something of your own to the list.

Do your listeners really care about such lists? Have you ever heard anyone talking about them? No. However, they may be interested in a good DVD to hire this weekend, the plot and who is in it . . . not simply what place it is in the charts. So give the listener that kind of information, or add something of your own. What film have *you* seen recently? Was it any good? Why? What were the best bits? What should people look out for? What mistakes were made, or what were the holes in the storyline that didn't add up?

And if you do do a Top Ten list, present the items from 10 (the least popular) up to 1 (the most popular) not the other way around.

## Entertainment news

Judging by the popularity of magazines such as *heat* there's certainly a call for this type of information and your programme controller will tell you whether it's appropriate for your station's demographic. Remember though, that if your station doesn't play Slipknot then there is no point telling listeners about the band's latest exploits. Similarly, if yours is a rock station, those tuning in probably do not want to hear about what Britney Spears has been up to.

**INFORMATION FOR INSPIRATION:** If you don't play 'em, why talk about 'em?

The only exception to this would be if the item is of general interest and appropriate to your audience for a different reason. For example, rock music fans may have been interested in the Michael Jackson trial because of his name and status and the implications of the case.

## Police File

Some stations, mainly BBC locals, broadcast weekly appeals from the local police, often called Police File Crimestoppers. Years ago these would be presented by the officers themselves in traditional mono-tones and with no relatability to the audience. They are now presented by a press officer down an ISDN line and are much more listener-friendly. Such features are good public service content and add to the localness of the station. If one is on your show, make sure that you alert the newsroom before each broadcast: it may be that the crime featured is one that could make a news story.

## Other unique features

Finally there are a few features that are particular to certain individual stations for specific reasons:

- o  Visitors' List − I was fortunate in 2001 to be asked to spend a week training staff at the radio station on the British dependency of the Falkland Islands in the South

Atlantic. Eight thousand miles from the UK and 300 miles off the coast of Argentina, one of their most popular features was who was visiting the islands each week. This was a hangover from the days before the British Army was based there, but was still of great interest to the Islanders. So, station staff regularly read out a passenger list of those on board the plane that was landing or ship that was docking.

▫ The Lamb Bank – There's an annual problem for sheep farmers in Cumbria as many ewes reject their lambs after birth and won't allow them to feed. Running from Christmas until May every year since 1973, the Lamb Bank on BBC Radio Cumbria gives out the number and breed of lambs, along with details of ewes in milk who may be able to feed them – a unique information exchange!

▫ Obituary notices.

'Obituary notices are one of the most listened-to strands on local radio and they're quite specific to Ireland. There's a tradition here to provide community support for bereaved families, through attendance at funeral homes and churches. So in these days of urban sprawl, the obituary service is vital for people to pick up that information easily and quickly.'

Clem Ryan, KFM (County Kildare) Station Manager,
X-Trax magazine September 2005

# 22 Presenting music

'The music is the star; the presenters are there
to entertain in an informative way.
The bulk of our speech content is material that helps
a listener enjoy the music more, so it's information
about the artists, the song and what's going on in
country music — it's not making jokes about what we
read in the paper that morning.'

Pat Geary, Station Manager, 3C Continuous Cool Country,
X-Trax magazine, August 2005

We have already looked at choosing music and scheduling it across the day, in this chapter I will give you some pointers for presenting music: introducing songs, outroducing them (what you say when you have played them), and some ideas on basic mixing.

## Introducing music

### The basics

It is the start of your hour and you have got a whole playlist of songs, but do not be tempted to tell everyone what they are. Don't promo a whole hour of music, because if the listener doesn't like anything you are promising, they may switch off. Remember: 'programme run-downs are for run down programmes'.

Instead mention two or three examples to whet the listener's appetite, and make those songs representative of the music you play. So, if you have a 'one hit wonder' (someone who only had one hit song) then it is probably not worth promoting, as it will be obvious to the listener what you are going to play. Instead choose two others that are different in tempo and tone from each other. Maybe a current and a '90s' track (if that example fits with your format), or a female artist and a boy band, or a pop hit and a classic ballad. But not more than three songs at a time.

Only mention artists, not songs. The reason is that it gives a greater chance that a listener will stay tuned to hear if their favourite is the one you've chosen. If you say it's *Material Girl* next, and someone doesn't like that song, they won't want to hear it. But if you simply say that Madonna's next, they will stay listening in the hope that it is going to be, for example, *Hung Up*.

Be careful about promoting songs later in the hour – there may be a chance that time restraints mean you won't get to one of them. That is going to make the listener angry that they trusted you and invested time in the station that they got no return on.

### What are you playing?

Although the terms are interchangeable, you do not play 'records' (as the music comes from CDs or hard disk), 'tracks' (as they are essentially not album tracks) and they are not 'tunes' (too cheesy). You play 'songs'.

## Specialist music shows

Presenters on this kind of programme will give a lot of background information to the aficionados listening. If that is you, you will certainly have to know and care about the music. That means a lot of research: surfing the net, subscribing to relevant publications, talking to producers and record companies and so on.

'The new release by Pure Tempest from the album *Days of Thunder* which is out on March the 27th on the Xylophone label, their first album with them, of course, since they ended their contract with Triangle, and that means it was recorded at the world-famous Cathedral Road studios in Norwich, and produced by Norma Collier. And I think you'll agree that you can certainly hear her influence coming through on the bass riff there . . .'

**INFORMATION FOR INSPIRATION:** This kind of link can give added value to the listener, and shows that the station is employing someone who knows and cares about the music they're playing. And that gives credibility to the presenter and the station.

On this kind of show, you may be able to use the 'expert listener' to help you with research. Ask them for feedback on new releases or to remind you of key dates or changes in band line-ups. Such listeners are very loyal and will probably listen for the entire show. This will boost your hours listening column in the Rajar diary, although there'll be fewer listening compared to a more general programme.

Listeners to specialist shows will pick up on the slightest inaccuracy. If you set yourself up as an expert your credibility has a long way to fall if you get something wrong and may take a long time to recover.

## A standard intro

Most people listening to most shows on most stations neither know nor care to know much about the music they are listening to. Giving too much information would be a turn-off for them. Most stations will not want you to say much more about the music than the name of the song and who sings it. Your listeners haven't tuned in to hear a lot of facts, or indeed your opinion of the songs you play.

Having said that you may want to occasionally mention information such as:
- The song's performance in the current charts.
- Its chart position in an older chart or year.
- A tour or an album.
- The artist's birthday if it's *today* (see links with the music below).
- A *new* news story about them.
- Trivia about the song or band (see trivia and clichéd links below).

'Occasionally' means that this kind of information may be mentioned on one song an hour, maybe two. No more, or you start to alienate most of your listeners.

This information can come from:
- Newspapers and gossip columns.
- Internet prep services.
- Artist's websites.
- TV shows.

Build up your personal collection of trivia. When I presented a '70s/'80s show on Essex FM this is what I did: every time I came across a snippet of information on a core artist I made a note of it so I could mention it the next time the song came around. (I know of another presenter who additionally dates each item when it is read, so he does not use it too often.)

## Some say . . .

It is usually better to announce the name of the song *before* you play it, and the name of the artist *after* you play it. That's because after someone's heard a song and enjoyed it, they are more intrigued to know who was singing it. This is especially important for new songs. If someone hates Kylie then announcing that this is her new song may turn that listener off. If, on the other hand, they hear the song and like it, they may be intrigued to hear who sang it. Adding a small amount of suspense may make them stay for another three minutes!

## The artists and title

Of course, you don't always have to give these details as they appear on your screen if you are being creative/compelling and easily understood/relatable.

Say you have just played *Summer Drive Home* by The Dollar Bills:

- 'The Greenbacks on Radio X . . .' you could occasionally use a shorthand for the group, if it's a recognised nickname. But you won't be the first to call Madonna the Material Girl, so please don't!
- 'Ahh, open-topped cars and girls in T-shirts . . . The Dollar Bills on . . .' a comment about the title of the song is another way of back announcing what you have just played, without actually giving the title. (Again, be aware of DJ clichés: 'The Beatles *Ticket To Ride* . . . and I never knew they visited the Isle of Wight . . .' and so on.)

## Classic songs

If the song is an all-time classic it may not need a name check. This will depend on your station House Style, but to back-anno Rod Stewart's *Sailing* or The Rolling Stone's *Brown Sugar* may insult the intelligence of your audience. Also, if the name of the song is the first or last words in the lyrics, be careful how you phrase your link, or it will sound as though you haven't been listening to the output: 'Now here's The Beatles and *Help* . . .'.

---

 **ACTUAL AUDIO**

PRESENTER: Here's Duran Duran and *Wild Boys*
SONG: 'Wild boys, wild boys, wild boys, wild boys . . .'

*Commercial station, November 2005*

---

## Trivia

This is another great way to occasionally talk about what you're playing: 'The Dollar Bills from a time when songs came out on vinyl. And the flip side to that song later became a huge hit for . . . who? I'll tell you after the travel news with Emma Leven . . .'.

I remember years ago several UK stations broadcast Casey Kasem's American Top 40 each week. One side of a break he would mention facts about the bands or artists that he was going to play the *other* side: a classic tease. I cannot remember those specific links, but it took me two minutes on the internet to find the *kind* of comments that he made – that you could:

- 'Next, the British band that had *thirteen* hits in the US charts . . . at the same time'.
- 'The first time female singers took the top three places in the charts in the US was in 1986. The songs were *When I Think of You* by Janet Jackson, *Typical Male* from Tina Turner . . . and the song I'm going to play next . . .'.
- 'The next song was written for a horror film, and was sent to the producers of a hit film about a girl who wants to be a ballerina, by mistake. And that's how it got to be famous.'

Note that these are not *trivial* facts such as chart positions or year of release which are both easy to come by and easy to forget. These are *trivia* (there is a difference) that perhaps set the song in a little more context and give the listener something of interest. They stay tuned till after the break to hear the answer and then they've learnt something of interest. They've been rewarded for the time they've invested.

## Stories of the songs
'Bill of The Dollar Bills says he wrote that song, not about cruising in the summertime, but about the front run-in at his boyhood home in Summer Drive . . . but people have misinterpreted it for years . . .'. Background to the song and how it got to be written, also gives it significance to the listener.

## Personal connections
Sometimes mention the memories the song brings back to you, or how you feel when you hear it. When you share your memory you'll trigger someone else's. And if you reveal something about yourself, the listener gets to know you better.

It could be the year that the song played all summer long. The one that came out when your daughter was born. The one that your dad always did a daft impression of. You get the idea.

- 'I remember when that was first out . . . August 2003 . . . odd because it was one of the wettest summers on record . . . The Dollar Bill's summer offering on Radio X . . .'
- 'I was 16 when I downloaded that song on my first iPod. We'd only just got broadband and I was at home in Worcester Terrace in Blankstown when . . .'
- 'Summer Drive Home . . . it's great isn't it, when you come back late at night from the day at the coast and can cruise along the deserted Blankstown Bypass without being forced to slow for other cars on the slip roads and roundabouts . . .'

More intimate stories and connections can be provided by listeners. Casey Kasem read out Long Distance Dedications on his American Top 40 and Simon Bates had Our Tune. Both tapped into human curiosity and helped make the songs have a personal connection with the whole audience, not just those who had written in.

## ACTUAL AUDIO

PRESENTER: That's Rick Astley. I was in a record shop the other day and he's got a new CD out. Dunno what it's called or if it's any good. So there you are.

*Commercial radio station, August 2005*

## Links with the music

You will, of course have done your research and programme prep to know that it's Bobby Brown's birthday today . . . so why not play a Bobby Brown song? Then perhaps mention his age and what he's up to now. Similarly, if an artist is touring locally, has a song that is being used on a TV ad, or won an award the previous night, play the song and mention the fact. That's not overloading the listener, it's putting the music and the knowledge in context. A good programmer will add information like this to the music playout screen so you can see it when the scheduled song appears.

## Info or advert?

Make sure your enthusiasm for the new song, or details of its release information, doesn't turn into a blatant plug for the artist. As you develop strong links with specialist record companies they may lure you with interviews, pre-release songs and so on. That is OK but you could be in deep trouble if you accept personal gifts to encourage you to, or thank you for, playing a certain song. (Some stations do not even accept the train fare for going to meet a celebrity to interview, as they feel that the integrity of the programme could be jeopardised if the interviewer wants to ask an awkward question.)

## Screen information

Songs will be marked on your computer screen with the name of the song, artist, intro duration, full duration and whether it ends or fades. I mention this because it is wise to double-check any of the information if you are not sure about it. I was once a presenter where I was taking over from someone who is now on a national station. As I drove into work I heard them introduce a song by a band that they had obviously never heard of and whose full name didn't fit on the paper print-out: 'And now here's a song from Everything But The G.I.'.

Intro times can be wrong, which will lead you to crash the vocals, and the E or F which signifies whether the song ends or fades may also have been entered incorrectly, so you may still want to double check each one by pre-fading the song first.

## Clichéd links

You're not the first to say 'Chicory Tip and *Son of my Father* – did you know that that sound is one of Rolf Harris' Stylophones?', call Errol Brown the 'Singing Malteser', or say after Shania Twain's *I Feel Like A Woman*, 'Yeah, so do I!' and so on and so on . . . so please don't!

## ACTUAL AUDIO

PRESENTER: That's Sting and *I'm an Englishman in New York*. Well, I'm not, he is . . . I'm a radio presenter in [town]!

*Commercial radio station, November 2005*

## Tortuous links

These are the kind where the presenter tries to tie one song into the next – at all costs!
'The Beatles there and *Ticket to Ride*. Well, you've got a ticket for the love train with me
Silky Smooth Steve Sanders, through till midnight, so hop aboard! Where do you want to
go? France? OK – how about Brittany? Here's Britney Spears . . .'

In fact, writing that makes me think of the spoof local radio DJ Alan Partridge!

## Bad songs

Never criticise the product. If you don't like the song that you're playing then make no
comment at all, certainly do not say on air that you don't like it. It's bound to be a favourite
of some of those listening and you'll have just spoiled their moment. You'll also have got
them wondering: 'If he doesn't like it, why's he playing it?' as most listeners don't realise that
the presenter doesn't pick all their own songs.

---

 **ACTUAL AUDIO**

PRESENTER: Simply Red and *Stars* – never thought I'd be playing *that*!
*Commercial radio station, January 2006 (after recent format change)*

---

## This one again . . .

You may have heard a song dozens or hundreds of times, but your audience hasn't. You work
at the station and hear it in the office, as well as driving there and on the way back. Plus
there is your three or four hour shift (during which you could play a chart song twice). So
as the burnout starts for you, listeners are only just getting used to hearing it.

## Levels and speed

The level of your voice should also be similar to that of the lead vocal on the song slightly
dominant yet clear and audible. The speed of your voice should be similar to the speed of
the song – a slower delivery for a slower song, for example. In general, be quick but don't
hurry. There is a difference between being succinct and rushing, which may cause you to
trip over your words.

## The penultimate words

Over the intro of a song do other information first (maybe a tease, competition phone-
number, what's on) and *then* the song information. Do the fillers then the facts, not the other
way around.

## The ultimate words

Most programme controllers agree that the last thing you say in any link should be the name
of the radio station. They say that way it will be more easily remembered. There are others
who say this should be the *first* thing you say – just make sure you know what your PC
wants you to do!

## All the way?

Do you have to talk up to the vocals on every song? No.

o    If you talk right up to the vocals (or jock the vocals) every time, it becomes tedious and repetitive.

o    If the singer starts at 15 seconds and you stop talking after 15 seconds, there is going to be a split second when both of you are on air at the same time. It sounds messy, and is known as 'crashing the vocals'. If you lose your train of thought mid-link and you take several seconds longer to end your sentence, you could end up trampling over the first few lines of the song. 'Vocal over vocal' is bad.

o    An intro is an integral part of the song. So, if you have a classic track that is a well-known crowd-pleaser (you will have to decide what this may be for your station's format) you will annoy a large percentage of your audience by talking over it. It may be Bachman Turner Overdrive *You Ain't Seen Nothing Yet*, Abba's *Dancing Queen* or Robbie William's *Angels*, such intros are distinctive and the first few chords are instantly recognisable, unless your comments spoil the experience for the audience.

o    Within each introduction there is often another 'music post' at which you can stop talking, as well as the start of the vocal itself. (A music post, or music marker, is when a song has a key change or other instruments appear mid-way though the introduction. Listen to Hot Chocolate *Everyone's a Winner* and you'll hear what I mean.) Working up to one of these posts can arguably be more effective and creative than going 'up to the vocals'.

o    Do not talk all over the start of *every* song, no matter its duration. What about *Together in Electric Dreams*? This is a song that has one or two other possible 'music posts' for you. Just because it has a 50 second intro, it doesn't mean that you have to talk for 50 seconds. Even experienced presenters don't talk right up to the vocals on every song. Remember the golden rule: say what you want to say and then stop. Fellow presenters (usually of the 'deejay' school of broadcasting) might think it is super-slick, but listeners will just think that your show is filled with 'pop and prattle'.

o    Other tracks you might play are instrumental, which brings me to another point: when do you stop if there are no vocals to hit? Either head for a music post, or don't do it at all. Otherwise you'll be tempted to wander and waffle.

Time after time, listeners say one of the things that most annoys them about DJs is that they talk over the introductions. Indeed some stations say their presenters should never talk over any music – that once the song starts, it belongs to the listener.

## What to do

If you have got an introduction of 15 seconds and you have got material which will take up to 14 seconds to read, then you can start the song (at a low level on the fader, of course) at the same time as you start talking. You may want to try practicing this with pre-written material first so you know exactly how long it will take to read (the guide is three words take one second to say).

If the script is only ten seconds, then you can stop talking at that point, bring up the level of the music to play for five seconds until the vocals start. Alternatively you can fill that five seconds with an ad-lib, 'And this is Kylie's latest, right here on 99.9 Radio Fab', which at three words a second will take you to the vocals.

After a while you will learn how to self-edit your link as you speak so you can add extra information, or take some out, depending on whether you're over- or under-running. If it is the latter situation, you will find yourself using one of a series of off-the-shelf stock phrases, such as:

o    The station name – 'This is Radio X' – 1 second.

o    The time – 'and it's eight minutes to eight' – 1.5 seconds.

- The station name and frequency – 'This is Radio X . . . 99.9FM' – 2 seconds.
- The station name, frequency and strapline – 'This is Radio X . . . 99.9 FM . . . the county's best mix of music' – 3 seconds.
- A trail – 'This is Radio X . . . where we've got the new song from The Crazy Frog after this '80s' classic from Black Box . . .' 5 seconds.
- . . . and so on!

If you have 20 seconds of script and the introduction is just 15 seconds, just start talking and after five seconds *then* you start the song playing, again at low level. This technique may be used in conjunction with another song: talk for five seconds over the back of Song A, then start Song B and stop playing (or fade down, or take out) Song A at the same time. It is tricky to start with but sounds slick if you are in control. The potential problem the first few times you do this is that with so much to think about (stopping and starting different tracks at the same time) your delivery may slow down or falter, leading you to crash the vocals. Quick tip: pick a station which plays a lot of music and as soon as each song starts playing, start talking. Identify the song and artist and then fill with other comments (trail, ident, your name, time, weather and so on), up to the vocals. Don't use the same content in every link though!

It all takes practice and a 'feel' for the music.

## Know when to shut up

It is a DJ cliché to fill, or pad, with inanities, just for the sake of talking up to the vocals: 'And this is Kylie's latest, right here on 99.9 Radio Active, the sound of the city, on Tuesday the fifth of May, with the temperature at 14 degrees and the wind direction south to south west . . . err . . . err . . .'.

Something some presenters do (which personally I find most annoying) when they have more time than they have things to say, is spread out their comments throughout the whole introduction. They don't add any extra information, they just leave lots of gaps in between the comments and raise the level of the music in between. This ducking in and out of intros is called 'riding the fader'. (Fig. 1)

**INFORMATION FOR INSPIRATION:** If you have opened the mic to speak don't bring back the music. In the same way, if you're talking over the *end* of a song don't stop and bring back the music. It sounds jerky, and you sound like a jerk.

## Intros and drop ins

You can play your recorded announcement over the whole of the introduction or just over part of it. The potential problem is that when you speak 'live' you can self-edit your comment to finish on time, but once you start the drop in, you are committed to letting it play to the end. And if you can sense that you started playing it too late and it will crash the vocals, there is not much you can do about it.

## More advanced

Once you have learned the basics of presentation then you can try some of the more advanced techniques such as fitting your voice *and* a drop in over the introduction to a song. The thing is not to run before you can walk.

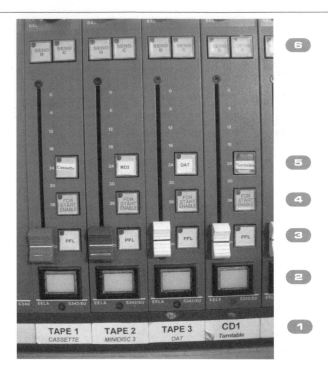

## Fader channels

The lower part . . .

1   The source option for each fader is shown here. So, either the first fader can play tape machine 1 (list default setting) or output from the cassette. All of these faders are currently closed, apart from the one for Tape 3 which is very slightly open.

2   The On/Off light. A presenter can raise the fader and then press this 'remote start' to play the source linked to it. The light will come on and stay on until the item is stopped.

3   As well as the fader control there's also the PFL button. Press this to hear the channel's source without putting it to air. Press it again to cancel the prefade (the little light on the button will then go out), then stop the source from playing and only then raise the fader!

4   Simply press this button to enable the

fader start: the source will then start playing when the fader is moved from its home position. The light will come on to show that fader start is activated.

5   Press these buttons to alternate between the main source and the alternative on each channel.

6   When a fader is up, the audio that it controls goes to the transmitter. But on this desk by pressing Send B or C, audio from that channel can *also* be sent somewhere else. So, if your podcast is a best bits of the programme compilation without the music, send the audio from your mic channels not only to the transmitter but also to a separate recorder which has been routed (or patched) through to the Send B (or C) switch. The programme sounds the same on air, but your recording contains only the audio that's been sent specifically to that machine.

The upper part of those same fader channels . . .

1 The balance control. Turn this to send more of the audio from that channel to the left or right of the listener's speakers.

2 The auxiliary control is used when that channel is linked with an effects machine to change the sound of that source, for example to give it more echo. By turning the aux knob further to the right, the amount of echo. By turning the aux knob further to the right, the amount of echo on that channel can be increased to make it sound as though you're in an empty room, or a large cave.

3 Press this EQ button to activate the knobs above it

4 The sound of each source can be altered by using these EQ buttons, which can change the low, medium and high frequency of the audio.

5 Pressing either of these button will send all of the audio from that channel to either the left or right speaker. If you have a stereo recording, you can make it mono by pressing both of these buttons.

6 Boost or lower the level that you are sending to the transmitter by rotating the Gain knob, but only after you've put the fader up completely. The home position for this control is at 12 o'clock.

## A final word

Master the basics by going into the studio whenever you can, watch what others do and ask them why they did something a certain way, then practice that technique yourself when the studio is free. When you listen to the radio at home, listen out for what the presenter does and try to work out how the sound was achieved. It won't be long before you become more confident in your presentation style as you master different ways of helping the programme flow.

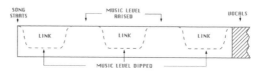

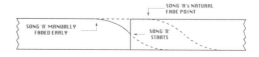

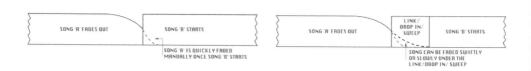

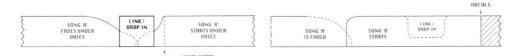

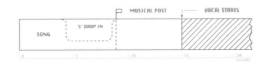

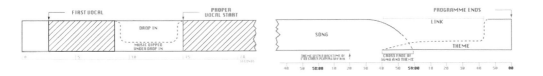

Various ways to mix songs with speech, drop-ins or sweepers

# Getting from one song to another

## The basics

Getting from one song to another is called a segue (pronounced seg-way).

There are different ways a song can start:

- With a musical introduction (most of them start this way, with the intro being anything from one second to over a minute).
- A vocal in — called a hard start (such as Owen Paul's *Favourite Waste of Time* or Simply Red's *Fairground*).
- *A fade in (Limahl's *Never Ending Story*, Sinead O'Connor's *Nothing Compares 2U*, *Telstar* by The Tornadoes, *Year of the Cat* by Al Stewart or David Bowie's *Space Oddity*).

There are two different ways a song could continue:

- An intro followed by the vocals (most songs are like this).
- *An intro, followed by a vocal, followed by some more music, then the song getting underway (such as the line, 'My life is brilliant' at the start of James Blunt's *You're Beautiful*).

* When songs start like this they may be edited to provide a power start, which I mentioned before.

There are basically three ways a song could end:

- A fade or soft out — marked on your screen as F (most songs are like this).
- A hard out — meaning that it ends or stops and marked as E or S (a large minority of songs end this way, such as Robbie Williams' *Angels*. *Penny Lane* by The Beatles is unusual in that it has a hard start *and* it ends).
- Sometimes there's an end/fade! This is unusual and is perhaps better described as a 'quiet end' or a 'soft end', such as Whitney Houston's *I Will Always Love You*.

There are several ways that you can get from one song to another (do a segue):

- Song A ends naturally, you start Song B (Fig. 2).
- This is perhaps the easiest segue. The temptation many presenters fall into is to start B just as A ends. It's actually better to feel the music, and leave a beat's pause between the two.
- Song A fades naturally, Song B is faded in (a 'cross-fade') (Fig. 3)
- Song A is yet to end but is faded manually, Song B is started (Fig 4).
  - Fade A at a natural point, for example, at the end of a chorus (best), or as the singer repeats to fade at the end of the song or (and this is least preferable) at the end of a line in a verse.
  - Don't fade mid-way through a verse as it sounds very poor.
  - Don't fade a song too early (less than two-thirds of the way through) as listeners will wonder why you have bothered to play their favourite song at all if you don't actually play all of it. In reality what has probably happened is that you have miscalculated your backtime (see p. 272).
  - Don't fade a song which ends, as this makes the audience feel cheated much more than if you do an early fade on a song which fades naturally.
  - Avoid letting songs fade too long by themselves. Take control and fade it out manually when the track itself starts to fade.

The problem with a cross-fade is that the two songs may jar musically when mixed together, even momentarily.

**ACTUAL AUDIO**

*All Night Long* by The Mary Jane Girls segued into *Domino Dancing* by The Pet Shop Boys without a drop in or speech link.

*Commercial station, November 2005*

- Song A is faded, Song B starts (Fig. 5).

In reality, of course, you would put a station ID in between the two songs (Fig. 6); that could be a sung jingle:

- Use a transitional jingle to go from a loud or fast song, to a quiet or slow one or vice versa.
- Playing a jingle as you fade a song can sound rather bad, as for a moment you will have two pieces of music playing at the same time, and it is unlikely that the tones will match.
- You would have three different tones of music within just a few seconds (the end of one song, a jingle, then the start of another).

Or it could be a dry drop-in, sweeper or your own voice link:

- If you have got a song which ends and another that starts, you can play the drop in between the two, very neatly (Fig. 7).
- You can use a drop to help hide the transition from one song to another: fade A, play the drop and mid way through it start B underneath. Bring up the level of B when the drop has finished (Fig. 8).
- Or play the drop over the last seconds of the fade, then as soon as the drop ends, start the next song (Fig. 6 again).
- Or you could fade A, start B, and play a drop over B's introduction (Fig. 9).

There are variations on that last technique. For example, if you have an intro of 15 seconds, and a five second drop-in you could:

- Play the drop-in over the first five seconds, then fade up the song for the remaining 10 seconds (Fig. 10).
- Start the song and, nine and a half seconds from the start of the vocals, play the drop in (the extra half second gives that space of a 'beat' that I mentioned earlier). You'll have 'backtimed the drop-in to the vocals'. Be aware that this technique can sound ridiculous if a three second drop-in is played at the end of, say, a 30 second introduction, and certainly if *you* suddenly appear and say something at this point (Fig. 11).
- Play the drop in mid-way through the intro (for example five seconds after the intro has started, giving intro/drop/intro/vocal all evenly spaced) (Fig. 12).
- Back-time the drop-in to a music post within the introduction (if there is one) (Fig. 13).
- Play the drop-in after a 'false vocal' and before the song starts properly (for example, after James Blunt sings 'My life is brilliant' at the start of *You're Beautiful*, or after the vocal start to Bon Jovi's *You Give Love a Bad Name*. (Fig. 14).

If the drop-in is longer than the intro you simply start the drop first, either dry (not over music) or over the end of the previous song. So, if the drop is 10 seconds long and the intro is five then play the first six seconds of the drop over the end of Song A, then start Song B when there are four seconds left to run.

It has to be said that in reality, many of these techniques sound rather ridiculous and are rarely heard on air. In the main, play a drop-in as you fade a song underneath it; to cover the join of two songs; or as a song starts.

**Remember**, don't use the same techniques relentlessly time and time again. Presenting segues requires practice and confidence. And as there really isn't time to rehearse all of your segues before you go on air (in fact doing that would make your actual broadcast sound dull and flat), you need to get lots of flying time under your belt first. When you are on air, you may be able to rehearse to a certain extent (for example talking over the introduction to a song on pre-fade) but you won't be able to practice all your segues because very often, the song you need to practice will already be playing on air.

# What to do when a song's playing

Work out what you are going to do next, and *how* you are going to do it. Structure your link, note down bullet-points bearing particular attention to these questions:

- What's the point of this item?
- What's the top line to grab attention?
- How can I flesh it out and add detail, interest and colour?
- What's the punch line or conclusion? How will I know if I've got there?
- What will I do *next*, once I've finished the link? (Are you going to go to another song or a break or a pre-recorded interview, or someone on the phone? Is that item ready? What will be the transition between the two items? If that item is live, for example, a guest, how will you get from *that* to the *next* item? There may not be an opportunity to think about it or set it up while you are conducting an interview.)

# Outroducing music

This is known as back-announcing or back-annoing. It is especially important to outroduce *new* songs: people aren't that interested beforehand. It is once they have heard it that they are intrigued and want to know who it is by. Doing this also keeps them listening longer too!

I don't think it is really necessary to intro *and* outro every song. If you do that you sound patronising, and also give the impression that you don't have anything else more worthwhile to say. Although there may be an excuse for in-and-outing *current* songs, there's not one for *classics*. Indeed, one radio group's policy was to 'not mention the artists and title at all (unless) . . . playing a brand new record or . . . a more unfamiliar oldie'.

Earlier I mentioned introing songs which have their title in the first line and what you should be aware of. A similar thing goes for outros too:

 **ACTUAL AUDIO**

(*New Temptation* by INXS repeats to fade)
PRESENTER: That's *New Temptation* . . .

*Commercial station, May 2005*

## Your speed and style

Alter your vocal delivery so it's in synch with the music you're speaking over. Your intro to Celine Dion's *My Heart Will Go On* will be at a different volume and speed than the one to Gloria Estefan's *Dr Beat*. The speed and volume of your voice should reflect the speed and style of the song.

## The order of the information

Earlier I suggested doing the fillers then the facts when introducing songs. With outroducing it's the other way around, do the facts (the artist and title) and *then* the filler stuff (the tease, the travel or the time, for example).

## What else to say

To avoid using the same 'that was, this is link', force yourself to think of different ways you can back-anno music (see what we looked at for 'intros' on p. 256 to give you an idea).

## Songs that fade

You shouldn't talk over the vocals at the start of any song, but you can at the *end* of a song that fades (though not one that ends). Don't talk over more than the last 20–30 seconds, even if it is instrumental at that point, or is merely repeating itself. The song will be someone's favourite. To promote your Sticker Patrol over the sax ending to *Baker Street* or *Layla* should be (and may well be at some stations) a sackable offence.

To keep the music flowing use the last 15 seconds of a song to talk over and then as it runs out, start the next song underneath your voice and talk over that introduction up to the vocals.

## Songs that end

A good rule of thumb is: don't talk over the ends of songs which end. On some classic tracks you should neither talk over the beginning nor the end. You'd be held in great disdain by your listeners if you told them about a funny thing that happened to you at Tesco's at the weekend as they were listening to the final notes of *Candle in the Wind*. If the song ends, let it do just that.

To stop a song that ends early, especially within 30 seconds of the end, is a heinous crime. Backtime properly.

**INFORMATION FOR INSPIRATION:** Poor presentation harms the station.

Beware of songs with awkward ends such as:

- *Mr Blue Sky* by ELO which has a climax, then silence, before music fades in again to a second crescendo
- *Too Sexy* by George Michael, which has a clip of a woman talking on the end after the singing itself has finished!
- *Barbara Ann* by The Beach Boys, *Hello Goodbye* by The Beatles, *Calling All The Heroes* by It Bites, all of which have false ends.

o  *Summer The First Time* by Bobby Goldsboro is an example of a 'story song', which tells of a young man's first sexual experience. It would obviously be wrong to cut this kind of song short.

# Backtimes and overruns

I have mentioned backtiming a few times, so let me explain what it is and how you do it.

It is the art of preparing so you don't run out of time at the end of the hour or the end of the programme. Finishing late sounds messy. You can't join a bulletin half way through, or have the newsreader say, 'It's a minute past ten . . .'. Indeed it may be that your show has a 'clock end' and you're cut-off in mid-stream if you don't finish your programme on time. Or perhaps you have to take another live source at a certain time. (This is called an opt-in and if it's at a specific time, has a clock in.)

Finishing early is downright embarrassing. Most presenters have at some time mis-read the studio clock or miscalculated a back time and been left with a minute or so to fill – rather more difficult than it sounds! Backtiming determines what time you have to start a sequence of events, in order to finish when you want to (on-time).

In effect it is no different from working out when you have to get up to get the chores done, do the shopping and walk the dog, before you have to leave for work.

For on-air backtiming you have to add together the durations of each item between where you are now and where you have to be at a certain time. It's tricky because you are dealing with units of 60 rather than 100, and because no song is a uniform length. But it gets easier with practice!

As you should do a mental back time in your head from the last 20 minutes of each hour, here is an example.

It is around 20 minutes to 2 and between now and the news (which you pride yourself on hitting on time) you have a travel bulletin at :50 and three songs following that:
o  X of 2:56 which fades.
o  Y which lasts 3:19 which also fades.
o  Z the final song of the hour which *ends* after 3:42.

Now, it's handy that Z *ends*, it just sounds neater than fading a song to the news. Indeed, some presenters swap their order around to specifically place an end-song as the last one of the hour.

There is also a nine second news jingle.

Working backwards:
o  The news starts at :00 so the news jingle has to start at 59:51.
o  Therefore Z has to start at 56:09.

The most important calculations are now done. Y and X fade anyway so to fade them early would be acceptable, as long as you have given them a decent play (see earlier).

Letting each of these go right to the very end would sound odd. The timings are based on the complete duration of each song, not where the best opt-out points are. So if you based a backtime calculation on the *full* duration you would have to let each track play to its bitter end with the song getting progressively quieter, which would sound pretty poor, but as we've seen, you can fade a song early.

So, back to our sums!

We have to start Z at 56:09, with Y starting no earlier than 3:19 before that (or we'll be left with a gap). That makes the new backtime 52:50 – the time we have to start Y by. Using the same calculation, X has to start no earlier than 2:56 earlier, giving us 50:04.

Make a note of when each item has got to start by and then count *forward* from your start-point to check that the backtime's accurate.

Of course, while all this number crunching is going on, the song on-air is counting down and getting closer and closer to its end; so as you can see, backtiming is rather like chasing your tail. If you leave it too late, you realise that you should have started the last song 10 seconds ago, and the moment has been lost: that song that you wanted to let end will have to be messily faded after all.

The above calculations do give us, remember, the times at which both those faded songs have to start by, which as I say, will cause us to have to play them to their bitter end. If we listened through to each of them we could work out the best opt-out points on each one and then build those timings into our equation instead, but that would be too long and tedious and would not be done in practice.

Instead, take a guess that we can fade X and Y about 30 seconds from time, giving us a start-time for this sequence of three songs and a news jingle of one minute later at 51:04. And to mask any clashes of musical tone or tempo, be ready to talk over or play a drop-in over the segues. So, if you can go to the travel presenter slightly early, which would usually be possible and ask them to 'be out (to have finished talking by a certain time) by :51, please' you should be on track to hit your back time. Easy!

As the 20 minutes reduces to 15 and certainly 10, re-calculate your timings.

Timing is of the essence if you are to present a professional programme. There must be no half-played songs, ad breaks must be broadcast on time and in full, the travel presenter must have all the time they need to tell of delays and diversions, and the show must begin and end when it is scheduled to.

(See Fig. 15 for a representation of starting a backtimed programme theme 1:40 from the end of a show.)

## Filling for time

This may happen when:

- You've not calculated your backtime properly.
- Someone else isn't ready for you to cross (or 'cross over') to them.
- A piece of equipment fails unexpectedly.

Look back at the section on stock phrases (p. 252) and also what I said about knowing about the station, the features, programmes and presenters. If all that's in your head, and with the knowledge you have about teasing and trailing, you should be able to ad-lib for a minute or more without any trouble.

# 23 Competitions

Every station in the country runs competitions (contests) in some way or another. Even Radio 4 has given listeners the chance to win a walk-on part in their serial *The Archers* (with the entry fee donation going to the Children In Need charity).

Competitions can be basic (the Mystery Voice) or more complicated (perhaps with a qualifying question, followed by several rounds against another contestant). They may be one offs ('Win a pair of tickets for tonight's performance of . . .') or more long-term ('Our jackpot is now at £3,000 . . .'). The prizes may be basic (The Breeze in Essex gave away 'gold plated' bath plugs) or expensive (holidays or cars) or exclusive (film premier tickets). They may take place on air (as most do) or off air (at an outside broadcast), or a mix of the two (an endurance contest such as 'touch the truck', with regular on-air updates from the event).

Although small competitions can occur at any time of the day (giving away CDs or concert tickets) the biggest ones are invariably scheduled at breakfast. That is because there's already a large number of people listening at that time, so there is a greater chance of some of them being Rajar diary-holders.

Other contests are usually run at regular times each day, so listeners can be 'trained' to listen and call.

The most effective competitions have a genuine editorial purpose and clear marketing objective. Perhaps to:

- Boost figures by attracting new people to the station.
- Keep existing listeners listening longer.
- Add fun, interest, excitement and suspense to the output, increasing the listeners' perception of the station as a place to go for a good time. (If the competition's confusing or dull then it's not worth running.)
- Provide awareness (a 'talkability' factor) in the community and on air.
- Make the station look generous when it gives away a huge prize.
- Or fun when it gives away a unique, smaller prize.
- Link with the station's core brand values.
- Give something for the station to promote (or talk-up) at other points in the day: either by repeating a recording of the contestant who won, or playing the qualifying question.
- To earn money for the station (a company might pay a commercial station to run a competition with its product as a prize as part of an awareness campaign, or might sponsor an existing contest).

Both at BBC and commercial stations, there is careful monitoring of the number of competitions that are run and the kind of prizes offered. It is possible that a station could have too many competitions – one a show, and not *every* show, is probably enough. More than this and the listener becomes confused with the number of different mechanics (what they have to do to win) that are being explained to them.

Even though competitions have their place, they do take time away from other things that the presenter could be talking about.

## Competition vs lottery

Simply put, one is something you can legally run, and the other is not. A competition is lawful if success depends to a substantial degree on the exercise of skill, although the exact definition of skill is hard to determine. The Gambling Act of 2005 passed up the opportunity to clarify this area of law and has come up with its own rather convoluted definition, which is expected to come into force in the autumn of 2007. Then as now, you will risk prosecution if the authorities believe there is insufficient skill. Insufficient skill could turn your lawful competition into an illegal lottery. A competition can also be unlawful if it asks entrants to predict the outcome of future events, for example, who will win the cup final.

A lottery is a scheme for distributing prizes purely on the basis of chance where participants have paid to enter. Small charity lotteries such as raffles are exempt (subject in some cases to registration with a local authority) as, of course, is the National Lottery. Just to complicate matters a 'free prize draw' where no skill is required (a winner is drawn at random by chance alone and no payment has been made to enter – and note that payment can mean a premium rate phone call cost) is lawful.

So, to sum up, you need to ensure that any competition you run involves sufficient skill and doesn't ask entrants to predict future events, to keep your station out of trouble.

## The mechanic

How the contest works, how it's run and won, is called the mechanic. Competition experts say there are only 11 basic contest formats in the world, which are listed below.

I have given examples from TV as they are more likely to be recognisable, but bear in mind that these contests or games, like the ones on the radio, may borrow from several formats, not just the one I have listed them alongside:

1  Fill the Blank – *Blankety Blank*.
2  Crack the Clue – *321*.
3  Cryptic Clue – *Treasure Hunt*.
4  Show Your Skill – *Hard Spell, X Factor*.
5  Ordeal – *Mastermind, Gladiators*.
6  Every Second Counts – *Beat the Clock*.
7  One to One (against another contestant) – *Ready Steady Cook*.
8  Play or Walk Away – *Who Wants To Be A Millionaire, Double or Quit*.
9  Total Chance – *Strike It Lucky, Deal or No Deal*.
10  Multiple Choice – *Who Wants To Be A Millionaire?*
11  50–50
   □  higher or lower – *Play Your Cards Right*.
   □  true or false – *Grab The Ads*.

So clash a few of these ideas, but don't steal them outright (many game show formats are legally protected, although in principle it's difficult to prove that someone's stolen an idea).

**INFORMATION FOR INSPIRATION:** Create a mechanic that is interesting and intriguing to those playing on air as well as those playing at home. Often the best ones are where there's simplicity with some suspense.

The mechanic must fit with the station (the host brand), the prize or sponsor (the guest brand) and the listener to be effective. It sounds odd to hear a question that has nothing to do with the prize, or a prize that has nothing to do with the format of the station, so make sure everything ties in. If the competition doesn't sound interesting and exciting, then it won't cut through the clutter to become compelling.

## The name

A good competition often has a catchy name that may tease, intrigue and is relevant to the mechanic.

You may want to consider one that:

- Is straightforwardly descriptive – *The Mystery Voice, Bullseye*.
- Adds tension or excitement – *Gladiators, University Challenge, Don't Try This At Home*.
- Is alliterative – *Going for Gold, Supermarket Sweep*.
- Uses an existing phrase – *Who Wants To Be A Millionaire?*
- Is a pun on the format – *Wheel of Fortune, Play Your Cards Right*.

## Four ways to call for contestants

How do people know to take part?

1 The Invitation – This is the most straightforward call to play. 'If you'd like to play Beat The Intro call now on . . .'. Take the calls as they come in and choose your contestant who'll be on air with you in a song or two's time.

2 Registration – Do potential participants have to register their entry in advance? Registration may be via a premium-rate phone number, the operators of which may send the station the name and number of a contestant that fits with pre-determined criteria (for example, a female from a certain town). Registration also captures the caller's information for future marketing, and helps make money for the station or helps finance the price.

3 Ring To Win – Some stations run contests where, say, the 99th caller will be the winner and that number is usually one that fits in with their station frequency. In reality most stations won't get that many potential contestants, and as their lines aren't able to cope with more than half a dozen callers at the same time, they will never know exactly who is caller number 99. The presenter or producer simply waits a while, perhaps clears down the switchboard a couple of times then picks a call at random. Saying 'caller 99' on-air sounds big, but the truth is that even if you get 99 callers, a lot of them will be the same listeners re-dialling.

4 Cue to Call – Players have to listen for a certain song to be played before they can phone and stand a chance of winning. This certainly helps increase your listening hours and that is why most 'cue to call songs' are played in the last 15 minutes of an hour (so the Rajar diary has as many ticks as possible). Obviously, the downside of playing the song too early in the programme or the hour is that listeners are then tempted to turn off.

There can be twists to this concept: you can choose a song that is on the album you are giving away; you can pick a song that has an appropriate title or fits in some other way to the prize ('Listen out for *Thriller* and call me when you hear it and you could spend Halloween at a haunted castle . . .'); a sound could be played rather than a song ('When you hear the alarm clock, call to win tickets to the New Year's Party', 'The thundering hooves could be your ticket to the races' and so on).

Some stations say that listeners should always be given at least two entry routes, to avoid discriminating against those without e-mail, for example. A typical competition would allow entry via the website (though unless it is a straightforward e-mail, a special page may need to be designed) and on the phone. Other options include entries by text or by post.

As well as the above, there may additionally be a qualifying question to get through to the main contest on air. This may be to weed-out those who, for example, have no interest in a day at the races, but enter anyway. On such an occasion your qualifier may be 'Which horse won the Derby in 1985?' Think carefully about setting qualifiers, they add another tier of complexity to the mechanic and are often unnecessary as statistics have shown that fewer than 1 in 800 people ever take part in station contests.

## The rules

Work out how people will play the competition – the mechanic. Contests must be very simple to explain and to understand. If the rules last more than 30 seconds or if there are too many rounds then it is probably too complicated and will take too long to run. Both are a turn-off for those taking part, those who would like to have taken part, and those listening at home who just want to get back to the music.

Some stations run group-wide contests. This is when listeners from all the stations are invited to call a registration line, but only one contestant is chosen to play from all those entries. A recording of them winning the competition is played on each station. Such networked competitions have rules about how the contest is promoted on air, so listeners in each area aren't given the impression that they stand a better chance of winning than in fact they do.

Seventeen competition considerations:
1. How people are eligible to take part (age might be a consideration).
2. If there's a deadline.
3. The duration of the entry period and the competition.
4. How many winners you need or want.
5. How they'll win.
6. Is there an element that allows everyone to believe that they *could* be a winner?
7. Is the mechanic interesting and fun?
8. Is the prize weird or wonderful? (See more on prizes below.)
9. What happens if more than one person wins?
10. What happens if there's a tie? Is there another question or another round?
11. What if a contestant drops out mid-way?
12. What happens if a contestant claims an answer's wrong?
13. What if they enter a second time?
14. Insurance: in case someone actually *does* win the car, or finds the Magic Million envelope.
15. Will the competition achieve your objectives?
16. Do the presenters know these objectives and the rules?
17. Has the contest been tested?

Much of this information should be made pubic on your website or in the reception.

As a presenter you should be aware that some competition mechanics are written in a script that you can't deviate from, so check before altering single word. There is a great difference between '. . . and you *could* win . . .' and 'You *will* win . . .'. Also a sponsor may have agreed a certain tag line (such as the company's positioning statement) that you will have to read word-for-word, which will also take into account regulations on the phrasing of sponsorship credits set down by Ofcom.

## Questions

Never refer to the question as 'easy' or 'simple' as you devalue the whole contest. If it's easy why should someone bother to enter? If you say it's easy and someone gets it wrong, how will they feel and how will you look? What happens to the station's credibility? That doesn't mean the question can't be easy or simple, just don't say so!

But don't make it too hard either:

---

 **ACTUAL AUDIO**

PRESENTER: 40% of Chinese people do what?

*Local commercial radio station, November 2005*

PRESENTER: The answer is 'red'. What's the question?
The answer is 'button'. What's the question?

*BBC Local station, January 2006*

---

Make the question appropriate to the station, the audience and the competition prize.

---

 **ACTUAL AUDIO**

(In a competition for tickets to the local theatre to see a musical.)
PRESENTER: What kind of animal is a chameleon?

*Local commercial radio station, September 2005*

---

## Suspense and surprise

Many of the great contests have a second level of excitement built-in: suspense. Think of *Millionaire* where the stakes get increasingly higher and of Chris Tarrant's teasing across the break.

Create suspense by giving the contestant an option:
o   Walk away or stay and play.
o   Take the money or open the box.

Consider that although too many wrong answers can have a negative effect on the competition as a whole, having some builds suspense and lets contestants show emotion.

Occasionally hold back part of the prize to give 'spontaneously' at the time of winning: 'You've just won tickets to the gig of Roddy Radio and The FM-inates . . . and . . . can I do this? Heck, I'm going to . . . I'm going to throw in £100 so you can go and have a great meal before you go to the concert . . .'. It creates excitement and unpredictability. And the listeners will love you!

## Contest production

Not all competitions have to have lots of whiz-bang production elements, but they should certainly have some of the basic ones to make it more interesting – more of an event. That might be a music bed, a drop-in and a winner's fanfare, for example. Production must be thought of at the same time as the name of the competition, the mechanic and the prize as they all go hand in hand. As well as considering whether you need any production elements, is the question of how and when the pre-launch activity starts, to build interest and increase the talkability factor.

# Promoting the competition

## Attention

> **INFORMATION FOR INSPIRATION:** Radio is a linear medium so first hook the listener, then say why you've told them, then what they've got to do.

If you say, 'Call me now on 01234 567890 and if you can answer the question "how long is a piece of string?" you could win a stack of CDs that weigh as much as you do . . .' you've put the reason for people to call (what they'll win) last! So, you told them how to enter, then what they have to do and then why, by which time, they will have missed the number to call!

Instead, say why they have got to enter (what they could win), what they have to do (the question) and then the way to do it (the phone number). 'Fancy winning a stack of CDs that weigh as much as you do? Then you may stand a chance if you can answer this question correctly: "How long is a piece of string?". If you think you know, call me on 01234 567890 . . .'. (Look back at cart and horse links and asking questions on p. 214 to see similar techniques.)

## Desire

Simply saying, 'Next, I'm giving away . . .' sees the situation from your view, that of the presenter. More effective is to talk from the viewpoint of your listener: tell them what they could win. Not, 'This is what we're giving away' or 'This is what we're doing', but rather, 'This is why what we're doing matters to you'.

Paint a picture! Sell the sizzle! Explain the benefit of winning.
So:
- Tickets to the theatre becomes 'Have a night out on us', 'Spend some quality time together' or 'Take your mind off work for a couple of hours'.
- A new car is 'Think of the money you'll save on servicing and repairs', 'You'll be the king of the road', 'Nothing less than you deserve'.
- A holiday becomes 'Free fun in the sun', 'A week of pina coladas and pampering', '. . . and with a kids club there as well, you've got all day to yourself'.

Get listeners to picture the scene and themselves in it and you've involved them.

**INFORMATION FOR INSPIRATION:** If they're *imagining* it, they're virtually *experiencing* it.

## ACTUAL AUDIO

PRESENTER: . . . and you could win a (station name) ski hat. Wow (sarcastically).

*Local commercial, station November 2005*

## Action

Don't use the word 'details' (it's so boring), just make it simple and straightforward. 'How you could win . . .', rather than, 'These are the details of what you've got to do . . .'. Then urge people to take part. Give the impression it is fun, exciting and challenging and 'You, yes you, could win'.

# Choosing a contestant

## Prize pigs

Work the switchboard to find the best listener to take part. You want them to sound fun, lively and interested, and to actually want to win the prize. Many times I have run a competition only to have the winner ask afterwards, 'What have I won?' or after having won tickets to an event say, 'Sorry, I can't go on that day'. You are then left with the problem of rerunning the competition to give away the prize that you've already given away!

Those contestants who have the competition line on their speed-dial, are called 'prize pigs' (because they're greedy for prizes – any prizes). They know that presenters want lively callers who will sound grateful, so they will put on that act to get chosen to play. They are not always loyal in the least and may call any station for any competition. So, contests that encourage 'extended listening' (such as listening to wrong answers to work out the right one) will dissuade them from calling.

You may have a book of recent winners or have a phone system which shows on a screen the last time each caller contacted you and why. Some stations have a rule that someone can't win twice within a certain period of time. But pigs call from other numbers or give you a false name or the address of a friend to get past this.

Consider why such listeners are 'banned'. If they win lots because they listen lots, then they are among your most loyal listeners and will evangelise on your behalf. In other businesses, such as supermarkets or air travel, repeat sales (for radio, read 'calls') are rewarded and the best customers given special privileges, yet many stations don't want them! Look after them well, even if you do stop taking their calls to air for a while, and consider letting them join your VIP club (see the section on UGC pp. 104–105), or sending them a prize pack out of the blue.

## Be picky

You may want to get a caller from a specific area. If the tickets are for an event in a specific town, they are more likely to be used by someone who lives nearby than someone who is at the other end of the county. Alternatively, you may have a large item to give away that will cost a great deal to post, and want a winner who lives on your route home! (Some stations have a policy that station staff always deliver prizes, to give personal contact to their listeners.) Or you may simply want winners from across your area so you don't alienate those in certain towns. This may be a major problem if your phone-in number is 'geographic' as listeners in the town in which you are based will get through faster than those who have to dial the full code.

## Get their number

If it fits with the competition mechanic, take the details of the caller before you put them to air. It avoids you saying on air, 'stay on the line so we can take your details', or off air asking them to 'stay on the line if you win and I'll come back to take your address'. Or, take their phone-number off-air and call them back later. Or record and edit the whole conversation so it sounds quick and slick, and cuts the clutter.

## Lucky lines

As I mentioned, there are no such things as 'lucky lines'. So, 'Get through on lucky line 99' is merely showmanship. If you do use this technique, use a practical number: one that is low and is more realistic. You can still screen the callers as they don't know what line they are on unless you tell them! Answer the calls in turn and speak to them: who are they, where they're from and so on. In those few seconds judge if they are going to be a good contestant. If they aren't then, 'Sorry, you're on line four' and go to the next caller (who may also be told they are on line four if they are not going to be good on air). Think on your feet, as you have only a few seconds to judge each caller. If you are using this technique, don't ask for the answer to the question in the screening process: if the caller is right they will be even more cross they didn't get on air!

Alternatively, set up several potential winners on the phone and tell them which line they are on and then on air say '. . . and the winner's on line 4!' at which time put up their fader to hear them whoop! Of course, you may only have that single contestant on the line, but it heightens the tension by giving the impression to them and the audience that you've got more.

Another technique is to line up several callers, the first two of whom have the wrong answer. Some people say this raises the excitement quotient for the listener and the caller. Others that your station is known for having losers as well as winners and that that could harm your 'happy radio' image.

---

 **ACTUAL AUDIO**

CONTESTANT: I don't believe it. You've kept me on all this time to tell me 'no'? You're having a laugh!

*BBC local station, February 2006*

---

## Education

Good callers educate other listeners to be good callers. In other words, put on the callers that you want to be on air and then you will get more like them. Choose someone with the right personality and demographic (never put someone to air who's outside either) and from the right area (never put someone to air who is outside your TSA). You often only have the length of one song to get all this done and find your potential 'star'.

Two more points. Ask the contestant to sound excited and guess the answer if they don't know it, and to turn their radio off.

## The caller on air

Never ask a caller a basic question on air that you (or your producer) haven't already asked them off air and know the answer to. Otherwise you get: 'How are you?' and the answer is, 'Well, not very well actually . . .' followed by a list of aches and pains. Or 'What've you been doing today?' answered with 'Not much . . .'. Ask them the boring stuff off air and identify some interesting thing about what they say, to ask them on air.

PRESENTER: What are you going to do with your £1,000?
CALLER: Go on holiday.
PRESENTER: OK, where, to?
CALLER: Dunno.
etc etc.
PRESENTER: Well, what about a skiing holiday? Or a safari? Disneyland? Barbados?
CALLER: Yeah, Barbados.
PRESENTER: And who would you take?
CALLER: My boyfriend.
PRESENTER: And what's his name?
CALLER: Dean.
PRESENTER: OK, when I ask you what you're going to spend your money on, it'll be really great if you can tell me all about your fantasy holiday with Dean, the white sand, the cool water, the cocktails on the beach . . .

If all this fails, and the caller ends up on-air and is poor, get rid of them as soon as is polite. No boring bits. No dead-end questions. No gaps. No awkward gear changes.

Another potential pitfall is echoing back what the caller has just said to you:

PRESENTER: Hello John.
CALLER: Hi, how are you?
PRESENTER: Fine, how are you?
CALLER: Good, thanks.
PRESENTER: Where are you calling from?
CALLER: Blank Village.
PRESENTER: Blank Village?
etc.

## Running the competition

One of the most important things to remember about the competition is not what the prize is or that you have lots of entries; it's that you make it an exciting and enjoyable occasion for the contestants. Note that I said 'contestants', even if you only have one on air with you. That's because there are many more people playing along at home, and you have to make the event interesting for them, too. Root for the caller to win. Be on their side. But don't give them the prize if they lose, as that devalues the whole competition.

# When it's been run and won

Most listeners know what is expected of them: that they have to whoop and holler once they have won. Many stations also ask the winner, 'What's the name of your favourite radio station?' The presenter wants to end the call on a high by having the caller promote the station that's just given them a prize but this can backfire. Radio X's caller could often answer 'Radio Y' instead, possibly out of confusion, excitement, malice or because that's the truth.

## Caller clichés

Don't let a listener reel of a list of hellos and that cliché 'and anyone else who knows me' at the end of the competition.

> 'Drawing attention to this phrase by saying 'you're not allowed to say that' not only prolongs the agony, it's also highly discourteous to the listener.'
> *County Sound Radio House Style*, January 1989

Similarly, don't make a big fuss when a caller mentions the name of the place where they work. Ask anyone what they do and most will include in their answer the name of where they do it. A quick mention of 'Hi to everyone at Wellington's the Chemist in the High Street' cannot possibly be seen as an endorsement of the work of the store: no one is going to shop there simply because they heard a comment such as that on your station. However, if you draw attention to the comment by saying, 'You're not supposed to mention shops', it makes the listener look and feel bad. If they start launching into a commercial for the shop on the other hand, interrupt them politely and move on.

# The prize

A great prize should be either:
- fun
- expensive
- or 'something money-can't-buy'
- and always: appropriate for the station's brand and the listener's lifestyle.

## Bigger is not always better

Life is strange: you try to give away a car and get no callers, but give away the presenter's pants and the switchboard lights up. That is because listeners have their own perception of the value of a prize, and it is not necessarily in financial terms. They also weigh up their chances of winning, consider the likely popularity of the contest and the difficulty of the questions.

People also have a 'self-destruct button' – 'I won't win a car, I never win anything. Pants? Yeah, that'll be it. I'll win a pair of pants!'

> **INFORMATION FOR INSPIRATION:** Big prizes can fail to make a personal connection with the listener.

## Small prizes that sound big

Cash handouts are fine, but unless they are really significant the perception of them is often lower than their actual value. In other words, sending a prize of £100 to a winner seems less exciting than a pair of concert tickets or a meal out which may actually cost less. A £500 prize is great, but the perception of a weekend at a country hotel may seem better, and actually be cheaper. Indeed, in February 2006 in his report *Materialism and the Pursuit of Happiness*, global equities strategist James Montier wrote that material goods and a fat bank account leave us flat, but experiences tend to be unique and the pleasure of a positive memory doesn't wear off.

Tangible prizes, that people can imagine themselves experiencing, are also easier to work into a mechanic and to talk up on air.

Often lots of small prizes work better than one large one, as there are more chances to win, more actual winners and therefore more people to spread the word about your station.

Some low-cost items are often perceived by listeners to be more 'winnable'. They work out that only one person will win the round the world trip and the chances are slim of it being them. However, the chances of them getting a book or CD are much greater, as those types of contest are run more regularly.

These smaller prizes are often obtained via monthly 'prize magazines' (such as *Q Sheet*, *X-Trax* or *Broadcaster's Bulletin*) which are sent free to radio stations. They advertise items that a station can ask for and even suggest a competition mechanic and 'peg' – the angle or reason to run the competition – to hang it on. It might be a new flavour of chocolate bar or the anniversary of the invention of the food mixer, with the chocolate or new model of mixer offered as a prize. Although you get the product for free, the company supplying it will want a mention on the radio (and to be sent a recording to prove it), and that will be worth much more to them than the cost of the product.

At larger stations, prizes will be organised by the sales or promotions department. At smaller stations there will usually be just one person who liaises with companies for give-aways. (If many different staff call for the same offers, the companies will be annoyed and the station appears to lack cohesion.)

## Clearing prizes

All competitions must usually be cleared with a senior member of staff for several impor-tant reasons. If yours is a commercial station there may be an understandable grievance that the prize you are giving away has been given to the station for free. Your sales and promo-tions team have targets to reach on how much money they have to bring into the station each month and they won't be pleased at seeing a possible opportunity (a lead) slipping through their fingers.

It is a little-known fact that the companies whose items are given away as prizes usually pay the commercial station to run the competition. The number of mentions and talk-ups (when presenters say how desirable the prize is) is carefully controlled by the promotions executive, so the company gets what they pay for, no more and no less.

Presenter mentions have more impact than an advert, as the listeners' favourite presenter is making what amounts to a personal endorsement of the product: added value is given to the company whose product is being given away. Promotions people argue that the company concerned should pay the station to run the competition as well as providing the prizes. You can see their point (their point, of course, also translates into your salary). So, don't be tempted to run a contest on air and give away any item that has been donated before checking it with the appropriate member of the team.

## Regulations

BBC stations have to tread very carefully in terms of competitions. They are not allowed to sell the competition in the same way that commercial stations do, of course, and there are more stringent regulations about the prize itself (they are not allowed to give away cash, for example), and what a presenter can say about the prize without veering into the area of advertising or endorsing the product. That is why many BBC stations buy the majority of their prizes and of course that is governed by budgets. More money being spent on a prize means less on programmes or staff: listeners and licence payers could justifiably ask questions about value for their money.

'Donations of substantial prizes cannot be accepted. Programmes should not broadcast brand names or any other details about a prize that might suggest endorsement of a product or service. In exceptional circumstances, for editorial reasons, some details may be given on the grounds that description of the prize would be inadequate without them. Brand names of household goods should not be given.'
*BBC Radio Five Live Style Guide*

Most stations have a policy that all freebies received (books, CDs, DVDs, tickets, etc) are the property of the station and not the person they were addressed to. So don't think that Christmas has come early when a big box lands on your desk!

## Prizes reflecting the brand

Are your winners getting prizes that represent the station brand or just ones that a keen marketing company has sent you and have been languishing in the back of the prize cupboard? I have heard a car alarm kit being given away on a school run competition, bottles of wine as another prize and how many key-rings does one person need? (They seem to be the only things in many small stations' prize cupboard!) Think about what your listeners do and what they would like to win to fit in with their lives. One station called this 'made-to-measure treasure', with a prize chosen specifically for each individual winner.

**INFORMATION FOR INSPIRATION:** Make the prize fit the brand, the programme and the listener.

## Money can't buy

Consider prizes that can't be bought. When he was the breakfast presenter on Breeze, in Essex, Peter Holmes gave his contest winners personalised bathplugs. They cost a few pence each and every listener wanted one. They were personalised, gold-plated (or rather 'gold-painted') on a stand and had an obvious connection with the time of day of the programme. They were promoted as being 'exclusive and elusive' which increased their desirability. Peter once held a party just for bathplug winners. Over 150 people turned up, all with their bathplug as the entry ticket.

Such prizes may have three attributes:

- Extremely limited practical value.
- Personalised.
- Inexplicably fun.

## Teasing and truthful?

Hopefully both, but not always. One radio station ran a contest and gave away a car. The winner received a *toy* car. She sued the station and won the value of a real one.

- Have you actually got the prize? Now. In your hand? If not then it is probably best not to run the competition. It has been known for promises from PR companies not to translate into reality.
- Finally, give something specific away, not just, 'Something nice from our prize cupboard . . . we'll see what we can find'. Say what it is, and why someone would like to win it.

Zoe Korth, Alex Williamson, Lisa Morgan with the Essex FM Black Thunder promotional vehicle. These highly-visible branded vehicles may be used on sticker promotions, publicity stunts and to deliver prizes. Courtesy of GCap Media.

## Despatching prizes

Never give away items that are going to be difficult or expensive to post (although some stations get their presenters to deliver prizes personally to the winners' homes). It is inevitable that the breakable items will get broken; recorded delivery is a good idea for expensive prizes.

Food and alcohol are probably poor prizes. You don't know what state they will arrive in, whether they will be edible, or who will open them (possibly someone who is under age).

---

 **ACTUAL AUDIO**

PRESENTER: . . . So, congratulations on winning. Our reception's open from 9–5 weekdays so you can pop in and pick up your prize.

*BBC local station, November 2005*

If the winner does have to come in to the station to pick up their prize, make it worthwhile. Ensure you are there to meet them and hand it over (not the 'anonymous' receptionist) and offer them a station tour and an explanation of how the studio works. Having winners pick up their own prize makes the station seem cheap and uncaring. They have to fit a visit to the station into their routine, and spend money on petrol and parking. The feeling the winner has, moves from excitement to regret. The competition climax turns to anti-climax.

> **INFORMATION FOR INSPIRATION:** Winning a competition on the radio should be an exciting experience for the listener. That's the whole experience: from them calling on the phone, to the postman calling on their doorbell.

Promote the station at every opportunity. Every letter, and especially prizes, should include two car stickers and a personally signed presenter picture. The increased postage cost will be negligible when compared to the extra promotion and connection you are building between listener and presenter.

# Post production

If a long-running competition is won in your show, you should be responsible for ensuring that the correct people are made aware. Alert the programme controller and the promotions team. They should arrange for a promo to be made of the 'winning moment' and alert other presenters so they don't still talk-up 'your chance to win'. You may also consider whether there is mileage in some press coverage. If it is a contest purely in your show, make a promo of the winning moment that other presenters can play.

With any long-running competition make sure the winning answer is repeated often for a day or so, to put listeners who missed the winning moment out of their misery!

# Finally

Never admit there has been a poor response to a competition, you only usually need one contestant anyway. If calls are always slow it may be because the mechanic is too complicated, or the prize isn't interesting enough (and that doesn't necessarily mean that it's not expensive enough) Are you talking-up the competition enough and in the most tantalising way? Consider changing some of these elements.

If you desperately need callers, recycle them from other occasions: when they do call, take their details and ask if you can call them the next day to take part. Ask the same question to those who call in for dedications and requests and so on.

Remember the two main criteria for a competition are.

o   What would they like to win?
o   How easy is it for them to win?

# 24 Basic interviewing

A little earlier I talked about setting up interviews, so now let's take a slightly closer look at how to actually *conduct* one. I'll take you briefly through the process of preparing for your interview and how to get the best out of your guest, and then the kind of questions that are best to ask them.

## Preparation

This is the most important factor in getting a good interview.

> 'Sometimes you hear a radio interview with a celebrity and you hear more of the presenter than the star. I do a lot of big pop interviews and I prepare the same way as I would for TV . . . and keep it all in my head. An interview is a conversation with someone; so don't look down at your notes.
> Keep eye contact and you'll get a better interview.'
> Katie Hill, presenter Capital Radio, Radio Academy event, November 2005

Get as much information as is appropriate, considering the time you have before the interview and its duration.

You'll certainly want to write some questions to ask your guest. Some presenters say that doing this makes it more likely that they won't listen to the answers and simply work their way down the list. I disagree to a certain extent. Although you should certainly not rely on a list of prepared questions, writing a list of key topics to be covered does several things:

- It forces you to think about the subject . . .
- the guest . . .
- and the aim of the interview.
- And gives you a safety net if the interview doesn't go according to plan, for example if either you or the guest clams up.

While you're drawing up the questions think about what *you* want to know the answer to, and what your *listeners* want to know the answers to. Don't be tempted to take the easy road by following the news release that the guest's publicity people sent you. Interviews are more interesting if they're inspired. Yes, you have to ask the obvious questions, but the successful presenter is the one who goes the extra mile the one who asks the question no-one else thought of, and gets a terrific answer.

## More UGC

User-generated content is a great way of asking exactly the questions the audience wants to know the answers to. Opening an e-mail account to which listeners can post their questions, has several advantages.

- o You can gauge the top talking topics in which most people are most interested.
- o It's a great resource for some more 'left of centre' topics that you may not have considered.
- o There's the opportunity for name checks for the listeners and the mention of local places.

# Before the interview

Chatting-up or 'shampooing' your guest is a valuable thing to learn how to do. One great and polite way to relax them is by using their name. Don't give your guest a list of questions you'll ask, but do give them an idea of what *kind* of thing you want. They'll respond better if they're prepared but not rehearsed. You may though want to give them the first question in advance, one that you know they know the answer to, so they can get into their stride and 'warm up'. But don't make it too wide that they don't know where to start: 'You've just got back from your tour of America. Tell me about it.'

It's usually best not to have an in-depth discussion before you start your interview as it risks your guest saying, 'As I said before . . .'

## The length of an interview

On a local music and speech station it's thought that each part of a conversation should last about the same length of a song, so about 3 minutes. You can then play a song and return to the guest for a second bite, but if you keep talking for more than a few minutes you stand the chance of driving away some of your listeners.

# The question section

## 5Ws and an H

The basic 'questioning words' are 'who', 'what', 'when', 'where', 'why' and 'how'. Each of them is used to get a different kind of fact about people, times and places and so on, but perhaps the most underused one is 'why'.

Starting a question with this word will often get your guest to explain themselves, and perhaps reveal a little about their motivation. Any question that gets a guest to open up in this way invariably makes good radio.

## Clear questions

Under stress your guest may find it difficult to concentrate on what you're saying: they're in a strange environment and may never have heard or met you before, so make sure that your questions are straightforward. I don't mean that they should be short necessarily (although some of them may well be), but that they should be *clear*. Don't have long rambling questions: 'I wonder what you would say to some people who might think, or even say that, and in fact I think I've read that many people do in fact take this view, that this film, or indeed the last couple that you've made haven't really been necessarily some of perhaps the best films of this type that, perhaps, could have been made with the budgets available at that time . . .'.

Don't ask more than one question at a time: 'Can you tell me how long it took you to swim the channel and how much money you raised . . . ?'. Which one do you want them to answer first? And when they've done that, your guest may well have forgotten what the second question was!

Another problem for novice interviewers is that they ask questions that, although short and to the point, are simply too wide: 'This weekend's carnival, tell me about it.' OK, it's not really a question but most people would treat it as such and try to answer it. But where do they start? When it's on, what's going to be there, how long it took to plan, the problems they had getting the floats ready on time . . . ? Help your guest by giving them a little bit of focus.

## Open and closed questions

Open questions are ones that encourage the guest to speak: 'How did you manage to stay up the flagpole for three days and nights?'

Closed questions are ones that may only get you a one-word answer! 'You were up the flagpole for three days?'

One type is good and the other less so.

Open-ended questions are especially necessary when working with children, as closed questions will invariably illicit a simple 'yes' or 'no' response, although adults will give you a full answer, even if presented with a closed question.

Here are some question-starters to have up your sleeve the next time you speak with little Johnny or Josephine.

- Tell me about . . .
- Tell me how . . .
- What did you see . . .
- Describe it to me . . .
- What happened . . .
- How did that make you feel . . .

## Listen for your next question

Listen to what your guest is saying to give you a clue to your next question. This way the interview sounds more like a conversation.

PRESENTER: So when did you become interested in music?
GUEST: When I went to a Tibetan retreat for three years.
PRESENTER: And why the oboe?

The presenter's completely missed a great follow-up question, which could have taken them in an exciting new direction. And that's probably the problem: the interviewer hasn't done enough homework to feel confident enough to leave their written list. They either feel as though they'll lose control of the interview or that they simply won't be able to get through all their prepared points.

**INFORMATION FOR INSPIRATION:** It's not the quality of the questions you ask, it's the quality of the attention you give the answers.

## Active listening

Effective listening will make interviewing easier, because it'll be more productive. You'll ask more incisive and pertinent questions, your interviewee will give better replies, and you'll end up with better audio. You need to listen with an open mind, not jumping to conclusions or anticipating what you think you're about to be told. Psychologists call this 'active listening'.

The tricks include reflecting on what you're hearing and recording it in your mind as a 'headline'. That way you'll end up with a mental list of bullet points.

**INFORMATION FOR INSPIRATION:** You need to not only hear the words which are being said, but also note what is *not* being said: the hidden meaning of the reply.

Give the guest your attention. Don't start fiddling, cueing a song – pay attention and practice SOLER.

- Sit up straight.
- Open posture (arms and legs uncrossed).
- Looking genuinely interested, listening attentively.
- Effective eye contact.
- Remaining relatively relaxed.

## You don't always need to ask your guest questions

Asking questions can sometime seem quite confrontational and can narrow conversations rather than open them up. Here are some other ways you can ask for information:

- Say what you want to know and why. 'Tell me how you came up with the idea in the first place, I still don't see how a grandmother could invent a revolutionary internet gizmo.'
- Ask them to elaborate on something they've already said. It shows you're interested in what they're talking about, and that alone should help them open up. 'Tell me more about your plans to tour south east Asia . . .'
- When they've only half said something, get them to tell you more: 'You say you're thinking of quitting your record label . . .'
- Ask open questions. Ask how they feel about something, their reaction to something, to comment on or talk about something else. We want someone who *reacts*, not just gives us *facts*.
- Focus on what effect the story will have on people's lives (remember relatability). Are there stories that can be told, or an example they can give rather than facts and figures? Is there a 'worst case scenario' that can be used to illustrate their point? Make the interviewee human.
- What's their opinion? How upset or cross are they? Or maybe they're pleased about a decision.

## Coach your guest

Inexperienced interviewees may need a little coaching to put them at their ease. They may forget what point they want to get across, be unsure where they're heading with a sentence, or talk for a long time but not actually say anything.

> **INFORMATION FOR INSPIRATION:** If someone's story is vague or dull, work hard for clarity and interest.

If you want them to sound up-beat and lively, tell them! If you do it politely and diplomatically they'll invariably co-operate. They'll take it that you're as much an expert in your field, as they are in theirs. (You're doing them a favour – they don't want to sound like a 'suit' do they?)

Ask them how they'd explain their story to the man or woman on the street. Remember, if *you* don't understand what they're talking about, with the benefit of your research and a distraction-free studio, what chance has someone listening at home with a crying baby, or someone trying to negotiate the rush hour traffic in the car?

You'll also get a better performance from a guest by getting them to, unwittingly, 'voice-match' you. So, if you speak to them in a bright and breezy way, with a lively attitude, and calling them by their first name, they in turn will give a much more lively interview. If you speak with a slow and quiet voice they will come down to match it.

## Interview clips

If you're doing a news interview, the newsroom won't want your voice recorded at all. You'll have to keep quiet during the answers, so there's not a 'yep', 'uh huh', 'OK, I see' all the way through, which would be distracting to the listener when the clip is played in the bulletin and the audience wonders where the other voice has come from. This is most unlike normal life where we're encouraged to keep giving signals to show we understand what's being said. Instead use non-verbal communication: keep eye contact with the interviewee, without staring them out; look in tune with what they're talking about – look serious when they're saying something serious, raise your eyebrows and start to smile when they're telling a humorous story; nod from time to time, to indicate that you're keeping up with what they're telling you.

## Reflect their answers back to them

Your guest will be much more assured that the interview's going well and they're giving you what you want, if you pick up on what's said, and feed it back to them. 'So, what you're saying is that if everyone in the county donated a tea bag each, we'd be able to save the Hairy Mountain Gorilla from extinction?' It all helps to nudge the conversation along.

You can use phrases such as, 'That sounds important to you' or 'I'd like to know more about that' to show interest and encourage them.

## Leave room

Don't feel obliged to jump in with the next question immediately after they've stopped talking. Staying quiet for a few seconds may just nudge them that little bit further to open up a little bit more. People hate silence, and the interviewee will feel as though it's 'their' silence and one that they should fill by talking a little more.

## Signpost some of your questions

Your stream of questions should progress in a logical and ordered, albeit conversational, way. If they don't then you need to signpost the fact, both for the interviewee and the listener. 'On a different subject, how's the family . . . ?'

## Two sugars

If you present your interview in short bursts with music in between you may be in a studio having an off-air conversation with your guest for the best part of 15 minutes before they're re-introduced to the listener. That's fine if the guest is interesting and you can easily make small talk, but you may feel your very life force being drained out of you if they're not.

You can busy yourself for a few of those minutes by explaining the desk and the equipment to them, then spend a while cueing the next song or checking the travel presenter is ready. Beyond that you may find that you have to ask them *off air* what you are later going to be asking them *on air*! To avoid this happening (and risking them saying later, 'As I said to you before . . .') you may want to set up a secret signal with your producer. This is something that I've done in the past: a call on the talkback to ask for a coffee for the guest and one for me 'with two sugars' (when I usually don't take any) was a signal for them to come in and either talk to me about an important programming issue or to join in the small-talk with the guest. One thing you can't do, of course, is to leave the guest alone in an on-air studio!

## Remember to T.A.L.K.

- Technical – don't get so engrossed in the conversation that you forget the technical aspects of your broadcast. For example, are the levels still OK? Has the guest moved away form the mic as they became more relaxed? What about the pans? What about the timing of the sequence: are you on time for the travel news? How long have you been speaking for in this segment of talk? Is there enough, or too much of interest to keep this guest for the allotted time? If not, how will you fill it?
- Aims – also keep considering what you wanted to get out of the interview in the first place. Are you still heading in that direction and staying on course? There may be situations where a guest says something so interesting that you decide to veer away from your planned question areas to investigate another train of thought. Usually that's OK, but not necessarily always. If you do change course, think how you may want to get back on track to end the interview where you had intended.
- Listener – don't forget them while all this is going on. What's actually coming out of the radio? Has the interview got a bit incestuous (you and the guest talking about 'in' subjects which exclude the audience)? Is the conversation flowing logically? Are there too many breaks and are they in sensible places? Is the listener getting from the conversation what they were promised, or what they expected, or is there a little bit more? Maybe a surprise revelation or personal anecdote. Don't forget to occasionally re-establish the name of the station and who the guest is, for new listeners who are joining all the time.
- Kill – what are you going to do when the interview ends? Will you merely thank the guest, or do a summary of the conversation, or mention their book or song again? Then what happens? Have you got the next item cued? And what about the item after that (you'll inevitably spend a minute or so thanking the guest off-air and saying goodbye)? If you're going to go straight into another speech segment, how will this sound to the listener? If that item is travel, from a remote studio, how will you be able to dial them up and check the line and presenter's name if you're talking on-air yourself?

# At the end of the interview

When you're nearing the end of the interview, don't say '. . . and finally.' The guest may give such a great answer that you *have* to follow it up! If you do say '. . . and finally' in a pre-recorded interview, perhaps to signify to a nervous interviewee that you are nearly done, make sure you leave a short pause at the end of those two words, for easy editing. Saying 'briefly . . .' or 'one last thing . . .' will also signify to the interviewee that you're nearly finished.

Finish the interview on a high note. Most people will remember how it started and how it ended, rather than the bit in the middle.

## Copies of interviews

It's very unlikely that you'll ever provide these at your station. It's usually an awful lot of time and trouble to cassette something up, and usually only done if the request comes from a valued contact.

There are various ways you can get out of agreeing to dub-off a copy:

- 'If you'd asked before I could've recorded it as it was broadcast.'
- 'Oh no. Didn't you ask a friend to record it for you at home?'
- 'I'm sorry, we don't keep copies of the interviews once they've gone out.'
- 'We're so high-tech here, you know we don't even use cassettes, so I can't dub off a copy for you.'
- 'I'm so sorry it's been broadcast now and we don't have any copies. Though there is a theory that all radio and TV waves go out into space and it's only a matter of time before they come back'. (This idea is one that scientists seem to agree on: that radio shows from the '20s are coursing through space at around 186,000 miles per second. And if space is curved as is thought and one day we work out how to travel faster than light, we'll be able to hear them all over again!)

# 25 Phone-ins

'Going round the LA Talk Radio stations a few years ago, they told me
how the Talk format started up. About 15 years ago the big radio
chains had bought up all the independent music stations, but were
still looking for more acquisitions. They knew music was a winner on-
air, but the only stations still to buy were AM speech licences. So they
bought a few to find out how they worked. They decided the stations
had too many people working on each programme and that their
main objective was to fill their running orders with items rather than
to grab listeners and hold them. They felt the broadcasters were a
smug bunch, positioning themselves above their listener, and the
experts were even more remote. The output was authentic
"speech" programming: interviews, round table discussions about
issues, an author explaining their book etc. It was expensive to do and
not enough people listened. So they started to pull over some of their
more experienced disc jockeys and put this to them: do a four hour
rock-and-roll show but without the music. Talk about the themes that
make rock music popular: love, conflict, growing up and life in general.
Sure talk about Bill Clinton, but not his fiscal policy, talk about whether
he's a rat. Talk about things that people talk about amongst
themselves and talk about them with your listeners, not "experts".
And talk about them the way normal people talk about them.
Audiences rose and overheads went down.'

Tommy Boyd, presenter BBC SCR, *The Radio Magazine*, June 15th 2005

## Doing a phone-in

They've been a staple diet of local radio programmes for years, but how do you actually do
a phone-in? I'm going to answer that and more – I'm going to tell you how to do them
successfully. So successfully that your show will be full of relevant, interesting and compelling
conversation that'll inform and entertain callers and listeners.

Phone-ins are:

- Cheap – all you really need is a presenter and a producer (who are rather more than
  their colloquial title 'phone flicker' might suggest) to take the calls. In fact often the
  presenter takes their own calls while a song is playing.
- Democratising – the vast majority of listeners will have a phone at home, most will
  have a mobile as well and that means that any of them can get on air with their
  comment or issue.
- Involving – the station becomes a forum, a place where people can share their views
  in the community.
- Flexible – you can get instant reaction to the day's news both from listeners, experts
  and those in power.

- Informative — with an expert in the studio callers can have access to information on everything from piles to postcards.
- A way to get local people on-air — there's a chance for people to debate and be heard talking about local issues in local accents.
- A place to challenge — those in power such as politicians and councillors, the mayor or even the prime minister, can be put on the spot.
- Not just for the callers — the presenter and the producer should also consider those at home. What's the listener getting from this call, or this programme? You're there for those who call and those who don't.
- Popular with listeners — with a strong but even-handed host, phone-ins are some of the most popular shows on radio.
- Difficult to do well.

## Types of phone-in

These can be categorised as 'open' in various respects:

- Open line — these are the type often heard on BBC local stations' mid-morning shows where the presenter sets up three or four talking topics to be discussed and then opens the lines for callers' contributions, and as such is the type we'll look at in depth in this chapter.
- Open door — an expert, perhaps a doctor, a gardener, a job adviser, or collector of old records) is invited into the studio to take calls and questions from listeners on their area of expertise. Although this type of show is a service for those who've called, it's particularly important to keep the programme relevant to those at home too. This is why many presenters introduce the expert and have a brief chat with them, but have listeners' questions taken off air. The show can then continue with its usual features and music, with the expert returning to the studio later in the programme to highlight any particularly interesting calls.

  Certain experts, for example a doctor or solicitor, should be wary of offering too much specific advice over the phone, as they won't have seen the patient's notes or read the background to their legal case. Other so-called experts should be warned about promoting their own private interests over those of the listener. I recall hearing a phone-in with an expert in old postcards who to almost every caller said '. . . well, I'd have to see it to give an accurate valuation. Why not pop into my shop at 35 The High Street . . .'.

- Open minded — many stations have programmes that are based around personal, emotional or sexual matters. Callers either phone with their own stories on a specific subject, or put a question to the host or to a panel of experts (perhaps a doctor and a relationship adviser) for their advice. Many of these shows are quite frank and are naturally scheduled in the evening. Unlike TV stations, radio doesn't have a specific 9pm watershed after which more adult material can be broadcast, although most stations would take that time as a good guideline.

- Open ended — these types of phone-in are increasingly popular, adding 'user-generated content' to the output. Although it's similar to the open line mentioned above, the topics thrown out to the audience to respond to are not hard news stories inviting opinion, but rather quirky subjects inviting personal anecdotes. The subject may be running throughout a whole show, with calls taken between music, travel and news. And those subjects and the calls that arise from them are invariably diverse and creative. 'Have you ever been bitten by an animal?' 'Can you do an impression of someone that only you know?' or 'When clothes attack their owners . . .' are all recent topics run by stations as I write this book!

All of the above formats are slightly different in their content, but they share common elements: the careful combination of time of day, presenter and topic. A lot of this will be determined by the overall station style (a gardening programme is unlikely to work on a station with a chart-based format because the target audiences are different). Other elements are much more subtle, but are for the same ends – maximising the audience.

## A sign of the times

People are able to listen to the radio during the day more than ever before. This is mainly because of the arrival of personal media (Walkmans, iPods and mobile phones), and also because stations are streamed on the internet, which means that office staff can listen as they work.

It's not difficult to see that access to phones has also increased. There are walkabout phones at home, which means contributors can do other things while waiting for their time on air rather than being tied to the wall in the hall, and there's also the mobile phone. It means that those who didn't in the past have access to a phone (for example, drivers and factory workers and the like) can now have access to the airwaves. And, in a twist unthinkable a few years ago, it means that some people can listen to a phone-in programme and then contribute to it, by using exactly the same device!

## The phone-in presenter

If you want to get into radio but feel as though you don't know enough about music to be a music show presenter and anyway, you talk too much and have an opinion on everything, why not consider becoming a phone-in host?

'Good talk radio needs a host with gravitas, personality, intelligence and imagination. On top of that the extras amount to nothing more extravagant than a switchboard, a good tech/phone op, e-mail and text interaction, and maybe some newspapers. Good talk radio can be done economically in this country . . . our friends in the USA do it very successfully with nothing more than the resources I've outlined, and in some cases even less.'

Duncan Barkes, head of Presentation, Spirit FM,
*The Radio Magazine*, 16 October 2004

You'll need:
- A good general knowledge.
- An opinion on virtually everything.
- To be able to talk knowledgably and entertainingly.
- Passion and an ability to argue any point with authority.
- An interest in what's going on and, especially for local radio, an interest in local news.
- Inquisitiveness so you can see questions that need answers on a subject which is new to you.
- To be fast and sure of foot – so you can think, talk and act on your feet.
- A good working legal knowledge – the next caller could say something libellous and you need to know how to react.
- An ability to be abrupt, or even rude, if the occasion demands (such as a caller who won't get to the point or refuses to answer the question).

Some presenters of phone-ins are fence sitters, or 'conductors' of the various sides of the debate amongst listeners, and don't get involved with airing their own thoughts. Others know exactly where they stand.

> 'I have never, ever been impartial because as a talk show host, you can't say "on one hand there's this, on the other hand there's that" . . . I don't want to be anodyne like that.'
>
> Jon Gaunt, presenter talkSPORT
> *The Radio Magazine*, 26 October 2005

There's a place for both styles. Some stations want a host who can field calls from all comers, and be a referee, while others prefer someone to be more confrontational and controversial — to say something that will stir up some emotion from listeners.

**INFORMATION FOR INSPIRATION:** A good talker is not necessarily a good phone-in presenter. They have to listen and communicate too. And a good thoughtful and considerate listener is not necessarily a good phone-in presenter either, if they can't talk.

## The phone number

Only give out the phone number, text number or e-mail address if there's a reason, not just as a verbal crutch to give you time to think of what to say next. It's pointless and makes you sound desperate. When presenting a phone in, there *is* a reason and you need to give it out regularly.

There will probably be a certain way you read the studio number. Often it's because the collection of digits has a certain ring to it, or because the number has been specifically chosen as it includes the radio station's frequency (LBC 97.3 is 0870 90 90 973). And it's always because the management team wants everyone to say the number in the same way for consistency, so the audience easily remembers it. For LBC the number is written up in the studio so everyone pronounces it the same way: oh-8-7-oh 9-oh 9-oh 9-7-3, rather than 'ninety ninety ninety-seven three' or 'nine hundred and seventy three'. Such detail should be written in the station's House Style Guide.

You can easily confuse listeners by giving out too many phone numbers and web addresses. Try to stick to just your phone-in and travel line number, your text number and your own web address. Other information can be posted on this site, which saves you reading out details on air, saves the listener rushing for a pen, and drives listeners to your station site which will please the advertises who are featured on it.

## Choosing topics

In a news and comment phone-in the topics have to be carefully considered. Setting up a discussion by the presenter may sound spontaneous but a lot of thought goes into each programme:

**The ten steps to top topics**
1. What are today's hot topics?
2. What are people talking about today?
3. Which ones are relevant for our listeners?
4. More specifically, do our target listeners *care*?
5. Do enough care enough to call and have a busy show?
6. Is the topic easy to debate without getting bogged down in detail?
7. Will people talk from personal experience, not just have a knee-jerk reaction?
8. What strong emotions does the topic deliver to engage and encourage listeners?
9. Is the presenter genuinely interested in the topic, to encourage and engage callers?
10. Is there a good mix of topics? National and local, light and shade, serious and fluffy?

Let's look at some of those steps a little closer:
- Step 2. There are two subjects people will talk about forever: the weather and the best route to get somewhere. But those topics wouldn't make a good phone-in.
- Step 4. You should consider not just those who are listening but also those who you want to listen longer. What topics will attract them to listen and call?
- Step 5. The more callers you have to choose from, the higher you can raise the quality of those who get on air.
- Step 7. The people who have knee-jerk reactions are usually jerks themselves.
- Step 8. Those emotions may be fury or frustration, but they may also be humour and happiness. Show the audience you care about the community by spending time explaining in a clear and compelling way the good stories as well as the bad.
- Step 9. If you, the presenter, are interested by the item, then you can make it interesting and listeners will be interested as a result.

**INFORMATION FOR INSPIRATION:** Know your position and know your opinion.

'How dare you not be honest with them as they are with you. It would be fundamentally unfair. The great jocks aren't shock ones; they're the ones who give something of themselves. But all the same, you've got to have impact.'
Jon Gaunt, talkSPORT
Radio Academy Speech Radio conference, 2005

See p. 164, the Emotion Quotient, for the four hot-keys for generating content that'll touch your listener. Focus on one or two of these a show and use the others for balance.

## Opinions and experiences
Topics which ask people for opinions often produce less-good radio, as they're often poorly thought-through, and with less emotion are less compelling. You'll encourage opinions by using phrases such as, 'What do you *think* about this?'

'(Pat Loughrey, BBC Director of Nations and Regions) wants to change the radio phone-in that he says too often presents ill-informed opinion instead of listeners' experiences.'
*Ariel*, 13th December 2005

Topics that affect people, or have affected them, are better 'phone-in fodder' than ones that merely ask for an opinion. That's because people talk more convincingly and knowledgeably when they speak from the heart — with a real-life event that has emotion and feeling. Personal experiences humanise a topic to create compelling radio that's interesting for the listeners as well as the callers. Remember the 'People Principle'; cover items about people and encourage experiences by using phrases such as, 'How do you *feel* about this?' The more personal a story, the more universal and relatable it is.

'I'm not a great fan of interviews in the traditional sense.
Too often they just produce predictable answers and plugs
for this book or that film. To me, real people with real
stories and opinions make for interesting radio.'
Clive Bull, Presenter, LBC 97.3, *The Radio Magazine*, 20 April 2005

## The selfish streak

Consider how the listener will view the topic that you're discussing. That's *the listener*, not the caller. What are they likely to get out of the item? Will they get emotional, become angry, upset, frustrated? Is there 'social ammunition': information of value that they can use in conversations with other people?

**INFORMATION FOR INSPIRATION:** Find the What's-In-It-For-Me Factor in every item to help focus and develop the item, and help keep callers calling *and* listeners listening.

## An open, open line?

Obviously make sure you're listening to the news, but don't fall into the trap of merely opening the phone lines and letting people comment on the stories. Think whether there's an underlying trend or cause of what's happened, can you take the story on?

 **ACTUAL AUDIO**

PRESENTER: Wherever you are, just give me a call . . .
*Local commercial radio station, November 2005*

For example, if there's been a road accident on a winter's morning you could ask why people don't clear their screens properly, all for the sake of saving five minutes.

## Where they go in the flow

As well as thinking of what stories to cover, also consider where they go in the programme and how much time they get. Balance your topics so you have a flow through the programme rather than a sudden gear change: people will stay with the station if one topic develops into another, but will turn off if it jars.

Most topics will start having equal time on your running order, but drop a topic if it's not hot, and stay with one that is. Plus, you may want to have a short 10-minute fun filler at the end of the show for people to react to: 'After the biggest jackpot win, what would you spend your millions on?'.

## Play your MyPod

With most stations playing the same songs, it's difficult for listeners to find true variety and distinctive difference between stations. With phone-ins as well as other programme elements, you can use a secret weapon that only you have: your MyPod.

Ask yourself how you would do an item different from anyone else. What is your personal take, your personal experience or viewpoint that no one else can attempt to replicate? Your Point of Difference.

Don't put a boring story in as a phone-in topic, just because it's a big story. If everyone else is talking about it, consider whether you want to as well. You may want to – you don't want to be left out – but can you add any more to the discussion? Can your listeners? Do you have a unique view? Focus and keep it fresh.

> **INFORMATION FOR INSPIRATION:** Ask, 'What is my point of difference?' between how you'll do the item and how everyone else will do it.

Although you should always be true to your on-air character, occasionally surprise people with your angle or your view.

> 'The balance is always between the obvious and the inspiring – we can't miss out the biggest story of the day, but how can we surprise our listeners? Once they guess our choice of stories and approach we're dead.'
> Jeremy Vine, presenter, BBC Radio 2, *The Radio Magazine*, 6 April 2005

Make the talking topics and the way you present them, personal, and you become more relatable.

## Setting up the topics

At the start of the show (or even in the programme before) you need to tell people what topics are up for discussion and invite them to take part. This is sometimes called 'the churn':

- The laundry list – this is the most straightforward way of mentioning the items. A simple list of fact followed by invitation: 'Train fares are going up again. What do you think? Call me on . . .' .You could get through your whole list of four or five topics in less than a minute. The trouble is that saying, 'Here's something you may want to talk about' is weak and isn't making an attempt to engage or entice. You don't say that in real life at work: 'Here's a topic for us to talk about'!

---

 **ACTUAL AUDIO**

PRESENTER: Tonight we're going to talk about communication . . . have you ever had good or bad experiences . . . let me know.

*BBC local station, December 2005*

---

▫ The flip flop — as above, but it takes a little more time as you'll be giving the pros and the cons of each side of the issue: 'Train fares are going up again. Companies say they need the extra revenue to improve services, but passengers' groups say there's been no obvious improvement since the last round of rises. Are you prepared to pay for a better service, and who do you think should be keeping an eye on the companies to make sure that passengers get what they pay for?'

▫ The personal view — this stall setting takes longer still but is usually most effective. Launch into a monologue, perhaps of a minute or two, on your own personal thoughts and experiences of the issue. It may not be immediately clear from the opening what topic you're talking about, but that'll help draw in the listener who'll become intrigued by the story. Tease them with the topic, dangle the angle, paint a picture and get them to think about it (without specifically *asking* them to think about it). Then pose a question and ask for calls. Give people a reason to call not simply because you thought it would be a good topic of the day — that just makes you sound desperate! This personal connection will either rile or enthral the audience who'll be encouraged to call to support the compelling views or shoot them down in flames.

*'Radio to react to.'*
The slogan of BBC Three Counties Radio

This technique isn't an excuse for you to spout your views without taking calls and hearing what other people have to say. The callers are the stars, and the presenter presents the callers. It's a dialogue not a monologue. Don't become a 'we talk, you listen' station.

It's a humbling experience to admit that you don't know and most talk show presenters are not humble. One of them is Jon Gaunt, ex-BBC Three Counties, BBC London and BBC Coventry and Warwickshire. He's strong-minded and opinionated. But occasionally he'll admit that he doesn't know what to think about a subject. 'Call me and let me know what you think, because I really don't know' is a line that you (occasionally) heard on his phone-in show. As a presenter, don't be afraid to admit that you don't know something. Better ignorance than arrogance. It shows you're human and it shows that you're telling the truth — and the truth is easier to remember than an artificial and controversial standpoint the next time that same subject comes up.

Those are three basic techniques and I'm sure there are some more that you've heard or can adapt. In short, as well as choosing items that are relevant, interesting and compelling, make that fact obvious to those who are listening. Tell them why the issue might matter to them, why they might be concerned about it. Raise arguments, either by posing specific questions or by getting listeners to react and respond naturally to what you believe.

A completely open open-line, where you take calls on all the subjects throughout the show, and in any order, may cause problems. Listeners could call with any comment on any issue at any time. That could either make for a lively and reactive discussion, or perhaps one that's confusing and disjointed. It would mean that you, the host, would have to be light-footed to jump from one issue to another. You'll have to continually explain the topic before each few calls as many listeners will have tuned in after the initial 'menu' has been presented.

There's certainly an argument for mentioning the topics together at the start of the show, but then having a running order in which you introduce them and the callers' comments on them, in depth. That gives the listener a feeling for the show at the start, and teases them with issues that'll be discussed later, and time to start considering their own thoughts and feelings before being discussed on air. You simply follow the initial churn with '. . . but first I'd love your thoughts on this . . .'.

Just before closing each issue, do a bit of 'plate-spinning' and start inviting people to call and contribute for the next one so you'll have someone to speak with a few minutes later. Finally close down each topic with a summary of the issues and say that it's '. . . time to move on . . .'. This is usually best done using the news or ad-break as a natural 'book end'.

## Resetting the topics

During the programme present the topic again (but don't re-read it word for word) and include a précis of some of the comments you've already received, perhaps even recorded and clipped:

'We're talking about school dinners and whether enough's being done to make them as healthy as they should be. Earlier we heard from Elizabeth in Southtown who said that her children's school has won a healthy eating award for its dinners, but Mark in Kingston Wells, you think that the meals are as bad as ever . . .'.

Putting their comments in context like this helps those at home (and especially those who've just joined the show) follow what's going on. It's like a story-so-far reminder that TV shows have at the start of each new episode.

## Are the phones broken?

If, after several mentions of a topic, no one is taking the bait, ask yourself why. Perhaps you wanted to cover the topic because *you* were interested in it rather than thinking about the listeners?

- Have you phrased the set-up in the most relevant and captivating way?
- Consider changing focus.
- Use another anecdote to illustrate your point.
- Add something new; don't just rehash what didn't work the first time.

If no one's calling about the topic, quietly drop it. Don't announce that you're dropping it or that no one's called about it so, 'you're obviously not interested'. Doing that shows your failure and if they don't care enough to call about it, they don't care enough to know that you're not running it anymore!

**INFORMATION FOR INSPIRATION:** If it's dead, bury it.

'The perfect radio show for me is one where you're just hanging out with the host. The less it sounds like radio the better. For my own show I always feel it's gone well if something I hadn't bargained on has happened and taken off. My producer Bob and I do a fair amount of preparation and talking through ideas, but the best night is the night when the plans get thrown in the bin because something even better has developed as the night has gone on.'
Clive Bull, Presenter, LBC 97.3, *The Radio Magazine*, 20 April 2005

# Screening callers

Let's be brutally honest, most people listen to a radio phone-in show for the host – not for the callers! Only a very small percentage of listeners ever pick up the phone to make a call (perhaps 1%). The show is actually for everyone else who listens. The callers are there to make the presenter look good because of what they've said or how they've said it. A boring person is not going to do that. A boring person is like a boring song – it gets turned off. Just because someone calls, it doesn't mean that they have the right to get on-air. If they're dull, don't add anything to the debate or don't fit your target demographic, don't put them on.

Instead you want callers who are going to talk meaningfully about their own experiences. Why what has happened has changed them, moved them or made them what they are.

'I'm not that interested in caller's opinions. To be honest, I couldn't care less what Doris in Ongar thinks about anti-social behaviour but if she can offer me a genuine insight into how it affects her life then I'll bite her arm off. I remember a lady who called in two hours after changing the locks on her flat because her 18-year-old had started stealing off her 12-year-old to buy drugs and she felt a failure. I was asking people about the best news they'd ever received over the phone and a dad phoned in to tell us about the call he got to say that his daughter's leukaemia had gone. He said

"I'm six foot three and built like a brick outhouse but I can't think of this without wanting to cry." He promptly burst into tears and I bet he wasn't the only one. Another example if you like, of stories being much more powerful than opinions.'

James O'Brien, LBC 97.3, *The Radio Magazine*, 14 September 2005

**INFORMATION FOR INSPIRATION:** Not everyone who has *done* something interesting, *is* interesting.

## First things first

Obviously the first thing is to answer the phone with an agreed phrase. It's very unlikely to be purely 'Hello?' but may be 'Hello . . .' together with the name of the station or the programme name. It's probably best to then get straight to the point and ask, without a beat, '. . . What's your point/question?'

Then go through this mental checklist of eleven questions every screener should ask themselves:

1. Is their comment new or a rehash of what you've heard already? If it's new, and especially if they disagree with the presenter's view or most of the other callers, put them on. A strongly-voiced and controversial view makes good radio.
2. Is their comment clear and valid? Most people aren't that interesting.
3. Do they add to the geographical mix of callers you've had so far in the programme? If they widen the net and especially if they're from part of the area you rarely hear from, they're more likely to get on, even with a weaker point. If they're from outside your area (even if they do listen on the internet) you probably don't want them on your local station unless their point is exceptional.
4. If your station covers a wide area, does this person add another accent to the mix? You may want to 'bump up' callers who fulfil these criteria.
5. Is it a woman? A senior phone-in producer at the BBC tells me that fewer women call his show, so when they do, they stand a better chance of getting on.
6. Are they part of your target age bracket? Are they old enough to have knowledge of this subject?
7. Is the line quality clear? If they're on a walkabout home-phone, speakerphone or on a crackly mobile they may not be any good.
8. Are they using the phone properly? Many people either have the mouthpiece too close to their mouth which causes distortion, or tucked under their chin which makes them sound distant and echoey.
9. Are they new? Some stations have specific first-time caller days to encourage those who are usually put off from calling by hearing the same voices time and time again. First timers add new voices, new experiences and new perspectives and that helps keep the show fresh.
10. Are they legal? If they're driving they have to be on a hands-free.
11. Are they standing? During the pending period before an election, check that they aren't a candidate, or if they are, that they aren't going to say anything political (see more in the chapter on the law, pp. 134–138).

Don't let the tail wag the dog. Too many calls go to air to satisfy the caller or to fill time on the show, rather than for the benefit of the show or the audience as a whole.

It's a self-fulfilling prophesy: each time you put a great call to air it teaches other listeners what they have to do if *they* want to get on. And vice versa.

**INFORMATION FOR INSPIRATION:** The best way to get great on-air calls, is to air great calls.

'If you put a bad call up, it won't give you another caller.'
Jon Gaunt, talkSPORT
Radio Academy Speech Radio conference, 2005

## Pre-interview them

If the caller is vague, a producer should work for clarity. Ask exactly what point they want to make: it helps focuses their mind and structure their thoughts and helps you both discover what their viewpoint. That way they're better able to say it succinctly if you decide to put them through. If they give a great reply or use a sentence that's enthusiastic, funny or outrageous then ask that they say that again when they're on air.

Too many times on the radio we hear something like this:

PRESENTER:  And on line 3 it's Larry in Lastownonearth. Hi Larry, how are you?
LARRY:  Oh, not very well, it's my corns . . .

Or

PRESENTER:  Here's Larry from Lastownonearth. Hi Larry, what are you up to this afternoon?
LARRY:  I'm just rehearsing my lines for my first recording of *EastEnders* tomorrow . . .
PRESENTER:  Great! So what do *you* think about rail fares?

The producer should chat-up the caller and find out what's interesting about them before they're put on air. The presenter should listen to the answer when they ask a question! It is your job as ringmaster to make the audience (the 'performing animals') perform to the best of their ability, to provide an entertaining show for the rest of the audience.

If they sound good, you and your show does too. You can bask in the reflected glory. Other listeners will begin to understand what's expected from them should they ever phone in.

Don't just process them – prepare them for their 'star turn' in the hope that they'll perform better.

**INFORMATION FOR INSPIRATION:** Phone-in listeners do your show for you. But only if you explain how you want it done.

## Set them up

Now take their phone number and name, obviously. If necessary, take it phonetically. It may be unusual or foreign, or even one that can be misread. That way, the presenter will introduce Sean as 'shawn' rather than 'seen', and won't stumble when they suddenly see the winner is 'Helen Shariatmadari'. You're not embarrassed and neither is Helen. It's insulting to hear unusual names followed by 'I hope that's how you say it . . .'. If someone's texted in, you have their number, call them back and check how they say their name.

Additionally note, again if necessary, if the caller is a man or woman. It may be that it's a man with a high voice and you don't want them to be embarrassed on air. It may be that you can't remember whether Leslie is the man's or woman's spelling of that name, and want to make sure that the presenter doesn't cross to them with an unfortunate remark.

The number is because:

- You may want to call them back to check that they are who they say they are.
- You want them later in the show, rather than right now.
- Taking their number sieves out the cranks who're dissuaded from calling.
- If someone malicious does get through to the programme, you have their number in case any follow-up is needed.

Tell the caller what you want from them:

- To speak up.
- To make their point succinctly.
- To call the presenter by their name.

Ask the caller to make sure their radio is off and to listen down the phone for them being introduced. This is because if a station was in delay, they'd be introduced in 'real time' several seconds before they heard their name on the radio. Even if the station's not in delay, there's still a split second between being spoken to on the phone and hearing it on the radio which causes confusion. Plus there's always the possibility of howl-round feedback.

Warn the caller they'll simply be cut-off at the end of the conversation (in other words they won't be handed back to you), so thank them in advance for their call.

Pass the caller's name and town through to the presenter together with what line number they're on. Do this via the shared computer system (a 'visual talkback') that can be seen in the studio. It may be that the presenter takes the calls sequentially or maybe out of order, and they can do that if they know where each contributor is on the phone-in panel. Also let the presenter know if the caller has a particular point that needs to be drawn out (perhaps they're calling to comment about abuse, but don't mind mentioning that they were abused as a child), if there's something else the presenter should know (for example, if they have a quiet voice or a stutter), or how good the call is. But keep these comments (or your shorthand for them) consistent so the presenter knows what you're referring to.

There are many computer-based switchboard systems for radio stations but they all work in a similar way. The screen will show you when a line is ringing: touch it once to answer it and speak to the caller, press it again to put it through to the studio. The presenter will put it to air by selecting it and raising its appropriate fader. A further touch will disconnect the call. More sophisticated systems will also log each call giving you information such as how long the contributor was waiting on the line before it was answered and if they've rung before. If they have (or at least if someone has rung from that same number) the computer system will show the caller's name and location, when they last called and what topic they called about. That kind of information is useful if you don't want to keep putting regular callers to air.

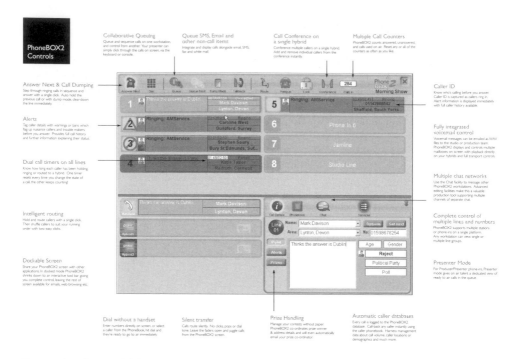

Promotional material for the popular PhoneBox call-answering system.
Courtesy: Broadcast Bionics

# The more calls the better?

Lots of calls do not necessarily mean a popular show. You may have lots of calls of the wrong type (see the checklist above): many people are on air (all the crank callers have realised that it's a free for all and are taking advantage), but too few are *listening*. Some topics attract lots of callers and few listeners, and others attract few callers and lots of listeners.

When I was a presenter at Mercury Xtra AM, a regular guest was a psychic. We had lots of calls from people wanting their personal readings, but I doubt many were listening at home because the information was of little relevance to them. When I was at Kfm we had a solicitor who talked about how to get the best deal from your divorce. No one called. That was probably because even though the subject was fascinating to everyone listening, no one actually wanted to discuss their situation on air. The fact that we had no calls didn't mean the subject wasn't relevant, interesting or compelling.

> **INFORMATION FOR INSPIRATION:** Flashing phone-in lights are not necessarily an indicator of a good show.

# Enough info

Producers should always make sure the presenter has enough information to cope if the quality or number of calls isn't high or if the phone system crashes. Can they carry part of the show by themselves? Has the presenter got enough back-up material to be able to talk about this issue, or enough other information to talk about others? Is there a guest that you can have on to talk about the topic (perhaps to help set it up)?

# Scheduling callers

Just as the music is scheduled, so too should callers be. You need a variety of content to help provide conflict, a variety of voices: younger and older (which fit your target demo), male and female; 'pro' and 'anti' the issue and so on. All these factors help provide both balance and momentum, making it more engaging to the listeners and provoking more callers. The music presenter has a variety of songs in a programme – you need a variety of callers.

So with each call you take you should not only ask:

- *Do* we get them on? But also
- *When* do we get them on?

Here's *Stewart's Scheduling System*:

- The first calls should be ones that disagree with the presenter to provide immediate conflict.
- The last call into a break (ads, travel, news, song, end of show) should be a short 'kicker' to end that part of the show on a high.
- The first call *after* a break should be a strong one to re-establish the show, the subject and the host.
- Look out for people with opposing ideas to go head to head.
- Consider controversial callers who'll heighten the debate (but look for balance within the programme).
- Be flexible – move callers around to heighten the debate.
- Push a call with passion up the list – fast-track exceptional contributors.
- Remember, callers on mobiles, or those waiting a long time, aren't automatically better callers.

Don't be afraid to keep callers on hold for the slot when their contribution will have maximum impact, or ask to call them back. Just keep checking calls on hold, are still on hold!

# On air

Your job as presenter is to get the best performance out of yourself and also the best performance out of other people. That means working a listener so they give you what you want to make entertaining radio. This, like everything that makes a difference and sounds good, takes a bit of work and practice, but it'll be worth it. Will the other listeners notice that you do it? Probably not. Will they notice if you *don't*? Probably.

## A balancing act

Make sure your phone levels are properly balanced. The quality of a phone-line means that it needs to be stronger than you on the studio mic to stand a chance to be heard on air. If you can't turn the phone channel up, turn yours down, and allow the processor to boost you both.

## Saying hello

Don't greet every caller the same way:

PRESENTER: Hello Susan, how are you?
CALLER: Hi Rob. Very well thank you, how are you?

PRESENTER: Fine thanks, what did you want to talk about?

If you or your phone-op has done their job properly and chatted to the caller off air, you'll at least be able to say 'Susan's on AllTalk FM now, and you want to talk about the price of petrol . . .' which will stop the 'hellos' in their tracks. You may be able to go one step further and cut out even more of the conversational pre-amble by saying: 'Susan's on the line now, and you've got a novel way of saving money on petrol, haven't you?'

Continue using their name throughout the conversation. It's calming and polite.

Build the name of the station into your introductions as a matter of course to continue basic branding.

## How are you?

Don't ask someone how they are, unless you really want to know the answer. It works the other way around as well, with listeners asking the host how they are, but there's not much you can do about that! As Mike Dicken on talkSPORT used to say to callers when they started a conversation with the phrase, 'Hello Mike, how are you?', 'My health is not in question . . .'.

## Voice match

Change your voice (its speed, tone and projection) to match that of the caller. It should be natural (we talk to our boss in a different voice to the one we use for our mum or sister), yet many presenters don't do this.

Voice matching is polite, and helps to establish a rapport with the caller and makes the conversation easier to listen to.

## Watch for windbags

Ever been at a party and got talking to someone who fills five minutes of space with one minute of information? Some callers are like that despite the best work of the producer to screen them out. Listen out for them and move on if necessary.

## Domination

Don't take over the conversation. The caller is the guest and is not used to speaking on the radio and getting over a point as succinctly as you are. Help them by chatting to them, asking them to explain, and gently probing their views, not by being argumentative. However, if they're talking nonsense or are too garrulous, get rid of them.

## Don't mention

Don't say that other callers are waiting. If you want to tell Tony in Todcaster that he'll have to wait till after the travel news, tell him on the phone, personally and privately, not across the radio: 'Tony in Todcaster, stay on hold we'll be with you after the travel news . . .'.

To broadcast that information tells all the other potential callers that they may have to wait (and waste time) before *they* get on-air. Hardly encourages them to call, does it?

And don't say, 'Mike from Molehampton, you're on line 14 . . .': you already know Mike's on line 14, Mike doesn't know and doesn't need to know, so why tell him? No one else needs to know either, so why tell them?

# Saying goodbye

Do you say it or not? Some programmers say you *always* should, others that you *never* should. I personally think that variety is the spice of life and you should use both techniques. Saying, 'Well, Sam that's an interesting point, thanks for calling with it, goodbye' is polite and gives 'closure' to the caller and the listener. However, there's another technique that will make the programme flow much more.

If you come off the back of one of the caller's comments and instead of talking to them, you talk to the rest of the audience (still, though on a one-to-one basis) you can segue seamlessly to another topic or caller.

To the caller: 'Sam what an horrific tale . . . (to the listener) and I wonder if you've had a similar experience to the one that Sam was just describing. Have *you* also come across an insect in pre-packaged supermarket food? If so call me now on . . .'. Or consider ending the call on the best bit (that's enthusiastic, funny or outrageous) and then going into a jingle, song or break, and saying thanks and goodbye to them *off air*.

# Recording calls

Although some programme controllers may object to this technique, having the conversation off-air, recording it, editing it, and *then* broadcasting it, can make the caller and the station sound fantastic. Although most phone-ins are live, a music-based show may benefit from this technique. You may have set a trivia question or competition or asked people to call with ideas for the name of a newly discovered planet or funny stories about when they were first kissed. All of these contributions are likely to be long-winded and contain a lot of chaff. You can take the call while a song is playing, re-route it through the off-air part of the on-air desk onto a digital recorder and then edit it. By doing this, you can put the wheat to air, and in the process maintain editorial control, the pace of the programme and the interest of the listeners.

Be ready to record every call that comes to you to stand a better chance of netting the best ones. As you do it, listen for the parts that can be removed to make the call shorter and stronger. There are various ways of doing this.

Distillation of the first part of a caller's contribution immediately makes the conversation tighter.

'Hi, how are you? You were talking about, earlier, about kissing? Well, I wondered if you'd like to hear . . . I mean I've got quite a good story. I don't know if it's any good but . . . you are? Well, it was about five years ago, well perhaps seven. Yes, seven, I was at school so it must have been in 1998, and . . .'.

You probably recognise that kind of caller: polite, but hesitant and slow. How much better a recorded and edited version would sound. You could distil their thoughts in to a more concise and understandable phrase of your own. Simply say the introduction live and then play in the recorded caller, starting with their voice to avoid a clash of tone on yours.

PRESENTER:  Now Marie's on the line from Callumham. Hi Marie, when was your first kiss?
MARIE:  I was at school so it must have been in 1998, and . . .

Another advantage of recording calls is that you can explore other avenues of conversation, which in a live situation you may have avoided for fear of discovering a cul de sac. By recording, you can probe for more information, without worrying about time. Let's take that call again.
MARIE:  **I was at school so it must have been in 1998, and it was one of those**

end of term parties and I was in the corner with **Darren Watkins** . . . I think
that was his name, anyway it doesn't matter . . .
PRESENTER: **What school was this?**
MARIE: **Blankstown Middle.**
PRESENTER: That's not around any more is it?
MARIE: No. **It's such a shame they knocked it down . . . I had so many happy
memories there . . .**
PRESENTER: Like what?
MARIE: **You know. Behind the bike shed!**

By keeping in the phrases in bold, and editing out the lighter type, your call will be
much stronger than if you'd taken the call live.
Editing:

- Makes calls more compelling by keeping the content relevant ('quality control').
- Saves time on air.
- Reduces the possibility of your listeners' attention wandering.
- Means you're more in control and can avoid legal pitfalls.
- Means you can explore other areas of conversation and work hard for clarity.
- Makes you sound better as well as the caller: a joke doesn't work? Cut it out!
- Is another way to weed-out the wheat and chuck the chaff. You don't have to use
  the poor callers at all.

Is this editing unethical? No. It's what happens in newsrooms all the time. What it does
mean is that you as a presenter have to do a bit more work to make your programme sound
better. Sounds like a fair exchange!

> **INFORMATION FOR INSPIRATION:** Editing calls can
> make callers, the station and you all sound fantastic.

## The rules of recording calls

All desks are set up slightly differently, but this is the main process:

- Check how much time you've got left on the song that's playing in which you can
  record and possibly edit your call.
- Switch your mic to the record channel.
- Check this has worked before you launch into your recorded call, which would other-
  wise go out live over the song that's currently playing. (Simply listen to off-air output
  and listen as you click your fingers.)
- Similarly check the caller's channel isn't going to air.
- Record and edit your call, keeping an ear open to what's happening on air – you
  don't want a song to end!
- Return your mic to the on-air channel, otherwise you'll go to back-anno a song and
  won't be heard!
- Give a live introduction to the caller and then play in the recording *starting with their voice*,
  so there's no voice clash of you, live, introducing you, recorded.
- There's no need to say that the call is recorded. Live is more interesting and exciting
  than recorded. *Who Wants To Be A Millionaire?* is recorded, but that doesn't reduce the
  tension. Simply play the call and allow the listeners to presume what they want to
  maximise their enjoyment.

# The index of eighteen callers to avoid

I said earlier that phone-ins are democratic, that anyone can get to air. Well that's not totally true. There are inevitably some people whose voices will rarely grace the airwaves of your radio station. They are:

1. The crank caller – with a ridiculously implausible story.
2. The rude caller.
3. The aged caller who is way out of your target demo, who sounds sweet, but loses their, err, train of thingy.
4. The underage caller with a story about sex and drugs.
5. The politician during election run-up.
6. The wannabe politician – ditto.
7. The windbag who talks until they think of something interesting to say.
8. The dullard for whom the word 'mono-tone' was created.
9. The unintelligible whose argument has more holes than a moth-infested, crocheted blanket.
10. The speakerphone caller who is too rude to actually hold the phone, and sounds as though they're talking from the toilet.
11. The mobile caller . . . whose call . . . keeps . . . hello? . . . hello? . . . breaking up . . . hel . . .
12. The heavily accented – who others simply won't be able to understand.
13. The regular caller. You say: 'Hello Jim. Again'. You *think*: 'I do have more than the same dozen listeners, don't I?'
14. The presenter's 'friend'. 'I met Andrew down at the cricket, bought him a pint, y'know. He said to call . . .'.
15. The slow coach. 'Yesterday Andrew was saying about . . .'.
16. The abusive caller . . . 'This is crap . . .'. Ignore them and move along.
17. The one-hit wonder, who talk about any issue, as long as it's their own pet peeve.
18. The needy . . . 'I just called for a chat . . .'.

# How to say no thanks . . .

So, how do you tell these people that they can't go on air? Well, you don't. At least not in those words.

Put them on hold for a few seconds and then go back to them and say:

- 'We've got several other calls lined up, and I don't want to keep you on hold if we can't fit you in, can you try again another day?'
- 'We're really busy on this topic today . . . I'll take your number and will try and call you back.'
- 'I've just lined up someone else who's making the same point . . . sorry.'
- 'I don't think your mobile line is clear enough to be able to take you to air . . .'.
- 'We've lined up as many callers as we need now thanks, and we're nearing the end of the show.'
- 'I've got to dash and answer some other calls, sorry!'
- 'I'll pass the comment on, thanks for calling.'
- 'Really sorry, we're running out of time.'
- 'That's great, thanks for calling, really appreciate it.'

- o  'You're in a really long queue, I don't want to crank up your bill . . .'.
- o  'Y'know what, we're just finishing this topic.'

**INFORMATION FOR INSPIRATION:** Radio is not been democratic. You don't put on every song that's ever been released, and neither should you put on air everyone who wants to say something.

## Finally

If you want to know what the listener's experience of all this is, call a phone-in show yourself and see the process the other way around.

# 26 Other kinds of show

## The zoo

A group of friends having fun, talking about what's going on through the eyes of their own distinct character – characters in a 'zoo programme' or 'team show' are cast according to a model that's been developed from TV and cinema. This originally American idea arguably peaked in British radio in the '90s with the studio 'posse' of Steve Wright In the Afternoon on Radio One, and then the emergence of Chris Evans' crew on GLR, Radio One and Virgin. The concept, of having more than one presenter on air at a time, is still used to great effect specifically on commercial radio and specifically in the morning.

For this part of the Handbook, I asked Will Kinder from Radio 1 to share some of his techniques that he used when he produced and appeared on air with Chris Moyles.

> 'Beware!
> Zoo radio is much more difficult than it sounds.
> Simply filling a room with people, all chatting sounds horrendous.
> Zoo radio takes a considerable amount of discipline and
> each member of the team must be as professional
> (and potentially talented) as the main presenter.
>
> Will Kinder, producer, Radio 1

## Why a zoo?

Zoo formats have more than two presenters: one main front person (someone has to be 'the air traffic controller' and decides what happens, where the live link is going, and where it lands) and several others who contribute to the output. The use of the word 'characters' is a deliberate one, as members of the zoo team are chosen for specific attributes, either real-life or imagined.

The different characters are necessary to:

- Appeal to the different characteristics of the listening audience, so everyone feels included and involved.
- Draw out different stories, perspectives and experiences. If all the characters are similar then their reactions to experiences are also likely to be the same, and that could make for boring radio.
- Highlight conflict, confrontation and contrast that engage the listener.
- Have the listener take sides, thereby having emotional involvement in the show.
- Give the impression to the listener that they're eavesdropping on a spontaneous conversation.

This is similar to a TV sitcom, where the characters have different personalities that cause friction and therefore humour. But having different characters isn't enough in itself. You also need your core listeners to care about them and relate to them, and have those characters say things that are relevant, interesting and compelling.

## The characters

The comedy is driven around the creation of three broad character types: The Intellectual (the clever person), The Idiot (the innocent fool) and the Mr I Am (the smart Alec).

The typical characters who are cast in a radio zoo-type show, may include:

- The main presenter who does the work of introducing the music and furniture features such as news and travel. They're often the warm and approachable person, but may also be slightly anarchic or renegade. Think of them as the 'kid brother' or 'kid sister'. (Mr I Am or the smart Alec.)
- The second presenter may be more 'ditzy', they often don't quite 'get it' and can be the perfect foil to their colleague. They may appear a little slow, but just as in life they occasionally get the upper hand and come out with a put-down for the main host that puts them in their place. This person may be the travel and weather presenter. (The Idiot or the innocent fool.)
- Another host may be more conservative. A little straight-laced and more traditional and easily offended in their values. Sometimes they may be the voice of sanity if the others go too far, but are often the butt of jokes (the Intellectual or the clever person).
- The fourth presenter in a zoo format may be the on the road reporter. They're not linked to the newsroom, but are out and about in the radio car doing stunts or vox pops with listeners on their way to work. They're a bit younger, and a bit cheekier than the others but just as warm and approachable.

Let's take those three main characters again:

- The Intellectual (the clever person) – sounds like Ross from *Friends* or Sergeant Wilson in *Dad's Army*?
- The Idiot (the innocent fool) – Sounds like Phoebe or Pike?
- Mr I Am (smart Alec) and Chandler or Captain Mainwaring?

Most successful sitcoms have characters who fit into these roles (to a greater or lesser extent). The characters have a brotherly/sisterly love, but disagree with each other. Some call it 'friendly friction', 'electricity', 'sexual tension' or 'striking a nerve' – they're all phrases appropriate for a zoo team.

## The conflict

Notice those words 'tension', 'friction' and so on. 'Argument' isn't there. It's important to have the right kind of conflict on your show so things don't overstep the mark and become too personal. Constructive conflict is about people's concepts, ideas, thoughts and views – things they can change. Destructive conflict comes from issues about a person that they can't change – such as their looks.

**INFORMATION FOR INSPIRATION:** In your show you need to constantly build up tension and release it, by creating constructive conflict and then resolving it in a positive way.

## The visitor to the zoo

Some of the most successful zoo shows (and other shows) create a club. That means that a listener needs to have a little bit of knowledge about the show and the characters to really get the most from it. It's a very fine line: there may be 'in' jokes that you might not get if you're listening for the first time. But as you invest a few days listening you feel part of the club too. This creates a strong bond between listeners and the show.

> 'The secret is to have lots of material that's accessible to all and a few moments and bits that are part of the club.'
>
> Will Kinder, producer, Radio 1

## Constructing a zoo

> 'I don't think you can construct a show. Sometimes you do and you luck out, but the best shows grow organically. It's like comparing Boyzone with The Beatles, who actually sing about shared experiences. Shows with mates are always going to be better shows.'
>
> Nick Goodman, former Capital Radio, speaking at a Radio Academy event, October 2005

Zoos or double-headers that work well are down to a lot of luck, hard work, and time. The luck that comes with putting two 'random' people together and expecting them to become friends and work well together on air. The hard work of finding the right combination of people, match-making if you like, who can do just that, and then creating the atmosphere to let them develop and discover their similarities and points of difference. The time? Well, it may be obvious in minutes that people won't get on, more realistically it might take a few weeks before people realise that it's just not working. There are several famous cases of this happening on major-market stations, where, because of no one's fault the chemistry just didn't exist. Of the cases I'm thinking of, sometimes the co-host who was dropped, sometimes it was the main host.

If you're a presenter and your programme controller suggests you'd work well as part of a team, make sure that you're in on that decision. Many co-hosts are, unbelievably, chosen without involving the main presenter.

## Hearing voices

Beware of too many voices. You could have a presenter, sidekick, producer, newsreader, sports presenter and travel person. That's a lot of voices and characters for listeners to keep up with.

> 'Try and limit the number of people on at any one time. For instance, during the news and sport sequence the sidekick and producer could be in the background. In other words it could be a large cast but they don't all need to be on stage at the same time!'
>
> Will Kinder, producer, Radio 1

## Be true to your on-air character

The key to a zoo format is that all characters remain true to their on-air personality whatever happens. In *Friends*, Monica was known as the overly fussy and tidy cook, who used to be overweight. Although she had other traits these were perhaps her main characteristics. To have her delivering a put down to another large person, or letting her flat go to rack and ruin would not have fitted with her character, so it didn't happen.

So, characters have to be true to their on-air self. Of course, the good thing about that is that sometimes it means that, when in character, you're able to get away with saying things that you would never be able to as yourself.

**INFORMATION FOR INSPIRATION:** Believable conflict isn't created because you take a view opposite to that of another team member. It comes from you saying something that's true to you — or at least to your on-air character.

## Naming names

Zoo or co-presenters should often address each other by name so listeners get to know the names and the characters that go with them. You may have similar voices and the listener may have trouble telling you apart. Plus, it's only courtesy: how often have you felt reticent to speak to someone at a party or meeting, because you haven't been introduced to them? When you know someone's name, you already feel much friendlier towards them. So keep letting listeners know who everyone is. By that I don't mean that you need to keep introducing them, simply refer to them by name frequently and naturally as part of your conversation:

'Hey Simon, did you see the match last night?'

'What are you talking about, Susan? That's ridiculous!'

This fits with the basic process of building a relationship: when someone knows you, they can decide if they like you. Giving your name starts building that rapport and forming a basic emotional bond.

Sometimes nicknames can quickly help develop a strong bond between a name and a character. It might be as simple as 'Producer Greg', 'Quiz Tony' or some other slightly more off the wall name that listeners are intrigued by.

'Moyles had a BA called Melinda. He was a bloke, his name came because he used to be the messenger ... his nickname was never explained on the show but it was always the first question he was asked. Nicknames are also something that tends to develop between friends so it strengthens the feeling of bonding for the listener.'

Will Kinder, producer, Radio 1

## Sycophants

There's a fine line between having co-hosts with whom you get along and those who are there purely to make you look and sound good. Although inevitably there'll be one main presenter, a strong team is one that's built on mutual respect. There have been situations in the past where the main presenter has belittled his colleagues on air (on one famous occasion getting a female co-presenter to admit that she'd slept with him the previous night), and there are many situations where the co-hosts are so in awe they laugh at the slightest hint of humour from the main presenter.

Remember there's a fine line between showing listeners you're having a good time and excluding them because they don't understand what is going on or feel uncomfortable.

> **INFORMATION FOR INSPIRATION:** Treat the listener as the third person in the studio.

Don't have such a good time in the studio that you leave out the other person in the relationship – the listener – otherwise they'll feel as though they've arrived late at a party, where everyone else knows each other, and will just want to leave.

## Follow my leader

If another character says on-air something happened – it happened.

 **ACTUAL AUDIO**

> PRESENTER: Well, we're getting dozens of calls voting in our Sunday love song poll. I'm joined by one of our telephone answerers. What are people voting for?
> PHONE OP: Well, we've had *two* callers . . .
>
> *BBC local station, October 2005*

Make your colleagues' life easy by reading them and working out where they're going with a link and follow them. If they say, 'The moon's made of cream cheese' they've said it for a reason. It'll be for a joke, a flight of fancy, a bit about 'what if everyday items were made from food', whatever. If you say, 'No, it's not' you've killed the item dead. That leaves them with nothing to say, you with nowhere to go and the listeners confused. Instead reply with, 'Yes, and . . .' to push the item further and help them get where they want to get.

In the Actual Audio above, the phone op didn't follow her leader: she contradicted him and made the station look unpopular. While you shouldn't lie, don't ever suggest that the response to anything has ever been anything less than impressive.

## Relatable revelations

A bit about you is stronger if you can get another character to start it. Let them provide you with the planned set-up for you to react to, rather than by crowbarring the subject into the conversation yourself.

For example, instead of saying, 'I had a really good weekend, shall I tell you why?', get your co-presenter to say, 'How was your weekend . . . you're all smiles this morning . . .' to which you can reply, 'It was great because . . .' which is a much more natural conversational flow.

## Humour in a team

If someone on your show, a colleague, listener, guest, travel presenter comes up with the best punch line or comeback, recognise it and respect it. They're probably better at you in timing, pacing and constructing their material. If you try to top them it will make both of you look stupid. Listen to the type of comments they make, what their favourite topics are and what their catchphrases are and learn how to set them up and help them. Even if the other person gets to say the punch line rather than you, the whole team wins. Don't feel as though you have to have the last word every single time.

## Top team tricks

There's a danger that team members may not be able to react to what a colleague throws at them during an on-air conversation, and that the whole link will crash and burn. You can't rehearse a whole show – if you do that it'll sound staid and stilted. Instead, give each other a tip-off. Speak with the other members and tell them *what topics* you're going to talk about, but not *why*. For example, simply saying, 'I've got something to say about skiing, queuing and pregnancy' is all that's needed. That will start sparking off some ideas for humour, personal stories and revelations that will help the whole link, without you all actually rehearsing it.

Here's another trick from Will:

'It's often useful to develop your "plot" for a team storyline before you begin it on air. For instance your plot might be to get the team's picture in the local newspaper. In this case talk to the newspaper and get them on board first, then start the storyline on air. There's nothing worse than starting a plot which fizzles out. A big, positive outcome makes your show look big and because you know it will work you'll be far more confident on air.'

Will Kinder, producer, Radio 1

(Also read the section on Breakfast Show Prep p. 100.)

## Invisible cues

This is the name given to the non-verbal cues that you give your co-hosts. When you have line of sight with the other person, simply use hand gestures: basic pointing to the other person when it's their turn to speak and their mic is on, or a raised index finger if you want to be allowed to join the conversation. The same gesture can be used if you are talking and leading up to a particular point or punch line and you don't want to be interrupted: the finger in the air makes sure the rest of the team are aware of your intentions so they don't trample all over you.

## Off-air bonding

Whether you're part of a new team, or a new member of an old team, or an old team you still need to get to know each other so well that you can anticipate each other's next move. Develop rapport and relationships by doing things together away from the station. Discover your colleagues' characteristics and form a trust with one another.

## Impro-ve yourself

What about taking an improvisation class? If you're part of a team, perhaps all of you could go together or separately. This isn't a chance to show off to the public, it's a chance for you to learn how to hone your skills:

- How to open-up conversational cul-de-sacs.
- How to listen out for humorous highways.
- How to build confidence in what you do . . .
- and what your co-host is doing that you may be able to react to.
- How to improve team rapport . . .
- and give ideas and opportunities to other members of the team.
- How to quickly recognise humorous possibilities, taking a small amount of material and building on it.

## Co-presenters

Co-presenters usually have equal billing and airtime on the programme – think of the *Today* programme on Radio 4, which is introduced as presented by John Humphrys and James Naughtie, who take it in turns to introduce packages and features, and carry out the heavy-weight (and sometimes less heavyweight) interviews.

On commercial radio the name of breakfast shows usually also hint at an equal part-nership: Jo and Twiggy on Trent FM and Danny and Nicky on Southern FM. But an equal partnership isn't always reality. The main presenter is usually in charge of the micro-phone faders and that inevitably means they have the last word on any link and can choose when to play music or fire an ad-break. This inevitably puts most 'partners' on an *un*equal footing.

# Requests and dedications

## What are they?

There's a difference between the two terms, which many people don't understand. A request is when a listener simply asks for a specific song, usually for themselves. A dedication is where they want any song, but to have a message broadcast alongside it.

## Their importance

> 'Perhaps the most important result of the successful record request programme is the listener feeling personal contact with the presenter via the radio. This is achieved by sincerity — too much and it becomes smarmy sickliness, too little and it sounds cold, casual and offhand.'
> BBC Local Radio Training Manual, 1987

> 'Perhaps most importantly, we put messages from families and friends on the radio for them. Even the most battled-hardened soldier sheds a tear when his children have a message for him on BFBS.'
> Damian Watson, British Forces Broadcasting Service,
> *The Radio Magazine*, 27 November 2004

Requests and dedis (dedications):
- Are an easy way to get listener involvement in your station.
- Make the listener feel good that they've a hand in what music is played.
- Get lots of place names mentioned.
- Are potentially great research on whether you're playing the right kind of music.
- Can be good audience builders.

An audience-builder? Yes, because the person the request is for may be a non-listener who's been told by a friend or relation to listen in to hear the song. The more you do (workplace requests, school call) the more personal recommendations the station will get. (It's sometimes the only reason stations do a Thought for the Day religious item, so the ministers tell their congregation to tune in).

Even if yours isn't a specific request programme, you'll still get calls from people wanting to hear a certain song. These kinds of calls are arguably more important than the ones to 'dedicated dedication' shows. That's because dedication shows are usually about the message or the person ('It's my mum's birthday. Can you play *Simply The Best*?'). Uninitiated calls are more likely to be for current songs that the listener simply likes most at the moment and it is these kinds of calls that are worth monitoring. To do this, some stations ask the presenters to show on a simple tick-list, the songs which are requested in this way, together with any other comments the caller makes about the song or the station in general. Other stations go further and occasionally have a longer questionnaire which the presenter asks the caller: what other songs do they like at the moment, which ones are they getting tired of hearing and so on. That information shouldn't be taken too literally, or carry too much importance, but put together with other research or maybe gut instinct, it can help mould the shape of the station sound.

## Off-air before on-air

Before you read anything on-air, read it to yourself off-air. Do you understand it? Can you read the handwriting? Is it rude?

## ACTUAL AUDIO

A BBC local radio presenter read out the following message from a 'listener' (actually one of their colleagues) on the Mother's Day request show, without realising it was a rude spoof:

PRESENTER: Please say a big hello to Connie Lingus who's 69 on Tuesday, she'll be enjoying my meat and two veg on Sunday at 12.00. Wish her all the very best and tell her I look forward to seeing her when she comes. Thanks ever so much, Ivan R Don.

If the message doesn't flow or is confused, re-write it. Don't make any mention on air about the sender's illegible handwriting. Check all the information is there so you don't say something like, 'Oh, that's funny, that's a dedication to Cheryl's mum, but she hasn't told me her mum's name . . .'. Always read through the letters first and highlight the facts you're going to say. You may want to check the pronunciation of a street name with a colleague who lives in the area or ask around the office for a suggestion on how to pronounce an awkward surname.

Don't give out full addresses on the air: mentioning the town or the part of town is fine but to give a street and certainly a house number is too much information. Consider this: '. . . a message to Vi Capstan of 35 Cherry Blossom Avenue, who's 78 today, and *who lives alone* since her husband Bert died . . .'. Or this kind of information revealed: '. . . and Jenny is six today and she and her friends are going to have a scavenger hunt in Nonsuch Woods later this afternoon . . .'.

## Producing the show

Basic courtesy should tell you that if you ask listeners to call you for a request or dedication, make sure you have time to play it. A basic understanding of radio will tell you that a long list of names, addresses and messages becomes tedious to the vast majority of listeners. Instead, try to theme them, or link them in some way: '. . . and there are several people with birthdays this week . . .', '. . . and now our regular anniversary section . . .'

Also try to get musical balance as you prepare the show, interspersing more recent tracks with classic oldies, faster songs in amongst the inevitable slower ones, male artists alternating with female ones and so on. Be wary of the most-requested songs such as *The Best* by Tina Turner which you simply can't play every week. Include that mention with one for another song and remember, the more often you play, for example, *The Best* on a request show, the more it'll be requested. That may mean that it's one that many people want to hear, but it'll also fast become one that many more don't!

## Phone-in requests

Don't just say something bland like, 'If you want a request, call me now on . . .' put an idea in someone's mind as to why they may want to call for a song for themselves or someone else. Paul James on BBC Radio Kent says, 'It may be three words like "I love you", two words like "thank you" or one word like "sorry".'

Perhaps go further and suggest other reasons why listeners may want to make that call beyond the usual birthdays and anniversaries.

- □ 'Perhaps you've heard a great new song we've been playing and want to hear it again so you can get your friends to hear it too . . .'
- □ 'Maybe there's a special song for you and your partner, where the words just sum up everything you feel about each other . . .'
- □ 'Perhaps you were out partying hard last night and made a bit of a fool of yourself and need to apologise to your mates . . .'

## The presenting style on a request show

This has developed over the years and even though it may feel odd to do, it works well on-air. You need to talk to both the sender of the dedication, the recipient and the rest of the audience all at once! And you need to, bizarrely, tell the recipient information they already know! 'Happy Birthday to Susan Fellows who's 55 today. That's from your daughter Katie, thanks Katie. You've written telling me all about your mum who lives in Robertstown. The whole family's coming round for lunch later, aren't they Susan? All eight of you. I hope they're enough chairs!'

## Ones you can't play

All programmes are entertainment and are there for the great majority of listeners. Request and dedication shows are no different, so sometimes there are songs that you simply won't play. These are ones that are so far from your core music list that even though to play it would cause delight for the person who the song is to and from, it would be a literal turn off for many more people. Requests alone cannot dictate the content of the programme. Indeed, neither can your own tastes, although your own tastes can *guide* it, and many stations don't play song requests as it compromises their playlist. If someone asks for a song that the station would never play, simply explain why you can't or say that you'll see what you can do.

Don't say that you haven't got the song they asked for. If that's the case (or it's not one that fits with your format), then simply omit the title of the request and play another by the same artist. If the artist is not one that you play, then don't mention the requested song or band but play one similar. For example, you could replace a song by Bobby Vincent for one by Simply Red but not one by Gorillaz. You can use this technique whether someone's written in or if they're on the phone: 'Ahh, we haven't got any Rolling Stones here, but what about a classic from The Who?' Obviously, this won't happen on air if you've pre-recorded the call or taken it off air first to prime them.

Don't play a song for other presenters on the station or your personal friends. No one else knows them, no one else cares and it smacks of incest.

## What if someone calls for a song you were going to play next anyway?

Simple. You don't tell them that it's all lined up ready to go, you tell them that you'll dig it out and will play it for them next. They'll go away a very happy customer!

## Recording request-line callers

You'll need to check your House Style Guide, but legally you can record those who phone you and broadcast the conversation. Even though it is against UK radio regulations to broadcast someone's voice without telling them, there is a 'loophole'. The ban was created in the 1990s to crack down on the growing number of complaints about 'wind-up calls' that were being broadcast without the victim's permission. However, it is generally accepted that if someone calls *into* a radio station studio they know that they could go to air either live or recorded. In other words that caller has, by calling the station, given implied consent to their voice being broadcast

# Remembrance programmes

Your station will probably carry the two minutes' silence on the Sunday closest to November 11th to remember those killed in war. Your national news supplier, IRN, SNR or GNS will provide you with a short opt-in from the Cenotaph just before 11 o'clock on that morning, followed by Big Ben and the silence. Alternatively, you could play in your own 'silence', either pre-recorded or perhaps live from a local memorial event.

It's important to remember that the silence is not completely silent. You'll hear ambient sounds such as birds, traffic, coughing and so on. This is important so listeners are aware that you're still on air and that their radio hasn't broken, and also so that the station's automatic alarm doesn't kick in and play an emergency tape of music. This would happen if a signal wasn't sent to the transmitter for a set period of time, so it's no good just to pull down the mic fader and transmit 'nothing' for two minutes.

Also be aware of what song you're going to go into and come out of the silence with. Consider a slow tempo song, or perhaps one with suitable lyrics, perhaps *Imagine*, *Greatest Love of All* or *Where Is The Love*.

# Christmas

Keep in the spirit of Christmas, whatever your religious beliefs. I remember hearing a story about a presenter who had as his guest the manager of the local post office sorting depot. He was asked about the number of cards and parcels passing through the office in the weeks leading to the 'big day'. Then the presenter said: 'What about all those letters addressed to Father Christmas, what do you do with them?' The post office manager didn't miss a beat: 'We deliver them to him at the North Pole . . .'. The presenter asked again. 'Yeah, OK, but really, what do you *really* do with them?' His guest repeated his previous answer. The presenter then said a third time, 'but what do you *actually* do with them?' to which the post office manager said, 'Look, I don't know what you want me to say, apart from that all letters addressed to Father Christmas or Santa Claus, are delivered to his home at the North Pole . . .'. The presenter had been asking a question that, although intriguing, could have spoiled Christmas for many people listening. The Royal Mail man however had given a first class answer.

# Swing shifts

You may get to be a freelance weekend presenter or a 'swing' presenter, who swings from presenting one show to another. Sometimes radio stations employ such a person full time, whose job it is to cover for ill or holidaying colleagues. It may be that one week you're filling on drive, the next week you're the lunchtime presenter. This is a great opportunity and although you don't have a show of your own and have to follow the format of the programme you're sitting in on (and downplaying your own personality as a result), you're showing the programme controller your versatility and getting valuable on-air experience.

If you're introducing a presenter who's sitting in on a show because the regular host is away, don't draw attention to their absence. 'On the Drive Show with John Simons this afternoon . . .' is fine. Some stations even keep the name of the show, even when the presenter's away: 'With John Simons on the Dave Juby Drive Show this afternoon . . .'. You don't have to say 'John Simons is sitting in for Dave Juby on the Drive programme while Dave takes a well-earned break . . .' or similar. Whoever's presenting the show is presenting the show! (Incidentally, 'well-earned break' is another DJ cliché, unless you're taking about a junior doctor or coal miner. Listeners believe presenters are pampered and privileged and will scoff at the idea that you think putting on a few songs for three hours a day makes a holiday well-deserved.)

# 27 When it all goes wrong

It's fantastic when you do a brilliant show:

> 'It was like great sex!'
> *Broadcast News*, film

But, things do go wrong:

> 'I find it unnerving if I pick up a cue or it goes on the screen
> and it's not right. It may be a sensitive interview and you get it
> wrong. It's to do with resources and people stretched
> to the absolute limit, but I still find it frustrating.'
> Maggie Philbin, presenter BBC Radio Berkshire,
> Radio Academy event, November 2005

In this chapter find out what can go pear-shaped and how to get out of the mess fruitfully.

## Putting the F into FM

Putting callers or guests live on air often brings with it the possibility of profanities. This is particularly so while on an OB with someone walking past a live mic shouting comments at the top of their voice — the radio equivalent to waving in the background while a TV reporter does a piece to camera.

We are, of course, in a world where swearing is more commonplace everywhere, but it remains absolutely unacceptable on radio usually at any time, certainly on a daytime programme.

> **INFORMATION FOR INSPIRATION:** Radio is often said to be more personal than TV, people treat it as a friend, and so swearing is much more intrusive.

But, if it does happen:
- A guest swears once and it appears to be unintentional — correct them on air and apologise to the listeners on their behalf.

○ It happens a second time – stop the interview immediately. Play a trail or song (as appropriate) and take stock. Speak to the guest off air making it very clear that the language is unacceptable and that it must not happen again. Ask them to apologise on air.

○ If they refuse to co-operate, or if there's a third occurrence, the interview must be stopped immediately – make a profuse apology on air and ask the guest to leave the studio.

The responsibility lies with the producer as well as the presenter. Producers should make sure all presenters are briefed, especially if those notorious for blue language are invited in.

---

 **ACTUAL AUDIO**

GUEST:  It's a whole load of crap, man.
PRESENTER:  Now watch your language, I'll give you one second chance.

*BBC local radio station, October 2005*

---

Sometimes it's you who utters the swearword!

'I've managed to say the worst swear word possible on air, but it was a mix-up of words rather than using it properly! I was talking up Friday Night Kiss which had a mixture of "big dance classics and up-front cuts". It was during the last bit when I got the words muddled up a bit. I just soldiered on and didn't laugh or refer to it! I actually remember being more annoyed that I clipped the vocals on the next tune because it had thrown me.'

Sam Heywood, presenter, 96.9 Viking FM,
*The Radio Magazine*, 30 March 2005

If you do trip up over a word when you're reading it's probably down to one of two causes:
○ You didn't prepare and read through the script off air before you read it on air.
○ You're reading it too fast.

**INFORMATION FOR INSPIRATION:** Always treat a microphone as live. If you make a habit of never swearing in a studio, then you reduce the chances of swearing on air, or leaving in a swear word when an un-edited piece is broadcast.

## The worst words

There are various regulatory bodies providing codes of conduct and a list of 'acceptable' swear words is available, but why risk alienating even a small part of your audience? That said, your use of language will partly be governed by the station you're on and the time of day (you would 'get away' with more on an overnight show than a family-orientated breakfast show, for example) and the cultural make-up of your audience.

The worst words (according to Ofcom's Language and Sexual Imagery in Broadcasting report, and particularly the ones below with asterisks) are likely to be:

- Insults — bastard, bitch, c***sucker, dickhead, motherf***er, p****teaser, slag, slut, w***er, whore.
- Body parts and functions – arse, arsehole, balls, b****cks, bum, cock, crap, c**t, dick, fart, knob, prick, p*ssy, sh*t, tits, tw*t, w*nk/er.
- Religious – bloody, God, Jesus, Jesus Christ, Jesus F***ing Christ, Jesus Sh***ing Christ.
- People with disabilities – mong, nutter, retard, schizo, spastic.
- Terms of racial or religious abuse – Chink, c**n, kyke, n*gger, Paki, pikey, spade, yid.
- Ethnic words – blaad claat, bumbu, chi-chi man, ho, hoochie, punani (don't use any word if you don't know what it means!).
- Sexually oriented – batty boy, bonk, bugger, dyke, faggot, f*ck/ing, poke, poof, queer, screw, shag.

Never use even use what you'd consider to be the mildest of swearwords ('damn') or blaspheme ('Oh God'). Many people won't mind, indeed won't even notice, but those who do notice will mind a great deal.

Be similarly careful over risqué items. If in doubt ask advice or leave it out.

(Also see pp. 134–138 on the law, especially pp. 134–136 on libel.)

# Silence vs dead air

'Silence' is when broadcasting 'nothing' is intentional and is working for you. For example, there could be a pause for dramatic effect, maybe you're leading up to a punch line, or want to show that you're thinking carefully about what someone's just said

'Dead air' is unintentional. It could happen when you're so busy cueing up another song, or talking to the travel presenter on the ISDN talkback, that you don't realise that the song on air has ended.

Many stations have an emergency recording that plays automatically if silence is detected for too long: when has there's been a problem in the studio such as the presenter's unwell, some equipment has failed or they've been 'caught short' (which is why most stations' toilets have an ouput speaker in them!)

> 'One of the hardest things in radio is going to the toilet. You're on your own for three hours and have to run out during a song and you can hear it playing in the loo and you think "come on!"'
> Katie Hill, presenter Capital Radio, Radio Academy event, November 2005

## When it all goes quiet

If an item fails to play, then go to something else. Don't panic or blame, just move on.

That sounds straightforward but in a time of panic your thoughts go out of the window. But you shouldn't be panicking. The perception of a presenter is that they're cool, calm and in control. Always prepare the next item, and the one after that. Remember, if you can get something to air in less than five seconds, it's probably best not to open the microphone at all. Talking while you re-cue something will make the re-cuing take longer. Just concentrate on the problem in hand.

It may be that someone at the station has heard your problem on the radio and is coming to your aid already. If not and you can't fix the problem yourself, call an engineer. You may be able to enlist the help of a producer by talking to them on air. Doing a seemingly normal link on the radio, but with your finger on the talkback button to the ops room, will draw their attention to your plight.

If it is going to be longer before something can go to air then you may need to fill. Open the mic and talk about what's later in the show or later in the day. Try to avoid talking about what's going wrong. Don't draw it to the audience's attention. Chances are they'll be none the wiser. Then, make sure all of this is written in the studio Fault Log so it can be followed up as necessary (it may be a recurring problem with one particular piece of equipment).

> **INFORMATION FOR INSPIRATION:** Mistakes happen but they're more easily dismissed if you don't draw attention to them. Don't refer to a mistake even if it was a major one. And if the listener wouldn't have realised, don't draw attention to it at all.

'Listeners and even programme managers
are very forgiving and hugely forgetful.'
Neptune Radio Style Guide 1997

## Apologising

It is rare that presenters apologise for a mistake. In general listeners rarely notice them, but they will if you keep telling them. If you have to correct information that was given out, avoid using negative words such as 'correct', 'wrong', and 'mistake'. Instead use phrases like, 'Can I just clarify . . .', 'I've got some more details on . . .'.

Perhaps you can change your angle so those who heard the previous (incorrect) information know of the change, but new listeners aren't any the wiser. Or simply give out the details again, together with the correction and make no reference to the change at all.

If there's a technical problem, a CD skips or a guest disappears from an ISDN line, move on. An apology may be necessary (though not always) but don't drag it out:

'We seem to have lost the professor so while we reconnect the line, let me tell you about . . .'

Never blame anyone for a mistake or a fault. It's a DJ cliché to blame 'sticky fingers', 'the producer', 'the engineers', 'gremlins' or, after tripping over a word to say, 'I'll just put my teeth back in'. If you tell the time incorrectly, just tell it properly and move on. There's no need for a comment such as, 'I'll learn how to tell the time soon'. You may make a brief generic comment about 'technical problems' to explain . . . but don't blame.

A professional presenter will have thought and prepared several steps in advance anyway and have a 'get out' – another song lined up, a trail to read or play or be able to ad-lib confidently. You may have to talk and sort out the technical problem at the same time, possibly while someone is telling you what to do via the talkback.

Alternatively, think whether any comment is necessary. If you introduce Jennifer Lopez's song and Will Smith starts singing, just back announce with the correct details, making no mention to what went wrong. If a song starts playing and then stops, slickly play another song you've cued up already.

**INFORMATION FOR INSPIRATION:** Think about what you'll say now, if things go wrong later. Practice those ad-libs so your lack of spontaneity doesn't tarnish your reputation.

## Dead-air checklist

- What is it that's gone wrong? Has the equipment failed to start ('failed to fire'). Are you absolutely sure that the item isn't going to air? (You may have knocked your headphone volume, may be listening to another studio's output by mistake). Check the main output level meters.
- How necessary is it that you go to this expected item now?
- Can you do a smooth link (or no link at all) to something else? If so, do!
- If not, identify the cause of the problem starting at the desk.
- Is the problem simple presenter error? Is the correct fader up? Have you left a prefade button on another channel on, which may cut the audio to speakers or headphones?
- Can you carry on talking while you fix the problem? Dead air for up to five seconds is unfortunate but probably doesn't need an apology. Much longer and you'll need to explain and/or apologise, but keep the language straightforward and don't blame anyone.

## How to fill to time

- Tease and trail items which are coming up later in your show.
- Tease and trail other shows and other features in those shows.
- 'Trawl for calls' on your talking points of the day.
- Do some of the material that you've prepared in advance.

## Corpsing

'There's one hazard that no amount of preparation can avoid:
the collapse into inappropriate laughter. The Today programme
website still treasures the moment when Charlotte Green kept
a cool head while reading a news item about a Mr Twatt.
And she would have sailed through it too, if it wasn't for the
next story — about a plucky sperm whale'
Roland White, *The Sunday Times*, 30 October 2005

That's bound to make many people smirk, but remember, smirking is bad for your health and you have to try and control the temptation. The smallest reference to something odd may start you laughing, or it may be a prat-fall by someone in the ops room, a funny joke a caller's just told you, or just because you're in 'one of those moods'. Obviously, there's room for humour on air, and many listeners like the occasional mistake. That's as long as it is not too often and they can understand what's happened. Otherwise they'll be more bemused than amused and feel excluded.

It's often best not to try to contain the laughter, but instead go to another pre-recorded item (preferably a song) and literally laugh-off the moment. Have a good guffaw, walk into another room, have a drink of water and try to re-establish yourself in time for the next link.

# Obit procedure

I have mentioned this a couple of times, in the context of your studio bible and music scheduling, so you may want to look back at those chapters too.

If and when a 'Category One' royal death occurs (i.e. the Queen, the Duke of Edinburgh, the Prince of Wales, the Princess Royal or Prince William), certain procedures need to be followed and there should be a clear allocation of responsibility for coverage at your station.

Procedures are less clear-cut for deaths in 'Category Two', which is likely to include:

- The Duke of York (Prince Andrew)
- The Earl of Wessex (Prince Edward)
- Prince Henry (Prince Harry)
- Countess of Wessex
- Duchess of Cornwall
- The Prime Minister
- The Leader of the Opposition
- The President of the USA
- The Pope
- The Archbishop of Canterbury

The coverage will depend on the circumstances surrounding the death.

Obit procedures are divided into three phases:

## Phase one

The news is suspected but hasn't been formally announced.

On no account flash the news. Refer to your Studio Bible about who to contact. There's no point mentioning the news and then not having any other information, so only hand over to the newsroom when you know they're ready.

Additionally:

- Be absolutely sure you know what to do if the announcement happens on your shift.
- Don't put anything to air unless it's from a specified source.
- Don't speculate.
- If you think an announcement is imminent then tone down your presentation in preparation. Consider dropping features, competitions, trails, sweepers, adverts, the news jingle, and start toning down the music.
- Know where the obit music is and which light is the obit light.

## Phase two

The announcement and the period immediately afterwards.

This period could be anything from a couple of hours or days, to (in the case of Diana, Princess of Wales) more than a week. Much depends on the prominence of the person, their perceived 'importance' and popularity, their age, if the death was expected, how sudden it was, what caused it, whether they died in public, whether anyone else was involved.

- If it's you who has to make the announcement, get it right, don't rush to be first. Use the agreed form of words (in the Studio Bible).
- Be set for regular bulletins, make no additional comments apart from what's been agreed and the station ID.
- All features, songs, ads, etc, are likely to be dropped.
- Later you may want to broadcast reaction from local dignitaries, religious people, MPs, etc.
- Then reaction from listeners – their memories, thoughts and expression of loss.

# Phase three

Returning to normal programmes. When this happens will be decided by a senior person at the station.

- Use 'bridging tracks' over several hours to ease the transition from the sombre music to the normal mix.
- Still be sensitive over what is said and the content of calls, guests, songs, etc. If in doubt be over cautious.

# Complaints

And then there are always the complainants.

If the complaint is serious, perhaps accusing you of being overtly political or being rude to a caller (both of which could be issues for Ofcom to investigate) then your own station house rules will tell you how to handle it.

Take a caller's details and the issue they're raising and promise them that the complaint will be looked in to (more user-friendly than 'investigated') and someone will get back to them. Never give them the impression that what they say isn't being taken seriously, or give them cause to take their complaint elsewhere.

Don't sweep the issue under the carpet, but deal with it honestly and openly with your manager. Don't try to deal with the complaint by yourself however awkward it may be to 'own up' to something you said on air which the programme controller hadn't previously been aware of. In my experience most complaints die a reasonably swift natural death if a senior manager handles them carefully. An explanation, apology (if necessary), and reassurance that the issue will be looked into and will not happen again is usually sufficient, without the need for official regulators to be involved.

There's usually a station procedure for dealing with all such complaints, covering what's said to the complainant, how it's said and who says it. In the most serious situations, for example, if legal proceedings are being threatened over a libel issue, the programme controller will contact the station's lawyer.

It is to be hoped that station management will give you all the support they can in such a situation, and it'll help if you're honest and straightforward with them from the outset. By apologising and explaining your 'moment of madness', or putting it into context, you'll stop the situation getting out of hand. If you give one story, and the logger tape shows you said something different, you could be in hot water. Lies, subterfuge and hoping the complaint will go away, usually makes the listener more determined to cause trouble.

Sometimes you'll be on an outside broadcast when someone will come up and criticise you or the station in general. React politely, and try to talk them round. It's usually best to see what they do like or what station they usually listen to and then make a connection with something similar.

THEM:  Your station's rubbish

YOU:  Hey, sorry you feel that way . . . why do you say that?

THEM:  You play all that slow stuff . . . I'm into classic rock.

YOU:  Wow, stuff like The Who and The Stones?

THEM:  Yeah . . .

YOU:  Well, they recorded several slow tracks that were classic rock songs in their own right. When was the last time you heard *Angie* by The Stones? Tell you what, I'll play it for you tomorrow just after four, give me a listen.

Or

THEM: You always play the same songs over and over.

YOU: Well, that's because most people only listen for a short time . . . but they always want to hear one of their favourites when they do. What do you like? Really? I'll play it for you tomorrow just before nine . . .

So, try to be polite, unaggressive and give on explanation to diffuse the situation.

If the comment's puerile, then overt politeness is usually the best policy. A caller rings and tells you you're crap; thank them for their comments and hang up. Then forget the call. Don't dwell on what they said as it might affect the rest of your programme. If they continue to call then tell your programme controller: there are ways to block or trace nuisance calls.

Incidentally, there's an anecdote of a survey that was carried out amongst listeners to America's shock jock Howard Stern. Most listeners said they hated him: he was rude, arrogant, sexist and so on. Yet these very same people listened day-after-day, year-after-year. They liked being offended!

## Apologies

Some presenters are too quick to apologise for things that *aren't* wrong! They either don't know the situation, or think it's easier to say 'sorry' rather than have to explain why the caller's not right.

A colleague told me of just such an incident. The station's newsreader had introduced a clip on newly legal same-sex partnerships with words similar to '. . . Michelle Mates of the Grantchester Gay Alliance says gay weddings are a good thing.' A caller phoned the studio and complained that the *station* had said that the weddings were good (in fact, the newsreader was clearly quoting an *interviewee*). The presenter said, 'You're absolutely right, we shouldn't have done that, I apologise, it won't happen again'. The station hadn't been wrong, but the caller had been given the impression that it had been.

Sometimes 'sorry' is too easy.

**INFORMATION FOR INSPIRATION:** Build a relationship with your listeners and they'll be more forgiving when things go wrong.

# 28 At the end of the show

## Goodbyes

Even if it's the end of your show don't say goodbye. You may be going somewhere (hopefully back to the office to have a review of your show and prepare for the next one) but the audience isn't. At least we hope they aren't! However, saying goodbye gives them the suggestion, and therefore opportunity, to tune out. It's like slamming a door in their face and is a potential exit point – something that we want as few of as possible.

> **INFORMATION FOR INSPIRATION:** As a 'programme junction' approaches you have to 'sell' the next show (especially during your last 20 minutes), to encourage the audience to ignore the exit point and make the station 'stickier'.

The station isn't a series of separate shows. It is a single radio station of which your show is only part. Seamless programming helps increase audiences.

> 'Never let them see the exit signs. We're searching for forward programme movement not opportunities to leave. The radio is just a domestic appliance, if it doesn't entertain, listeners will leave it.'
> *BBC Radio Devon House Guide, 2004*

So don't say goodbye, but something more like, 'I'm back tomorrow at ten . . . but keep listening to Radio X for Gemma Johnson and your chance to win a thousand pounds in our new Ring To Win ticket giveaway . . .'.

> **INFORMATION FOR INSPIRATION:** Listeners join and leave all the time. You don't welcome them when they join, so why do it when you leave?

## Handovers

I've mentioned this in passing elsewhere: the banter between presenters as one ends their programme and the other starts theirs. It's a good way of throwing ahead to what's to come, of introducing the new voice, for creating a 'family feel' and a seamless segue from one show to another.

On Radio 2 the handover between Terry Wogan and Ken Bruce works well: Terry makes a comment which he throws to Ken, there is a few seconds of banter and at the optimum time (usually after a punch line) Ken plays his jingle and goes into his first song.

It's great if the two presenters are in their own studios, or one is a guest in the other's but that doesn't always happen. Instead, you hear conversations with colleagues off-mic, or on mics set at different levels, chat that's incestuous or goes on too long.

A handover that is much more than a minute is probably too long. After that you'll probably be talking about inconsequential subjects. It's not, after all, as though each of you don't have three hours in which you can talk! Keep asking yourself: is what the other presenter saying, in my show, relevant, interesting, and compelling?

Hot-seat handovers can be trickier. These are where one presenter follows another in the same studio. As you're clearing up your debris, your colleague is behind you with their cues, coffee and probably comments, too. It can be all too easy for them to chip in with an off-mic aside, either invited or uninvited. This sounds poor and unprofessional.

**INFORMATION FOR INSPIRATION:** It's still your show, so don't allow uninitiated comments from 'guests' to intrude.

It is a courtesy to help the next presenter as much as possible by tidying up in good time, turning on the air-conditioning so that they have a fresh studio, and alerting them to any broken equipment broken (which you've also written in the Fault Log).

If *you* are the incoming presenter in a hot-seat changeover, make sure you don't disturb the current presenter too early or too much. Do as much of your prep in the office before you go in (although you will have told them in good time that you're in the building in case they become concerned at your late arrival).

Remember: professionals prepare.

## After the show

The best times are when you come off air knowing that you've given your all and that the listeners and callers responded to you well and the whole show just buzzed.

It's good to keep evaluating what you're doing on the show. Whether you're a producer or a presenter, always strive to do a better one the next day.

There are several ways this should be built in to your own routine and that of the station:

- Programme review meetings.
- Your own ROT sessions.
- Snoop sessions with your programme controller.
- Long-term appraisals.
- Listener panels.
- Surveys (including Rajar).

## Programme reviews

Some presenters, especially those on freelance contracts, rarely stay at the station more than an hour after they've finished. I've known some who have their coats on for the last ten minutes of the programme so they can make a speedy getaway (and others who record the last few links so they can go before the programme's even finished.) The term for this is 'show and go'.

However, it's important that all those involved in the programme (presenter, producer, phone-op, programme controller) get together to discuss what worked well and not so well, and also *why*, and to set up features for the next day's show. This should happen soon after you come off air and shouldn't need to last more than half an hour to an hour.

A programme review (the term 'post mortem' is dated and negative – it makes it sound as though the show was so bad someone died) may include the following points:

Presentation
- Did the presenter feel well briefed?
- Was there appropriate research and questions?
- What about the links? Were they too long? Was there too much fat in them before the point was reached?

Originality
- How creative was the show?
- Was it imaginative in content, the type of guests, the angles, and the structure?
- Had it responded well to items in the news that people were talking about?
- Were there any moments that were 'surprising' or 'magic'?
- What emotional links were there with the audience? (Did it provoke, challenge, and entertain?)
- Was there impact? A 'wow factor'?

Speakers
- Were the guests good and reliable?
- Would they be used again?
- Are their details in the contacts file?
- Did the strongest callers get on air in the best possible order?
- Did the presenter get enough information about them and were they used well?

Technical
- How competent were the presenter and producer?
- Consider elements such as levels, dead air, timings and accuracy.

Music
- The three R's: rotation, repetition and requests.

Running order.
- Were items in the best order?
- Consider the placing of music, ads, calls, links, guests, competitions.
- Was there a sense of movement? Was it momentum or confusion?

The listener
- What did they get out of it if they were listening at home?
- How would it have sounded to them?
- Were they involved?

Teases and trails
- Were these done, and done well?
- Was there a difference between the teases and the trails?

Commercials
- Were the commercials in order?
- Were there product or voice clashes?
- Any out of date ads or ones with the wrong copy?
- Have they been reported?
- What about the built (pre-recorded) trails for the station?

Competitions
- Was it run and won?
- How did it go?
- Has the prize been sent?
- What about the next competition — is the mechanic understood?

Overall
- Did the show meet its aims?
- Did it reach the target audience?

Prep
- What ideas have you got for tomorrow, next week, and next month?

Many of these feedback points are a matter of personal feeling: one person may say a song is repeated too much on the station, another may disagree. The producer may say that the items were in the in the best order, the presenter may have preferred another sequence. But you still need to talk them through to get different viewpoints as those are what the listeners will have.


# Your own ROT

Use the snoop machine to record your own ROTs (recording off transmission) so you can listen to yourself from another perspective; in other words, as the listener does.

Don't listen to that day's show on the way home: it's too soon to be objective and you'll remember what was going on in the studio while you were doing each link. Give it a few weeks and then listen, but build up a library of tapes so you've got one to listen to each week, each from several weeks ago.

Ask yourself questions similar to the ones above. Monitor yourself truthfully and get other trusted people to give you feedback as well, so you don't fall in to annoying habits.

A good exercise for new presenters is to transcribe a link word for word, and then cross out everything that was unnecessary. You soon realise how many words are wasted.

Listen to presenters on other stations outside your immediate area. Drive there or listen on line. It's not copying, it's getting inspiration: you may hear something that you think would sound better if you did it *your* way, with *your own spin*.


# Snoop sessions

## The four Cs

A snoop (an aircheck) is similar to the programme review (and the self review), but as a one-to-one with the programme controller. Their job is to carry out the four Cs: to critique, congratulate, cajole and coach — constructively.

'I once had a snoop session at Radio 1 in which a very senior bod stopped the tape after five minutes and gave me this feedback: "You're very good with the buttons" . . . and that was it.'
Wes Butters, former Radio 1 chart show presenter,
*The Radio Magazine*, 26 October 2005

Wes was critiqued (to a very limited extent), and congratulated but wasn't cajoled or coached constructively. All of these elements are important. (I have a similar story when a senior management figure said to me that my bulletins were good that morning. I asked why and the reply was, 'You just sounded good'.)

Critiquing is the session itself, which should include the bad points from the show as well as the good ones (perhaps in a 'shit sandwich': congratulated on what was done well, then less well, then some more congratulations).

Cajoling and coaching is done by explaining why an element would be more effective if it was done a certain way and by setting targets for you to reach.

All this should be done constructively over time, with thought and offering explanations. It is inevitable that when you start there will be lots of elements of your show which will need improvement, but you'll become better, faster when these are pointed out, if you're shown what you could have done instead. This will improve your confidence. When someone says you did a good show, remember how that makes you feel. Ask them what they most enjoyed and try to make your next programme come up to the same standard. In contrast, if a show is a complete lemon, learn from that too.

I don't think enough radio station managers take time to actually listen to their product, and if they do, they listen in the office while they're doing the rotas or organising a road-show. In other words they're not listening *as the listeners do*. They need to get out of the office, and hear their breakfast show as they sit in traffic jams, the morning programme as they walk around the corner shop and so on. Such days should be entered into their diaries as set 'research days' at least once a month and not be moved. They're a vital part of helping the manager see the wood for the trees and enabling individual presenters and the station as a whole, to develop.

Of course with use of automation, a programme controller can in theory give an aircheck to a presenter before a show is even broadcast. Pre-recorded links can be checked for content and corrected on the spot. Never again should a poorly thought-out link go to air, or one in which the station's name doesn't appear, go to air. 'Pre-air airchecks' could make a voice-tracked station sound perfect!

# Long-term appraisals

Re-evaluate everything you do about every six months. It's natural that some of your features may be getting near the end of their natural life, so try to end them while they're still popular rather than when people are fed up with them. Some successful features can run for years and years, but it's much more usual to rest them to introduce others, or drop them completely.

# GETTING IN

What's in this part:

o Where the possible openings are and how to prise them wider so you can get in.

o How to put together your demo to show what you can do.

o The pros and cons of going freelance and getting an agent and accountant.

# 29 Where to start

Barely a week will go by when someone at a radio station doesn't get a phone call, e-mail or letter asking them how they get to be a presenter. Indeed, many times the request is as straightforward as, 'I think I'd be good on the radio . . . have you got any jobs?' that before they've ever spoken into a microphone.

Earlier in the book we looked at the overall radio landscape in the UK, here we'll look more closely at how to make a start at each of the different kinds of radio station.

The advice given is general for an entry point for most people. There will always be the exception: the person who wins a TV reality show who gets given a radio programme the next week, or the musician who fancies playing CDs rather than playing on them. Some of these people, who stumble into radio (or who have it thrust upon them) may be good but many more have their show just as long as their '15 minutes of fame' lasts and then are dropped.

Remember, for every one of these people plucked from obscurity, there's also the Chris Evans of the broadcasting world. Chris was a huge success and made millions from his radio and TV shows, but even though his fame came fast he was not an overnight success. He put in the years working as a tea boy at a commercial station in Manchester, learning the 'rules of radio' first. There are many more who also put in the time, effort and dedication and are quite happy working at their local station, and have no desire to break into the big time.

What route you take will depend to a large extent on your own personal circumstances. For example, your age, current job, family circumstances, whether you mind moving house and so on. There's the danger that, after resigning from your current job to follow your radio dream you realise it's just not for you, in which case part-time weekend work is probably a good way to start to see whether you'll be bitten by the bug. However, your career will take longer to develop.

As automation becomes more and more common, a natural entry-point for many aspiring presenters has closed. There was a time when shows, pre-recorded on spools of tape, needed to be played out usually at weekends or Bank Holidays. On other occasions, stations had non-stop music hours for which a technical operator was needed to play songs, jingles and ad-breaks. As I've mentioned, computer playout systems can do all this, saving expense for many stations. However, some BBC local stations still prefer a real person to play in programmes and calculate backtimes. The human system also means phones can be answered and up-to-date weather reports broadcast – things that automation hasn't yet managed. There are, then, still opportunities as a tech op, although they're disappearing fast.

'I'd make radio stations broadcast live 24 hours a day, because there's no new talent coming through. I blame the big groups who either pre-record stuff or let the computer play out the music. When I started in 1993 all stations were live and you'd get a kid coming into do overnights; they'd then move to a bigger station doing overnights, and move up that way. But where do you get the talent from now? Most stations stop live local broadcasting at 7pm. So I think they should be made to broadcast live 24 hours a

day, seven days a week. A lot of the little ones do, but there's
nowhere for people to step up to after that because you can't
go from doing overnights on Yorkshire Coast Radio straight
to doing drive at a big regional station.'

Joel, presenter Radio 1, *X-Trax* magazine, September 2005

Another role for a TO, and one which is more prevalent in BBC local's speech-heavy stations, is driving a show for a presenter who may have come into radio from another field and therefore are unfamiliar with the desk and unable (and sometimes unwilling) to learn. Their 'attitude' could be your opportunity!

A further situation in which a tech op would be used at a station is when there's an outside broadcast. An OB TO drives the studio desk when the presenter is out in the field, mixing the live reports with other elements. As the TO is in the studio to play in songs if the line goes down (signal is lost between the venue and the station), they may occasionally also get to go on-air.

> **INFORMATION FOR INSPIRATION:** Many presenters
> start off as a TO and it's a well-established route from working
> on someone else's show to getting one of your own.

Like a technical operator, a promotions assistant is also a good off air way to get on air. It's not as obvious a route, but you'll still learn loads about the station and show that you're keen to learn, are good at organising events, and can keep going when the promo van gets stuck in mud, the new T-shirts have the old station logo on them and the signal from the OB is lost five minutes into a two hour show!

Treat your time at the bottom of the ladder as an opportunity to learn more about your next steps, and the ones after that. To a large extent in this business you make your own luck – some ways to get the break are listed on the following pages.

# How to get in

## BBC radio

Some of the jobs at the BBC are advertised in the media section of the *Guardian* and *Independent* newspapers on Mondays. Other publications are *The Radio Magazine* (the website has the address for subscriptions), *RadioJam* (a weekly e-mailed newsletter which includes jobs) and the internal BBC newspaper *Ariel*. You can subscribe to this or you may be able to pick up a free copy at your local BBC building. Most of the jobs in *Ariel* are for experienced internal candidates only – the ones open to the public will be shown via the BBC jobs website. Some are for presenters but others are 'foot-in-the-door' positions, such as receptionist, phone-answerer or charity co-ordinator.

Most jobs, though, are offered to people already at a station who want an on air role as the next stage of their career. It may be a keen helper on the Saturday sports show, a phone-answerer or receptionist. Don't underestimate the advantage to your career of being in the right place at the right time and the realisation that *that* is not always down to luck.

Also watch out for the BBC talent programme which is advertised widely but especially on the website. This competition gives the opportunity for people to get short-term employment in the BBC in various roles of radio and TV.

## Commercial radio

Most of the commercial radio jobs are advertised in The Radio Magazine, fewer are shown in the Guardian or Independent because of the expense of national advertising. You may stumble across a job on the individual websites of the stations but that will be a long and arduous process.

Most vacancies at commercial stations are filled through word of mouth, moving presenters between stations in the same group, poaching from other stations, or giving a break to someone who has sent in a demo or who is already helping around the station.

There are several websites that advertise jobs in BBC and commercial radio, such as that for the Radio Academy.

See: www.radioacademy.org; www.bbc.co.uk/jobs; www.theradiomagazine.co.uk; www.radiojam.co.uk

## Travel presenters

One very good way into getting a show of your own is to contribute to someone else's!

Trafficlink is the company that provides road news for BBC and commercial stations across the country, from its main base in London and other studio centres around the UK. (Read the section on travel news to remind yourself what they do, see pp. 235–246)

You have to be on the ball to cope with different stations, presenters and personalities every few minutes. You'll be shown how to read the road news, which is written in a form of shorthand to make compiling it faster. You'll need to be able to ad-lib around the information and have to sight-read news as it flashes on your screen while you're on air.

You'll be known to presenters and management teams at various stations as they'll become aware of your voice and style of reading. Chat to the presenters off air before you go on air, so you'll get to hear of any opportunities that may be coming up. You may even be able to get to go in to a station and get someone to show you how to use the desk and put together a demo.

See: www.trafficlink.co.uk

## Community radio

Part of the reason for awarding community licences is to get more people involved in making radio. That's a gift for someone just starting their broadcasting career. Ofcom says that in awarding a licence they'll take into account 'an applicant's proposals to allow for access by members of the target community to the facilities to be used for the provision of the service and for their training in the use of those facilities. It's a characteristic of service that members of the target community are given opportunities to participate in the operation and management of the service . . .'.

See: The Community Media Association: www.commedia.org.uk; www.ofcom.org.uk

## RSLs

These legal stations may offer a great opportunity for you to get in to radio at the grass roots. Several hundred of these short-term stations are set up each year and if you get in with one of them you may not only get some broadcasting experience but also get to help with formatting the station or writing the proposal for a licence. If the RSL is a forerunner of a full-scale licence then you stand a good chance of a job if and when they win it. As RSLs are specifically locally based stations, you'll be more likely of a role with one if you live in or are very familiar with the broadcast area.

Keep a watch on the Ofcom website to see which groups have just been given licences. See: www.ofcom.org.uk

## Student radio

This is a great start to your broadcasting career, so if you're going into higher education try to choose a university that has its own station. These are run for students by students and their standard of broadcasting can be very high. There are around 70 in the UK, and the SRA holds conferences, training events and awards ceremonies

See: The Student Radio Association: www.studentradio.org.uk

## Hospital radio

Many of today's radio presenters started in hospital radio, including myself. Most are hugely professional and have equipment and output that rivals that of professional stations. They have a large team of dedicated volunteers who broadcast for several hours each weekday and throughout the weekend. Many have computer playout systems and do sterling work entertaining patients and staff, and raising money for the station and the hospital. But getting on air with them may take some time. It's understandable that there has to be a waiting list for presenters, and those who've been with the station the longest should not be forced out by newcomers (although many stations regularly change their schedules to give everyone an even chance).

It's also understandable that every volunteer has to serve an apprenticeship, usually in the form of walking the wards collecting dedications and shaking a collecting tin at fairs and fêtes, before being allowed on air. That means it may take several months or years before you get a programme of your own, but don't be disheartened. In between ward rounds you may be able to sit in one someone else's show and see what happens. If you suggest some ideas, offer to help in research or are willing to answer the phones then you'll get on much faster than those who don't.

Hospital radio is the place that you can develop from a club or party DJ to being a broadcaster. You will learn how to talk on a one-to-one basis to people. You will learn how to structure a programme hour and work around furniture. You'll learn the basics of interviewing guests and interacting with other volunteers at the station.

Any work you do at the station will be on a voluntary basis and you'll certainly end up out of pocket (not only in time but also in petrol and car park costs if nothing else), but it'll give you great experience for your CV and will provide a place where you can put together a demo.

Some stations recruit at 16 but the trend is slowly moving to 18+. This is partly for legal reasons over who is responsible for those who are legally still children. And because of the nature of the work (being around vulnerable people, those in bed and in various states of undress, and access to children's wards). It is also increasingly likely that all volunteers will soon have to go through a police check before being accepted.

There are around 480 hospital stations in the UK, so there's bound to be one near you. When I contacted the HBA in spring 2006, they had 243 member stations, so that's a great place to go for addresses and contact details.

See: Hospital Broadcasting Association: www.hbauk.com

The studio at the hospital station Radio St. Helier. Note the old cart machine next to the more modern computer playout system

## Pirate radio

It's not a very good idea to get involved with these outfits if you want to make it as a legal, professional broadcaster. If you're found and fined, or even imprisoned, then your career is as good as over. Some pirates broadcast because they feel as though there aren't any stations playing their kind of music or presenting it in their preferred style. If that's you then go down the legal route and apply for RSLs and a formal licence, or swallow your pride and get some experience at an existing station and try to change attitudes and content from the inside.

## Club and party DJ

You may already be a club DJ and want to get into broadcasting. There are similarities but actually very few of them! The style of presentation; the use of your voice, technology and timings; paperwork and protocol and interaction with the audience, are all markedly different. The path travelled between the two jobs is one taken by many, but few make it to the end unless they have some broadcasting experience as well as that of playing music. Start working as a hospital radio volunteer, get a demo recorded in a radio style and take it from there.

Being a party DJ is perhaps closer to being a radio presenter. You play a wider variety of music, learn how to use the microphone and get to interact with the public more, even if it is only by presenting the bride and groom and their first dance or three cheers for Uncle George's 80th. Help out with a mobile disco outfit and help lug the gear around for little or no money and after a while you'll learn what plugs in where and how the bits of kit fit together. A basic understanding like this will stand you in good stead at any radio station or on an outside broadcast! Then ask if you can try your hand at segueing a few songs, or practice before the guests arrive or the club opens. After a few months you could fill in for the main DJ when they take their break — it's all experience that will make a difference when you try and get your foot in the door at a radio station.

## Talking newspapers

This is, of course, not broadcasting at all as you'll be involved in recording articles from a local newspaper onto cassette, copies of which are sent to local blind people. This will help you learn how to use your voice to deliver stories as well as microphone technique and timing. Again, it's another line on your CV that shows a potential employer that you're keen to follow your chosen career path.

See: The Talking Newspapers Association UK: www.tnauk.org.uk

# Broadcasting courses

These can be a very good way into radio, but choose the course wisely. There's often no accreditation for those 'be a presenter in two-days' type courses and even though there are some which are well known and very professional, you may spend a lot of money to sit in the back bedroom studio of someone who was last in a radio station a decade ago, and that was to buy a T-shirt. Having said that there are some which are very good: the Radio School run by ex-Radio 1 presenter Bruno Brookes is one, the National Broadcasting School is another. And there are those which are linked to radio stations such as Chrysalis Radio's Radio Schools and the Guardian Media Group's Radio Training Academy.

See: www.radioschool.co.uk; www.nationalbroadcastingschool.com

CSV (Community Services Volunteers) is the largest independent media-training group in the UK and offers media training to charities, community groups, the unemployed and disadvantaged. These courses are usually free, certainly cheap. www.csv.org.uk (click on Media Clubhouses).

The Community Media Association also runs low-cost training for those who want to get in to radio, and there's lots more advice on training on the Skillset website www.skillset.org (and click on radio). They also run the Open Door competition which gives thousands of pounds of free training to those people who can show they're keen and have some raw talent. The Radio Academy runs regular masterclasses: www.radioacademy.org/masterclasses

## University courses

To make it as a good producer or presenter, you'll need experience in life as well as in radio. That's why many potential employers will take a second look at an application from someone who's completed a degree course; even if the subject is unrelated to media, it still shows that you can apply yourself, have intelligence, can study and set targets and so on.

Alternatively go on a specific media studies, broadcast journalism or communications course to get more of an overview of the industry and its place in society.

Questions to ask:

- Is it a theoretical course ('the role of reality TV') or is there hands-on work (actually making a radio feature or programme)? A good course will give you at least 50% practical time.
- What are the skills it teaches, and what equipment is used? Is it up-to-date and what the industry is using?
- Who are the trainers and tutors? What's their background? Have they actually been in the media? Better still, are they still working in it? Are outside speakers brought in?
- What about placements? Where are they? Are they arranged by the students or through the college? What kind of places have they been at recently? Does the university have any other media links?
- What happens after the course? What's the qualification? Where have people recently got jobs? Can you speak with them to ask about the course? Will tutors help you get a job?

# Work placements

Badger your local station for a work placement, but apply early and be politely persistent. If you're at school, most of your friends will be applying for the same places and many stations only have one person at a time on a placement.

Be prepared to be interviewed for the placement. Competition is fierce even at this level, but reading this Handbook and showing your commitment through hospital radio will stand you in good stead. Make sure you actually listen to the station you're applying to and have something to say about it!

When you get to the radio station, offer to work in as many different departments as you can in the time that you have. You may want to be a presenter but you'll benefit from seeing how the other parts of the station work to contribute to the show. Remember: even though the presenter is at the sharp end of the station there's a lot going on behind the scenes to make their show what it is. Without other departments the presenter wouldn't know what songs are the best ones to play to attract the audience, would have no one to interview, no competition prizes to give away and no adverts to play. And that final point, of course, would mean that they wouldn't be paid!

Look around the other departments and get to know what the presenter's colleagues do in the newsroom, promotions department, sales team and so on — you may find one of those jobs more interesting than that of a presenter or producer.

Some more tips to make your placement a success:

- Do everything with enthusiasm and to the best of your ability.
- Do what you're asked, and then stay late to learn what you want to learn.
- Learn by observing as well as asking.
- Make yourself invaluable — master a task so you're always asked to do it.
- Use your initiative — if you see something that needs to be done, do it.
- Don't clock-watch — be there even when you don't have to be.
- Approach experienced staff with questions.
- Have an understanding of the big picture about radio as a whole.
- Do the crap, the calls and the coffee — it's not all action all the time.
- Always turn up on time.
- Always think of the long-term goal.

I once judged a media competition where the winner got £10,000 of training in radio, TV or production. Many of the applicants had done no voluntary work or industry placements at all, and their lack of commitment meant they stood no chance of winning the prize on offer.

**INFORMATION FOR INSPIRATION:** After your placement, ask to work at the station for free, write for your school or college magazine or help organise a charity event. They all show you have the drive to make it and to get into radio.

Skillset, the body that oversees media training in the UK, reckons 40% of radio jobs are never advertised, they go to someone who was 'in the right place at the right time'.

See more on work placements on www.bbc.co.uk/jobs/workexperience

# Volunteering

'I wasn't paid for three and half years but you can't
buy that kind of experience.'
Chris Evans, presenter Radio 2, *Desert Island Discs*,
Radio 4, November 2005

There is, of course, a fine line between taking advantage of the station wanting another pair of hands and them taking advantage of you! Some stations rely heavily on volunteers: we saw earlier that RSLs, community stations and some smaller commercial stations are staffed almost entirely by them. If you feel as though you're getting experience, then by all means stay. If you feel that you're being asked to do the mundane and menial jobs too often (you should expect to do them sometimes) then have a quiet and polite word with someone. Don't just complain, but suggest what else you could do as well, or instead of, that would help the station and yourself.

If nothing changes you'll have to ask yourself whether your time is worth the amount of experience you're getting. If you decide to leave, then ask for a reference that you can take to another station for more experience or some actual cash.

But bear this story in mind:

'A former tea girl has been unveiled as the new host of
Forth One's Drivetime show. Yasmin Zemmoura, who started
at the station running errands for the presenters, was to
present her first show between 4pm and 7pm today'
*The Scotsman*, 31 May 2005

# Demos

It doesn't matter how good you think you are, or how good your friends and family tell you you are, what you have to do is persuade a potential employer. Although some presenters are poached from station to station, many jobs are got through a 'demo tape'.

'Demo' is short for 'demonstration' and the 'tape' bit has stuck, even though nowadays you're more likely to submit the example of how you sound on a CD, minidisk or MP3 file.

I've been sent many demos over the years, some by people asking for work and more recently by people wanting feedback on their style before they apply for a job. And it is a truth that's universally acknowledged amongst programme controllers – the first few seconds of the demo are what count. As the maxim goes, you don't have a second chance to make a first impression.

Your demo is your audition. It's just like what an actor goes through before getting a role on stage. But the great thing about a radio audition is that it's not live, it's recorded, and that means you can spend as long as you like getting it just right to give you the best possible chance of a job.

## Your voice

'Firstly, it's a great, distinctive voice (that makes a great demo). You can tell almost immediately if the person has a passion and a belief for what they're doing. We listen to the radio to be entertained, we want to feel good, be it through the music or through the broadcaster; so they've got to sound like they care and talk naturally. So many of the tapes we receive are of people with no comedy background, trying to be funny and in turn all that achieves is making you feel like the person is talking down to you. If I hear potential, I like to meet them to see what they're like. Are they in it for the right reasons, are they intelligent, do they see this as a real career . . . 'cos let's face it, if you're starting out you're generally coming from a position of little experience about how to present yourself and we all need guidance'

Paul Jackson, PD Virgin Radio, *The Radio Magazine*, 4 December 2004

Programme controllers are very busy so if they don't like what they hear in the first 15 seconds, your demo goes into the bin. Sound natural and communicate.

## Be yourself

You can have an unusual voice and still make it in radio, but it's tone, delivery and clarity as well as personality that is the first and most important thing. That personality should be yours. You may be a 'wannabe' presenter but the station won't want a 'wannabe' Chris Moyles or Terry Wogan. Those two presenters are hugely successful at being themselves on the radio. You would just be a pale imitation. Certainly learn from their style, and work out what they do and why it's successful and apply *that* to yourself – don't just copy them. Bring your own X factor to the demo.

## Focus on the format

Understand the station you're applying to. This is basic courtesy and after reading this book and listening to the station on the web there's no excuse for not understanding formats and which one is being used at your station of choice. Do not send clips of you interviewing a local author to a chart-based station, do not send a recording of a super-slick segue with drop-ins and whooshes to a BBC local station, unless that's the style they've specifically asked for.

**INFORMATION FOR INSPIRATION:** Sound like a presenter on the station you're pitching to — and that includes your choice of songs.

## Links

Think carefully about including any dubious material or innuendo in any link. What went down a storm in your late night show on student radio may be too near the knuckle for a controller who's looking for a family-based breakfast show presenter. Similarly, avoid including any link that comments on political or religious matters or indeed 'the news' at all. Err on the side of caution.

## Confidence

Other qualities I would listen for in a demo would be your maturity and intelligence; by that I don't mean that you have to sound 40 and quote from an encyclopaedia, but you should sound as though you know what you're talking about, have confidence in your delivery style, and confidence in driving the desk – did that jingle or sound effect start bang on time, or did you hesitate for a split second beforehand?

## Wits

I would expect you to be able to show me that you can be quick witted (perhaps with a comment that sounds off the cuff, maybe interacting with a caller or another presenter), are creative (this may be as basic as finding a new 'in' to a what's on), and can read from a script (so I know you can read and know about intonation of the written word). Use the section on links in this Handbook to make each one on your demo as different as possible.

## Time checks and IDs

I would suggest not putting these in, as they'll make the programme controller think of who they've got in that slot already. Let *them* decide if they want you and where to place you in their schedule, not you.

It is best not to include jingles on your demo. There are packages of 'off-the-shelf' jingles that you can buy, but they often sound a little cheesy and, of course, will sound odd if you're pretending to already be on the station to which you are applying. If you're sending a copy of the demo to several stations, don't mention any station name at all. Show yourself in the best possible light. No fluffs or verbal slips here – what does that show about you that you think your best work contains mistakes?

## Where to record it

After reading this handbook and following the career advice that is most appropriate for you, you should have got through the door to some kind of studio. There you'll be able to ask for some spare time to record your demo. If that's not the case then you may have to spend some money on studio time with an independent production company, or go on the kind of course that offers a produced demo at the end. But you may end up paying a lot of money for very little, so surely a few nights a week for a few months at a local hospital station is time well spent both for the patients and your future career.

## What to record it on

Many job adverts will specify the format that is preferred for your demo – cassette, CD, minidisk or even MP3. Ignore this at your peril as demos that are in a different media will go straight in the bin. That's not a euphemism, they really will: programme controllers have so many applications for jobs that they just don't need to be bothered with people who can't follow simple instructions. If you're sending a demo on spec then call and ask the programme controller or their PA what format they prefer to receive and then mention that advice in your covering letter. It'll show initiative and will cover you in case you were given the wrong information.

> **INFORMATION FOR INSPIRATION:** Never send an audio file to a radio station unless asked for. It may very easily clog or crash the system because of its size and you won't be popular.

Whatever the format, ensure it's clearly and professionally labelled. You may need to borrow or invest in a computer program that prints CD labels and inserts for the best possible image. A flashier all-colour design won't necessarily help you get the job so keep the design clear and clean. On those labels (one in the box and one on the CD) include your name, telephone number, the date (the same one as your covering letter, you want to show this is a recent example of your work recorded especially for them, not one that's off the shelf) and the duration of the piece. Remember in radio durations are written in shorthand so follow the format where three minutes twenty-seven seconds is shown as 3' 27". If there's room enough to be able to read it, include a brief list of the items on the demo ('song intro, competition caller, segue, creative what's on, programme trail') so the controller has an idea about what to expect.

Make sure the demo has actually been recorded. Some home-burned CDs don't play back on other machines, so double-check on several other players.

## How long should the demo be?

It is generally accepted that a demo should be no longer than four minutes. That may not seem long, but if advertisers can sell a car or insurance package in 30 seconds then it should be plenty of time, and it will force you to only include the best bits!

How can it be so short if you include a song intro and a segue as suggested above? Because you'll edit out most of each song, by fading it out just after you stop speaking and fading it in before your next link (as appropriate) and cutting out most of the middle (the term is 'telescoped'). The programme controller knows what the song sounds like, they want to hear you, not Kylie! Similarly, don't include ad breaks or news bulletins, although the programmer may want to hear a fluent (and possibly creative) weather report.

If the programme controller likes what they hear, they'll probably ask for an unedited two-hour tape of your on-air programme – they know that a demo can be 'dummied-up' to show you in the best possible light!

## Finally

Wait until you're sure this is the best demo you can do before you send it off: this is your audition! Listen back to it a few days after you've recorded it. Ask for feedback from friends and family or colleagues at your hospital radio station. They may notice a verbal tick (such as 'kind of thing', or 'y'know what I mean?') or that you're talking too fast or haven't explained something very well. Maybe a punch line was more pathetic than punchy. Then get ready to send off a copy of the demo, not the original!

# CVs

There are many specialist books, and some companies, that will tell you many different ways of how to prepare your CV, so I won't outline them all here. However there are some basics:

- Write it on a computer with a clear layout with lots of white space.
- Use the spell-check.
- Write in clear and straightforward sentences, but use appropriate words to show your enthusiasm – 'ambition', 'creativity', 'successful' and the like.
- Highlight any radio courses you have been on, or media qualifications you have. Mention your work placement.
- Note any interests that may have a bearing on a job in the media – maybe you're a prolific collector of specialist music albums, write articles for a local newspaper or website or run a mobile DJ business. Maybe it's public speaking, drama, sports, or music.
- Talk up the good points, play down others but don't lie.
- Print it on good quality paper to a maximum of two pages.

# Covering letter

Keep this short and to the point, make sure you address it to the correct person (by name, not 'Dear Sir or Madam') and that you've spelt their name correctly. Remember to highlight your appropriate experiences from your CV, the more skills you can offer them the more work they could offer you.

Use the word 'opportunity' rather than the more formal 'job', or the desperate-sounding 'break' and mention that, although you understand their workload, you'd welcome feedback on the demo if at all possible.

# The whole package

Put your CV, demo disc and covering letter all together and send it off; preferably first class as it looks more professional.

The whole package should be as eye-catching as possible, but that doesn't mean that you need to spend hours on a desktop publishing system experimenting with different colours and fonts. Have all the written items properly printed on good quality paper, with a font that's easy to read and ink that doesn't appear as though it's about to run out. Look in a large stationers for a plastic wallet for all the paperwork especially one that includes a section into which a minidisk or CD can be inserted.

> **INFORMATION FOR INSPIRATION:** Remember you'll be competing against other people after the same job — your application has to stand out from the crowd. This demo is your audition or first interview for the job, an interview where you're not asked any questions, just given free reign to sell yourself. What a terrific opportunity!

# The follow up

Follow up your package with a phone-call about a week later. If you leave it any longer, a standard 'we'll keep your details on file letter' may already be winging its way to you.

Radio people are very busy. It is sensible not to call very first thing soon after 9 am. It is likely they will want to get their feet under the desk as the day kicks off, reviewing e-mails, reading the post and so on. At 10am many programme staff will be in a programme review meeting and talking about more long-term events, which will last about an hour. From 1pm there could be a working lunch or at least a chance for them to get out of the office, and from 4 pm they'll be finishing off that day's work and setting up more for the next day. So, the best time to call is probably late morning or mid afternoon.

Ask if the programme controller has managed to hear your demo yet and made any decisions. You may also be able to ask for feedback on it, good or bad. However, the harsh reality is that, despite showing keenness and a willingness to learn, the programmer is likely to be very busy and unable to take calls.

Experiences with more pushy 'wannabes' has also taught many of them not to enter in to a discussion (or in some circumstances, argument) about the merits of including a particular link on the demo. Reaction to a demo will help increase your chances of a future job. However, put simply, if you regularly ignore phrases such as 'they're really busy/in a meeting/can't come to the phone right now' and continue calling a programme controller's office, you'll do your career chances more harm than good.

If you've not applied for a specific job but are writing on spec then you may be more fortunate in speaking to the programmer. Ask whether they've heard the demo, whether you could pop in for a chat and a look around, and ask about any opportunities. Offer to work for free if necessary (a great inducement for any radio station). This is especially needed at weekends, evenings, bank holidays, for charity 'radiothons' – in fact at any time that may be 'undesirable' for the regular staff.

The important thing is that you've made contact. That's pretty much a foot in the door. Don't waste the opportunity. Don't let the controller go until you've moved the situation on by asking one of the questions in the paragraph above.

Make a note of the call afterwards. Who it was that you spoke to and what they said. Then if you want to follow up the follow up and ask if there's been any change, you know who to speak to and how the conversation was left last time. Otherwise it's easy to forget who said what to whom.

There'll be a great number of refusals before you get a break so be prepared. It may be that there's just no opening for you at that time, or it may be that your demo or CV is not showing your talents in the best light – ask a friend or colleague to go through it for you and highlight where you may have let yourself down.

# Create your own luck

Keep plugging away. Look for chinks of light – other opportunities in broadcasting where you can show off your skills. Is there a job for a receptionist, or someone to work in the shop (a few BBC stations have these)? Turn up to outside broadcasts and see if there's something you think that needs to be done. Although you may not be thanked for muscling in on the day, introduce yourself and ask if you can write to them and offer your services in the future to rig and de-rig. Keep your eyes and ears open for any of these types of leads.

# You're in — almost!

Someone's interested and has asked you in to 'have a look around and a chat'. Don't waste this golden opportunity.

Do more research on the station, listen regularly (especially on the day) and dress for the station's format. A suit and tie may not be appropriate attire these days for anything but the most formal interview situations, but neither is anything unwashed or unironed. If you're going to a chart station, dress in trendy casual clothes that a member of that audience would wear. This may be smart jeans and T-shirt and would surely be a different outfit from the one you'd wear if you were going to see a management member at a local BBC station where proper trousers, shoes and shirt may be more appropriate. Women can take their lead from the description for men. Avoid too much after-shave or perfume!

There are plenty of good books on interview technique, as well as others on body language and how to make conversation and so on. This is not one of them. However, there are some points which may be useful for the situation of going into a chat at a radio station.

- Arrive in good time. Ask for the toilet and check your appearance and breath. In reception read the memos on the notice board as there might be some more ammunition you can use in your conversation.
- Chat to the receptionist and the person who collects you. They may let something slip about new positions or opportunities. You'll certainly be ready to impress them by having a conversation and they may be able to mention that to the controller later in the day. (The impact of a comment such as, 'They seemed really nice and chatty' from a receptionist can never be underestimated.) You'll also be able to show that you were friendly to them: 'I was speaking to Trish on reception as I was waiting and she mentioned that . . .'
- If you're offered a drink, take one even if you don't really want it. A lot of social 'bonding' happens over a coffee or glass of water. People loosen up and become more friendly . . . and it helps spin out the chat for longer.
- Shake hands firmly, speak clearly, sit up, look into their eyes and keep your body language open (no crossed legs or arms).
- Show that you've done your research on the station. If the subject of the breakfast show comes up, mention the name of the presenter in your answer and comment on a feature or competition they recently ran. Doing this proves that you listen and understand the station.
- If touring the station ask plenty of questions. Be keen to show an interest, but how you do it will show that you understand the workings of radio stations in general. For example, 'Do you just have one on-air studio and have the presenters hot-seat, or is there a second one?' Use the proper jargon (see the Glossary).
- Have a list of points or questions that you want to raise and make sure you ask them . . . Among these will be a way of moving the conversation on to the conclusion that you want. Don't leave having had a chat and a look around and nothing else. 'Can I help out on that show at a weekend?', 'You must be busy over the summer with all those OBs, can I come and help out on some of them . . . I don't mind about not getting paid', 'Perhaps I can call in again with an updated demo in a few months' time?'
- Afterwards, whatever the outcome write and thank the people who you met for their time and help. Like first impressions, last ones also count for a lot and even if this time things didn't work out, you never know where you might meet someone again at another station.
- Accept almost any offer from any station. Small things grow to be big.

# 30 More career advice

## Promoting yourself

Know where you want to go with your career, have some kind of game plan. It may be that you want to stay at Hometown FM for the next 20 years, and if you do that's fine. It'll mean that your children will be settled in the same schools and you'll be there to see them at the end of the day and so on. But if you want one day to be on National FM, work out how you think you'll get there.

The best and most straightforward way of promoting yourself is by doing the best possible job while you're on air. You never know who may be listening. Many times a presenter has been headhunted by a programme controller who heard them while driving through the area. With webcasting, similar situations are likely to happen even more regularly. You never know who may be listening and call you on the phone-in line and ask you if you're inter-ested in moving to a bigger market or better slot. It does happen. So, the best advert for you, is you. Remind yourself: today, I must present my best possible show. And say that to yourself tomorrow as well.

And then the next day, because you're only as good as your last show. Others, no less accurately, say you're only as good as your last ROT. So be prepared. Snoop yourself regu-larly. Radio stations rarely give warnings of redundancies.

As well as presenting a good show there are other ways of promoting yourself. I've already written about the about the value of roadshows and personal appearances and how meeting your listeners can help you present a better-targeted programme, and increase your ratings. But there are other tricks you may want to consider (some of these may need permission from your station's manager) to increase your profile at the station and the pounds in your bank.

- If you open a local fair or fête, take along a camera and ask the organiser to take a picture of you cutting the ribbon, riding on the dodgems or handing over the giant cheque. Then write a news release and send it to the local newspaper. Chances are they'll use it.
- Send the occasional news story about yourself to the locals. Think what's happened to you. Martin Day at Essex FM got a lot of publicity when he started to learn how to fly a light plane, and then a few months later when he crashed it. On a national scale, Chris Moyles said only he could reverse the slipping listening figures and become the 'Saviour of Radio One' if he was given the breakfast show. He was, and he did, boosting his image and bank account in the process. But only send items that project the image that you want to foster. If you're the trendy young jock, opening your child's school fête won't be as appropriate as introducing an act on stage at the local Battle of the Bands night.
- Publicity stunts may be arranged to raise the profile of you and the station at the same time. Maybe it's because you love a song so much you play it five times an hour and are 'suspended', or you lose an on-air bet with a fellow presenter and have to run to work in your underwear.

- Could you write a weekly or monthly column for the local paper? They may not pay you (and your copy may have to be approved by your station manager), but you'll get free publicity.
- Maintain a profile among your colleagues by contributing articles or letters to the trade press such as *The Radio Magazine* or *RadioJam*.
- It's very important to meet and keep in with other people in the same field – they may recommend you for a job or appear on an interview panel. One of the easiest ways of doing this is to join a broadcasting organisation such as the Radio Academy, which has regional groups around the UK. If you're a student, membership is at reduced price and all members have free entry to meetings where guest speakers discuss various aspects of the business. Such groups may be particularly useful to you if, as a freelance, you find yourself treading a rather lonely path, not feeling part of any one station.

# Going freelance

As you become better and more successful at your job you may find it more financially advantageous to go freelance. That would mean giving up the security of a monthly salary paid by one station and have the opportunity to work for several stations and negotiating a fee for each job (although some stations won't employ you if you can also be heard on a neighbouring station).

## Why it's best to be a staffer
- There's more security. You'll be given more notice about any redundancy, and get compensation.
- Someone else does all the paperwork such as tax and National Insurance (freelancers aren't earning any money when they are sorting and filing their receipts and invoices).
- You always know where you're working and the shift pattern, what will be paid into your account and when. (Freelancers have to work hard to sell themselves to lots of stations, or get an agent who may find work for them but that comes at a price.)
- There's often a recognised career ladder to work your way up.
- There may be in-house training that's all paid for.
- You won't have to scrabble around for work or reduce your rates when jobs are thin on the ground.
- Paid holiday (for freelancers, if they're not working they're not earning).

## Why it's best to be a freelance
- You can negotiate different rates for different jobs. If you're on staff as a journalist and you're asked to cover the drive show for a week, your pay remains the same. As a freelance you'd be able to ask for more money for the presenting job which may involve more expertise.
- If you don't like the job you don't have to do it. A staffer may be told to present the overnight show on Christmas morning. You will be able to say 'no thanks'.
- Flexibility and variety: you could be doing different things on different days of the week with different companies.
- The more you work the more you earn.
- Some of your expenses (such as travel and clothes) may be tax deductible, meaning that your 'take home pay' is even more.

As you can see there are good points and not so good points about going it alone. If you're talented and lucky then success may be yours, if you're not then it may be tough.

## Other work

As well as presenting you may decide to do voice-overs, do research, be a master of ceremonies, host events and trade exhibitions, front corporate videos or train others and become a lecturer. But work will only come to you if you go out and find it. You have to let people know that you're around, what you can do and what your availability is. Bookings may start off slowly, but if you do a good job on one occasion, other events will follow as re-bookings take place and word gets around.

One of the most difficult things to do is the cold-call: phoning stations, companies or agents and asking if you can send them a demo. Of course, you don't need their permission to send one, but it'll mean so much more if you can address your letter to a specific person, and it's even better if you've had a chance to introduce yourself to them on the phone first. You'll be in constant competition with other freelancers also trying to get the same job, so the first impression you make with each station is very important.

# Getting an accountant

Find one who works with other presenters and who knows the allowances for your kind of job. Other freelance presenters shouldn't mind passing on details of who they use.

As well as doing a lot of paperwork for you, a good accountant may be able to reduce your tax bill on items that you buy which are essential to your job. These may include a car and petrol, a portable recorder and headphones, clothes you need for public appearances and their laundering, subscriptions to trade organisations and tickets to industry events. On top of that there may be allowances for voice training, stationery, and for their own fees!

# Getting an agent

The job of an agent is to find you more work. In return you pay them a percentage of any fee that they get you. This may be around 15%, although some agents charge a fee of *all* your earnings, even if you secured the work yourself. So, if you sign up with an agent and you're on £20,000 a year, their fees are going to cost you £250 a month for the entire period of your contract at the station.

If you're a freelancer you may be wary of cold-calling other stations and doing the hard sell of yourself and negotiating a fee. An agent should have lots of contacts, so will have little or no problem in putting you forward for various jobs. They will be among the first to hear what work is available and because they may have others like you on their books, they are often able to make money through doing very little work. Placing one client in one job does, after all, leave a vacancy for another presenter elsewhere.

A good agent will represent you at meetings to discuss your salary and other perks, and know the best way to counter the 'there's no more money in the budget' argument. Indeed some stations prefer liaising with an agent so the relationship with the presenter (what the Americans call 'the talent') isn't soured.

An agent may also act as your manager and give you career advice, such as changing your on-air style, your name or aspirations. They should always be looking forward to your next step. That next step may be to a larger station, which they can sound out on your behalf, and in confidence.

If you do decide to approach an agent (and it's not usually necessary, especially at the start of your career) then pick one who is used to dealing with radio presenters. It makes no sense to have someone who deals with look-alikes or circus sideshows, as they'll have no contacts in your line of work.

Always keep your agent informed about your career. What developments have there been with your job, where are you working, how much for? It's all information they'll use to negotiate your next gig. Give them regular copies of updated demos, pictures, newspaper articles, refreshed CVs and so on, so they have all the tools to sell you with.

Beware of the bad agent who says that work is 'just around the corner' when in reality they're pushing a bigger name with whom they can earn more money, or the ones who charge you extra for phone calls and stamps: all that should be covered in their commission, or the ones who want you to pay them up front.

Also be wary of these sharp practices:

- Some agents tie you in to a contract with them even if they don't find you any work, or offer you jobs that they know you'll turn down just so they can say they found you *something*. Make sure you are free to move agents if nothing's forthcoming after a set period.
- Some contracts may require you to pay a commission to your agent as long as you work for the station at which they negotiated your original booking, even if you get a new agent to negotiate a new contract with the employer after the original agreement expires.
- Some contracts forbid you from talking with or taking advice from others in the industry. It's an attempt to try to isolate you from others and keep you dependent on that single organisation.

## Unions

Consider, too, whether becoming a member of a union is for you. For a small monthly fee (which may be tax deductible) you could have the support of perhaps the NUJ (National Union of Journalists), or maybe that of Bectu. If you consider yourself more of an actor and have or can get an Equity card then it may worth keeping up membership of that union. You may need all the support and advice you can get if an employer breaks a contract with you or refuses to pay you what you thought had been agreed.

# THE BACK ANNO

# The back anno

Well, that's about it. Our journey is nearly over.

Apart from a few appendices, the glossary and index, that's it from me.

I hope that you got what you wanted from the Handbook and that you refer to it often during your new career in radio.

I wish you the very best of luck as you enter the business. Set your sights high and be the best you possibly can. Aim to present a great show every time (curiously the best shows are usually presented by those who plan the most). The key is perhaps to Prepare, Practice and Perfect, and with this Handbook you'll be able to do just that.

Let me leave you with a final thought.

Don't forget what I consider to be the keys to great radio:

Make everything:

o   Relevant.

o   Interesting.

o   Compelling.


Regards


*Peter*


PS

If you've got any comment on this edition of the book, or suggestions for the next one, or questions about your career, drop me a line at EssentialRadioSkills@hotmail.com or via my website www.PeteStewart.co.uk

And that's the same address if you'd like a subscription to my monthly e-mail newsletter of news and ideas for broadcasters. It's free, you can unsubscribe at any time and your address will not be forwarded to anyone else, or if you'd like a personal programme review, voice training session or station consultation.

(By the way, the answers to the trivia questions in the chapter on presenting music were The Beatles in 1964, *True Colours* by Cyndi Lauper and *Maniac* by Michael Sembello. The film was *Flashdance*.)

# Appendices

## Appendix 1

### Radio format categories

| Format | Abbreviation | Example BBC | Example Commercial |
|---|---|---|---|
| Adult Contemporary | AC | Radio 2 ◇ | Virgin, Heart, Real, Magic* |
| Alternative | Alt | 6Music | Xfm |
| Asian | Asn | Asian Network | Sabras, Sunrise, Club Asia |
| Childrens | Ch | BBC 7 ◇+ | Capital Disney+ |
| Contemporary Hits | CHR | Radio 1◇ | Capital Radio* |
| Classical | Class | Radio Three | Classic FM |
| Community | Comm | | BCB Radio – Bradford |
| Country | Ctry | | 3C+ |
| Dance/Urban | Dan | | Galaxy, Vibe, Choice, ◇ |
| Easy Listening | Easy | | Saga |
| Ethnic | Ethnic | | London Greek Radio |
| Full Service | Full Ser | (BBC local stations) | Leicester Sound FM |
| Gay | Gay | | Gaydar+ |
| Hot Adult Contemporary | Hot AC | | |
| Jazz | Jazz | | Jazz FM♦ |
| Multicultural | Multi | | Spectrum |
| New Music | NM | Radio 1◇ | |
| News | News | | LBC News 1152 |
| News/Talk | N/T | Radio Five Live, Radio 4 | |
| Oldies | Gold | | Capital Gold, Classic Gold |
| Religious | Rel | | Premier, Cross Rhythms |
| Rock | Rock | | Kerrang!, Planet Rock+ |
| Soft Adult Contemporary | Sft. AC | Radio 2◇ | Star |
| Soft Rock | Sft. Rck | | The Arrow+ |
| Speech/Adult Contemporary | Sp/AC | | Century |
| Sports/Talk | S/T | Five Live Sports Extra+ | talkSPORT |
| Talk | Talk | | Talk 107, LBC 97.3 |

*   Most commercial music stations describe themselves either as AC (GWR FM) or CHR (Radio Aire).
♦   In 2005, Jazz FM changed its format and its name to Smooth FM
+   Digital/satellite station
◇   Some stations have 'cross-over' formats, for example Radio 1 is described as NM/CHR, and Juice 107.6 as Dan/NM

Stations which share the same name, but which broadcast on different frequencies to different parts of the country, invariably share the same format, so most frequencies have been omitted from this list.

Various sources including: UK Radio Guide – Summer 2005/6; Ofcom report *Preparing for the Future*, 2005; and www.radiocentre.org

# Appendix 2

## DJ clichés

Listeners want to hear you the person, not your impression of what a DJ sounded like in the mid-seventies. Talk to real people like a real person does. It's called communicating!

DJ clichés are what some radio presenters say because they think they're the first to think of them, because they once heard someone else say the same thing, because they think that's what radio presenters do, or because they don't know any better.

### At the start of the show
- 'Welcome along!'
- 'Good afternoon *everyone* . . .'
- 'I'm Peter Presenter through till three . . .' (who will you be after that?)
- 'Great to have you along'

### Introducing songs
- 'Here's a little bit of . . .' as in 'Now here's a little bit of The Darkness'. (If you're only playing a little bit, why are you bothering? You've probably messed up your back time.)
- 'Good old . . .' as in 'Now here's good old Ozzy Osborne . . .'
- Calling Madonna 'the Material Girl'.
- Singing along to or talking along to song lyrics.
- 'That's the sound of . . .'

### Before an ad-break
- 'Keep it here'.
- 'We'll be back after the break', 'after the news', 'after these messages', 'after the commercial break', 'after we've paid the rent'.

### Blame after a mistake
- 'Sticky fingers'.
- 'The producer'.
- 'The engineers'.
- 'Gremlins'.
- 'I'll just put my teeth back in'.

### The post
- 'Snail mail'.
- 'An e-mail has flooded in . . .'

### Phones
- 'They're lit up like a Christmas tree'.
- 'They've gone into meltdown'.
- PRESENTER: 'So, how are you?'
  CALLER: 'Oh, OK'.
  PRESENTER: 'That's great!' (or 'that's grade' in a pseudo-American accent.) 'Great' can grate.
- When a caller mentions the name of the company where they work: 'You can pay me later for that mention . . . ha ha ha . . .'

### Your name
- Calling yourself by a nickname other people use for you: 'Hi, it's the Hairy Cornflake here . . . !'

### Time Crimes
- 'Coming up on 8:20', 'It's 20 after 8', 'It's 11 past 8', 'It's 40 before 9', and so on.
- 'Here's a time check. . .', 'Here's the time . . .' Just give the time!
- 'It's 8:26 . . . *that's the time*'
- 'The top of the hour', 'The bottom of the hour'.
- 'It's 8 minutes *past the hour of. . .*' or '8 past the hour of . . .' (without the word minutes mentioned).

- 'It's *time for* the news/the competition', etc.
- 'It's the 12th of November 2005' (eleven months in, I know what the year is!)

### Other clichés and crutches

- 'Travel-wise', 'weather-wise' and so on.
- 'Talking' as in 'We're talking antiques', 'We're talking books'. What is wrong with 'talking *about* books'?
- 'Thru' as in 'Monday thru Friday'.
- Referring to Wednesday as 'hump-day'.
- Saying 'The weekend is just around the corner'.
- Referring to items as 'official' as in 'the official weather station'/'the official weekend station' and so on.
- Anything along the lines of '. . . It's Britney Spears' birthday, so *if you're listening* Britney, happy birthday . . .'.
- 'Radioland'.
- 'A big shout out to . . .'
- 'Don't touch that dial'.
- A prize that's 'up for grabs'.
- 'That prize will be winging its way to you . . .'

### Nearing the end of the show

- 'Darren Deejay is here in 22 minutes . . . 18 minutes'. . . just ten minutes', time', etc, rather than mentioning specifics.

### At the end of the show

- 'This has been Peter Presenter . . .' (see above)
- 'Until tomorrow at 12, I'm Peter Presenter'. Who will you be then?
- 'That's it from me'/'I'm outta here!'

# Appendix 3

## How to cope with killer breakfast (or overnight) shifts

'When you're doing a job you love it's easy to get up at whatever time of the morning. At some points it becomes quite hard, like if I've been out the night before, but I try to be home and in bed at a reasonable time, about 10. The best thing is getting a siesta in the afternoon, when you know everyone else is still in work. Weekends are recovery time and I get to have lie-ins.'

Zoë Hanson, Presenter Capital Radio,
*The Radio Magazine*, 19 February 2005

Breakfast may be peak listening time on radio, and you may get paid a little extra for doing it. In the summer you have the afternoon to relax in the sun, and can actually get to the doctor and the bank in working hours. And it can be great if you have kids: you get to meet them from school and put them to bed.

But you're tired by mid-afternoon and have to go to bed early. Parties are a no-no and your odd sleep pattern continues even when you're on holiday. You sleep all day and spend the night shift or breakfast shift semi-awake – bleary-eyed and cranky, in a semi-darkened studio with only Sam the security guard and Chris the cleaner to keep you company.

Working on a morning show can be exhausting, lonely, and thankless, but it can also be rewarding.

How do you survive them? I did earlies for eight years, so here are my suggestions that may just help:

### Waking up

- Getting up and skipping breakfast, driving straight to work and doing a show won't get the best out of you. You need at least a 40-minute wake-up time. watch the news, have something to eat and a good cup of coffee and check your e-mails.
- A walk to work clears the head and allows you to come up with ideas. In summer, relish the nicest part of the day.
- Use a pre-icer or a blanket on your car so you don't have to scrape in winter.
- Get up as soon as the alarm goes of. Trying to grab another 30 seconds' snooze is both pointless (it makes you feel no better), and dangerous as you may oversleep.
- Make sure your alarm clock is away from the bed, so you have to get up to turn it off. Consider setting a second (battery) alarm to go off 5 minutes later. There's nothing worse than waking up and realising you're on-air in less time than you have to get to work.
- Set your clock radio to a really annoying radio station.
- Buy a sunrise alarm clock for the winter. It really helps avoid that painful moment when you turn on the light and it tricks you in to thinking it's morning for a few seconds.
- Don't sleep-in on weekends if you can avoid it.

### Food and drink

- Eat right. Try to maintain a balanced healthy diet. Take a packed lunch so you avoid the snack machines (it's especially important to remain disciplined). Take a regular vitamin supplement if necessary.
- Coffee, tea, caffeine in fizzy drinks and nicotine won't do you any favours when you get home and want to sleep, since it'll still be in your system. Instead cold water (as cold as you can manage) will increase your alertness and concentration. Other substitutes are fresh orange or grapefruit juice.
- Don't think coffee or Red Bull will work instead of sleep!

### Your health

- Your body works better if you're fitter. Experts say take exercise five hours before you want to fall asleep; so, as you leave work, a quick gym session or a walk home might help you sleep better.
- Many people enjoy exercise more on these shifts than they do on a daytime shift. The gym is generally empty between 10–4 and it's cheaper!

### Your voice

- Try and talk to yourself on the way to work! Go through some mock links and generally get that voice box into gear. Your mouth and voice won't be exactly raring to go that early in the morning so make sure you've got the most important body part that you need to be a presenter properly warmed up.

### After work

- Be careful driving home. You start to feel drowsy, and it can be really dangerous.
- When you get home, don't sit down, otherwise you won't be bothered to go out again (to the gym, the shops) or even get up again.
- If you do nap in the afternoon, do it for no longer than an hour. Set the alarm.
- Consider taking up some afternoon classes to pass the time and relax you.

### Family and social life

- Perhaps early shifts are for those with very understanding partners, or who are single.
- What about the missed TV shows because you have to go to bed early? A TiVo or Sky+ is essential so you never have to sit through dreadful, mind-numbing daytime TV again.
- Don't forget to live a little: it won't hurt to have to a late night every so often – you've got to live a bit. You'll find your own body rhythm and work out what's best for you.

### Going to bed

- Find a sleep pattern and stick too it. A mid-afternoon power-nap seems to do the trick for some; some simply function well when they've had a good night's continuous sleep.
- Blackout curtains and eye masks (like the ones you get on planes) seem to be essential. So would earplugs, but they'd cut out your alarm too!
- Tell friends when you usually go to bed, so they don't call just as you're dropping off to sleep.

# Appendix 4

## How to learn the most, the fastest, when you move to a new station

**THE AUDIENCE**
- ☑ Where do they work?
- ☑ What do they do at weekends?
- ☑ What matters to them?
- ☑ How long do they listen for?
- ☑ What do they want out of life?

**GEOGRAPHY**
- ☑ The most travelled streets, major hold-up areas, motorways, traffic hot spots and accident black spots.
- ☑ The local names for some of the junctions or cut-throughs
- ☑ Features such as hills, mountains, lakes, reservoirs – and local names for them.

**MEDIA**
- ☑ The other local radio stations and their target audiences. Are any of them in direct competition with you? How do you compare?
- ☑ TV stations: do they have any local personalities, for example, weather or sports presenters?
- ☑ Local newspapers, when they're published. What kind of following do they have?
- ☑ What does the listener watch on TV?
- ☑ What papers and magazines do they read?

**BUSINESS**
- ☑ How far do the people travel for work? Is it a commuter belt/dormitory town? What colour collars are they? Average income?
- ☑ Biggest employer/s. Is it just one trade (a single-product factory) or a wide range of jobs (airport)? What's its past and possible future?
- ☑ Shopping. The high streets and centres. Are they trendy malls or run-down precincts? What are they called and where are they?

**ENTERTAINMENT**
- ☑ What is there? Entertainment centres, leisure parks and nightclubs.
- ☑ Annual events: major ones such as Wimbledon, Epsom Races or smaller events like a famous pancake race, marble championship or blessing of the catch at a fishing village. Big fairs or carnivals. Popular pastimes such as sailing or choir singing.
- ☑ Theatres and cinemas. Which ones are the multiplexes and which ones the fleapits?
- ☑ Get specifics: not just 'the park' but 'the Festival Leisure Park' or 'The Dolphin Sports Centre'.

**YOUTH**
- ☑ Major schools, colleges, universities. Which ones are private? How are they perceived locally?
- ☑ What are some of the local schools? Which ones are 'the best' and 'less good'?
- ☑ Where do pupils go to hang out? The sea front? The 'mad mile'?

**POLITICS**
- ☑ Notable political figures. The MPs, where they represent and what party they support.
- ☑ What political colour is the TSA?
- ☑ What ethnic minorities are in the area? What's the make up? Where are they from and where are they living now? What's their history in the area?

**SPORT**
- ☑ What are the big teams and the big rivalries? How are they doing in the leagues? What are the teams' nicknames and where do they play? What are their mascots? Are they followed with passion? What's their past and future? Who are the big players on and off the pitch?

☑ Is there a quirky local sport?
☑ Where are the sports centres?

**NEWS STORIES**

☑ Major city projects and development plans. New road systems, housing estates, a leisure complex or shopping centre.
☑ Scandals. In politics, business, sport, health, leisure . . .

**GENERAL BACKGROUND**

☑ Famous residents. Does your station have a list of personalities with local connections? Do they still have strong links with the area? Are they supporters of the station?
☑ Well-known local characters. Are there any heroes or legends?
☑ The weather. Is the area particularly prone to fog, floods and so on.
☑ Transportation. The names of the local bus and train companies and any recent problems. What are the main routes that people take?
☑ Trends. For example, is the seaside resort 'in' or 'out'? Why? What's hot and what's not?
☑ What things, events, places or people in the area does everyone joke about?
☑ What do they *never* joke about?
☑ History and local legends.
☑ Weird pronunciations of local places.

# Appendix 5
# Contact details

## Regulation

*Advertising Standards Authority* Regulates broadcast advertising. www.asa.org.uk
*BBC* www.bbc.co.uk and www.bbcgovernors.co.uk
*Broadcast Committee of Advertising Practice* Sets, reviews and revises the advertising codes for radio ads. www.cap.org.uk
*Department for Culture, Media and Sport* The government department which regulates BBC and commercial radio in the UK. www.culture.gov.uk
*Ofcom – The Office of Communications* The independent regulator for UK radio www.ofcom.org.uk

## Other industry bodies

*Advertising Association* Represents advertising and promotional marketing industries. www.adassoc.org.uk
*BBC Training* Some free courses via this website, as well as details of paid-for courses open to anyone from any station. www.bbctraining.com
*Broadcasting Journalism Training Council* Accredits 30 journalism courses. www.bjtc.org.uk
*Commonwealth Broadcasting Association* Offers consultancies, training, bursaries and fellowships and awards for broadcasters in Commonwealth countries. www.cba.org.uk
*Community Media Association* The voice for 'cultural and creative expression, community development and entertainment'. www.commedia.org.uk
*CSV* (Community Services Volunteers) The largest independent media training group in the UK. www.csv.org.uk
*Digital Radio Development Bureau* Promotes digital radio take-up. www.digitalradionow.com
*European Broadcasting Union* Negotiates broadcasting rights, co-productions, programme exchanges, etc. www.ebu.ch
*Hospital Broadcasting Association* Supports and promotes hospital radio stations. www.hbauk.com
*National Association of Broadcasters* Promotes and protects the interests of radio broadcasters around the world. www.nab.org
*Radio Academy* The body for radio professionals. www.radioacademy.org
*Radio Advertising Bureau* Promotes effective radio advertising. www.rab.co.uk
*Radio Advertising Clearance Centre* Clears special category radio adverts. www.raccc.co.uk
*RadioCentre* Formed in 2006 from the merger of the Radio Advertising Bureau and the Commercial

Radio Companies Association, its members consist of the majority of UK commercial radio stations, whose interests it represents. www.radiocentre.org

*RadioJam* Weekly newsletter on the radio industry, including jobs. www.radiojam.co.uk

*Radio Joint Audience Research* Manages the audience measurement system and is jointly owned by the CRCA and the BBC. www.Rajar.co.uk

*The Radio Magazine* The industry's trade paper. www.theradiomagazine.co.uk

*Skillset* The body that oversees media training in the UK. www.skillset.org

*Student Radio Association* Represents student radio stations. www.studentradio.org.uk

# Glossary

This really is an A–Z of radio, an extensive list of definitions and terms used in and around radio stations.

**AAA** A music genre: Adult Album Alternative.

**AC** A music genre: Adult Contemporary.

**Accapella** A jingle with no music, just singers.

**Acoustic screen** A mobile screen covered in sound-absorbing material which is used to shield a microphone from noise from another part of the studio, or to help deaden a studio's acoustics.

**Actuality** The recording made of an event or speech. It can be used as background sound under a voiceover or as an insert into a package.

**Ad** Shortened term for advertisement or commercial. In the US: 'spot'.

**Ad lib** Talking without a script, possibly from bullet points but in the main, improvised.

**Ad log** A computer-generated daily list of the station's adverts indicating when they should be played. Although the songs are automatically loaded by the playout computer, the presenter is required (as part of their contract) to sign the log to indicate that the ads were played at the specified time, as a contractual agreement with the advertiser who is then billed.

**AGC** Automatic Gain Control. Equipment which equalises the differences in volume, by automatically adjusting the levels to reduce dramatic changes.

**Analogue** The traditional delivery of radio output, through an aerial. It is prone to interference and lacks the sound quality of digital.

**Angle** Also execution, or line. The approach that is going to be taken with a story. For example, who is going to be interviewed and the line of questioning that is going to be used.

**AOR** A music genre: Adult Orientated Rock.

**Apps** See racks room.

**As-live** Pre-recording an item to give the impression when broadcast as though it is happening live. Such a technique can add an edge to the show but may also be misleading.

**Atmos** Atmosphere. General background noise or hubbub.

**Audience figures** Important for commercial stations as they prove to advertisers how many people are likely to hear their sales pitch, and therefore how much money can be charged for each spot. Important to BBC stations to help justify the universal licence fee. Usually given either as the *actual* number of people listening (reach) or as a percentage of the *potential* audience (share).

**Audio clip** Or just clip. A short piece of usually spoken audio, perhaps taken from an interview or other source (for example speech or TV programme).

**Automated** A pre-recorded show that plays out from a computer. The links are recorded and inserted into the appropriate place in the running order so when the different elements are played in sequence it gives the impression of being live. A presenter can be employed for say one hour to record the links for a four hour show, saving time and money.

**Average quarter hour** A typical listening period of 15 minutes, by which basic listening ratings are derived.

**BA**  In BBC radio, a broadcast assistant.

**Back-anno**  Back announcement (also outroduction): what the presenter says at the end of a report or song, which explains what was just heard. A shorter version of an introduction which in effect is announcing an item backwards.

**Backpack**  A low-powered portable transmitting device, stored in a special backpack, which enables a roving reporter to report live on air. (See COOBE)

**Back timing**  Adding together the durations of several programme elements and subtracting them from the time that they all need to have finished by, thereby working out what time they need to start.

**Barter**  The swapping of airtime (advertising space) in return for an on-air service, to avoid money being paid by either party. For example, a travel news supplier may give their service for free, and in return be given 30-seconds of additional airtime which it can sell to an advertiser and keep any income it receives.

A contra deal usually refers to a similar swap but for off-air products or services: for instance an ad campaign for a local garage run for free, in return for the servicing of the station's pool cars.

**Base**  The location of the radio station, as in 'I'm having trouble sending a radio car signal back to base'.

**Bass**  The lower end of the musical scale.

**Bed**  As in music bed. A piece of music (sometimes other audio such as natural noise) played under speech. An example would be a 'travel bed', the music played underneath traffic reports. Beds are underscores of full themes which allow the speech to be heard more clearly.

**Benchmark**  A radio feature that airs at the same time each day or week, is synonymous with the station and often sponsored.

**Bid**  As in 'I've put in a bid for the prime minister . . .'. Asking for an interview with someone.

**Bit**  A (usually) pre-produced comedy segment.

**BJ**  In BBC radio, a broadcast journalist.

**Bleed out**  Or bleed through, breakthrough or cross talk. When audio from one source is unintentionally heard in the background of another. It may be when a producer's talkback message is heard on air, or when a phone call is heard behind as a song as the conversation's being recorded.

**BNCS**  Broadcast Network Control System. Used in BBC radio, this is the control system accessed by a screen in the studio through which the presenter can dial outside sources on the ISDN.

**Board**  1. US term for a studio desk (running the board).

2. A BBC term for a job interview.

**Book**  A Rajar survey period: 'The latest book shows that we're losing listeners . . .'.

**Boomy**  A low, echoey acoustic either from a voice or in a room.

**Break**  A series of commercials.

**Briefing sheet**  A producer's job is to give the presenter all the information that they will, or might need to carry out the interview. This will be written on a briefing sheet.

**Bumper**  US term. The jingle played in or out of an ad break.

**Cans**  Slang for headphones.

**Cartridge**  Or cart. A plastic box containing a loop of tape that could automatically re-cue once used. The duration of the tapes were between twenty seconds and five minutes, allowing jingles, adverts or songs to be recorded on them. Rarely used nowadays.

**CHR**  A station music genre: Contemporary Hit Radio.

**Clean feed**  This is when a producer sends the sound of the programme down a phone or ISDN line, so a contributor can hear questions put to them. Importantly the feed *will not include what it is said by the contributor*, only what the presenter says. Clean feed is used when there is a delay on the line (it is impossible to speak coherently if you hear yourself being sent back to you a second or two later) or when the feed is being heard through a loudspeaker (when otherwise, feedback would be caused). Compare with cue feed.

**Clippings**  A collection of articles clipped from newspapers or magazines as part of research or show prep.

**Clock start**  A precise start for an event or occasion, such as joining up with the rest of the network.

**CMA**  Community Media Association.

**Codec**  A device used to dial up and convert signals from analogue to digital, and send them down a special telephone line, such as an ISDN. You need a codec to encode the signal at source, and another to decode the signal at the destination. (Codec stands for 'code-decode'.)

**Commentary**  A running, often live, report, description or explanation of an event as it happens, such as a sports event or royal visit.

**Competition book**  Kept in the studio or ops room, detailing competitions, winners and the despatch of prizes.

**Compressor**  An automatic volume device which stops the signal becoming either too high or too low.

**Com prod**  Commercial production. The department at a radio station where adverts are made.

**Console**  See mixer.

**Consolidation**  When stations or station groups merge or are taken over. A larger group with fewer overheads invariably makes more money.

**Contra**  See Barter.

**COOBE**  Pronounced 'cooby': Contributor Operated Outside Broadcast Equipment. The equipment used by reporters wanting to connect through ISDN when they're out in the field (see backpack).

**Cough button**  A switch which cuts a microphone while it is depressed, allowing the presenter to briefly cough or clear their throat.

**Crash**  Term used when a presenter is still talking when the vocals start on a song (crashing the intro), or when the presenter misjudges the amount of time left on the programme and is taken off-air mid sentence by the next programme starting on time.

**Cross**  When one presenter introduces or hands over to another: 'to do a cross', 'let's cross over to . . .'

**Cross fade**  Reducing the level of one piece of music while introducing another track at the same time.

**Cue**  Confusingly this has three different meanings.

1. The introduction to a report or interview (the same term is used whether the introduction is written or read).

2. The signal given from a producer to presenter (usually a finger pointed in their direction, or a green light, a cue light) to start to start a link, or from presenter to producer (usually a hand signal) to start playing an item.

3. An abbreviation of cue programme when the output of what is being broadcast is sent

through to a contributor's headphones, so they are aware of when they are being introduced. In such a situation they'll also hear themselves (as the audience will) when they start talking.

**Cue light** A light, usually green, activated when the contributor is required to speak.

**Cue feed** Compare with clean feed. This is when a contributor to a show who's broadcasting from another studio, is sent the audio of everything that's being transmitted, *including what they say*. This is when they are listening via headphones to hear the questions.

**DAB** Digital Audio Broadcasting. The broadcast of high quality sound using digital technology rather than radio waves (which are analogue signals). Now just known as digital radio.

**DAT** Digital Audio Tape, pronounced dat. A high quality cassette for digital recording.

**Day part** The general time of day in which programmes of a certain format are broadcast. For example, some stations' breakfast shows are 6:00–9:00, others are 7:00–10:00 (their individual time-slot). The day part is referred to simply as 'breakfast' for easy comparison.

**Dead air** Silence on air due to equipment malfunction, such as a playout system which has crashed or a fault with the transmitter. Different from silence which is meant to have occurred, for example when a presenter decides not to ask another question in the hope that a guest adds to their answer.

**Dead side of a mic** The side which is not sensitive enough to pick up sound of broadcast quality. Usually the best side is marked with a label.

**Delay** The system that is set up to stop a broadcasting being transmitted, usually for around 10 seconds, to reduce the possibility of a defamatory comment (or 'prof': profanity) going to air. Usually, although not always, used in phone-in programmes.

**Demo** As in demonstration. A recording of the presenter at work, showing their abilities to a potential employer. An audition. Often referred to as a demo tape although invariably on CD, minidisk or MP3 file.

**Demographic** As in target demographic – the outline of an average, or target listener. Factors such as their age, marital status, income, family size, sex, social grade, ethnic origin and job are used to construct the profile. That profile is used to help format the station to such a listener and also helps sell the station to the advertiser who knows who'll be hearing their advertisement.

They are divided according to the following criteria:

A – higher managerial or professional profession

B – intermediate managerial or professional

C1 – junior managerial, supervisory or clerical

C2 – skilled manual employees

D – semi skilled and unskilled manual workers

E – state pensioners, widows and casual workers and the unemployed (including students)

**Dep** To dep for a presenter is to deputise for them – to stand in on their show while they are on away.

**Desk** Or mixing desk. Sometimes called panel, board or console. The main piece of equipment in the studio through which are channelled various sources to be mixed for broadcast.

**Desk output** What you are sending to the transmitter from that studio (compare with off-air output).

**Digital** Digital signals are basically on/off pulses which can be squeezed, mixed up with others and still end up as a good quality sound at your radio set. Once compressed, lots of them need relatively little space for transmission.

**Digital radio** Either the piece of equipment used to pick up digital stations (a digital radio set) or the overall term used to describe the process of delivering high quality sound (and text) through multiplexes.

**Digital recording** This replaced recording on tape to give a high quality recording through the use of encoded numbers, which can be re-recorded many times without loss of quality.

**Disco** Apart from discotheque it is also short for a discussion usually involving three or more people.

**Doco** Pronounced docco. Abbreviation for documentary.

**Donut** A jingle that starts and ends with singing (usually over music) but which has a music-only hole in the middle without singing, over which a presenter can speak, or play a drop-in.

**Double header** A programme for which two people share the role of presenter often but not always a man and a woman.

**Down the line interview** Conducted with the presenter in the main studio and guest in a remote studio, connected via an ISDN link.

**Drive** To operate the desk controls in a studio. This may be done by a tech op, either for a presenter who is on an outside broadcast or for a presenter who is in the studio but is untrained or unwilling to drive themselves, perhaps to give them more time to concentrate on the content of the show.

**Drive-time** The generic name, and sometimes the actual name of the programme on a station which is broadcast during the afternoon rush hour, usually between c 5:00 and 7:00 pm, which is usually the second most listened-to programme of the day. This is partly because of the sheer numbers of people who are available to listen at that time. It can also be used to refer to the time of day itself rather than the programme. Can be shortened to drive.

**Drone** A long, low single note that is played behind competition questions to heighten the tension.

**Drop-in** A dry recorded announcement, for example the station's phone number.

**Dry** Speech without music (it is usual to have a dry drop-in).

**Dry run** A rehearsal.

**Dub** Simply to copy audio from one source to another, usually, though not always ones of different types. That is possibly from one minidisk to another, but more often from, say, a minidisk to cassette.

**Emergency tape** A recording (formerly on tape but now more likely to be on minidisk or CD), to be played in the event of station evacuation so that output is still being transmitted. There may also be a recording of solemn music in the event of the death of a member of the Royal family, which may be called the obit tape.

**Ends** Description of a song that stops, rather than fades.

**End stop** The home position of a fader channel. In fader-start mode, an item will begin playing as soon as the fader's moved from the end-stop.

**ENPS** Trade name for the Electronic News Production System, which is the computer program on which BBC and commercial stations often process the text of their news bulletins and programme running orders. Often stations can view stories and running orders which are stored by other stations in the network.

**EQ** Equalisation. This control of each fader channel on a desk boosts or reduces bass and treble sound to alter the tonal quality.

**Evergreen** Usually a speech item that is not time-specific. It can be produced and then held until it is needed, for days, weeks or even months. However, check before transmission that it is still usable and has not dated.

**Fade**  A song which gradually reduces in volume towards the end.

**Fader**  The vertical slider which controls the volume of a selected source through the studio desk.

**Fade in**  Music or speech which starts quietly and then increases in volume.

**Fall off the air**  When a transmission stops unexpectedly.

**Feature**  Usually the pre-recorded, packaged report of voices and other audio that tells a story. Can also be the term to describe a live item in the programme such as a competition, although not fixed furniture such as news and travel.

**Feed**  The supply of audio either from an outside source to the radio station (such as from a remote) or from the station to another location (the live news bulletin back to the OB).

**Feedback**  1. The process by which the sound from a speaker is fed through a microphone, which is then heard out of the same speaker. It produces a high-pitched howl hence the alternative term howl round. Usually heard when a phone-in contributor has their radio on in the background, while they are broadcasting on the same station.

2. Comments on the performance of a presenter or producer, given by a programme controller.

**Fixed spot**  Also called furniture. The regular items in a programme that have fixed time slots and which can't be moved, such as news and travel.

**Fluff**  Mistake.

**Focus group**  These groups are used to find out qualitative information (not *what* station people listen to but *why* they listen to it.) A small group of people (usually 6 to 10) are asked their opinions around a certain topic. An expert who remains objective throughout moderates the focus group. Focus groups normally take between 1–2 hours, and several groups are usually run on a particular topic. The moderator then analyses these to understand the key themes and trends.

**Foldback**  Foldback allows the studio speakers to be kept on, even when the mic is on. But you have to be careful to set the level so that foldback does not cause feedback.

**Format**  The set structure of a programme or station that lays out the content and style usually to achieve a standard house-style, which helps identify the station. Factors considered in a format will be such things as the mix of music, the duration and regularity of news, travel and weather reports, and possibly the content and length of links.

**Frequency**  1. The rate at which the station is being transmitted.

2. Used when describing the total number of times a listener is likely to have heard an advert or song.

**Furniture**  Regularly scheduled features such as news, travel and weather bulletins, which cannot be moved.

**FX**  Or SFX. Short for sound effects, which add to pre-recorded packages or live broadcasts.

**G7.11**  The technical way of describing the format of calls made to a telephone line.

**G7.22**  The format used for sending audio down ISDN lines.

**GNS**  General News Service. Based at BBC TV Centre (TVC) staff here collate the national and international news for BBC local radio stations (see IRN, SNR).

**Goodie girls**  The young women who hand out stickers on OBs. This is now a rather politically incorrect term, and promotions staff is often preferred.

**Graveyard shift**  The time of day with fewest listeners, usually overnight.

**Green room**  The room or area where guests wait before being shown into the studio.

**GTS**   Greenwich Time Signal. The pips heard on BBC stations (although they are also available at other times too) to signify accurately the top of the hour.

**Hammocking**   To have a popular programme either side of a less-popular one in the hope that the audience will remain throughout.

**Handover**   The on-air conversation between presenters as one ends their show and another one starts.

**Handover sheet**   Or simply a handover. It is a 'story so far' explanation from one producer to another and could list information such as items confirmed, what bids are in for who, who is calling back, what production elements still need to be recorded or edited and so on.

**Hand signals**   Non-verbal communications between producer and presenter to signify such things as 'Wind up the programme now', or 'Do you want a cup of tea?'

**Hard disk**   The computer storage area that holds audio and text.

**Heritage station**   One which has been around for a long time and, it is suggested often does better in Rajar surveys simply because people remember its name more readily.

**Hit the phones**   Or phone bashing. One or more people having a concerted effort to track down a contact or interviewee as a matter of urgency by calling as many possible sources as possible.

**HOT**   Short for Hands Off Tape. The notice put on a studio desk or equipment to show that it is in use, even though the operator may be temporarily absent.

**Hotline**   Or Batphone or Boss Line. The ex-directory studio phone that flashes (rather than rings) and dedicated to important calls.

**Hot seat changeover**   If there is only one main studio, presenters have to perform a hot-seat changeover, when one presenter is tidying up at the end of their show the next one is setting up theirs in the same studio.

**House style**   The way a particular station sounds. Some stations are very disciplined and have very tight house styles, even down to what presenters say out of songs, or what jingles are played and when.

**Idents**   Or ID. Either said or sung, live or recorded, these are mentions of the station name and frequency, to publicise those facts to listeners. May also be used as a way to transition from one item to another.

**ILR**   Independent Local Radio.

**Imaging**   The jingle package used by a station to identify itself and create its style.

**INR**   Independent National Radio.

**In the can**   The phrase used when a programme has been recorded or edited and is ready for broadcast.

**Intro**   Abbreviation for introduction. The instrumental start of a song before the vocals start. Computerised playout systems will show the presenter how long this is on each track so they can prepare their link without a crash.

**IR**   Independent Radio. Commercial (i.e. non-BBC) radio. Includes ILR (Independent Local Radio) and INR (Independent National Radio).

**ISDN**   Integrated Services Digital Network. The high-quality phone-line used for carrying audio to and from radio stations, for example from a remote studio such as a travel centre or district office.

**Jack**   A radio format popular in the US and Canada, whose stations attempt to replicate the sound of an iPod (playing a wider variety of songs than has been usual).

**Jack field**  The junction box where audio signals arrive at the station's racks room or in a studio, before they are redirected to different channels on the studio desk. It looks rather like an old manual telephone exchange.

**Jingle**  The overall term for musical idents on a station, which publicise such information such as the name of the station or presenter, the frequency, the area served and so on.

**Jock**  Alternative to presenter, host, talent and certainly DJ or disc jockey.

**Kicker**  A funny story at the end of a news bulletin. Also called a tailpiece or an and finally, the latter because of the words often used to introduce the item.

**Landline**  The cable system once used to carry high audio quality signals to and from a radio station. Now almost universally replaced by ISDN.

**LCR**  London Control Room (BBC). The staff who route (patch) audio from one BBC building to another.

**Lead**  (Pron: leed) 1. The first story in a bulletin or programme.

2. The opening sentence of a cue.

3. A follow-up for a sales executive about a potential advertiser.

**LED**  Light Emitting Diode. The series of lights which show information such as audio level or signal strength.

**Level**  The volume of a source, such as music or a voice. It must usually peak (depending on the desired effect and the other sources being mixed) between 5 and 6 on the meter. Also used when appraising the volume of a source: 'Let's take some level . . .'

**Limiter**  A processor that automatically limits, or reduces, a high volume signal to avoid damaging sensitive equipment or listeners' ears.

**Liner**  Announcements (such as station name, frequency, a promotion or contest details) written by the programme controller and read by the presenter in a certain order at a certain time, usually word for word.

**Line-up**  The list of presenters on a station.

**Line up tone**  The tone sent down a line from, say, another studio, to signal that a connection has been made. It is of a set frequency to allow levels to be set accurately.

**Link**  The adlibbed or scripted words between songs or to introduce features such as competition or travel news.

**Lip mic**  A noise-excluding mic used when lots of background noise is present, for example during a football match commentary.

**Listener**  1. As defined by Rajar, someone over the age of 15 who listens for at least five minutes in a fifteen minute time segment.

2. In radio it is quite common to talk about listeners in the singular, as in 'What value does this item have for the listener?'

**Listings**  The published lists of radio (and TV) programmes.

**Live**  Not recorded. A programme that is transmitted as it takes place.

**Live copy**  An advert read by the presenter live, rather than pre-recorded. (There are certain restrictions in doing this in the UK.)

**Log**  1. To record on paper or a computer system the use of music so that royalties can be paid to its composer and publisher.

2. The automatic recording, usually done on video or onto computer hard disk, of the complete output of a station, kept in case of query or complaint.

**Market**  The radio station's area.

**MCPS**  The Mechanical Copyright Protection Society which collects dues for its publisher and composer members.

**MCR**  Master Control Room. A central area where the producer sits and answers phones, and advises the presenter. It will have line of sight to the presenter and have a talkback to them. The MCR may also contain a live mic too. Also called the MCA (Master Control *Area*), ops room or production area. Jokingly referred to as Mission Control Room.

**Meat puppet**  (US) Derogatory term for a presenter (also mouth on a stick, also talent).

**Meter**  The device that measures the level of a sound source. The Volume Unit (VU) meter gives an average reading, the PPM (Peak Programme) meter gives the highest volume reached.

**Mic**  Short for microphone.

**Mic rattle**  The noise picked up by a microphone when its cable, or another item such as hand jewellery, is knocked against the mic cover.

**Minidisk**  Or simply MD. A small CD-type disk for recording and playback using a laser.

**Mixer**  The main desk in a studio also called a desk, console or panel. Various sources arrive at the mixer, each with their own channel (volume control) to allow their sound to be balanced.

**Mixing**  Combining two or more sources. This may be as simple as dipping (reducing the volume of) a music bed for the travel news presenter to speak over, or a more complex tapestry of sound in an audio feature.

**Mono**  A combination of left and right channels.

**MOR**  A musical genre: Middle of the Road. Mainstream music.

**Multiplex**  A group of stations broadcast as a single entity occupying one digital channel.

**Music line**  High quality line, either a physical landline or ISDN, intended for music use, rather than speech but can be used for either.

**Music log**  A computer-generated daily list of the station's playlist.

**NCA**  The studio from which contributors speak to other stations in the BBC network (Network Contribution Area).

**Needle time**  The total minutes a station is allowed to broadcast commercially recorded music.

**Networked**  A live programme which is broadcast on several stations in the same group at the same time.

**Newslink**  A commercial placed just after the news bulletin and sold at a premium rate.

**NPA**  The BBC term for the news studio from where bulletins are read (News Production Area).

**OB**  Outside Broadcast (also called a remote, although this is more an American term). A programme or production originating away from base, indeed from anywhere that is not a permanent studio.

**Ofcom**  The UK regulatory body for all telecommunications, including radio. It has the power to advertise, award and monitor radio licences.

**Off-air output**  What is actually being heard by the listener, rather than what is being sent from the studio (which may be in delay or before compression).

**Off-mic**  The term used when someone deliberately or unintentionally is picked up by a microphone without them speaking directly into it. It has the effect of reducing the volume of that voice and also making it sound thin and hollow.

**One-legged**  Sound unintentionally only appearing in either the left or right channel.

**Open ended**   A programme with no specific end time, usually used in the event of breaking news or an emergency.

**Ops Room**   See MCA.

**Opt-in**   Taking a programme feed from an external source, for example one which is going to several stations.

**Opt-out**   A programme or part of a programme for a specific region or transmitter only.

**Out cue**   The last line in a report, so the presenter knows when they are cued to speak again.

**Output**   What is actually broadcast.

**Outside source**   A source coming from anywhere rather than the studio desk, for example an outside broadcast or remote studio.

**Over modding**   When sound levels put through a desk are too high and distortion occurs.

**Over running**   When a programme or music is expected to exceed its planned finish time.

**PA**   Personal appearance by an individual representing the station.

**Padding**   When the presenter is forced to ad-lib without warning to fill time, usually when a machine has malfunctioned and time is needed to cue another track.

**Pan**   By altering the pan button, you will make the sound appear from the left or right speaker channel.

**Panel**   Another name for the studio mixing desk: work the panel or panellist (a technical operator).

**P as b**   Programme as broadcast. What actually went to air, rather than the intended or planned running order. This detailed list includes staff and running orders so the correct people are paid.

**Payola**   The illegal practice where in the past, record companies paid stations to play (and therefore advertise and make popular) their artists' songs.

**PC**   Short for Programme Controller. Usually a title in commercial radio (BBC local stations have the term SBJ programmes) who is responsible for the station output and therefore, the presenters. Might also be called a PD – Programme Director.

**Peak**   The ideal maximum level for a single source. This may be reduced under certain circumstances, for example when mixing one source with others.

**PFL**   Pre Fade Listen, also cue switch, pre-hear, and audition. The button on a studio desk, linked to each fader, which allows a source to be heard by a presenter in the studio (either through their headphones or through studio speakers) without that source going to air. PFL also allows the presenter to check the level of an audio source to prevent distortion or, via the talkback, to speak with a contributor on a phone line or in a remote studio.

**Pgm**   Short for programme.

**Phoner**   Or phono. An interview on the phone, rather than in the studio or down the line which uses an ISDN line.

**Phone screener**   Or phone op or phone flicker. The person who takes the calls into a programme, and passes information such as the caller's name and topic to the producer who will decide whether they are to be put to air, and when.

**Pitching**   Suggesting an idea for a programme or competition and so on, to the presenter or programme controller.

**PLG**   Playlist Guide. A system used by BBC stations to schedule music.

**Plug**   Or puff. A free advert

**Podcasting** Recordings of professional broadcasts or those compiled and presented by amateurs on their home computer. They are converted into MP3 audio files, which can be downloaded onto an iPod (or similar device) and listened to whenever and wherever one likes.

**Point** Promoting or teasing a feature on the station, i.e. to talk about.

**Popping** The small but annoying explosive sound heard when someone speaks too closely or too loudly into a microphone and harsh letters (themselves called plosives) such as P and B force a sudden rush of air from the mouth that's picked up by the mic.

**Post mortem** See programme review.

**Pot** An earlier point at which to stop a pre-recorded interview to save time. This process relies on precise timings and accurate out words, e.g. 'pot at 2'34", out words "that's exactly what happened in this case"'. At that point the presenter quickly closes the fader so that no more of that interview is heard. Also, missing the pot: failing to shut the fader in time, often because it was too tight because there was not much space between the last word and the next.

**PPL** Phonographic Performance Limited. Licences the broadcast of music both for radio and TV stations and in shops and pubs.

**PPM** See meter.

**Pre-fade** Listening to a source off-air, before opening its fader, to check content and levels.

**Pre-fade to time** Also back-timing. Starting an item, usually music and whose duration is known, off-air, so that it ends at the time needed.

**Prep sheet** A sheet or sheets of paper for an interview. It contains facts such as background information, questions, angles, an introduction, contact details and so on.

**Pre-recorded** As opposed to live or recorded. An item, perhaps an interview or an entire show, recorded in advance of transmission.

**Prime time** The time of day with the most listeners.

**Product clash** When two similar companies are in the same break (for example two car garages).

**Production** 1. Audio created using studio equipment and electronic effects.

2. A finished pre-recorded show ready for transmission.

**Programme review** The what went wrong/what went right discussion after a programme between a presenter, producer and manager about which elements of the programme worked well, and not so well, and why. Previously often called a post mortem.

**Promo** Promotion or trail. An advertisement for another programme or feature on the station or an event which the station is involved in. Presenters are often asked to record a promo for their own programme, which is played in others' shows.

**PRS** Performing Rights Society. Representatives of musicians and publishers and the company that collects royalties due to them from when their compositions are played on air.

**PSA** US: Public Service Announcement. UK: What's On.

**Q and A** Question and Answer. Where a presenter interviews a reporter on a story, rather than an expert or someone directly involved.

**Qualitative** Qualitative research captures people's attitudes and preferences through quotes and comments, usually by interview or focus groups. Generally qualitative research answers the question why, not just *what* people think or do.

**Quantitative** Quantitative research delivers percentages and statistics. Generally it gives us information about what people think/feel or do rather than answering the question *why*. Opinion polls are a typical example.

**Quarter** The rolling three-month period during which the Rajar audience survey is conducted. Quarter 1 is the survey for January, February and March, Quarter 2 is for April, May and June and so on.

**Quarter on quarter** The comparison of Rajars statistics from one three-month sweep to the next (see also year on year).

**Racks room** Or simply racks. The room at a radio station where all the source feeds arrive before being redirected to the various studios. The studio feed of mixed signals will also go through here, often via a compressor, on its way to the transmitter. In this room you will also find the station's main phone exchange system, computer playout hard drives and so on, all mounted on racks in large units. In the BBC this is often called Apps – apparatus room.

**Radio mic** A microphone attached to a battery and aerial which allows a presenter to move around, for example, an OB event.

**Rajar** Radio Joint Audience Research Limited. The body owned by both BBC and commercial radio (through its trade organisation The RadioCentre), which measures audience figures for radio stations. In the US the group that measures audience figures is Arbitron.

**Reach** The percentage, or actual number, of total listeners in the TSA (Total Survey Area) who tune in to a station in a specified period.

**Recce** Reconnaissance visit to the proposed site of a roadshow or outside broadcast to visualise and anticipate any potential problems.

**Recorded** An item recorded as it is being transmitted (as opposed to pre-recorded).

**Recorded as live** A pre-recorded event which will need little if any editing before transmission.

**Relay** A programme originating in one studio or at one station, being sent to and broadcast simultaneously from, another station.

**Remote** US term for an outside broadcast.

**Residual** The fee an artist gets each time a programme is repeated.

**Reverberation** A type of echo.

**Reverse talkback** The talkback system from the studio to the production room (rarely used term).

**Roadshow** An outside event held to publicise the station, not necessarily broadcast.

**ROT** Recorded Off Transmission or Recording Of Transmission. Recorded output either to edit and use again (clip and turn around), for archive, or to give to a contributor by way of thanks and souvenir.

**Rotation** Also turnover. The time between a song being played and it being scheduled for broadcast again: a three-hour rotation.

**Royalties** The money paid to the PRS for the use of music on air.

**RSL** Restricted Service Licence. A short term, low power radio station, the licence for which is obtained through Ofcom, which usually broadcasts for a specific event or to gauge reaction ahead of the submission of an application for a full-scale licence.

**Running order** The planned order of items in a programme.

**Running time** The duration of a programme.

**Run through** A rehearsal.

**Sable** A computer system used to easily log music returns (PRS, etc). Each track or jingle has a small supermarket-type barcode, which is swiped to enter its details. Used by BBC stations in conjunction with PLG.

**Satellite studio** A small contribution studio away from the main radio station.

**SBJ** In BBC radio, a Senior Broadcast Journalist, one of whom usually has special responsibility for programmes.

**Schedule** The planned order and overall content of programmes on a station in a week.

**Segment** A block of time between adverts for a potential feature, or sometimes a generic term for a feature itself. Also called a slot.

**Segue** Pronounced seg-way. Two pieces of audio following immediately one another, without a pause. Usually used when describing two pieces of music played one after the other.

**Selector** Trade name for a popular music-scheduling programme, which provides a list of music to be played to any given format instructions decided by the music scheduler.

**Self op** Self operated – when a studio is driven by the presenter rather than by a tech op: 'a self-op studio', 'the programme is self-opped'.

**Setting up** Setting up an interview is to organise it, to book the guest and write the material for the presenter.

**SFX** Short for sound effects.

**Share** The total listening time for a station as a percentage of the total amount of time spent listening to all radio by people in its area.

**Show prep** Show preparation. Everything you read, watch, see, hear and do is a potential source of material for your show.

**Signature tune** The theme tune to identify the start and end of a programme.

**Silence** See dead air.

**Simulcasting** The same programme being broadcast on two or more frequencies (or two or more stations) at the same time. Also called shared programming or a share.

**Sky News Radio** Provider of national news to commercial radio stations. Part of Sky News.

**Slogan** Also positioning statement or station strapline. It is the phrase heard on jingles and sweepers and often written under the station logo, that helps establish and maintain the brand by showing what kind of station it is ('Your better music mix', 'Live news and sport').

**Sound reflection** When sound bounces off hard surfaces. Desks, walls and floors in studios are covered with material to reduce this.

**Snoop** A device which automatically records the programme output as soon as the mic fader is lifted, and pauses it when it is closed.

**Snoop session** A discussion between the presenter and line manager about what worked well and not so well in the programme, conducted with the snoop recording as an aide memoir (or evidence). Also aircheck.

**Song clash** When two songs featuring the same singer appear close to each other on your playlist (for example, a song by Destiny's Child followed soon after by another featuring Beyoncé Knowles).

**SOC** Standard Out Cue. The agreed phrase said by a reporter which is a cue to the presenter that the live or pre-recorded item is near its end. Also called a payoff.

**Socio-demographic groups** See demographic.

**Solus** By itself. Some commercials are solus, the only ad in a break, to make them stand out more. Advertisers pay extra for this.

**Split headphones** Listening to the output of a different transmitter in each ear, especially during a break to ensure that all the ads have fired.

**Stab**  Short jingle, played at full volume, usually used at the end of bed (which has been talked over and played at a lower volume). This technique gives the impression of completeness, as though the presenter has talked to time to the end of the bed.

**Sting**  Short jingle.

**Strand**  A regular programme feature.

**Streaming**  A live feed of a radio programme over the internet.

**Studio**  Either the room from where the presenter broadcasts or where the producer is while directing the show (with the presenter in another studio). Other terms: cubicle, booth, workshop, which tend to mean slightly different things to different people and at different stations or in different situations.

**Sustaining programme**  A live show from another station that's broadcast, usually overnight, to save a recorded programme going out.

**Sweep**  The period during which the audience numbers are measured.

**Sweeper**  A jingle often played between two music tracks.

**Swing jock**  A presenter whose role is to fill for ill or holidaying presenters and who does not have a regular show of their own. In the US this is known as a jock-in-a-box: a presenter who can fit any slot given to them.

**Syndicated**  Another word for a networked show. One programme being simulcast (simultaneously broadcast) on several stations in the same group (either commercial or BBC). Station-specific commercials, jingles, drop-ins and links can be played from a central computer giving the impression of being local to several stations at the same time.

**Tag**  A short commercial or sponsor credit played at the end of a feature, for example the recorded announcement at the end of a commercial station's travel bulletin.

**Take control**  Putting your desk to air and taking over station output from another studio or presenter.

**Talkback**  Internal communication system between one studio and another, or between one studio and other operational parts of the radio station building via which staff can talk to each other. Sometimes called a squawk box.

**Talkback programme**  (Aus) A phone-in programme.

**Target audience**  This is a group of people to whom the radio station is aimed. Having a target audience makes it easier to visualise the sort of people the station is aiming at and helps shape what the station can do to best meet their needs.

**TBU**  Telephone Balancing Unit. The device which balances the output of a phone-in line and the studio output.

**Tease**  A short verbal trail which promotes a future feature on the station, usually without giving away too much information, hence its name.

**Telescoped**  A snoop tape or demo recording that contains links, but not music or commercials. A condensed version of the programme.

**Throw ahead**  To promote a forthcoming item. Also to talk up.

**Time slot**  See day part.

**TO**  1. Technical operator or tech op. The person who drives a studio desk for the presenter (often in the BBC called a Tech BA short for technical broadcast assistant.)

2. Short for talk over when a presenter speaks over some music.

**Tone**  The sound sent down a line (such as an ISDN line) which allows level to be set, and also indicates that the line is open and connected.

**Top 40** A music genre: current chart hits.

**Traffic** 1. The department at a commercial station which schedules the advertisements. Can cause some confusion with those who collate and present the traffic or travel news.

2. Those people at the BBC who book studios and lines to other remote studios.

**Trail** An advert promoting a forthcoming feature or programme on the station.

**Transmission area** The area served by a station, not necessarily the same as the area in which the station can be heard. There may be dead locations in the transmission area where the station cannot be heard, and other places well outside where the transmissions can be picked up. (Compare with TSA.)

**Transmission time** The hours a programme is broadcast. Shortened to 'tx'.

**Treatment** The style of a radio report or feature, such as a short 30-second voiced report by a reporter ('a voicer' or 'voice piece'), a series of linked interview clips ('a package'), a phoner, doco or disco.

**TSA** Total Survey Area (this is different from the transmission area), defined by the station or the licence, within which the Rajar figures are calculated. A reduction to a smaller region (or 'core' area) is likely to increase your reach and share, as more people are likely to listen to you in that area.

**TSL** Time Spent Listening. The Rajar statistic 'Average Hours' shows how long a typical listener listens. This is often called 'Time Spent Listening', or TSL.

**Twig** Another term for an aerial.

**TX** Transmission.

**UHF link** Ultra High Frequency link used for getting an audio signal or material back to the studio from another base, such as a radio car or outside broadcast unit.

**Under run** When a programme falls short of its planned duration.

**VCS** The storage, editing and playout system used by BBC Radio News and Radio & Music departments.

**Voice clash** When the same voice-over artist appears in the same break (or worse, on two ads in a row).

**Vox pop** A collection of clips of members of the public giving their views on a certain subject. Some sweepers include these with comments about the station. Latin: 'voice of the people', also called 'streeters' referring to the usual location where they're collected.

**VU** See meters.

**What's On** Or PSA (Public Service Announcement – American). An item such as charity event, entertainment guide and so on, read out to inform listeners.

**XD** The studio ex-directory hotline for emergency calls. Often called the 'Bossline' as it's used by the programme controller to congratulate or castigate a presenter mid-programme, and because it flashes rather than rings, 'The Batphone'.

**Year on year** The comparison of current Rajars statistics with the same time the previous year (see also 'quarter on quarter')

**Zoo** A programme presented by a team of presenters, all with different characters.

# Index

# Quotes

"An invaluable guide to help those with talent make good in the best business there is."
**John Bradford – former Director, The Radio Academy**

"Anybody who dreams of a career in radio, simply must pick up a copy. If they're genuinely keen on the profession, they won't be able to put it down."
**Richard Park – Programme Director, Magic, London.**

"Peter is a first rate broadcast trainer. His courses here always attracted top marks from attendees. His knowledge of and passion for radio are evidenced on every page of this excellent book."
**Paul Brown – Chairman, The RadioCentre**

"I don't care what the level of experience – the one thing everyone involved in radio can benefit from is to stop, get off the treadmill, stand back and look at what we're doing, how we're doing it, why we're doing it, and different ways of doing it. This book takes the lid off all those areas for those of us in radio, and for those wanting to climb in."
**Martin Campbell – Head of Radio Contents and Standards, Ofcom, the independent regulator for UK radio**

"If you're just starting out in radio *Essential Radio Skills* covers everything you need to know in order to produce and present good radio. Based on the author's experience of working for both BBC and commercial stations, the book is full of clear and practical advice which is delivered in an informal and easy to read style."
**Skillset – the skills council for the UK audio visual industries**

"This is the most comprehensive book any budding radio presenter can have. I would certainly recommend anyone looking to enter media via Hospital Radio to get themselves a personal copy."
**Mike Skinner – Public Relations Manager, Hospital Broadcasting Association**

"A well-written and helpfully laid out 'manual' for anyone wanting to get in to radio or improve their skills...Get it and get on air!"
**Jan Mikulin – Marketing Manager, Student Radio Association**

"There is a demand for radio to up its game and offer more content-rich programming as it competes with other media. To help achieve that aim, this handbook provides one of the most comprehensive foundations I have read. If you have an interest in radio that you want to develop further, you won't want to put this book down. If you want to get on in radio, you'll take it to bed with you, and quite possibly use it as a pillow too!"
**Paul Boon – Editor, *The Radio Magazine***

"There is a distinct difference between the theory of great radio and the practice of it. Listening to stations today that difference is rarely just a gap; more often it is a gaping chasm and invariably an abyss. Peter's book really helps turn theory into great practice. Maybe...just maybe...if enough presenters read this, they can avoid the abyss."
**Phil Angell – Group PD, UKRD Group Ltd**

"Why, why why, wasn't this book around twenty years ago when I was first starting out in Hospital Radio? This book could have saved at least five years of my life, and stopped me making so many mistakes in my early career! A must for anyone just starting out in radio, or who needs a reminder why they wanted to get into this industry in the first place!"

**Sean Dunderdale – Director of News, Lincs FM Group**